THE *Bride* FACTORY

This book is part of the Peter Lang Media and Communication list.
Every volume is peer reviewed and meets
the highest quality standards for content and production.

PETER LANG
New York • Washington, D.C./Baltimore • Bern
Frankfurt • Berlin • Brussels • Vienna • Oxford

Erika Engstrom

THE *Bride* FACTORY

Mass Media Portrayals
of Women and Weddings

PETER LANG
New York • Washington, D.C./Baltimore • Bern
Frankfurt • Berlin • Brussels • Vienna • Oxford

Library of Congress Cataloging-in-Publication Data

Engstrom, Erika.
The bride factory: mass media portrayals of women and weddings /
Erika Engstrom.
p. cm.
Includes bibliographical references and index.
1. Mass media and women. 2. Weddings in popular culture.
I. Title.
P94.5.W65E54   302.23082—dc23   2011046157
ISBN 978-1-4331-1746-6 (hardcover)
ISBN 978-1-4331-1745-9 (paperback)
ISBN 978-1-4539-0568-5 (e-book)

Bibliographic information published by **Die Deutsche Nationalbibliothek.**
Die Deutsche Nationalbibliothek lists this publication in the "Deutsche
Nationalbibliografie"; detailed bibliographic data is available
on the Internet at http://dnb.d-nb.de/.

Cover concept by Erika Engstrom

The paper in this book meets the guidelines for permanence and durability
of the Committee on Production Guidelines for Book Longevity
of the Council of Library Resources.

© 2012 Erika Engstrom
Peter Lang Publishing, Inc., New York
29 Broadway, 18th floor, New York, NY 10006
www.peterlang.com

Printed in the United States of America

Contents

Acknowledgements

NO WOMAN IS AN ISLAND. I BORROW THIS FROM JOHN DONNE AS IT IS (A) TRUE and (b) reflective of the process required for writing this book. Many kind and intelligent people helped me put this manuscript together, and I thank them sincerely. This book began as an outline on a paper placemat during lunch with my dean, Martha Watson. She supported me from the very start, both with her wisdom and her desire to see me succeed. Even though it's taken quite a while to get here, she has always encouraged me, and for that I am forever grateful. My fellow "book club" member David Hassenzahl helped me through the first stages of the proposal. He'll never know how much I appreciate his smarts and friendship (well, *now* he does). Book author extraordinaire Terance Miethe generously read parts of an initial manuscript. He continues to share his knowledge of book publishing and keep his door open. I thank my long-time colleague David Henry for his advice and critique, as well as his encouragement and enthusiasm. I am lucky to have him on my team. I revere feminist scholar Linda Steiner, who so graciously agreed to read some of my stuff at the last minute during a conference we were attending, and advised me to consider the openness of hegemony as I deconstructed the media presented here. Her suggestions serve as the bases for discussions of alternative media in Chapters 6 and 7. During an earlier iteration of this manuscript, one anonymous reviewer in particular pointed me in the direction of some incredibly useful material, which I include in the first chapter. I believe the manuscript is much stronger for it, and for that I am so very appreciative. I thank Mary Savigar, my editor at Peter Lang, for her responsiveness and support throughout the publication process. Her calming effect helped to ease the first-book jitters. Along the way, people have given me materials that they thought I could use in writing this book. And they were right. I thank Jane Marcellus for her feedback on a conference paper that became an article that became parts of this book. She might think it was no big deal, but it was. My colleague Tara Emmers-Sommer provided me with an example of a non-bridal bridal publication. My dissertation adviser at the University of Florida, the late Mickie Edwardson, sent me a large package of bridal magazines just months before her sudden passing. She was a great, great teacher and a fantastic person. I regret that she didn't get to see the finished product. I am lucky to know Mary-Lou Galician and Sammye Johnson; both have supported me emotionally and professionally. I am unworthy of their kindness. I thank my partner, the bright and beautiful Ted Greenhalgh, for being my best friend and companion for nearly twenty years. He considers the writing of a book by a professor to be a given, so the completion of this one is a matter of course. Finally, I dedicate this book to my parents, Alex J. Engstrom and Margaret M. Engstrom, née Hisayo Mizukami. They raised me in a covert feminism whose tenets were education, independence, and awareness of one's worth. I owe them everything.

1. Introduction

You can find them at any supermarket, newsstand, or bookstore. You see them more and more on television, on both broadcast and cable networks, and on the Internet. They are everywhere, and they offer the promise of a dream come true, the pinnacle of female existence, romantic perfection, and happily ever after. "They" are bridal magazines, web sites, and television shows, and they comprise an ever-growing segment of the mass media industry.

One need only scan the covers of bridal magazines, watch movies and television programs that include weddings in their story lines, or come across variations on the same theme in reality television programs to see over and over again the prototype of the white wedding: bride dressed in white and bridegroom in suit or tuxedo repeating vows in front of a group of family, friends, and acquaintances, and then celebrating their newly consecrated marriage with a party consisting of a layered cake, music, and dancing.

The white wedding has become the standard for the ritual of marriage, and increased in popularity as the 20th century progressed. This book examines its portrayal as an unquestioned, common sense aspect of everyday American life. The evidence for the popularity of the white wedding comes from the commonality of its depictions in mass media and documentation in news coverage of the profits it generates as an industry totaling in the billions of dollars annually. The media side of the wedding industry has given us an ever-increasing array of manuals for creating the perfect wedding: *Brides, Modern Bride, Elegant Bride, Southern Living Bride, Bridal Guide, Martha Stewart Weddings,* and *The Knot* all serve as guidebooks for the female Holy Grail—the meticulously planned big, white wedding. Their Internet counterparts, such as *TheKnot.com*, encourage brides-to-be to shop for all their wedding accessories and create their wedding registries online. Box-office hits of the 1990s, such as *My Best Friend's Wedding*, *Four Weddings and a Funeral*, *Runaway Bride*, and the 2002 box-office success *My Big Fat Greek Wedding*, offered nearly uniform portrayals of wedding pageantry.

Such fictional displays often belie the quality of the love relationship between bride and groom, as demonstrated in the glamorous wedding depicted in the 1994 film *Muriel's Wedding*, in which Muriel fulfills her lifelong dream of becoming a bride, even as she enters into a sham marriage that ultimately fails. In a sense, the "true" story of Muriel Heslop's wedding allows moviegoers perhaps a more honest depiction of weddings than reality television versions by showing that shaky relationships remain so despite having the validation associated with wedding spectacles. One can see fictional wedding stories such as *Muriel's Wedding* as offering at least some hint of life after the wedding, something reality television weddings that purport to show us "real life" do not.

Wedding-related television series and specials have dotted the television programming landscape in recent years as well. These include the Fox network's series *The Wedding Bells*, and its past reality offerings *Surprise Wedding* and *Married by America*, as well as NBC's *Race to the Altar*, ABC's *In Style Celebrity Weddings*, and A&E's *The American Wedding*. The Learning Channel's *A Wedding Story*, Oxygen's *Real Weddings from The Knot*, FitTV's *Buff Brides*, and WE tv's *Bridezillas* give viewers a look at the backstage goings-on of one of the most revered front stage performances of a woman's life. In 2010, the E! Entertainment Television reality series *Bridalplasty* became the object of criticism by other media organizations. As a new low in the reality competition show subgenre, it promised its female contestants the prize of plastic surgery and a dream body along with a dream wedding (Hutchison, 2010). Indeed, this program illustrated just how divorced from marriage weddings had become: even though she was already married and had a baby, one contestant felt she deserved her special day because her actual wedding did not live up to her dream.

"Dream" weddings serve as the ultimate goal of bridal-themed media. Big and white, set in large churches with massive guest lists, the white weddings depicted in the ever-expanding array of bridal media cultivate a stereotype of the wedding wherein traditions rooted in archaic gender roles have become the norm. All involve numerous bridesmaids and ushers, expensive receptions, and traditional, gendered rituals, such as the giving away of the bride (usually by a male). Rather than serving as the beginning of married life, current mass media present the wedding as the denouement of romantic relationships.

They reinforce and endorse the idea that romantic relationships should and must lead to marriage, which requires a public display—the wedding. At the same time, these media forward cultural meanings and values about women and the way they should play the role of bride on their wedding day.

From left to right, Rachel Griffith, Daniel Lapaine, Toni Collette and Bill Hunter in P.J. Hogan's MURIEL'S WEDDING.

MIRAMAX

A Miramax Films Release © 1995

FIGURE 1.1. *Muriel's Wedding*

The comedy *Muriel's Wedding* featured social reject Muriel's (Toni Collette) lavish, dream wedding set to the pop tunes of ABBA. Her sham marriage to a South African swimmer (Daniel Lapaine) ended shortly after the nuptials. At least this fictional wedding story gives viewers a look at married life after the big wedding Muriel dreamed of and saw as her life's goal (Copyright Miramax Films, 1995).

The wedding industry is big business, but, contrary to what has become "tradition," weddings did not always involve the amount of time and money stipulated by social etiquette and rules enforced today by bridal magazines and planning guides. In the case of the so-called "middle class" wedding in the United States, for example, weddings prior to the 1830s were "simple affairs, usually conducted in the home, unmarked by stereotypical costumes, and often planned as little as a week beforehand" (Freeman, 2002, p. 25). Church weddings were rare, and Thanksgiving was a favorite time for weddings because it served as a ready-made family gathering (Cole, 1893). The wedding process has been subject to revision and transformation since the 1830s and

1840s (Penner, 2004), with weddings modeled after those of elites during the Victorian era providing the model for the commercialized version familiar in the 20th century (Howard, 2006). By the late 1930s, research on wedding expenditures, such as that by Timmons (1939), who reported a mean average wedding cost of $400 for his sample of family and acquaintances of his students, reflected the burgeoning list of accoutrements needed for the proper wedding.[1]

By the start of the 21st century, the bridal business had come to be termed "recession-proof," generating some $50 billion a year (Penner, 2004). As Schley (2006) reported in "Invitation to the Wedding Business: Oxygen Campaign Revolves Around Nuptials," by 2006 the Association for Wedding Professionals had estimated it at $80 billion a year. In 2007, the average American wedding cost $28,730; by 2009, that average fell to $19,580, a reflection of the economic downturn ("Avg. Wedding Cost 1945–2010," 2011).[2] Even with a decrease in the average price of weddings—which in 2009 still ranged between the cost of a new car or substantial down payment on a home—weddings remained a highly lucrative business. Indeed, by 2010, wedding spending had gone up again, with the average wedding cost climbing back up by 22.9% from the previous year to $24,066, according to The Wedding Report, a research company that follows wedding industry trends and spending ("Average Cost of a Wedding Increases 23%," 2011).

Despite a decline in marriage rates among U.S. adults aged 25 to 54 between the years 2000 and 2009, reflected by a larger proportion of never-married adults in this age group (Dougherty, 2010; Mather & Lavery, 2010), one need only monitor the number and variations of wedding-themed media products to see that weddings themselves remain highly popular as celebratory events that promote the desirability of marriage. As cultural products of symbolic meaning, bridal-themed media offer a means by which we can discover the narrative of the modern woman within American society. Indeed, bridal media offer what Boden (2003) called "the pleasure of ultimate femininity" (p. 61).

Bridal media also reveal what mass communication in general says about women and men as they shape 21st century society. To the uncritical viewer, bridal media, in the form of wedding-related magazines, television shows, and movies, provide entertainment, yes, and even admiration for the pretty clothing, the fancy settings, and the overall glamour that big, white weddings provide. However, only by closely examining the underlying messages forwarded in such stylized depictions can we understand how the wedding serves as a metaphor for society as a whole, reflective of commonly accepted cultural practices, meanings, and values.

This book examines portrayals of gender within the world of bridal media. I use the term "bridal media" to refer primarily to nonfictional, informational mass communication, namely, magazines, Internet web sites, and reality television programs that use the wedding as their central content. Though aimed at females planning to marry in some type of formal wedding, the target audience realistically can consist of anyone, regardless of relationship status or gender or even sexual orientation. Bridal magazines and their Internet counterparts offer a mercantile-related purpose by showing their audiences specific items available for purchase, whether as part of their editorial or advertising content.

Reality television wedding programs purport to offer their viewers a slice-of-life perspective of real women preparing for their real weddings. More so than fictional versions of brides in films and television dramas and sitcoms, reality television versions of weddings include actual persons. The portrayal of these real women serves as my focus, as I seek to discover the commonalities and differences between various wedding-focused programs in the reality television genre. In this manner, this book serves as an examination of actual wedding practices as depicted in popular culture, specifically in nonfictional accounts of weddings in news stories, bridal magazines, and reality television programming.

The portrayal of women in bridal media reaffirms the assumed identity that "society" expects women to take: that of the beautiful, ecstatic bride. The allure of what Wolf (2003) called "Brideland"—the "world of lush feminine fantasy eerily devoid of men" except as "shadow figures"—allows women, even those identifying as feminist and decidedly financially independent, to leave behind feminist consciousness and allow their inner Cinderella to reveal herself in her "true aristocratic radiance" (p. 61). The problem with Brideland lies in its power to obscure and distract; the relationship being validated by the wedding becomes secondary, with Brideland serving as a transient utopia in which class mobility becomes attainable, if only for just one day.

Unlike the nature and history of marriage, only recently have scholars seriously examined the wedding as an important cultural artifact and practice. For example, Leeds-Hurwitz (2002) examined weddings in her ethnographic study of the bricolage of the rituals incorporated in cross-cultural weddings. Research on brides in particular includes Goldstein-Gidoni's (1997) participant-observation study of Japanese wedding parlors in *Packaged Japaneseness: Weddings, Business, and Brides,* and Boden's (2003) examination of wedding industry portrayals of the bridal role in Great Britain in *Consumerism, Romance and the Wedding Experience.* Boden described how British bridal magazines have created the "superbride," a role which allows women to control every aspect of their weddings while still immersing themselves in the feminine pleasures of the fairy-tale wedding in which they play the role of "star." This concept of superbride serves as one of the themes analyzed later in this book.

In *Cinderella Dreams: The Allure of the Lavish Wedding*, Otnes and Pleck (2003) examined the bridal industry and history of wedding merchandising in the US. They concluded that weddings allow women, who now can earn their own money and spend it as they please, to escape the mundane aspects of daily life through the planning and creation of fantasy weddings. The history of wedding consumerism in the United States also served as the focus of Howard's 2006 book, *Brides, Inc.: American Weddings and the Business of Tradition*. Jellison (2008), in her historical treatment of the white wedding, *It's Our Day: America's Love Affair With the White Wedding, 1945–2005*, traced the history of the white wedding in the United States from the end of World War II to the present, concentrating on how weddings developed from simple, in-home affairs to lavish, materialistic displays of "family togetherness and material abundance" (p. 61).

The materialism associated with modern weddings also served as the subject of a popular book by Mead (2007), *One Perfect Day: The Selling of the American Wedding*.[3] On this same topic, Winge and Eicher (2004) specifically examined the appeal of fantasy and theme weddings in "The American Groom Wore a Celtic Kilt: Theme Weddings as Carnivalesque Events." Winge and Eicher looked at how weddings that employ specific themes, such as "medieval" and Mardi Gras, allow couples and guests to play out roles they otherwise could not. These various works demonstrate that the role of the bride creates a sense of temporary celebrity for women. This celebrity status strongly appeals to women, and helps to perpetuate the long-dreamed-of "princess" persona.

Feminist scholars also have begun to study the wedding industry in terms of the gendered messages contained in wedding rituals, preparation (such as the process of choosing a wedding gown), and weddings portrayed in mass media. In *Here Comes the Bride: Women, Weddings, and the Marriage Mystique*, Geller (2001) pointed out that feminists have ignored the bridal industry as a subject in need of critical examination. In addition to a historical review of wedding rituals and their meanings, as well as her own experiences as a would-be bride at bridal salons, Geller analyzed weddings and marriage as presented in popular films. She concluded that wedding-related media and social practices combine to socialize women into believing that their personal fulfillment as a gender depends on becoming a man's wife, and that they can achieve this by having a lavish, white wedding.

While Geller approached the "marriage mystique" from a personal perspective in order to explain the appeal of the wedding and the bridal role among women today, Ingraham (1999), in *White Weddings: Romancing Heterosexuality in Popular Culture*, critiqued the entire wedding industry. Ingraham based her book on the theory of materialist feminism, which argues that "the nexus of social arrangements and institutions that form the social totalities of patriarchy and capitalism regulate our everyday lives by distributing cultural power and economic resources unevenly according to gender, race, class, and sexuality" (p. 19).[4] From global economics to popular films, Ingraham analyzed aspects of the bridal industry as she searched for reasons why women adhere to cultural practices that enforce consumerism while promising womanly fulfillment.

Several researchers have studied the wedding and the portrayal of brides specifically within the context of the media industry. For example, Lewis (1997) examined the gendered messages contained in wedding photography. Wedding photography, contended Lewis, illustrates perfection, "ideal" body language, and glorification of the bride, and legitimizes consumerism through the acceptance of its high cost and necessity. In terms of print and film, Freeman (2002), in *The Wedding Complex*, used performance theory to analyze literature and films in which weddings serve as the plot line, and concluded that weddings and marriage privilege heterosexuality. Jellison (2008) also examined bridal advertising, magazines such as *Life*, Hollywood movies, and, more recently, reality television programming in terms of the conspicuous consumption and idealized versions of brides they exemplify and endorse.

Here, I analyze how bridal media, in the form of news, magazines, and reality television, portray women in modern American society. Specifically, I demonstrate how these portrayals instruct women about the significance of the physical requirements of brides, which includes submitting to the rules of the disciplined female body and the requisites of beauty and cosmetics. Feminist and feminine-related messages exist simultaneously in these media, as they depict brides as agents of control over their perfect day who at the same time succumb to traditionally feminine roles. Throughout this book, I analyze the bridal role in terms of the woman-centered messages that surround the wedding as reflected in the text and visual components of today's mass media, which really are giving their audiences new versions of an old story.

The Wedding Appeal in Mass Media

Historically, the wedding has served as a common and popular topic of news coverage. For example, Stephens (2007), in *A History of News*, traced accounts of celebrity weddings to news pamphlets of the 1500s. Stories of prominent weddings of royalty "commanded readers' attention as spectacles in an age when spectacles had not yet been cheapened by overexposure" (p. 93). "News reports of royal pomp and circumstance," Stephens noted, "dwelt on the details because the events depicted were more extravagant and magnificent than anything else in their readers' experience" (p. 93). Those magnificently staged events served mainly to cement state alliances. The practice of giving away the bride continues, in symbolic form, the use of women as items of exchange under patriarchy. Indeed, Coontz (2005) noted that marriage based solely on love represented a revolutionary way of thinking when introduced in the late eighteenth century.

The tremendous television audiences of contemporary royal weddings, such as those of Lady Diana Spencer and Prince Charles in 1981, and Prince Andrew and Sarah Ferguson in 1986, attest to our common attraction to the notion of the "fairy tale" wedding. Both events featured ancient and solemn rituals, horse-drawn carriages, multitudes of well-wishers, elaborate costumes, and cathedrals. Charles and Andrew were real-life princes who married their true loves (or so we thought). Their weddings served as hyperbolized examples of the "fractured" fairy tale: though heralded by extravagant wedding pageantry, both royal marriages ended in divorce.

The media frenzy surrounding the 2011 wedding of William, elder son of Princess Diana, and Kate Middleton, the wealthy "captivating brunette" ("Kate Middleton: Snapshot," 2011) of common heritage, evoked familiar themes from past royal weddings. Entire web sites devoted to keeping readers up to date on the intricacies of their wedding created an anticipation of the big event.[5] Royal weddings reify the fantasy associated with weddings, and through imitation the wedding practices of the elite trickle down to the "common people." Print examples that evidence the popularity of weddings include covers of supermarket gossip publications that advertise the details of the nuptials of Hollywood celebrities, the American version of "royalty."

Though the lowly reader would never receive an invitation to such galas, magazines such as *People* provide the entire inside scoop. The August 14, 2000 cover of *People* read, "Brad and Jennifer's Wedding! The Guests, the Rings, the Vows, the Menu—All About How the Happy Couple Got Hitched!" (alas, by 2005, Brad Pitt and Jennifer Aniston had divorced; their "love story" had been replaced quickly by the hot romance of Brad and his new love, Angelina Jolie, nicknamed the "Brangelina" phenomenon). The highly publicized, $6 million Italian castle wedding of international superstar Tom Cruise to the much-younger Katie Holmes (the media dubbed the duo "TomKat") in 2006 created a media furor. Readers of the December 4, 2006 issue of *Life & Style Weekly*, which featured the headline "Katie Speaks: My Dream Wedding!" (underscored by an accompanying gender role-rich caption, "I felt like a princess—now I want more children!") found out that in addition to exchanging "diamond-studded white-gold Cartier wedding bands," Tom and Katie's "five-tiered white chocolate wedding cake was decorated with marzipan roses and white chocolate chips, and filled with white-chocolate mousse and cream"

("Katie: My Dream Wedding!" p. 28). Such reports fulfill an ages-old curiosity about celebrity weddings by divulging all the intricate details about guests, rings, vows, menu, cake, wedding dress—all while bestowing tremendous importance on the material aspect of these weddings.

Bridal magazines forward a materialistic agenda by focusing on various requisite wedding accessories. The repetitive message they espouse dictates that women look their best on that one all-important day of their lives. Numerous advertisements for wedding gowns, party favors, and diamond rings announce themselves between articles on how brides-to-be need to prepare for their wedding months, even years, in advance, with special emphasis on their physical appearance. Rather than focusing on the meaning of marriage as a lifelong relationship, this form of bridal media, like others, instead concentrates on the material aspects of the wedding (Filak, 2002).

Cinematic versions of the wedding follow a familiar script, as do network and cable television programs that offer their viewers the big, white, romantic wedding in prime-time comedies and dramas, often with the wedding serving as a show's season or series finale. Daytime soap operas feature weddings on a regular basis, as characters marry and remarry, furthering the idea of marriage as the culmination of romance and the supposed key to happiness. Television commercials often use the wedding as the backdrop to pitch not only diamonds, which "are forever" (and, thus, provide the promise of a marriage that lasts forever), but also automobiles (groom drives the featured car to get to the church on time), credit cards (father contemplates how he'll pay for his daughter's wedding), and beer (bride dunks her head into a tub of ice to retrieve the touted bottle of imported lager). Obviously, the wedding narrative serves as a familiar and attractive draw for audiences, not only in terms of box-office and television ratings success, but for advertising as well. Taken together, repeated images of movie and TV weddings offer a composite, idealized version of the marriage ceremony, which serves as *the* example for how couples ought to design their own ceremonies.

The desire to achieve the "perfect" wedding, to the exclusion of the goal of building a strong relationship with one's mate, serves as a potential way for some brides to exhibit selfish, demanding behaviors. Such instances serve as the basis for "Bridezillas and Groom-monsters," on the web site *Etiquettehell.com*, which relates wedding "horror stories." Victims of wedding abuse post their hellish experiences with demanding brides—and the occasional boorish groom—who overstep the bounds of good manners, many times with the result of broken relationships and the loss of friends. These media versions of "bad brides" offer cautionary tales about how not to behave. Accounts of bad taste exhibited by out-of-control brides, such as outright money-grubbing in the form of demands for monetary gifts in invitations and choosing bridesmaids based on their weight, served as the subject not only of Spaemme and Hamilton's (2002) semi-comical book *Bridezilla: True Tales From Etiquette Hell*, but also a 2003 Fox television network special of the same name and a subsequent series on the Women's Entertainment (WE tv) cable network. While the authors of the *Bridezillas* book offered a humorous retelling of weddings gone awry, their real underlying message actually forwards the pro-social idea that the resultant marriage and quality of relationships with family and friends hold much more importance than materialistic concerns.

"Real" Media Weddings

Signorielli and Morgan (1996) stated that television serves "as the primary manifestation of our culture's mainstream" (p. 117). Television, as a primary medium that disseminates cultural values in our society, then, promotes the mainstream, or "relative commonality of outlooks and values" (p. 117). The seemingly exponential increase in the amount of wedding- and bridal-themed television programs thus serves as evidence of the popularity of the wedding in the US at the turn of the 20th century.

Recent television wedding documentaries combine entertainment and news-style reporting on all the behind-the-scenes details involved with putting on the big event. These programs offer viewers what Calvert (2000) termed a "video vérité" (similar to the film version of cinema vérité) account of weddings of celebrity and noncelebrity couples. Some, like VH1's *Rock 'n' Roll Weddings* and the Lifetime channel's *Weddings of a Lifetime*, focus on expensive, glamorous affairs that epitomize the fantasy, fairy-tale wedding. Others, like The Learning Channel's *Wild Weddings*, serve as compilations of home video "bloopers" similar to ABC's long-running *America's Funniest Home Videos*, providing viewers with lighthearted accounts of wedding disasters, such as the hailstorm that ruined an outdoor wedding, or the clumsy waiter who dropped a huge, expensive wedding cake.

The wedding theme also has served as the focal point of game show-based reality programs based on the idea of "winning" a potential romantic partner. Popular for decades, these shows, such as the classic *The Dating Game*, featured contestants vying for the big "prize"—a date with a member of the opposite sex. In 2003, the Bravo channel's *Boy Meets Boy* followed a similar theme. With the reality genre's rise in popularity during the early 2000s, programming in this category in recent years has offered contestants the prize of marriage, complete with an all-expenses-paid wedding. *Who Wants to Marry a Multi-Millionaire?*, perhaps the most famous, or infamous, of these programs, combined the game show with another television genre, the beauty pageant; it became a ratings blockbuster and subsequent debacle for the Fox network in 2000. Later offerings, such as ABC's *The Bachelor* and *The Bachelorette*, and Fox's *Joe Millionaire*, capitalized on viewers' attraction to the notion of women, and men, competing for the hand of an eligible bachelor, or bachelorette. Even the "loser" of the first season of *The Bachelor*, Trista Rehn, became a "winner" by appearing as the star of the first season of *The Bachelorette*; her triumphant return to reality TV land resulted in a much-hyped, "fairy-tale-come-true" wedding to her chosen suitor, Ryan Sutter.[6]

Married by America, which aired on the Fox network in 2003, put couples who underwent a matchmaking process into instant engagements. A panel of relationship "experts" reviewed each couple's interaction and prognosticated their chances for a long-term relationship, eliminating those who appeared incompatible. Couples who actually married and stayed married for one year would win a substantial cash award. Alas, Fox kept its money, as none of the couples actually went through with a wedding. Also in 2003, NBC's *Race to the Altar* pitted already-engaged couples in competitions involving dangerous-looking stunts, with a sumptuous dream wedding serving as the champion couple's prize.

Several of these programs garnered media commentary by television critics, who pointed out that such shows reflect the status of women in today's society, and differences in social class between the men and women who appear in them. For example, Stanley, in her November 20, 2002 *New York Times* editorial on the imbalance of social status on *The Bachelor*, noted that the bachelor on this program (read: "prize") usually has an Ivy-League education and/or a high-paying career, such as lawyer or investment banker. In contrast, the women selected as "contestants" do not hold equal credentials. Indeed, would a woman in a similar position even consider, or be considered, for the show? Stanley's observations touch on issues similar to those I examine here, namely, what this type of programming says about our society's view of women, gender stereotypes, and the importance of marriage.

The number of wedding-related reality programs that focus more on the how-tos of planning a wedding, and the day-to-day details faced by couples planning their weddings, has increased in recent years. These include the popular daytime ratings success *A Wedding Story*, on the cable outlet The Learning Channel (TLC), which offered viewers a highly stylized version of home videos that compress several days' worth of activities into just 30 minutes. *For Better or for Worse*, also on The Learning Channel, served as a sort of game show, in which relatives of the happy couple took on the planning of their weddings, with a budget of "only" $5,000. The relatively small amount of money allotted to the wedding served as the planners' major challenge.

The Oxygen channel, which targets women viewers, in 2003 began offering *Real Weddings From The Knot*, a program that followed couples for several weeks before their wedding day. FitTV's *Buff Brides* documented the
physical makeover of women who wanted to get in shape in time for their wedding day; the wedding gown itself served as the major impetus for attaining
physical fitness. Further illustrating the popularity of weddings and all things
bridal, in late 2007, TLC, the purveyor of women-targeted, slice-of-life programs, debuted *Say Yes to the Dress*, a program about women's experiences buying wedding gowns.[7]

Beyond other bridal media, these treatments of the wedding planning
experience provide instruction in the guise of entertainment, thus combining
a how-to aspect with the added "drama" of real people's experiences. In this
sense, the nature of television itself becomes another aspect of the appeal of
wedding media. "Live" and videotaped programs make television more plau-
sible than movies: Feuer (1983) observed that "from a certain technological
and perceptual point of view, television is live in a way that film can never be.
Events can be transmitted as they occur; television (and videotape) looks
more 'real' to us than film" (p. 13). Taking this notion further, videotape and
live broadcasts serve as the preferred modes of reality television shows because
they leave viewers with the impression that television can capture "real life"—
that is, people acting naturally, unaware that others are watching them.

Thus, rather than watching a taped, highly edited version of what happens
to and is done by the people in these programs, the noncritical viewer perceives
a picture of the world as it supposedly exists, and the weddings in reality TV
shows offer a glimpse into how "real" weddings look and should look.
Furthermore, these programs reaffirm the familiar narrative of the wedding.
The "happily ever after" ending then becomes folded into our idealized
notions of the wedding, and to a broader extent, romantic love.

Researchers have begun looking specifically at reality television's treatment
of the wedding narrative. As weddings relate to consumerism, Rebecca
Stephens (2004), in an essay on TLC's reality series *A Wedding Story*, commented on how that program implied that "creating the 'perfect' wedding
might lead to an equally 'perfect' life ever after—and that perfection equals
consumption" (p. 201). Levine's (2005) study of the reality-based television
program *Weddings of a Lifetime* on the Lifetime cable channel addressed the
appeal of the heterosexual romance as well. Consisting of a series of special
weddings, several of which took place at Walt Disney World with Cinderella's
castle as backdrop, *Weddings of a Lifetime* featured "real" fantasy weddings,
which Levine found as illustrating the "ongoing circulation of a Disney specialty, the traditional romance narrative" (p. 78).

Weddings and fairy tales have long been intertwined. Propp's (1968) analysis of fairy tale narratives revealed that for male heroes, the reward for the fulfillment of a task is a bride, a kingdom, or both.[8] In fairy tales involving a female protagonist, this marriage-as-reward motif appears as well, but rather than embarking on her own adventure, she waits for a daring prince to rescue her from oppression or a disenfranchised status in which she is the victim, the subject of others' actions. Thus, even as Cinderella eventually is rewarded (with the help of a fairy godmother's supernatural powers) for her suffering with happiness and marriage, she *receives* a man's love, and becomes a "beloved object" (Zipes, 2006, p. 120). Further, the standardization of the fairy tale, exemplified by Disney films especially, disallows character development so as to render story characters as types, noted Zipes (1997, p. 93).

Galician (2004) explained how fairy tales, or "wonder tales," relate stories through symbolic characters not meant to represent realistic persons (p. 35). Marriage in these stories frequently represents the transition from childhood to adulthood, while also inculcating in children "class rituals and customs that reinforced the status quo" (Zipes, 2007, p. 18).[9] According to Zipes (2007), the "sense of wonder" and astonishment in these stories comes from a "marvelous object or phenomenon" of unquestioned "supernatural" origin, and conveys the idea that no matter one's place in society, happiness is possible (p. 5).[10]

The description of weddings as fairy tales thus reinforces notions of magic, wonder, and an escape from reality while also reaffirming the marriage-as-reward motif. Bacchilega (1997) described fairy tales as offering girls and women an "exquisitely glittery feminine kingdom" (p. 5), an image that invokes quite readily the fantasy weddings proffered in bridal media. While we may see fairy tales as sweet and seemingly innocuous, they perpetuate a dominance of thought regarding happiness and the idea that mistreated women will one day be rescued from the drudgery of day-to-day life, the Cinderella fantasy that underlies the white wedding appeal.[11] Indeed, one might find highly interesting Marina Warner's (1995) work on the gendered aspects of fairy tales in *From the Beast to the Blonde: On Fairy Tales and Their Tellers*. In the chapter titled "Reluctant Brides," she analyzed the recurring theme of young women who actually fear the thought of marriage to a "beastly" man (such as in "Beauty and the Beast").[12]

By framing weddings in terms of fantasy and fairy tales, bridal media in turn ensure that women "buy into," literally, the notion that their lives are unfulfilled until they find a man who will propose marriage to them, and they finally have the wedding they have meticulously planned since childhood. Hence, we hear how women have "dreamed of their wedding day" since they were young girls, not how they dreamed of obtaining a good career, or of developing a happy and healthy relationship with someone (of either sex), or of living a life unencumbered by any commitment as a truly *free* agent. As a counterpoint to female desires, one rarely hears of men speaking of their dream wedding since they were boys.

Today, reality television versions of the wedding in the US give millions of viewers a stylized picture of the most intimate, yet public, moment of people's lives. When added to the milieu and reach of wedding-related messages disseminated by other mass media, they further enhance common perceptions about the way human beings express and acknowledge feelings of love and commitment. Media versions of weddings also reflect current gender norms and roles, those associated with divisions of labor and expectations of behaviors, wants, and expertise. For women, weddings serve as a site where gender socialization comes to the forefront.

Informed Inquiry: Feminism, Femininity, and Hegemony

"Weddings, marriage, romance, and heterosexuality become naturalized to the point where we consent to the belief that marriage is necessary to achieve a sense of well-being, belonging, passion, morality, and love," asserted Ingraham (1999, p. 120). Wedding stories, true and fictional, sustain our commonly held beliefs about the quality of human life in general. I write this book to explain the ability of bridal media to evince Ingraham's observation about how accepted beliefs and practices become so. Three underlying themes guide my investigation into the world of bridal media:

1. Feminism, the composite beliefs and practices that forward the progress of women.

2. Femininity, the traditionally accepted traits and characteristics associated with women and their life roles.

3. Hegemony theory, which serves as a way to explain why we accept certain ideas and social mores as common sense.

The wedding serves as a nexus where these three themes meet. Hegemony relates to feminism in that the workings of civil society affect feminist progress. Hegemony also allows for counterhegemony in the form of resistance or rejection of common sense. In subsequent chapters, I demonstrate how these themes interconnect and surface in bridal media.

Feminism

Weddings have served as a traditional concern for women ii
ety, formalizing feminine and masculine roles as reflected
itself. As Lewis (1997) noted, "Although there are exceptions, ...ai wedding, which blends the public and communal with the domestic and personal,
is relegated to women and embraced by women" (p. 184). Thus, just as Foss
and Foss (1989) contended that research done for and about women assumes
a feminist stance, research on weddings becomes a feminist endeavor. To
open this inquiry, I rely on a definition of feminism provided by Dow (1996)
in *Prime-Time Feminism: Television, Media Culture, and the Women's
Movement Since 1970*: "a set of political ideas and practices . . . dedicated to
the progress of women and the transformation of patriarchy" (p. xxiii).

Feminism, as noted by Gamble (2001), starts from the perspective that
women are treated inequitably within societies organized around male viewpoints and concerns—patriarchy—and seeks to alter arrangements in the public and private spheres that rely on sexual difference. Under the rationale that
men are strong, active, and rational and women are the opposite (weak, passive, and emotional), women become aligned with negativity, that is, "everything men are not" (p. vi). In a patriarchal society, wrote Gamble, "women
are denied equal access to the world of public concerns as well as of cultural
representation," and changing that situation serves as feminism's goal (p.
vii). Feminism thus becomes useful as a theoretical and practical approach to
studying mass media portrayals of women and women-centered concerns, to
which a study of the treatment, definition, and image of "bride" relates.

The "wave" paradigm relies on a general timeline illustrating the progression of "feminism." As Baumgardner and Richards (2010) in *Manifesta:
Young Women, Feminism, and the Future,* wrote: "In the most basic sense, feminism is exactly what the dictionary says it is: the movement for social, political, and economic equality of men and women" through specific periods in
history (p. 56). The French term *feminisme* described the activities of women
suffragists in the late 1800s; in France, noted Baumgardner and Richards, it
was a "cool word, like calling someone hip or savvy" and "denoted youth, psychology, sexiness, financial independence, and self" (p. 51). Although the first
documented use of the actual word *feminisme* in the US appeared in 1906,
they cited the time period between 1848 and the mid-1920s as associated with
the First Wave of feminism, whose members worked to attain the vote for
women as well as the Equal Rights Amendment.[13] During that time, marriage
for women was a given; efforts to give women the right to vote as well as to
divorce and keep their own property also marked that time. The Second
Wave, which began around 1970 and continues to this day, saw not only con-

certed efforts to establish reproductive freedom, job equality, and the continued fight for the Equal Rights Amendment, but was (is) also an era when one could "make a living as a feminist intellectual" (p. 76).

I find of twofold import Baumgardner and Richards's (2010) observations about how marriage served as a target for change during feminism's Second Wave. First, women who wanted to make marriage (previously cast within a patriarchal structure) an equitable arrangement reimagined its division of labor as political. Second, eschewing marriage altogether and remaining single became a way to avoid the gender-based problems associated with the institution itself. Whether through conscious attempts to create egalitarian arrangements and changing marriage, or liberating oneself from it altogether, the subject of marriage—at least in terms of heterosexual personal relationships—automatically becomes a feminist concern that has implications for women and men who desire gender equality. Concerns related to egalitarian ideals in turn serve to provoke an inquiry such as the current one that addresses practices surrounding weddings that supposedly anticipate the lived lives of persons in marriage.

"Born with feminism simply in the water" (Baumgardner & Richards, 2010, p. 83), Third Wave feminism describes what might be considered feminism "today," a version marked by individualism but with a political consciousness. Writing in 2000, when *Manifesta* was first published, Baumgardner and Richards (2010) termed Third Wavers the "core mass of the current women's movement." This Third Wave thus builds upon the achievements of the Second Wave and constitutes a cohort of those raised in the wake of and enjoying the benefits of the previous wave (p. 400). Femininity does not mean antifeminist, and one is free to enjoy "girlie" culture which celebrates stereotypically "feminine accoutrements . . . be it Barbie [dolls], housekeeping, or girl talk" (p. 400).[14] In this way, it still retains at its roots the essence of feminism as a means by which to effect egalitarian ideals in a wider scope. Gamble (2001) noted that this Third Wave of feminism "acknowledges that it stands on the shoulders of other, earlier, feminist movements," and helps to describe a time and thought after the Second Wave that allows for celebration and critique of previous waves, as well as new strategies that bridge the gap between theory and practice to achieve equity for all human beings (p. 54). It is, as Gamble concluded, "another way for feminism to accommodate itself to changing times" (p. 51).

The wave paradigm attempts to locate feminism's broader aims within some kind of historical progression. These demarcations have no specific, concrete boundaries regarding age, time period lived, or even goals; one can self-identify as part of the Second Wave, Third, or even Fourth,[15] or disregard these altogether and simply say, "I am a feminist because I believe in equal rights for women." Or, one could, being conscious of feminism's achievements, goals, or failures (or even not), proclaim that feminism is over and outdated. This view that women at this point in history no longer *need* feminism has become defined, however vaguely or disjointedly within feminist scholarship and popular media, as postfeminism. While Third Wave feminism acknowledges that the work of feminism is not done, postfeminism distances itself from "old guard" feminism that saw patriarchy as oppressive and cast workplace issues such as equal pay for equal work, sexual harassment, and childcare, as well as personal issues such as marriage, control over one's own (female) body, and housework, as ways in which gender inequity was maintained.

According to Gamble (2001), postfeminism rejects the notion that women are victims unable to control their own lives. Gamble pointed to its origins in the media during the 1980s; postfeminism became a way to declare that feminism was obsolete. In her 1991 bestseller *Backlash: The Undeclared War Against American Women*, Susan Faludi explained how the gains of the Second Wave had become dismantled as traditionally feminine ideals reemerged in various facets of popular culture and media in the 1980s. Gamble (2001) stated: "For Faludi, postfeminism *is* the backlash" whose "triumph lies in its ability to define itself as an ironic, pseudo-intellectual critique on the feminist movement, rather than an overtly hostile response to it" (p. 45). For Gamble, postfeminism "embraces a flexible ideology which can be adapted to suit individual needs and desires," resulting in a literally post-feminist time and thought, a heterosexist world in which its members are unwilling to criticize pornography, date rape, and passé issues related to gender inequity and oppression (p. 44). Thus, one might see postfeminism as telling women to "get over it" and move on; these are no longer big deals that deserve outrage, criticism, or calls for action.

In her 2004 article, "Post-feminism and Popular Culture," McRobbie described how this "non-identity" with and distance from feminism had carved a "cultural space" within which postfeminist themes had found not only a venue but also popularity, with the success of "gentle denunciations of feminism" embodied in the books and subsequent films associated with *Bridget Jones's Diary* (pp. 255–257). The heroine of postfeminism works for a living, depends on no man for her financial security, yet longs and yearns and dedicates considerable effort to getting a man. For McRobbie, the fictional world of Bridget Jones creates a virtual parallel of the postfeminist mindset, replete with the tropes of freedom and choice connected with a world which allows the dismantling of feminism because, to borrow from Baumgardner and Richards (2010), it's been "in the water" (p. 83) for so long.

This postfeminist cultural space, noted McRobbie (2004), normalizes pornography, dismisses objections to the objectification of women, and emphasizes the individual's pursuit of self-improvement free from the critique of gendered power relations. Looking through a postfeminist prism, the hipness associated with *feminisme* a century ago has become decidedly unhip, and to criticize "choices" that reflect the antithesis of feminism's core ironically appears as *anti*-feminist. In this new media environment, stories and issues about women and their concerns both acknowledge and distance this new state of the world from old-school feminism, lest the new "hip" woman appear the stereotyped bitter man-hater.[16] The dismantling of feminist politics and absence of critical thinking that mark postfeminism thus open the door for a re-emergence of *feminisme*, though McRobbie foresees self-censorship as a dampening agent:

> Feminism is cast into the shadows, where at best it can expect to have some afterlife, where it might be regarded ambivalently by those young women who must in public venues stake a distance from it, for the sake of social and sexual recognition. (p. 255)

I see bridal media's popularity in the late 20th and early 21st centuries in the United States as indicative of a postfemininst cultural environment. Bridal media encourage women to thoroughly and unquestioningly take part in archaic, patriarchal rituals in which they still take the role of object of exchange between men, "the traffic in women" that Rubin (1997) proposed serves as the glue upon which societal relations in patriarchy depends: of the gifts exchanged to cement kinship bonds and alliances, women are the most valuable. I find useful to this discussion McRobbie's (2004) explication of postfeminism's "double entanglement" of (a) neoconservative values regarding gender, sexuality, and family life, and (b) the liberation represented by choice and diversity in domestic and kinship relations that provides an additional way to look at traditional marriage, which weddings validate, as positive and desirable (p. 255). Thus, a postfeminism lens would picture bridal media as enhancing the desirability of marriage as a means to validate heterosexuality, especially for women, and traditional weddings as a means by which same-sex couples can highlight and call attention to their right to marry just like everyone else.

"Feminism remains a pretty simple concept," wrote Faludi in 1991, "despite repeated—and enormously effective efforts to dress it up in greasepaint and turn its proponents into gargoyles" (p. xxiii). While "postfeminist" describes the historical moment in which I examine the appeal of bridal media of the mid-1990s through the first decade of the 21st century, currents of feminism remain alive and well in alternative forms of bridal media, such as the web sites *Offbeatbride.com* and *FeministWedding.com*. To say that all bridal media reflect the "backlash" against feminism would be erroneous, as feminists have married and do marry in weddings while wearing white wedding dresses. Evidence of the work by young women who identify with feminism, whom one can term as Third Wavers using the wave paradigm, negotiate the assumptions of wedding etiquette while maintaining their core feminist values appears most notably on the Internet. Wedding web sites in this vein offer alternatives for couples who wish to marry yet still hold values associated with the Second Wave, such as equity in domestic labor and "evergreen" feminist issues such as deciding to keep or change or even modify surnames after marriage.

In this book, I examine the themes common to media treatments of the wedding to demonstrate how the cultural space carved out by bridal media remains an open field for both feminism *and* postfeminism, in the forms of critique, consciousness, and portrayals of women that cast them as both feminist and feminine. The pursuit and endorsement of femininity within postfeminism appears to undermine the achievements of the Second Wave. I see the post-Second Wave "return to femininity" described by Faludi (1991) even more present today, with the backlash against women to have not faded in the least. If anything, bridal media have taken the ideals embedded in the notions of true womanhood and the depiction of the perfect bride to ever more lofty heights.

Indeed, femininity lies at the very core of bridal media: the modern woman can, thanks to the perceived accomplishments of feminism, now *choose* to pursue physical beauty and *choose* to take on the role of bride. This choice, however, does not necessarily mean freedom, but actually binds the bride to what Otnes and Pleck (2003) called an "'ethic of perfection'" (p. 8). This pursuit of the perfect wedding and perfect bridal appearance actually limits her, and disguises the labor and effort required to obtain that perfection as something she deserves, a reward for achieving her new status as wife.

Femininity

Femininity "is to be consumed with (heterosexual) sex, romance and beauty," wrote Ussher (1997, p. 75). Among myriad media representations of femininity, bridal media exemplify all three components, perhaps even to the point of serving as the ultimate source for feminine representation. This triad serves as a useful way to lay out how mediated portrayals of weddings accommodate postfeminist notions described by McRobbie (2004): heterosexuality (sex), the desirability of finding a "good catch" (romance), and the worship, enjoyment, and value of female physical beauty. Within a postfeminist framework, noted McRobbie, these desires serve to re-regulate young women by creating new pathologies that define females as lacking *something*.[17] In the world of wedding media, those somethings take the form of a husband, marriage, a wedding, the perfect wedding, the perfect dress, or any of the endless items deemed absolutely necessary by bridal merchandisers via the forms of media that promote their products either directly (advertising) or indirectly (editorial-based accounts of actual weddings).

As Letitia Baldrige (2000) noted in *Legendary Brides*, the wedding serves as a high point of a woman's existence: "No pageantry unfolds with more drama, and no one remains unaffected by witnessing the celebration. It is, after all, one of the most beautiful moments in a woman's life" (p. 8). With all its emotions and romantic idealism, the wedding ceremony certainly can touch even the most hardened of hearts. The performance of love and imbuement of romance conveyed by media accounts of weddings reflect an emotional generality that Berlant (2008) identified in *The Female Complaint: The Unfinished Business of Sentimentality in American Culture* as an anchor of women's culture, a "mass-marketed intimate public" (p. 5) that promotes "a core form of gendered personhood for women" (p. 170). As a phenomenon of a capitalist culture industry, women's culture offers women, regardless of race or socioeconomics, a sense of belonging; it provides a site where disparate women connect with other women via a shared knowledge and common emotive experiences.

In women's culture, feminine worth depends on a sense of being needed by someone, noted Berlant (2008), and identification with the modern love plot requires that its adherents keep open to the idea that love is a means by which women are rescued from their current (single) life and have the chance for a new (married) one. Berlant pointed to women's culture as providing the central fantasy that allows the complex woman to become "a vague or simpler version of herself, usually in the vicinity of a love plot" (p. 7).

Radway's (1984) analysis of the romance novel illustrated this regulating process of women's culture that reaffirms "woman" as incomplete without an *other*: "Even more successfully than the patriarchal society within which it was born, the romance denies women the possibility of refusing that purely relational destiny and thus rejects their right to a single, self-contained existence" (p. 207). Berlant (2008) addressed how being needed has become a demonstration of feminine worth; she observed that the "unsutured" woman is seen as lonely, falling short of attaining the "feminine good life" (p. 171). Weddings might shine the spotlight on the bride, but she cannot take on the role without being "sutured" to an *other* (a man). Thus, women's culture defines feminine identity while simultaneously ensuring the continuation of patriarchy by reinforcing the notion of the "incomplete woman." Natharius (2007) further underscored this when he argued that popular film portrayals of the single career woman reinforce the idea that such a woman lives by herself and supports herself only "because she does not have a man to take care of her and make her dreams come true"; the stereotype of the successful but unhappy single woman has become an assumptive theme within a patriarchal culture (pp. 182–183).

Within traditional Western gender ideology, borne of patriarchy and which continues to the present, women become socialized to believe that finding a man is an important life goal. This remains an important facet of the feminine identity because it upholds patriarchy and the social order in which men still call the shots and women take their secondary roles as wives and helpmeets. The white wedding perpetuates the traditional gender rubric, Jellison (2008) noted, by reifying the husband-provider/wife-consumer model of post-World War II gender prescriptions (p. 3).

Feminist scholar Adrienne Rich (1980) used the term "compulsory heterosexuality" to describe the social mandate that we find partners of the opposite sex. Rich pointed out that under this requirement, a woman must find a man—to desire, to seek, to "catch," and to marry—in order to be considered a "real" woman, thus forwarding a heterosexist agenda which privileges male-female couples, the ideal composition of romantic relationships. As Ingraham (2008) observed, the bridal industry and the media environment surrounding it promote heterosexual normativity through portrayals of the "heterosexual imaginary," the idea that one's well-being depends on maintaining a heterosexual romantic relationship (p. 26). One can view the bridal role, now commonly portrayed as desirable and, indeed, mandatory, as a manifestation of hyperfemininity: the exaggerated adherence to stereotypically feminine gender roles, especially the need to obtain and sustain a romantic relationship with a man. Indeed, for the hyperfeminine woman, whose idea of success is finding a man of substantial economic means, marriage and the taking of the role of wife serve as her sole source of achievement (Murnen & Byrne, 1991).

I argue that bridal media collectively have become *the* epitomic example of women's culture, a genre of popular culture that promotes, defends, and celebrates femininity. If, as Berlant (2008) contended, femininity works as a "normative gender practice" that enforces the view that romantic fantasy ought to constitute realism (p. 304), then the totality of bridal media is its greatest weapon and Brideland is its Nirvana. In a postfeminist media landscape devoid of critique, the wedding serves as a microcosm wherein performative aspects of gender reestablish sexual difference, a process through which the external "effects" an internal core, as described by Butler (1999, p. 173). Performance of gender in this most public of arenas *requires* the reifying signals Butler lists as part of the creation of "gender": the acts, gestures, corporeal signs, and other "discursive means" by which (hetero)sexuality is regulated (p. 173).

Similarly, the roles of "bride" and "bridegroom" require external cues, ones that, unsurprisingly, signal gender. The ability to reject traditional behaviors associated with divisions of labor becomes difficult even for those who perceive wedding planning as genderless. For example, Currie (1993) found that couples who claim to have egalitarian domestic relations before their wedding ironically become trapped in an unequal division of labor in planning their first public act as a married couple. Regarding this imbalance of work illustrative of heterosexual couples, women devote inordinate amounts of time and physical, emotional, and mental energy to the planning of what advertisers, and others, call "her day"—the pinnacle of her life. Planning, which involves time-intensive, domestic-oriented tasks such as shopping for and selecting menu items, choosing a venue, assigning clothing for the participants, and determining ceremony accoutrements, typically falls to the woman. In contrast, her husband-to-be usually just needs to make sure he arrives at the ceremony on time and in correct "uniform," with even these responsibilities assigned to the best man, so that the groom need simply appe   In a real sense, the public and private spheres we associate with men and women become performative when the woman takes on duties related to food, clothing, and shopping (related to the domestic/private), while the man's main duty is to make a *public* showing. While the bride may overshadow the bridegroom's appearance on the wedding stage, her duties prior to her public appearance illustrate the extra work she has done privately, away from public view.

Femininity need not limit itself to this gender binary. Even as gendered behaviors and heterosexuality serve as the composite interactional plane for their enactment, the aspects of fashion and beauty surrounding weddings also appeal to non-heterosexual women. For example, Walker (2000) described her own experiences as a lesbian-feminist bride in "Feminists in Brideland." As an out lesbian, Walker confessed, her only regret was "my chance to be a bride" (p. 219). Not only did she get her chance, but she explained how she was able to find alternatives to the traditional wedding gown that matched her fashion taste and desires while also preserving her feminist sensibilities. The appeal of the bridal identity—historically based in heterosexual marriage—thus does not necessarily contradict the mantle of a feminist female. I see Walker's bridal story as illustrative of a kind of circular thinking, reflecting a Third Wave feminist perspective with postfeminist tinges: one may proclaim to be a feminist and advocate feminist values *and* still participate in a patriarchal-based practice in which feminine beauty is exalted, because one is a feminist, after all.

The desire to be beautiful illustrates the problematic aspect of femininity when approached with the perspective that its bases lie in instilling in women a feeling that they lack something. The entire beauty industry exists to address the lack of beauty—or at least, to literally make up for this lack through surgery, weight loss, hair color, cosmetics, face creams, eye creams, body creams, hand creams, and infinite other products designed to "complete" a woman. While the marketing of such products deliberately uses femininity as a tool to tell women they need them, Faludi (1991) pointed out that beauty product manufacturers do not actually conspire together to coerce women into purchasing them. Rather than a concerted effort to oppress women by creating artificial needs that "correct" their unattractiveness, the business of beauty relies on the bottom line: making a profit. This "soft selling" of femininity illustrates the cumulative effect that results from consensual acceptance of certain beliefs and practices—to the point that they become part of everyday life. Similarly, bridal media work separately yet collectively to reproduce dominant ideology while "gaining the tacit approval of those whom the ideology suppresses," as described by Dow (1990, p. 262). This process is known as hegemony.

Hegemony

The term "white wedding" evokes a familiarity, requiring little in the way of definition when used to describe a form of social event marking the marriage ritual. It has become a commonsense term, a concept already imbued with mutual understanding between sender and receiver: we know what the white wedding entails—we see it everywhere in bridal media, which in turn, we also see "everywhere." The billion-dollar wedding industry combines with a category of mass media comprising entire publications, periodicals, films, and television programs dedicated to the reification of the fairy tale, offering as a result evidence of the acceptance of marriage and high-priced weddings on a societal, indeed, international scale.[18] Where does this rubric get its power so as to warrant such desire, such acceptance, such attention? How does the magical domain of Brideland mesmerize women who claim anti-bridal attitudes? I use these questions as a starting point to explain why I believe *hegemony* applies so aptly to the study of feminism and femininity in bridal media.

Hegemony as a theory finds its origins in the critique of Marxism by Italian intellectual and head of the Italian Communist Party Antonio Gramsci, imprisoned under the regime of Benito Mussolini. Gramsci's writings in prison in the 1920s until his death in 1937, known collectively as the *Prison Notebooks*, provide a means by which to think critically about the workings of society and state that could not be explained by Marxist theory, according to Forgacs in *The Antonio Gramsci Reader: Selected Writings, 1916–1935* (Gramsci, 2000). Gramsci sought to discover why socialist revolutions had failed or been defeated in capitalistic Western nations, given the Russian Revolution. While strong on general predictions about capitalistic development and the connection between economic crises and political transformation, Marxist theory "was weak on detailed analyses of the forms of political power, the concrete relations between social classes and political representation and the cultural and ideological forms in which social antagonism are fought out or regulated and dissipated," wrote Forgacs (p. 189). To fill that void, Gramsci relied on non-Marxist philosopher Benedetto Croce's insights into the "ethico-political sphere," a theoretical plane consisting of the ideological, moral, and cultural "cements" that bind a society's participants to each other (p. 190).

Gramsci cast his explanation of how power works in a society along two levels: the private sphere of civil society and the political society of the state. "These two levels correspond on one hand to the function of 'hegemony' which the dominant group exercises throughout society and on the other hand to that of 'direct domination' or command exercised through the State and 'juridical' government" (Gramsci, 1999, p. 145). The first level, civil society, results as a function of class, wherein a ruling or dominant class exerts power based on consent. The second level, the state, exerts power through organized government and the law. The former becomes the site where the afore-mentioned ideological, moral, and cultural cements of society become organized, and where hegemony operates to create a status quo and a shared knowledge regarding social life.

Gramsci thus developed "a criticism of the state as a hegemonic super-structure of power," summarized Zompetti (1997, p. 72). Lears (1985) pointed out that this involves not a simple model based in a single, monolithic super-structure, but "a complex interaction of relatively autonomous spheres (pub-lic and private; political, cultural, and economic) within a totality of attitudes and practices" (p. 571). According to Gramsci (1999), hegemony works, both functionally and successfully, because the "subaltern"—those outside the hege-monic structure system—pretty much lets it. Thus, in addition to the appara-tus of the state (which has coercive power), the subaltern functions based on what Gramsci defined as, "The 'spontaneous' consent given by the great masses of the population to the general direction imposed on social life by the domi-nant fundamental group; this consent is, historically, caused by the prestige (and consequent confidence) which the dominant group enjoys because of its posi-tion and function in the world of production" (p. 145).

Gramsci (1999) identified "functionaries" as a category of intellectuals that serve as the dominant group's deputies; they exercise "the subaltern functions of social hegemony and political government" (p. 145). This particular class of intellectuals collects, organizes, and conveys knowledge that reflects the dom-inant group's interests. In a sense, these would be the "middlemen" (or, more correctly, "middlepersons") between those in power and those who are not (the subaltern). Within the context of cultural work, Carragee (1993) explained, the production and reproduction of social relationships in a capitalistic society "plays an essential role in establishing the legitimacy of the social order" (p. 330). Gramsci (2000) pointed to the press as part of the "formidable complex of trenches and fortifications of the dominant class" that maintains the "ideo-logical 'front'" of those in power (pp. 380–381). Gramsci saw the press as the most dynamic part of the ideological structure composed of civil society and the state, but not the only one: "Everything which influences or is able to influence public opinion directly or indirectly belongs to it" (p. 380).

Gramsci's concept of power and order regarding the role of the press and the mass media industry in general serves as a key theoretical approach in media and cultural criticism. Mary E. Brown (1989), in her study of soap operas and women's culture, described the notion of hegemony as cultural leadership, a concept central to her investigation and to cultural studies in general. Others have viewed hegemony not as a fixed, abstract concept, but as a continual process that results in commonly held meanings within a society. For example, Dow (1990) referred to hegemony and hegemonic processes as "the various means through which those who support the dominant ideology in a culture are able to continually reproduce that ideology in cultural institutions and products," a process that depends on the unspoken, implicit consent of those to whom those institutions, such as mass media, convey that ideology (p. 262).

Hegemony becomes a useful way of analyzing how mass media frame the contemporary wedding because it helps to explain the process of cultural production. As Carragee (1993) noted, hegemony "provides a framework for examining the mass media's ideological role by focusing on the relationship between the mass media and power" (p. 331). Those who control the mass media present viewpoints they know will be accepted by most of the people who receive their message. In order to sustain their existence within a capitalistic system, media producers avoid "rocking the boat," and, instead, seek to create messages that will not be rejected. Thus, the tendency to maintain the status quo becomes a means by which media convey those least-objectionable messages while ensuring they stay in business. Forgacs, in *The Antonio Gramsci Reader* (Gramsci, 2000), encapsulated the relevance of mass communication to hegemony theory this way: "Gramsci's interest in popular culture was bound up with his conception of revolutionary change as a process in which popular mentalities and behaviour are transformed" (p. 363). Thus, bridal media offer a cultural space wherein hegemonic notions about gender, feminism, femininity, and the way a society validates personal relationships all converge and provide a mirror about what values and practices have become unquestioned aspects of social life.

Wedding as nexus

Marriage serves as an example of hegemony—most people do marry, and accept it as the way of formalizing romantic relationships. Marriage in its current form exists to serve particular interests, namely, those belonging to the dominant social order constituting a range of interested parties that discursively construct marriage as the foundation of family life (Ingraham, 2008; Leonard,

2006). In *Public Vows: A History of Marriage and the Nation*, Cott (2000) summarized how marriage illustrates both the private and public spheres of society by noting that marriage represents personal love and commitment while also offering legal benefits for its participants. In this manner, marriage reflects hegemony of civil society and the state while simultaneously providing a means to organize the sexes: "So far as it is a public institution, it is the vehicle through which the apparatus of state can shape the gender order" (p. 3).

Marriage, by assigning roles of husband (provider) and wife (dependent partner) to men and women, thus provides a regulatory function regarding what males and females are supposed to do—how both sexes "act in the world and the reciprocal relation between them"—while also upholding the state's interests regarding the stability of gender relations and establishment of kinship (Cott, 2000, p. 3). What Michael Warner (2002) called the "menu of privileges" offered by the state through heterosexual marriage provides an implicit and explicit means of discrimination against nonheterosexual relationships, thereby further upholding a certain social order beyond just that regarding gender (p. 274). Marriage then becomes a class issue, in that those barred from legal marriage are relegated to a lower class. As an exclusionary practice, it is a "marker of class privilege," according to Foster (2005, p. 76). Ironically, if homosexuality is considered a progressive sexual movement, the view that marriage has become the only legal sanction for nonheterosexual unions is "unacceptably conservative" (Butler, 2002, p. 236).[19]

While some may reject the notion that domestic relations require what Cott (2000) termed the "imprimatur of public authority" (p. 225), or even the idea of monogamy altogether, most people would agree that marriage serves as the way one would go about making a relationship "official," while doing so makes the relationship legal as well. Even as half of new marriages in the US end in divorce, Cott noted, marriage remains a desirable way to formalize the love relationship, with the money spent on elaborate weddings serving as "ballast destined to keep the marriage afloat" (p. 225).

We see hegemony illustrated in the idea that the responsibility for proposing (heterosexual) marriage falls to the man in the relationship, rather than both parties discussing and agreeing to this formal step. Similar to the "Heterosexual Script" (Kim et al., 2007), which mandates an active male role and passive female role, I see a "marriage script" that has become an implicit part of the narrative assumed in bridal media.[20] After the man asks her to marry him, the marriage script goes, the woman, overjoyed at the prospect of avoiding spinsterhood, happily accepts and then turns her thoughts to "the wedding."[21]

Indeed, the novelty of women proposing marriage, so foreign and challenging to our assumptions about gender, served as the gimmick for a Fox television special in 2000 called *Surprise Wedding*. One by one, the nervous brides-to-be, dressed in wedding finery, proposed to their unsuspecting "grooms," who were duped into appearing with their girlfriends on what they thought was a makeover show. Adding to the excitement, these hopeful brides surprised their unsuspecting men in front of a studio audience of hundreds. Aside from switching gender roles, as the women in *Surprise Wedding* did, one also can defy convention by choosing cohabitation over legal marriage. Couples who choose to live together and not marry, then, question hegemony and challenge the mainstream.

Hegemony surrounds every aspect of wedding planning. Indeed, when people learn of a couple's engagement, they usually then ask, "When is the wedding?" Here we find the application of hegemony to real, everyday life: hegemony serves as the motive, the origin, the commonsense, taken-for-grantedness implicit in wedding planning. Every etiquette book and magazine targeted at the bride serves as a channel for hegemony; these guides provide us with social knowledge and rules on how such an event must be presented.

Historically, treatises on proper manners served as conduits between the nobility and the upper middle classes; courtly customs and behaviors of the rich were adopted by the less wealthy classes. In *The Civilizing Process: The History of Manners*, Elias (1978) traced how books on proper manners became a way of "civilizing" the societies of Western Europe during the Middle Ages. He noted that people in the "example-setting" circle do not need such books to instruct them on how to behave (p. 100). Rather, the non-nobility and upper middle class imitated courtly manners, with etiquette books serving as their guides. In turn, as imitation seeps into the rest of society, the distinction between the classes requires further refinement and development, noted Elias (p. 100).

Much like the treatises on proper manners Elias (1978) described, today's wedding media offer tips on how to have the same kinds of weddings enjoyed by celebrities and royalty. The dominant class in today's age would be the parties who have an interest in maintaining hegemonic notions about proper weddings, namely, businesses and corporations who profit from wedding expenditure. For television networks and production companies, the relatively low cost of producing reality shows that result in high ratings, and, in turn, advertising income, makes it worthwhile to capitalize on the popularity of weddings. Such programs serve as thinly disguised commercials, in that they blatantly feature wedding gowns, rings, catering, and other wedding-related expenses and items as much as, if not more than, the marriage ceremonies that provide their denouements.

As media products, bridal magazines, web sites, and television programs thus offer benefits to an array of interested parties. Bridal magazines blur the line between the editorial and the commercial, benefiting not only their publishers, but also their advertisers. Indeed, bridal magazines essentially serve as extended advertisements for the wedding industry: "The ad, the edit, it's all the same," summarized one industry insider (Kuczynski, 2000).[22] Bridal media producers in turn serve as Gramsci's "functionaries" by organizing the knowledge about "correct" weddings as dictated by the profit-seeking bridal industry and its professionals, such as dress designers, consultants, bridal salon owners, and presenting that knowledge to media consumers. The "big, white, romantic" wedding so naturally has become the norm in American society that wedding-related media emphasize the merchandise associated with weddings rather than the marriage resulting from the event (Gibbons, 2003).

Aside from their profit-making aspects, bridal media can serve a broader purpose regarding marriage, by either forwarding or withholding certain viewpoints about gender equity and civil rights, such as legal recognition of same-sex marriages. Those forwarding a conservative, religious agenda might consider portrayals of the traditional white wedding (of heterosexual couples) most often seen on television as reaffirming "family values," values that dictate that marriage be reserved for a man and a woman. Indeed, such sentiment holds political implications, as when President George W. Bush declared during a White House press conference in July 2003, "I believe marriage is between a man and a woman, and I think we ought to codify that one way or another" ("Bush Wants Marriage Reserved for Heterosexuals," 2003). His comments drew praise from conservative groups, illustrated by the statement, "The president has taken a courageous stand in favor of traditional marriage," from the Traditional Values Coalition, a church lobbying group. One might argue, then, that weddings that follow tradition (and traditional religious practices) provide an affirming message that demarcates gender roles, sustains the nuclear family, and preserves marriage as an institution for heterosexual couples only. The naturalness of marriage forwarded in bridal media illustrates how hegemony functions in civil society while also upholding the apparatus of the state.

Hegemony and feminism

"For the first time in western history women have the option not to marry," observed Geller (2001, p. 292). The dominant portrayal of weddings reinforces this notion for women by making the bridal role so appealing. In "Marriage Envy," Suzanne Leonard (2006) explicated how the "manufactured needs" created by media in postfeminist society tell women they need to get married and become wives and mothers (p. 57). In her essay, Leonard addressed the mass media's fostering of wedding perfection and the search for "the one" (man), a theme underlying reality television programs such as *The Bachelor*. These programs frame marriage as a rare commodity—enhancing its allure to the point that not having it relegates the single woman to the status of a lowly and pathetic figure. Indeed, McClanahan (2007) dubbed programs of this type "Must Marry TV." Bridal media in the form of novels about brides and weddings (known as "bride lit") "grafts romantic fantasies onto the wedding narrative," allowing women to indulge in consumerist and emotional pleasure by reliving wedding "mythology," asserted Leonard (2006, p. 59).

According to Leonard (2006), the excuse of personal choice allows Third Wave feminists to ignore the problematics of marriage as a site of privilege, proof positive that "when handled by women as savvy as themselves, the institution need not impose unwanted roles or responsibilities" (pp. 52–53). She asserted that naturalizing the desire for marriage creates hierarchies among women that categorize them as those who are married vs. those who are not, instilling jealousy and competition between women (antithetical to feminism as a movement unifying women). This marriage envy—and, I would say, wedding envy—is a symptom of what Leonard saw as "a broader and perhaps even more troubling breakdown in the female imaginary, in that the only possibility open to women through postfeminist culture, it would seem, is to dream of their wedding day" (p. 60). In other words, the world "after feminism" has enjoyed an almost too-successful result from the efforts of past waves of feminism, to the point that women today have little left to aspire to than a lush social affair that recognizes their achievement in a final frontier where marriage has become the ultimate prize for enduring the long years of singlehood.

The celebration of femininity cultivated by bridal media and the negative implications of "marriage envy" today makes even more relevant Gramsci's writings of nearly a century ago. His call for women to attain "genuine independence in relation to men" reflected a feminist approach; this advocacy for women to see themselves differently in their sexual relations further underscores the importance of gender equity (Gramsci, 1999, p. 587). According to Gramsci (2000), a "new feminine personality" was required for an "ethical and civil order" connected to what he called the "sexual question"—the issue of gender and the role of women in the creation of that ethical and civil order (p. 587). Indeed, Slaughter (2011) wrote that Gramsci "almost employs a feminist perspective as he reworks Marx in understanding the 'woman question'" (p. 263). I see Gramsci's views regarding the need for a new feminine (female) personality as similar to Kipnis's (2006) conclusions concerning the incompatibility between feminism and the attributes associated with femininity today, especially in terms of the former's aim to eliminate female inadequacy and the sustaining of female inadequacy that the latter contends underlies femininity in its current incarnation.

Hegemony, wrote Dow (1996), allowed her to "understand and to analyze why women themselves have historically been the most powerful enemies of feminism" (p. 17). Dow did not doubt her female students' ability to look critically at the media and to resist the power of persuasion that media messages contain, but she did admit to questioning the "quality or power of that resistance in the face of the repetitive and consistently reinforced hegemonic media messages that they consume" (p. 18). The need for a feminist-based critique of wedding media and marriage itself becomes heightened when one observes how immune from criticism the bridal industry appears to be in works by those who study it. Marriage envy, noted Leonard, has become one way for noncritical writers to explain away and discount the serious questioning of marriage engendered by feminist critiques such as Geller's (2001) in *Here Comes the Bride*.[23]

Counterhegemony

Widely held and entrenched, hegemonic views of appropriate gendered behaviors have taken centuries to evolve into common sense. The problem with common sense lies in its unquestioning acceptance. Landy (1994) described Gramsci's term *senso comune* as comprising a "collage of opinions and beliefs that fails to be not only coherent but also critical" (p. 29). The uniformity of portrayals thus becomes problematic when little or no alternative images are included among the dominant order. When considering mass media and the creation of cultural work, there is no monolithic state wherein specific cultural norms are specifically and consciously discussed, mapped out, and then incorporated into what we call "entertainment" or "news." Rather, producers, writers, photographers, and editors find programs and ideas that a disseminator, such as a network or publisher, considers sellable. Clearly, there exists some kind of appeal to women of seeing other women prepare for their dream weddings, otherwise these programs and publications would not exist.

Lest this assessment of the functioning of hegemony within the world of weddings and its associated media outlets appear grim, there is an "out," so to speak. Hegemony does not imply a totally dominant ideology against which resistance is futile. "Rather than assuming an all powerful, closed text," noted Dow (1996), hegemony "presumes the possibility of resistance and opposition" (p. 14). Regarding change, hegemony also highlights the interaction between media institutions and "alternative social movements that challenge the political order" (Carragee, 1993, p. 17). In this sense, the potential exists for mass media also to include, to varying degrees, viewpoints and perspectives that counter hegemony and open the way for new ways of thinking. The possibility, potential, and *existence* of alternative wedding formats allow hegemony to occur because hegemony is always "leaking."[24] People can choose not to marry, for example. Couples who choose to elope clearly counter the hegemonic expectation of a wedding.

However, since it "de facto represents a tradition," observed Geller (2001), "no wedding, conventional or innovative, occurs autonomously" (p. 259). Even as counterhegemonic wedding ceremonies on the surface look untraditional, they tend to incorporate all the same rituals and artifacts associated with the stereotypical big, white wedding. In this manner, hegemonic practices become circumvented by active consumers who "make (*bricolent*) innumerable and infinitesimal transformations of and within the dominant cultural economy in order to adapt it to their own interests and their own rules," as described by de Certeau (1984, pp. xiii–xiv). Counterhegemonic efforts thus make use of imposed culture and practices by providing a means of what de Certeau described as an "escap[ing] . . . without leaving" (p. xiii); the active cultural consumer thus adapts the texts of the dominant social order when challenging that social order outright is not possible.[25]

Bridal media at this point in history have reached a point where criticism of the current high-priced wedding has started to gain ground—in the form of news stories and even depictions within the bridal media "universe" that counter the prevailing common sense. Eventually, when those alternatives to the most heard and seen version of the wedding reach a critical mass, the dialectical nature of hegemony allows for changes. Thus, as Lull (2011) stated, "Hegemony fails when dominant ideology is weaker than social resistance" (p. 35). Should enough people see a different form of weddings as desirable and practical, then the typical wedding might not involve what we have considered as traditionally required artifacts and practices. So, while hegemony explains why we tend to see so many similar weddings in various media forms, it also allows for counterhegemonies propagated in texts that offer ideologies of resistance—these, in turn, create an open door to new ways of thinking.

Author's Perspective

I write this book from the point of view of a feminist, a media scholar, and as a married woman. Like so many young women, I had an interest in wedding apparel while on shopping trips with my mother, sneaking a try-on of the veils in the bridal section of department stores, watching the royal weddings of Princess Diana and Sarah Ferguson on television, and attending weddings as guest and bridesmaid.

My interest in television weddings began when I started watching *A Wedding Story* on The Learning Channel in the mid-1990s, when I was an assistant professor and in a serious relationship with the man who is now my husband. I became re-attracted to the idea of a wedding and bought bridal magazines looking for "the dress"—only to become disillusioned by the price and prospect of wearing an expensive, uncomfortable garment for even just a few hours. I happened upon The Learning Channel's *A Wedding Story* while channel surfing. I found it highly appealing, both in its visuals and the way in which couples expressed their love for each other. After a few episodes, I noticed some gender-based patterns in the way couples got ready for their weddings. It seemed that while the women took hours getting dressed and having their hair and makeup done, the men were out playing golf or touch football.

As a communication professor, I thought the program would serve as an excellent way to research the portrayal of gender roles in the mass media; my own "wedding story" informs this inquiry. As a woman in a romantic relationship, I began to realize that all the associated time, cost, and effort that went into "a wedding" did not fit into my and my partner's values, our individual life goals, the purpose of our life together, or our ideas about money and time and how to spend them. As a financially independent woman, asking my parents to fund a wedding fell outside my reality.

Since my partner and I already lived in Las Vegas, where "quickie" weddings comprise an entire industry (and which easily could serve as the subject for another book on weddings), our spur-of-the moment, no-frills ceremony went against the ideal promoted in bridal media: no wedding gown, no tuxedo, no guests, no planning, no Elvis impersonator (he wasn't available), no rented artificial flower bouquet (it cost extra). My students enjoy hearing the details of our wedding story; some think it's terribly romantic and "cool," although I do get the occasional sympathetic "awwww" response from my female students because I didn't get "my special day," illustrating again the power of the hegemonic view.

I constitute part of the target audience of bridal media; as such, I am, as Zompetti (1997) put it, "a functioning part of a community" (p. 66). As a critic of these media, I acknowledge my ethical responsibility to take a position on the subject matter that I criticize. I do not write this book as a diatribe against weddings or marriage. Rather, I contend that the expectation of conspicuous consumption and the amount of time and energy devoted to wedding planning can distract women as a sex from gaining true equity in a still-patriarchal society. Like Wolf's (2002) beauty myth, I see bridal media as creating the wedding myth—the promise to women of one perfect day of happiness and joy as long as they devote the required time, money, labor, and emotional effort to it. The wedding myth tells women that they are incomplete without a man, incomplete without a wedding, and incomplete without the physical beauty associated with being a bride.

In this book, I examine what bridal media are telling their audiences. Even though I might see myself as the counterhegemonic bride, the very fact that I got married illustrates the "escap[ing] . . . without leaving" that de Certeau (1984) described; I am married (to a male) and thus participate in the dominant ideological order represented by legalized marriage. I cannot change this, nor do I wish to remove myself from the living arrangement I have chosen. However, I can speak to the problems I see with the way marriage has become equated with the need for weddings in which women, especially, willingly allow themselves to take part in practices that nullify their worth as individuals and continue to support patriarchal ideology. I see that even as women work so hard to gain an education and equity and fair treatment in the world, messages surround them every day that continue to tell them they *need* a man to be happy and that their value as human beings lies not in their abilities, but in their physical appearance as a bride and role as wife. The financial expense and unpaid labor mandated by bridal guides and wedding media further undermine the concerted efforts of like-minded, independent women—and men—who seek to create an egalitarian society. This is why I view the seemingly trivial, mundane, and feminine world of bridal media as an important site for feminist critique and study.

Preview of Chapters

So, how do bridal media reflect women's status in the society of the United States at the beginning of the 21st century? The answer requires first an examination of how various forms of mass media have portrayed weddings in the past. In Chapter 2, "From Princess Brides to Everyday Celebrities," I review the development of the white wedding standard as news media portray it today. Working from historical news accounts, I trace the history of the big, white wedding as it originated in New York high society. I explain how bridal media allow ordinary, noncelebrity women to achieve a modicum of fame on their special day through newspaper wedding announcements. I present case studies of mega-famous brides and describe the media coverage surrounding their weddings; such examples illustrate the importance of the role of bride over the other roles or notable achievements of these famous women. In particular, I discuss media hype surrounding notable royal weddings since the 19th century that stand out as examples of how the bridal appearance creates and enhances feminine identity.

In Chapter 3, "The Bridal Media Milieu," I describe the range of wedding-oriented media available within the American mass communication landscape today. These include bridal magazines, Internet web sites designed for brides, and the numerous network and cable television programs in the reality genre.

These all demonstrate that the wedding, and its accompanying hegemonic notions, is alive and well. I also discuss wedding-related television programs, beginning with *Bride and Groom*, a reality-based program originating in the 1950s, and other programs on cable networks that offer a wedding as the grand prize for couples competing against each other.

In Chapters 4 and 5, I explore common themes regarding the portrayal of everyday brides and the larger feminist and feminine implications of specific, slice-of-life wedding planning programs, namely, TLC's *A Wedding Story* and *Say Yes to the Dress*, Oxygen's *Real Weddings From The Knot*, WE tv's *Bridezillas*, and FitTV's *Buff Brides*. These programs follow brides weeks, days, and hours prior to their wedding and provide data for examining the bridal process. In Chapter 4, "Creating the Perfect Bride," I analyze media portrayals of women as they take on the role of bride and create the physical aura embodying this signifier based on four themes: the wedding dress as magic, the disciplined female body, physical beauty, and perfection. I use narratives in specific episodes to illustrate not only the hegemonic notions of what a bride should look like, but the acceptance of such ideals by brides as they literally work their bodies to conform to the wedding dress they desire. In these bridal media, then, we see an almost factory-like operation on the wedding day, with the bride as the resulting "product."

In Chapter 5, "Working the Part: Bride as Actor," I examine the bride as actor, in contrast to the past chapter's examination of her as object. Using the content of wedding reality programs, I look at how these programs portray brides as persons prior to their status as wife. I discuss how the superbride allows for the incorporation of behaviors associated with masculinity (and, taken to its logical conclusion, leadership) into the feminine identity of the bride. In Brideland, Wolf (2003) noted, men do exist, but as shadow figures in service of the bride. The examination of gender performance within the setting of the wedding could stop at analyzing the facets of femininity emphasized in bridal media, but weddings and their portrayal in various media provide a space where one also can look at portrayals of masculinity. As Edwards (2006) noted, simplistic equations that define masculinity and men in terms of the public sphere, and femininity and women in terms of the private, have become more complex, even if these generalized distinctions have not yet become dismantled. I describe overarching themes present in these programs regarding the contribution of the men who appear in them—and their perceived importance both as participants and onlookers—in this form of media that purports to reflect "real life."

In Chapter 6, "Alternative Brides and Grooms," I examine reality television examples of brides who serve as exceptions to the rule among the over-

whelmingly similar weddings presented in magazines a[...]
Specifically, I offer three examples of reality television wed[...]
the big, white wedding. First, I discuss the story of reluctant[...]
who in an exceptional episode of TLC's *A Wedding Story*, expressed a r[...],
trary viewpoint. I then describe how the homemade, homestyle wedding of
Jessa and Jeff from Oxygen's *Real Weddings From The Knot* serves to counter
the hegemonic versions that reflect consumerism. I discuss the presence of both
hegemony and counterhegemony in Bravo's *Gay Weddings*, a slice-of-life reality wedding series that featured gay and lesbian couples. Alternative feminist
media that offer advice and resources for feminists who want to get married
in a wedding constitute a subgenre of bridal media. I examine the content of
these sites of resistance to reveal their counterhegemonic messages. These
include media platforms that explicitly challenge wedding hegemony by using
the concept of feminism, and those that offer alternatives to the big, white wedding in more covert, entertaining ways.

I close this book with a discussion of the implications of mass media versions of the white wedding for the future of feminism. In Chapter 7, "Modern
Women, Traditional Brides," I provide an overview of more recent forms of
bridal media that both continue to affirm the generic big, white wedding now
so common among the middle and upper classes, as well as those that offer
evidence of counterhegemony. Even as this book concentrates on the vastness
of the bridal media universe and the hegemonic messages it conveys to women,
venues for change exist that counter those hegemonic messages and present
images of women that go beyond the bride. These venues communicate ways
of creating and maintaining egalitarian and equitable relationships between
individuals, regardless of gender or sexual orientation. Finally, in Chapter 8,
I offer my assessment and personal observations based on my analyses of
bridal media throughout this book.

Notes

1. Penner (2004) noted how weddings had few rules during the early part of the 19th
   century. Howard (2006) noted that prior to the 19th century, weddings were more
   informal, held at home with some kind of dinner. The elite weddings of the upper
   class served as models for today's white wedding. In Chapter 2, I provide details from
   their coverage in big-city newspapers during that era.
2. Here are the average wedding costs according to "Avg. Wedding Cost 1945–2010"
   (2011), a graph available on the web site *The WeddingReport.com*: $26,450 in 2005,
   $27,590 in 2006, $28,730 in 2007, $21,810 in 2008, and $19,580 in 2009.
3. Mead's (2007) first-person, journalistic treatment of weddings in *One Perfect Day:
   The Selling of the American Wedding* "comprises a journey through the wedding

industry, exploring the degree to which weddings have been transformed by outside interests into machines for making money" (p. 10).

4. For more on materialist feminism, see Hennessy and Ingraham (1997), *Materialist Feminism: A Reader in Class, Difference, and Women's Lives.*

5. *People.com*'s Kate Middleton site (http://www.people.com/people/kate_middleton) described her as having "sporty elegance" that makes her a "natural" wife for the prince. Though not of royal heritage, Middleton hardly could be described as "common," being the daughter of a millionaire who attended the most elite schools in Great Britain. *Yahoo.com* offered web surfers an entire site, *The Royal Wedding* (http://royalwedding.yahoo.com/), with numerous links about the wedding, including royal etiquette, Kate's life story, media coverage, and wedding guests.

6. The Trista-Ryan wedding became fodder for gossip magazines such as *Us Weekly*, which featured their wedding plans with the headline "Our Dream Wedding Details!" on the cover of its September 8, 2003 issue. In the December 15, 2003 issue of *In Touch Weekly*, their wedding served as the cover story. The magazine headlined the story as "Wedding of the Year!" and gave readers the inside scoop on "their love," "the laughs," and "the fantasy honeymoon."

7. The Learning Channel's (TLC) past and present offerings in their "Personal TLC" lineup of daytime reality programming include *A Wedding Story, A Baby Story, A Dating Story, A Reunion Story*, and *A Makeover Story*. Maher (2004) termed TLC the "compulsory heterosexuality channel."

8. Davis (2006), in *Good Girls and Wicked Witches: Women in Disney's Feature Animation*, analyzed these classic fairy tales as interpreted in Disney animation films. She noted that in later Disney movies such as *Pocahontas, Aladdin*, and to some degree, *Beauty and the Beast*, the overarching quest for a husband/prince, such as that of *Snow White*, becomes secondary to other themes.

9. Zipes (2007), in *When Dreams Came True: Classical Fairy Tales and Their Tradition*, pointed out that fairy tales served as a pleasurable socializing process for children (p. 18).

10. Propp (1968) earlier noted how the supernatural and fantastic, such as talking animals, serve as key characteristics of fairy tales (p. 5).

11. Jellison, in both *It's Our Day* (2008) and "The Commercialization of Weddings in the Twentieth Century" (2010), cites Cinderella as a motif in the wedding world.

12. Marina Warner (1995) also addressed the "negative female power" (p. 222) in fairy tales featuring stories in which women mistreat other women, such as the evil stepmother and stepsisters in the story of Cinderella.

13. See also Wood's *Gendered Lives: Communication, Gender, and Culture* (2010) for an overview of feminism movements.

14. Girlie culture reclaims girl culture—practices and consumption related to enjoyment of "being a girl." Rather than rejecting femininity, it has become embraced and celebrated as one of the strengths of women. Baumgardner and Richards (2010) described this aspect of the Third Wave in length. One might also recognize the term "girl power" as being related to this amalgam of girl culture and feminist consciousness.

15. Baumgardner and Richards (2010), in the preface to their 10th anniversary edition

of *Manifesta: Young Women, Feminism, and the Future*, wrote of hearing "murmurs of an emergent Fourth Wave (tech savvy and transpositive)" (p. xi).

16. I borrow the exact term "bitter man-hater" from an anonymous student evaluation I received for my course on gender and communication. This reflects the challenges of teaching with a feminist viewpoint in a postfeminist world.

17. McRobbie (2004) noted that popular texts normalize women's "gender anxieties" in such a way that "well-regulated liberty" ultimately backfires (p. 262): single women still are the exception, not the rule; a woman without a man is abnormal and needs to correct the situation in order to rectify her pathology.

18. Foster (2005), in *Class-Passing: Social Mobility in Film and Popular Culture*, noted how weddings become a way to "class-pass." By spending money in accordance with bridal rules and attaining the fantasy, upward mobility becomes a reality, even if only for a day. She also called the importance placed on wedding expenditure a form of "terrorism procured through mass participation in events that demand silence around class" (p. 76).

19. See also Michael Warner (2002), "Beyond Gay Marriage," for an explanation of how same-sex marriage has become a legal issue rather than a broad-based movement by gay and lesbian activists. Warner pointed out that "the culture of marriage, in fact, thrives on stories of revolt against it," illustrating the historical incongruity between legal marriage and romantic love (p. 271). Foster (2005) also pointed to the conservative nature of same-sex marriage (p. 76).

20. The "Heterosexual Script" reflects ideals of masculine and feminine behavior, in terms of the role taken by men as sexual pursuers and women as passive "waiters," who wait to be approached for dates or marriage. This script limits sexual activity on the part of women, while reinforcing the idea that men are supposed to be sexual and base their masculine self-concept on sexual conquest. See Kim et al. (2007) for more on how television programs convey this script.

21. Kim et al.'s (2007) content analysis of what they term the "Heterosexual Script" in network television shows found a recurring theme regarding men's supposed responsibility for making the first move in a relationship. I found this pattern of male initiative in marriage proposals also borne out in reality television wedding programs in "The 'Reality' of Reality Television Programs" (Engstrom, 2007).

22. This quote came from John Balen, associate marketing director for *Modern Bride* magazine, in Kuczynski's (2000) *New York Times* article, "A Little Light Reading Anyone?; When Weighty Issues Are the Magazines Themselves." The article focused on hefty magazines, including the February/March 2000 issue of *Brides*, which contained 1,271 pages, only 90 of which were editorial.

23. In "Marriage Envy," Leonard (2006) pointed to the intertextuality between the work by Otnes and Pleck (2003) and that of Geller (2001), noting that the former's misreading of Geller's critique of marriage illustrates the use of marriage envy as a method to "silence the author trying to rethink or reorganize" the institutional function of marriage (p. 50).

24. I am indebted to feminist media scholar Linda Steiner for pointing this out to me (personal communication, August 12, 2007). The openness of society allows for "leakage" to occur, in that hegemony is not enforced by coercion but by consent.

Those who do not find the status quo acceptable thus can reject it, modify it, or pick and choose what they find applicable to the functioning of their own lives.

25. The focus of de Certeau's (1984) work in *The Practice of Everyday Life* centered on how we consume media to create everyday life; in other words, we "poach" on the property of others—mass media products—and in turn create a new product: ways of doing things, ways of thinking, ways of "doing" life. Lull (2011) made a similar point in "Hegemony."

2. From Princess Brides to Everyday Celebrities

HISTORICALLY, NUMEROUS FORMS OF MEDIA HAVE FEATURED THE WEDDING. These have included news accounts of weddings in print media, from the *acta diurna* of Roman times to wedding announcements now so familiar to newspaper readers, and 20th century media coverage of celebrity weddings, such as those of royalty and Hollywood couples in newsreels and on television. The multifaceted appeal of weddings as news and their inherent news values, such as prominence and the unusual, provide media organizations with ample visuals and details that attract audience attention.

Besides the spectacle of notable weddings, news stories place descriptive emphasis on the main character of the wedding, the bride. What do they emphasize regarding her as an individual, in addition to her role as bride? By examining other facts included in this type of news, we can ascertain the status of the sexes. Since wedding news mostly concentrates on the appearance of the bride, rather than on the bridegroom, we can discern the importance that the physical has on women. Wedding news in the form of newspaper wedding announcements also reflect certain aspects of the status of men and women. As published gossip, this news form becomes a mirror of not just wedding practices as they exist in contemporary culture, but also of changes in the news coverage of women, especially regarding their identities apart from that of bride.

In this chapter, I look at weddings as news. First, I review some notable weddings from the past and how they captured the attention of the news media. I then present examples of wedding announcements from U.S. newspapers that illustrate how bridal news has evolved from concentrating mainly on descriptions of brides to more detailed information about couples who get married. I find of special interest the way wedding news has come to make room for other aspects of weddings besides the who, where, and when aspects of news reporting. As the following discussion unfolds, I aim to show how news of weddings incorporates both the femininity associated with bridal media and indications of feminism as reflected in the inclusion of additional information about brides (and their grooms) that illustrate women's progress in American society over the past century.

Published Gossip and Princess Brides

In *A History of News*, Mitchell Stephens (2007) noted that weddings as news appeared as early as the *acta diurna* ("daily acts") of the people of ancient Rome, which included news of marriages. Later, news pamphlets of the Middle Ages provided detailed accounts of noteworthy weddings. Stephens explained that royal weddings became news, and important news at that, because of their implications on the common people's daily life. Royal marriages represented embodiments of treaties, in addition to any personal significance they held for the contracting parties. Officially sanctioned newsbooks of the day not only were distributed to support a government/monarch's treaties, but they also gave readers what Stephens termed "published gossip" (p. 92). For instance, in the newsbook issued for the 1508 "marriage" of Henry VIII of England's 12-year-old daughter Mary to 8-year-old Prince Charles of Austria, readers learned about the seating arrangements at the wedding celebration (p. 92).

Published gossip of royal weddings, in addition to providing the reading public with the spectacle and magnificence of pageantry associated with ruling powers, allows for the satiation of normal human curiosity regarding the major events in the lives of people they know (Stephens, 2007). Whether gossip concerns one's king or queen, or movie stars and celebrities, this parasocial interaction—the concept of "knowing" famous people and feeling some kind of connection to and curiosity about them—contributes to the appeal of published gossip. Details about such events, especially those of royalty, the rich, and the famous, become not only interesting, but the behavior of celebrities in turn provides guidance for "everyday" folks. Details about the weddings of well-known people thus hold a special appeal: "Those who read about a royal wedding may use elements of the ceremony as a model for the proper conduct of their own infinitely more humble affairs," Stephens observed (p. 94).

Besides serving as models for the ordinary bride's own wedding, celebrity weddings and news accounts of weddings fulfill that ages-old human curiosity to know what other people are doing. Getting the inside "scoop" on details about the bridal gown, who is wearing what, the ceremony play-by-play, the wedding cake, and the guest list has become part of what readers and viewers of royal and celebrity weddings expect to learn about, and the media are happy to oblige. Wedding news also tells us something about the status of women. The focus on a celebrity bride's apparel, especially her wedding dress, returns us to the all-important aspect of the female: her physical appearance.

The weddings of past high-profile, world-renowned women were media sensations in their day. Among the earliest of these to have garnered an incredible amount of press coverage was that of Great Britain's young Queen Victoria in 1840. Hers became the exemplar of today's "traditional" white wedding dress.[1] The first royal bride to break from the tradition of wearing heavy brocade, the young Victoria instead ordered "a lovely white satin gown trimmed with sprays of delicate orange blossoms," noted Baldrige (2000, p. 12). According to Baldrige, white silk or satin dresses had been the *de rigeur* material for a woman's "best dress"—that is, the one considered her fanciest— since the 1820s (p. 12). Historically, according to Amnéus (2010), colorful and even black gowns were favored for weddings, as shown in paintings from Renaissance times; white was not the traditional color, as white cloth was difficult to keep clean.[2]

The white dress worn by the Queen of England for her wedding thus became the model for the white wedding gown that has become the ideal, and white became the color of choice of affluent brides by the mid-19th century (Amnéus, 2010, p. 36). Thus, the custom of wearing one's "best dress" became replaced with the notion that a special, white garment was required, and this in turn has become "tradition." However, as news reports of high society weddings in the American press in later decades would show, not all fashionable and well-do-do brides chose white. As later demonstrated in this chapter, stylish brides also chose hues in peach and blue. Thus, individual brides have chosen other colors for their wedding day outfit, and continue to choose hues other than the required white, just as Victoria had eschewed the traditional heavy brocade.

Extensive coverage of Victoria's wedding appeared in the February 11, 1840 edition of the *Times* of London and even her wedding cake became a media preoccupation (Allen, 2003).[3] "This media frenzy set the standards for all subsequent royal weddings during the Victorian period—and there were quite a number, as all of Victoria and Albert's nine children married," noted Allen (2003, p. 464); from 1858 on, royal weddings received "lavish" newspaper spreads, with entire issues devoted to those celebrations (pp. 464–465). These spectacles in turn affected the weddings of everyday people, resulting in the notion that "if the Queen's daughter could be given away by the family-of-England, England's daughters could become Queens-for-a-day in a wedding ritual that was at once different from ordinary life and its apotheosis," concluded Allen (p. 468).

Thus, weddings simultaneously allow women, especially, to enjoy the celebrity associated with a spectacular, once-in-a-lifetime event, while at the same time get married like everyone else. The influence of the royal weddings, but especially the wedding of Victoria in 1840, had a real and lasting effect on what we now perceive as the must-have element for any proper and real wedding in the US today. As Jellison (2008) contended, "Rhetoric justifying this sale and purchase of lavish weddings suggested that a white-gowned bride, multitiered cake, and exchange of shiny rings represented American tradition" (p. 3). It was Queen Victoria's wedding that "made these elements of the so-called white wedding fashionable among elite Britons and Americans," Jellison continued (p. 3).

The relatively more recent royal weddings of Diana Spencer and Sarah Ferguson commanded audiences of millions, thanks to their live satellite television broadcasts. Princess Diana's wedding gown became the subject of the 2006 book *A Dress for Diana*, authored by the designers of the dress, David and Elizabeth Emanuel (ironically, the couple eventually divorced, as did Diana and her prince). The wedding of the world's most famous woman, whose fame and celebrity continues more than a decade after her tragic death, attracted an estimated 750 to 800 million television viewers worldwide (Baldrige, 2000, p. 147; Emanuel & Emanuel, 2006, p. 205). Of those, an estimated 55 million viewers watched the royal wedding in the United States alone ("55 Million Saw Wedding," 1981).

Unlike royal weddings of the news pamphlet era, the wedding of Diana to Charles did not commemorate any territorial treaties or national alliances, although it was noted that the wedding was historic in the fact that Diana was the first English woman to marry an heir apparent to the British throne since 1660 (Apple, 1981a). The pomp and circumstance surrounding their wedding certainly rivaled, if not surpassed, the media frenzy of the past. Baldrige (2000) used the terms "fairy tale," "magic," and "storybook princess" to describe the wedding and Diana as bride (p. 140). Front-page newspaper articles of the Charles and Diana wedding, such as in *The New York Times*, played up the romantic and fairy-tale aspects. When these articles are examined more closely, one can see how the framing of the couple's "love story" reflects a patriarchal tone, especially in terms of Diana's portrayal. For example, in "Amid Splendor, Charles Weds Diana" on page A1 of the July 30, 1981 edition of *The New York Times*, R. W. Apple framed the wedding as a "fairy tale come to life," in which Prince Charles takes a wife: "In a blaze of martial and spiritual pageantry on a glorious summer morning, the Prince of Wales took as his wife today a shy and charming member of one of the kingdom's greatest families." Charles was described as "handsome" and Diana as "the lovely 20-year-old Diana Spencer, daughter of an earl." In the page A1 story "Charles and Lady Diana Wed Today" in the preceding day's edition of *The New York Times* (July 29, 1981), Apple had enhanced the fairy tale aspect of the wedding by telling readers, "And romantics found an extra sweetness in the obvious fact that Prince Charles, a highly popular figure, is marrying for love and not for dynastic convenience."

Diana's identity prior to her marriage did not even come close to matching her identity as royal bride. Her role as bride and wife of the Prince of Wales, the future king of England, became her sole occupation. Certainly one can argue that Diana later had a career as a working royal, but her role as princess bride epitomizes Jellison's (2008) statement that famous brides in general (if one can even include Diana in the same category) are never more famous than on their wedding day: "Assuming the role of wife as her primary post-wedding identity, each woman relinquished her claim to a public persona that could be entirely separated from that of bride" (p. 143). Given that Diana's pre-wedding persona mainly stemmed from her identity as the royal fiancée, one can see her identity as a bride and the continuing fascination with her bridal image as justifying such attention, making her even more historically significant in the study of weddings and bridal identity.

The New York Times' news coverage focused on the trappings of the event, rather than on Diana as a separate person who was entering into a high-profile marriage. Although she was a 20-year-old female, Apple portrayed her as almost juvenile. Indeed, she seemed trivialized when compared to her husband. Regarding her additional identity aside from bride, she was termed simply as a "former kindergarten teacher" (1981a, p. A1) who, like "many another young bride" was "taking a cooking course" (1981b, p. A1). The difference between the manly Charles and the young, demure Diana becomes even more apparent in the description of the ceremony itself: Charles was described as saying the words "I will" "huskily but firmly" while Diana said the words "in a little girl's tentative voice" (1981b, p. A1). The descriptions of their wedding apparel further highlighted the contrast between little-girl Diana and manly Charles. While Charles wore a "full-dress uniform of a Royal Navy commander," complete with medals, Diana wore a gown "of frills and flounces, pearls and crinolines" (1981b, p. A1).

The amount of attention paid to Diana's bridal appearance emphasizes to an almost hyperbolic degree the importance of a woman's "personal front" (Goffman, 1959, p. 24).[4] The wedding dress of the world's most famous woman, whose celebrity and appeal cannot be denied, has become legendary itself. The "flounces and frills" of that famous dress also seemed to overwhelm the woman within, as the dress itself garnered as much press attention as the young bride. Much was made of the record-breaking length of the dress's train; at 25 feet, it was the longest for a royal bride. According to Emanuel and Emanuel (2006), a previous royal bride had a train 23 feet long. The Emanuels also chose ivory for the dress color, after discovering that there was no protocol requiring any specific color for a royal wedding dress; they wanted Diana "to look like no princess had ever looked before" (p. 148). "That royal wedding dress had an enormous impact on wedding fashion," they claimed, starting a trend in non-white dresses not only in ivory but in other shades (p. 158). The Emanuels' goal of creating "real magic" and a "sense of fairy tale" by going against the then style of traditional A-line, formal dresses apparently succeeded, based on press reports (p. 158). For instance, Anderson's article on the dress in *The New York Times* on July 30, 1981 opened with the lead sentence: "For her long walk up the aisle that transformed her into a princess, Lady Diana Spencer, in the most romantic storybook tradition, wore a sequin-and-pearl-incrusted dress with a 25-foot train" (p. A10).[5] The horse-drawn, Cinderella-like carriage that delivered Diana to the cathedral completed the supposed fairy tale.

Diana continues to serve as an exemplar of the princess bride, both figuratively and literally, with several books on celebrity weddings all noting the grandeur that surrounded and continues to surround weddings of notable brides. Jellison's (2008) historical examination and popular treatments such as those by Baldrige (2000) and Schreier (2002) have looked at celebrity weddings as forwarding the essence of the bridal image: that of ideal perfection. Prominent weddings of the 20th century—such as those of British royalty, the American elite (notably those of the Kennedys), and Hollywood movie stars—all essentially repeat the same story of romantic love culminating in the big, lavish, "perfect" wedding.

Although the eventual outcomes of several of these love-story weddings have belied the image of fairy-tale romance and the happily-ever-after ending, the image of those perfect brides still holds the attention of bridal writers years after their historic nuptials. Entire books have been devoted to the wedding gowns of Princess Diana and Princess Grace. The wedding gowns of both women also have been displayed for public viewing. Diana's wedding gown was displayed around the world to raise money for charities, and is now part of a permanent exhibit at her ancestral home of Althorp (Emanuel & Emanuel,

2006). The gown of Princess Grace also serves as a museum piece; news coverage of her gown predated the media frenzy surrounding that of the young Diana Spencer some three decades later.

The publicity preceding Grace Kelly's 1956 marriage to Prince Rainier of Monaco serves as an example of the appeal of the wedding in mass media. Details about the wedding and the secrecy surrounding the soon-to-be-princess's gown melded the idea of "breaking news" with published gossip: "Newspapers across the U.S. issued almost daily bulletins" in late winter and spring of 1956, according to Haugland (2006, p. 22). The minutest details became newsworthy, noted Haugland, and included gossip about the 12 hours a day Kelly was devoting to the planning of her wedding, analyses of the guest list, speculation about her film career (which ended after the wedding), inventories of the wedding gifts, and information about Kelly's life and royal titles after marriage.

Kelly's wedding dress played an equally, if not more, important role in her royal wedding as she herself did. Described in Schreier's 2002 book *Hollywood Gets Married*, the famous gown/costume "used twenty-five yards of peau de soie [a soft silk, satin weave with dull finish], twenty-five yards of silk taffeta, one hundred yards of silk net, and three hundred yards of antique Valenciennes lace" (p. 11). The story of Kelly's wedding gown serves as the subject of Haugland's glossy coffee table book, *Grace Kelly: Icon of Style to Royal Bride*, published in 2006 to mark an exhibition featuring the famous gown at the Philadelphia Museum of Art. Kelly had donated the dress to the Museum, and it served as the centerpiece of the exhibition, along with her bridesmaids' dresses. So intricate was the design of Kelly's gown that the book itself devoted five pages to architectural-style diagrams of the multipiece costume, which included a bodice, attached underbodice, skirt support and slip, cummerbund, skirt with smoothing petticoat, a ruffled petticoat and attached foundation petticoat, and train insert.

"Many elements of her wedding attire—delicate pearl-bedecked lace, an extravagantly full-trained skirt, a gracefully flowing veil, and a crown-like cap—are still considered the ultimate in romantic bridal fashion," contended Haugland (2006, p. 70). An additional fact highlighted by both Haugland (2006) and Schreier (2002) was Kelly's famously tiny waistline and how the dress was too small for "normal" mannequins. The display mannequin used by the Philadelphia Museum of Art for the dress's exhibition was too large; it had to be cut down to fit the less-than-21-inch waist of the gown. Kelly's weight loss prior to the wedding was attributed to the stresses of wedding planning. Diana also lost weight prior to her wedding, resulting in last-minute alterations to her gown, as related by the Emanuels (2006) in *A Dress for Diana*. In Chapter 4, I discuss how weight loss actually has become a required checklist item of the wedding to-do list, with the idea of deliberately losing weight in order to fit into one's bridal gown serving as the central theme of the reality television program *Buff Brides* as well as the subject of bridal magazine articles.

Kelly's image encompassed the ideals of feminine beauty; the "Grace Kelly look" epitomized the actress's cool demeanor, elegant posture, and fashion sense. Looking to capitalize on the fairy-tale wedding between the Hollywood movie star and a real-life prince, Max Factor announced a new cosmetics line formulated to match Kelly's wedding gown (Haugland, 2006). The Grace Kelly look soon dominated the beauty industry, and the wedding fueled the connection between the perfect bridal appearance and the perfect wedding. After all, the media portrayed her role of princess bride as Kelly's ultimate role, surpassing all her film roles and any real life roles she, or anyone else, could have imagined had she continued with her movie career.

Haugland (2006) reported that Kelly herself was portrayed by the media first as a Hollywood actress and secondly as Princess of Monaco, with the most emphasis placed on her bridal appearance. Kelly served as an example of the modern woman and traditional bride: she combined the images of a woman who had achieved the highest honor of her profession by winning an Academy Award with her role as a real-life princess bride. The book's subtitle, *Icon of Style to Royal Bride*, reflects how Kelly's personal front as actress and bride overshadows her talent as an accomplished film actress. In sum, the celebration of Kelly's physical appearance as "icon of style" and her ultimate, celebrated role as "royal bride" negates the achievements that brought her acclaim while reaffirming the societal approval and expectation that women marry, and, better yet, marry very well. In a real sense, the independent woman who left her home in Philadelphia to find success in Hollywood gave up her career to become a wife and mother. The fairy-tale wedding, however, did not necessarily mean a fairy-tale "happily ever after." "With her marriage, Grace Kelly left her film career behind; as princess of Monaco, she devoted herself to raising her three children and fulfilling her duty to her husband and adopted country until her life was cut tragically short in September 1982," concluded Haugland (p. 70).

The term *costume* aptly describes Kelly's "real-life" wedding gown, as the garment itself bridged her onscreen and "real-life" identities. Kelly's gown was the creation of designer Helen Rose of MGM Studios, which financed the creation of the gown as a gift to its famous star. Hollywood studios under the star system regularly furnished their under-contract movie star brides with studio-created gowns. These *gratis* incentives helped actresses maintain their wholesome image while providing studios with publicity for both their stars and designers (Haugland, 2006, p. 31).

FIGURE 2.1. Icons of style

Art meets life: MGM Studios created the weddings gowns for two Hollywood legends. "Icon of style" Grace Kelly (left) donated her wedding gown to the Philadelphia Museum of Art. Her 1956 real-life fairy-tale wedding to Prince Rainier of Monaco was a media sensation; details about the dress were the subject of daily news bulletins. The studio also created the wedding gown for the first marriage of Hollywood legend Elizabeth Taylor (right), which coincided with the release of the 1950 film *Father of the Bride*, starring Taylor and Spencer Tracy. Publicity photos of Taylor's dress were used to market the film and the gown itself in department stores (Copyright MGM).

Another example of a studio-created wedding gown was that of actress Elizabeth Taylor for her first marriage in 1950. Department store tie-ins promoted both the gown and the movie Taylor was starring in at the time, *Father of the Bride*. Naremore (1993), in *The Films of Vincente Minnelli*, described how publicity photos were distributed to women's clothing stores in towns where the film was playing, further enhancing both Taylor's image as young bride onscreen and in reality. Her real-life marriage to hotel heir Nicky Hilton ended in divorce. Her dress, however, became a way to promote the idea that "regular" women also could experience the glamour and fantasy that the bridal role promised.

The spectacles of these and other weddings of the rich and famous provide media with relatively simple narratives to report on, and an abundance of details to write and talk about. The visual appeal of wedding costumes, emotion-eliciting ceremonies of prominent celebrities, and rich, detail-filled descriptions of these lavish events as a whole provide news media with expedient pictures and easy storytelling. With the added elements of love and romance, news of the weddings of famous people makes for ample fodder to give a gossip-hungry audience. Thus, the media attention given to celebrity weddings both reaffirms cultural gender norms and practices in terms of what Boden (2003) termed the "crucial elements of the successful wedding" (p. 54).

The use of celebrity weddings as models for one's own, slightly less impressive wedding illustrates the historical process wherein practices of the upper classes became modeled by the "subaltern," those outside the dominant class. "Currently, the popular media and its depictions of appropriate or inappropriate wedding consumption heavily influence the wedding industry and the demands of consumers," noted Boden (2003, p. 54). Indeed, in the cases of Princess Diana and Grace Kelly, copycat designers made re-creations of their one-of-a-kind wedding gowns within hours of the designs being revealed by the press (Emanuel & Emanuel, 2006; Haugland, 2006).

As Amnéus (2010) observed, in terms of the history of weddings in the US during the 19th to 20th centuries, much of middle class wealth "was focused on imitating social superiors"; among requisite items needed by proper weddings, "wedding dresses were, perhaps, the article of clothing in which this aspiration reached its height" (p. 37). The need for a special bridal gown, as opposed to wearing one's best dress, allows for not only an elevation of status but "contextualizes" the bridal role on a "grand scale" (p. 53). Thus, even the commonest of brides could emulate royalty, just as Queen Victoria had inspired the white wedding dress that has become "traditional" and required, and Diana's dress of flounces and frills influenced wedding fashion during the 1980s.

On April 29, 2011, another fairy-tale "wedding of the century" garnered worldwide press and public attention. William, the 28-year-old son of the late Diana, married 29-year-old Catherine "Kate" Middleton, the daughter of self-made millionaires, in a spectacle of royal pageantry before an estimated audience of between two and three billion people (Kay, 2011; Lyall, 2011). On the Internet, the wedding set record traffic on the service provider Yahoo, with live streaming to an estimated 1.6 million concurrent video views; the event broke the previous record set by the 2011 World Cup (Choney, 2011). Broadcast live in the US, the wedding garnered wall-to-wall coverage by network and cable news channels, with re-broadcasts of the wedding offered for several days afterward. Royal wedding–themed programming, pre- and post-wedding on U.S. cable outlets such as Lifetime, TLC, WE tv, E! Entertainment, National Geographic Channel, and BBC America provided audiences with retrospectives on past royal weddings, royal wedding history, and documentaries about Princess Diana.[6] Love and romance permeated such media offerings, with titles such as *Royal Wedding of a Lifetime: William & Kate, A Love Story* on Lifetime, *William & Kate: A Royal Love Story* on TLC, and *A Modern Fairytale*, a special edition of the news magazine program *20/20* on ABC.

Expectedly, comparisons to the wedding of Diana and Charles some 30 years earlier abounded in the press, especially the true love shared by William and Kate as opposed to the charade and subsequent disaster of the bridegroom's mother and father. The U.K.'s *Daily Mail* ran a story with side-by-side photos of William and Kate's balcony kiss at Buckingham Palace and Diana and Charles's in 1981 (Kay, 2011). William and Kate kissed twice on the balcony; it was instantly deemed an "historic" event (May, 2011). The shadow of Diana permeated the news coverage as well—it was her engagement ring from Charles that William presented to Kate when he proposed to her in October 2010; Diana's favorite hymn opened the wedding ceremony at Westminster Abbey; Kate's mother wore a dress by one of Diana's favorite designers (Kay, 2011).

FIGURE 2.2. Wedding of the Century
"Wedding of the Century," Parts I and II: The press made numerous comparisons between the wedding of Charles and Diana in 1981 and that of their son William to Kate Middleton in 2011. Photo: AFP/Getty Images.

Alessandra Stanley (2011) of *The New York Times* noted that it was a "do-over" for the Diana-Charles marriage, whose wedding story was "presented as a gossamer fairy tale and turned out to be a horror story" (p. A6). Rather than a marriage of royal convenience, William and Kate truly married for love, media commentators concluded, with Kate well prepared for her new life as a member of the British royal family. Stanley summed up the television coverage between the BBC and U.S. networks by noting that the British coverage focused on the wedding as a historical, pageantry-filled event, while the American news anchors looked for signs of William and Kate's true love.

Prior to the magical day and the familiar, romance-imbued aura surrounding royal weddings, press coverage of the new Duchess of Cambridge (William and Kate were bestowed the titles Duke and Duchess of Cambridge by Queen Elizabeth II) reflected a slightly different tone than that of regal future queen. Comparisons between Kate and Diana were expected and the media did not disappoint, with programs such as WE tv's *Kate: The New Diana?* and Lifetime's *Royal Weddings of a Lifetime: A Tale of Two Princesses.* Similar to the pre-wedding news coverage of Diana, mainstream and tabloid stories especially in the British press focused on Kate's background—or, more accurately, her lack of a career. The press gave her the unflattering title of "Waity Katie," portraying Catherine Middleton as a well-educated but spoiled and lazy rich girl, a bride/queen-in-waiting who seemingly just waited around for some eight years for William to propose while not pursuing a "real" career of her own, in articles with titles such as "Short History of 'Waity Katie" (Cochran, 2011), "From Waity Katie to Princess Catherine" (Katz, 2011), "Waity Katie Needs to Get a Life" (Elser, 2009), and "'Waity Katie' to Wed Her William" (2010).

Such criticism appears reflective of the expectation that educated women in a 21st century world would have careers and be self-supporting, even if they do come from wealth. In "Wedding or Not, It's Time Waity Katie Grew Up," columnist Sandra Parsons (2010) of the U.K.'s *Daily Mail* appeared especially harsh in her criticism of the future queen of England. By 2010, the time of William's proposal, Kate had been out of university for five years, and "failed to knuckle down and find a job"; at the very least, Parsons wrote, Kate could have done some charity work.

Similar criticism came from Australia's *The Punch*, when Daniela Elser (2009) criticized Kate's apparently non-serious attitude toward working: Kate's "brief foray" as a fashion accessories buyer essentially meant she was paid just to go shopping. Noting how the Queen was keen to have members of the royal family seen as hard workers, Elser commented that "people want an (at-least titular) future ruler with a bit more going for her than an ample cleavage and an average arts-degree." Although Kate did graduate from the

University of St. Andrews in Scotland, these accounts infer that her real "job" was waiting for William to ask her to marry him.

Once the wedding day arrived, however, the focus moved from Kate's waiting to her physical appearance as a regal bride, with perhaps even more attention paid to her wedding gown. Just as Diana's wedding gown was shrouded in secrecy prior to her wedding day, press reports about Kate's bridal attire gave the public speculations about who would design it and what it would look like ("Dress Prediction: Final Rumor Round-Up," 2011). Only when Kate stepped out of the Rolls-Royce that delivered her to Westminster Abbey did St. James's Palace release the official details. An E! Online article, "Kate Middleton's Wedding Dress Revealed! And It's *Amazing*!," underscored the excitement and anticipation stoked by the press; Kate looked "elegant and stunning," the "breathtaking" gown was, aptly, "fit . . . for a princess" (Stewart, 2011).

In addition to witnessing the gown's "reveal" during the live broadcast, one could find a plethora of intricate details regarding the garment's construction and materials used—it was a "long-sleeve lace, ivory and satin gown with flattering V-neckline and 8-foot-long train" (Stewart, 2011); the material was more specifically a "gazar" with a satin bodice (Zap, 2011). Kate wore "a Cartier 'halo' tiara lent to [her] by the Queen" (Zap, 2011), "which Queen Elizabeth [had] inherited on her 18th birthday" ("A Dress for the Ages," 2011). Notably, comparisons to Grace Kelly's gown enhanced the image not only of Kate's wedding gown, but of Kate herself as a royal bride; she symbolized the elegance and style of Kelly. References to Diana's presence throughout the day itself completed the circuit between these high-profile, royal mega-brides ("A Dress for the Ages," 2011; Alphonse, 2011). Kate's lack of career forgotten, the wedding day and subsequent news stories framed her as an "elegant and stunning" bride (Stewart, 2011) with a "'queenly' poise" (Stanley, 2011) for her new occupation: princess (or, more correctly, duchess).

Taken together, the manufacturing of the Duchess of Cambridge's identity once again erased, in a sense, her individual identity, replacing it with an idealized version of the perfect, royal bride. Although she was "Waity Katie" no more, her identity as bride and even as the Duchess of Cambridge contrasted with how some press accounts described William. For example, a *Vanity Fair* article referred to Kate only as "Princess Catherine," while describing William as a "helicopter search-and-rescue pilot in the Royal Air Force" (Sacks, 2010).

Further, if clothing serves as a symbolic representation of roles within a particular situation, the apparel associated with "bride" and "bridegroom" would logically communicate those roles. If one considers how other meanings are communicated by clothing besides those that are situation-specific, we see the inclusion of more roles for William than for Kate. Kate wore a lace-drenched, ivory silk wedding gown—a costume associated with "bride" only—while William wore a uniform reflective of his position in the working world—a position illustrated by his wedding outfit: "the bright scarlet coat of an Irish Guards mounted officer" (Lyall, 2011). In short, Kate's attire reflected her main occupation based on gender (bride) while William's reflected a range of roles apart from bridegroom, specifically those of a highly-trained member of the military as well as future king, with his uniform representing to some degree the state itself. Indeed, his father (Prince Charles), uncle (Andrew, the Duke of York), and grandfather (the Duke of Edinburgh) wore military uniforms in past royal weddings.

Tradition and pageantry aside, William and Kate's wedding occurred amid a media environment that offered numerous outlets one could access to watch the ceremony, and learn about all the details that have historically garnered curiosity by onlookers. In addition to live broadcasts on television, one could watch the proceedings online and purchase special commemorative issues of gossip magazines as souvenirs and mementos of the wedding of the 21st century. For example, the May 16, 2011 *People* magazine "special collector's issue" of the wedding reinforced the true love theme of this royal marriage with the headline: "William & Catherine: LOVE REIGNS!"; the subtitle copy framed their wedding as having "sweeping grandeur" and "sweet romance." In addition to articles on William and Kate's wedding, the issue also included "A Dress for the Ages," a four-page article on Kate's wedding gown, and "The Princess Wedding Diaries," which included a page devoted to Diana's dress and the secrecy surrounding it, further romanticizing and mythologizing the importance of the wedding gown as a vital element of not only royal weddings, but any wedding. The enormous publicity given to this most recent "wedding of the century" demonstrates the timeless appeal of royal weddings and weddings in general. Further, the amount of attention surrounding Kate and especially her wedding gown underscores that weddings tend to elevate the bride to a new stature. This was even more apparent in that Kate came from a "common" family, with her surname of "Middleton" offering a reading that invokes a sense of her (initially) middle-class background.

Jellison (2008) contended that in the 21st century, female-centered events such as weddings—those that center on *women*—are not only rare but are also unchallenged. That is, it is rare for a woman to be the center of an event (like the wedding) and no one questions the "rightness" of weddings (a woman-centered event). In a world in which patriarchy exists as the dominant form of society, weddings allow women to serve as the center of attention. As a woman-centered event, the wedding provides a venue where, no matter what her social class, achievement, wealth, or any number of social indicators, the *bride* plays the central role. The amount of news coverage of extraordinary weddings further enhances the status of brides, especially when those brides are young and beautiful, and, as these examples illustrate, have incredibly expensive and intricate garments made for them to play their role in the event. The specific way in which such events are covered by news outlets amplifies whatever common sense surrounds weddings—the dress, the reception, the ceremony—as well as ideals regarding romance. The extra special status given to the bride furthers the notion that women can have, and deserve, a special day. The problem is that the role of "bride" becomes almost generic, in that despite whatever individual and extraordinary traits a bride might possess in reality, they become obscured through the prism of the bridal image.

Wedding Announcements: *Acta Diurna* of Modern Times

Wedding news also has taken the form of the wedding announcement, another venue upon which women take center stage and which contributes a sense of celebrity to the "everyday" bride. As a reflection of wedding practices through the years, newspaper wedding announcements illustrate not only changes in wedding practices, but the way in which women have been portrayed in news media in general. In contrast to wedding news of celebrities, these accounts of noncelebrity weddings usually follow some uniform format, wherein the bride's and bridegroom's names, family backgrounds, and other information become public through publication in local newspapers. An examination of wedding announcements makes apparent the bride's importance as the central character of the wedding narrative. This type of news also reflects wedding practices and becomes a record of the history of weddings among the "ordinary" public.

However, even as wedding news in this form reflects an overall uniformity regarding wedding elements, there are exceptions to the rule that illustrate that not all weddings are the same. The examples presented here come from three major newspapers with searchable archives representing to some extent the Eastern, Midwestern, and Western United States: *The New York Times, Chicago Tribune*, and *Los Angeles Times*. Examples come from the society page sections of these newspapers, which represent upper class as well as what can be considered middle class weddings. What is of interest here is not only the details of weddings as published in newspapers, but also the additional information included, most notably personal information about the parties involved. Besides descriptions of brides and their appearance, these media portrayals provide a way to gauge other identifying aspects of women. In this sense, not only does looking at the seemingly mundane wedding announcement allow us to examine the femininity surrounding the bridal role, but it offers a means for tracking how wedding news also reflects feminist-related notions regarding women's societal roles beyond wife and mother, such as their educational attainment and career achievements.

Using the search term "wedding announcement" in the historical archives of *The New York Times*, the earliest article I found, "Married," appeared on page 4 of the October 29, 1851 edition. "Married" consisted of a very simple, 12-line item listing four marriages, their dates (one having occurred that past April), the names of the reverends who performed the ceremonies, and the grooms' and brides' names in capital letters. While all the listed marriages included the grooms' first and last names, two of the listings referred to the bride's first name only, followed by "daughter of" and her father's name only. For example, all the reader knew about the wedding of James O. Sheldon to Louisa, "daughter of James McCall," was that they were married by "the Rev. Dr. Potts on Thursday, 23rd." Of these four listed marriages, only the first contained any details; the rest simply stated the basic information. The first wedding listed was that of Robert Mackey to Louisa Stewart. The article does not include any details of the ceremony or even a mention of any reception. The only information available to the curious reader is that "after the hymeneal ceremonies were performed, the happy couple left the city for a wedding tour in the sunny south."

While this rather bare-bones news item listing four weddings consisted of a mere five sentences, with two of those five sentences devoted just to the nuptials of Robert Mackey and Louisa Stewart, it reflects more than just the fact that four couples in New York were married that year. The reference to two of the brides as "daughter of" a male rather than including their last names indicates that their status was such that their full names were not important enough to be included. Indeed, later news accounts described in this chapter referred to single women as only "Miss" plus surname, rather than as persons with both a first and a last name.

While the no-nonsense "Married" article from 1851 provides almost no detail regarding the weddings of the four couples mentioned, an article appearing just two days later in the same newspaper described in great detail a wedding in the woods of northern New York state. Reprinted from an article in the *Potsdam Courier*, "Pioneer Wedding" appeared on page 4 of the October 31, 1851 edition of *The New York Times*. The article described the undated wedding of Mr. Theodore Wentgott to Miss Sarah Cole, both of Charlottesville in Franklin County. The outdoor wedding on "the banks of the Raquetta River" in "a temple not made with hands" involved some 25 guests from the two families. After the ceremony, the account told readers, "a brace of hounds were now let loose and soon drove a couple of deer into the river" where the guests "captured" them and, with a supply of trout, these "were served up as the wedding supper."

In addition to the freshly caught game described in "Pioneer Wedding," the reception apparently also included music (provided by a violin) and dancing. No mention of the bride's apparel nor of any other details of the bridal party appears in the article, except for how the bride, the "now Mrs. W," cooks. The writer, a personal friend of the groom, relates that "the way she does up" venison and trout "cannot be surpassed." The festivities came to a close when the new couple was escorted to their shanty in the "beautiful and romantic" vicinity of Tupper's Lake. Rather than a wedding announcement, this particular account of a woodsy wedding serves more as a description of country life than as any real gossip, unlike the wedding announcements of later times and of today. There is no mention of the bride and groom's ages, nor anything else about them or their families. Indeed, the only information the reader gleans about the couple is that the bride was a good cook.

Using the same search term "wedding announcement," the next article I found in the archives of *The New York Times* was "The World of Society," on page 14 of the paper's October 4, 1885 issue. By this time, the *Times* apparently had enough gossip to fill an entire column on society goings-on, including a several-sentences-long description of a recent prominent wedding, as well as wedding announcements of society notables. These items were presented among two "important" dances, French recitations, several lawn tennis matches, and a theatre opening, among other social news of the day.

Though still rather brief and short on intricate details, "The World of Society" paid rather close attention to the wedding of Miss Alice Taintor Leland, described as "the eldest daughter of Mrs. Charles Leland of New York," and Mr. Charles Whitman Munroe, son of Mr. John Munroe, "the Paris banker." Names of the best man and ushers are included, but no mention is made of any of the bride's attendants, if any. The only details regarding the wedding ceremony itself was that it was held on Wednesday at Trinity Church, which was "tastefully and elaborately dressed with palmetto branches," and that the reception at Mrs. Leland's cottage was attended by 150 guests.

In the pages of the *Chicago Daily Tribune*, forerunner of the *Chicago Tribune*, however, society weddings by the 1870s already had included several intricate details of bridal apparel along with the sumptuousness of wedding receptions. For example, using the term "wedding announcement" in the *Tribune*'s archives, I found the earliest account of a society wedding in the *Chicago Daily Tribune*'s November 15, 1874 edition. In what appears to be the first column of society news titled "The Social World," it begins with a promise to readers to document Chicago society by "recording its most interesting events, trying to do justice to all that may come within our notice" (p. 5). Among these events of notice were weddings, with news of such occasions ranging from simple announcements to detailed accounts providing readers with information mostly about the who, where, and décor. By tracing these news accounts of society weddings, one can also see the evolvement of the treatment of women in the news.

Much like "The World of Society" from the 1885 issue of *The New York Times*, this particular edition of the *Chicago Daily Tribune*'s "The Social World" column on page 5 dated November 15, 1874, included several wedding announcements of both recent and upcoming nuptials, along with other detailed accounts of Chicago's high society. Among the tidbits describing dances, children's birthday parties, club meetings, and anniversary celebrations was the first of several similarly short descriptions of recent weddings. Under the heading "Dickinson-Reynolds," readers learned of the Tuesday evening wedding of "Miss Reynolds" and "Mr. Dickinson" at the home of the bride's father, Mr. James P. Reynolds. A light meal provided by the caterer "Wright" was offered, and "Sanders" supervised the "tasteful and appropriate" floral decorations. While it may have been assumed that readers of this particular section of the newspaper knew about the proprietors, Wright and Sanders, the lack of first names of the wedding couple also points to an assumption that readers would know who they were as well. This rather cursory and familiar account of the Dickinson-Reynolds wedding tells us nothing more about the bride, or the groom, for that matter.

However, in the very same column, out-of-town weddings also were included that gave readers much more detail. Under the heading "Abroad," numerous details about the "principal wedding in Cincinnati" of Miss Julia Ottenheimer and Mr. Morris Rosenfield of Peoria included number of guests (200), toasts given by guests, and the fact that the wedding presents were "numerous and valuable." The bride's costume   as described in detail as well, in the stead of any illustrations: she wore "an elegant white silk, trimmed with satin and point lace. The corsage was cut in the Marie Antoinette style, the whole completed by a long tulle veil, and garniture of orange blossoms." However, as in nearly all the early, big-newspaper, wedding news accounts I found, details regarding the bride and groom that normally accompany journalistic reporting required for descriptions of persons in news stories, such as their age and other pertinent information, were ignored.

The gossipy nature of the reportage of weddings deemed to be newsworthy enough to be included in columns such as "The Social World" also reflected the worth of women as brides—especially when one examines how women are described. In the same November 15, 1874 *Tribune* column that included nine announcements of recent and upcoming weddings in the Chicago area, the "Abroad" weddings included two that were to occur on the Pacific Coast. The reader does not find out where these two weddings will happen, but does get specifics on the two brides. One of these big-name weddings is that of "Senator Jones" of Nevada, whose first name is excluded, and "Miss Georgia Sullivan," an heiress. Miss Sullivan, the writer notes, in addition to having a wealthy father, inherited her fortune from her grandfather, and thus had "escaped the stigma of fortune hunter." Senator Jones, one gathers, is a catch, and Miss Sullivan apparently did not need him, thus making their impending union a true "love match."

This account of the impending Sullivan-Jones wedding does not mention the date of the wedding itself. It does, however, include quite a bit of information about Miss Sullivan, notably this includes her looks and age; 20 years old, she is reported to be a "brunette with blond hair" of "medium height with slight, graceful figure." As a "lady of high culture," the writer predicts she will do well in Washington, DC society. Her trousseau, the writer further reports, includes three dresses worth $1,000, with the wedding dress from Paris expected to be "unusually elegant." The focus on the 20-year-old heiress contrasts with the lack of details regarding Senator Jones's age, physical description, or wedding costume. The price of Miss Sullivan's trousseau and the speculation that her Paris-made wedding dress will be elegant becomes the focal point of the wedding news, further highlighting the assumed feminine interest in her attire, as well as her physical attributes.

The impending wedding of Miss Clara Sharon and Mr. Frank Newlands "agitating California society" planned for that December followed the Sullivan-Jones item in the "Abroad" section of this edition of the *Tribune*'s "The Social World." The 19-year-old Miss Sharon, according to the report, is the daughter of William Sharon, a "wealthy capitalist," while Mr. Newlands, no age reported, is "a young lawyer of much promise." There is some hint as to Miss Sharon's identity besides her age and wealth, as the article notes that she had a "cultured education in the convents of San Jose and Benita" and is described as "stately and dignified but with a sprightly and vivacious manner." Her wedding trousseau reportedly cost $10,000, and the elegant Sharon mansion was becoming fitted up with "palatial splendor" for the wedding. Here the description of the bride includes more information than just her age and wealth; the inclusion of her schooling adds a hint that there is more to the bride than the perfunctory description of brides in wedding news of the day.

Both of these high-profile, out-of-state weddings really had nothing to do with Chicago, but perhaps were deemed interesting enough for the readers of page 5 of the *Tribune*. "The Social World" as a record of the times not only provides a picture of the weddings of the very rich and notable, but also of local couples, although certainly not those considered as working class. This has changed, as today one can find wedding announcements in almost any local newspaper, big or small.

The inclusion of price tags for these rich brides' trousseaus also reflects the importance of money spent on weddings considered worthy enough for mention in "The Social World." News reports of the past and present highlight prices of wedding gowns and other accoutrements of royal and celebrity weddings, while those of ordinary couples do not include such gauche details. More than a century later, reality wedding programs such as those discussed in the next chapter again highlight the cost of wedding gowns and accessories, which not only demonstrates that spending money is all right, and even encouraged, but that the high cost of weddings is worth it. After all, the wedding is the one time all women become "princesses" for a day.

The same "Abroad" section of the *Tribune*'s page 5 "The Social World" column from November 15, 1874 ends with the wedding announcement of another out-of-town wedding, that of Mr. W.L. Bowers of Liberty, Indiana and Miss Florella V. Appleton. Miss Appleton "is spoken of as a lovely blonde, and wore a silver-gray silk." The only other information about this wedding was that the ceremony took place at 7 P.M. on the 11th of November at the First Presbyterian Church, and the reception was held at the home of Prof. H. R. Smith. The lack of information about the groom—or other information about the bride besides her hair color and minimal description of her wedding attire—contrasts starkly with the heiress weddings reported in the same column.

One can consider these highly descriptive accounts of weddings as the counterpart to today's reality television nuptials. In the age before photographs became commonplace in newspaper wedding announcements, readers relied on the reporter's eye to get the full picture of the splendor associated with society weddings. Those of 1870s Chicago society reflected displays of wealth associated with upscale weddings as this type of news became more detailed. For example, the article "Weddings" on page 5 of the December 11, 1874 edition of the *Chicago Daily Tribune* featured four weddings, two very lengthy accounts and two rather short ones. The rather substantial items included not only the details of ceremonies, but the complete list of wedding gifts from the wedding of Mr. B. M. Wilson and Miss Frances Huntington, daughter of Alonzo Huntington, Esq. Such detailed accounts of wedding presents provide a glimpse into the consumerism surrounding large weddings at that period of time.

The Huntington-Wilson wedding at the cathedral of Saints Paul and Peter took place Thursday, December 10, 1874 at 6 P.M. before a "large number of the bride's friends." The account then provides a detailed countdown of the bridesmaids and ushers as they proceeded down the aisle, followed lastly by the bride and groom. During the ceremony, the reporter writes, the bride "looked a little nervous but very lovely." The account makes no mention of the groom's appearance whatsoever, nor of any other information about him except that he spoke "with a quiet intensity in his tones" during the wedding ceremony.

Of the bride, however, the reader learns much more, with the focus on her appearance, but not her age or schooling. Besides being the daughter of Mr. Alonzo Huntington, Esq., she is "of medium stature, slight in figure, with dark eyes and hair and a bright, vivacious countenance." Under the subheading, "The Dresses," details of her wedding costume comprised most of the references to her person:

> The bride was attired in an elegant dress of white silk, made with a long Watteau-plaited train, and a tablier of vertical puffs, with knife plaitings of silk and tulle around the bottom. The corsage was finished with lace, while the tulle bridal-veil was confined by a coronet and sprays of orange blossoms. ("Weddings,"1874, p. 5)

Descriptions of the bridesmaids' dresses followed. Readers learned about the other family members' outfits as well. For instance, "Master Alonzo Huntington" wore a white silk suit of knee breeches, which "was sufficiently unlike the ordinary full dress to deserve mentioning," and the mother of the bride wore a "French dress in two contrasting colors." Without the benefit of illustrations, the emphasis on details certainly gave readers, whether part of Chicago society or not, some guidance as to how well-to-do weddings, and perhaps even their own, should look. Further, one can surmise that the article was written for female readers, due to the lack of details regarding the men's costumes, except for that of young Master Huntington, who, one assumes, wore something different than the older ushers.

In the same *Chicago Daily Tribune* article, the lengthy account of the Huntington-Wilson wedding required several subheadings in addition to "The Dresses." Readers learned about "The Reception" at the Huntington residence, "The Floral Ornaments," and "The Presents," which consisted of a lengthy list of wedding gifts and from whom they were received. For example, a "Miss Stewart" (no first name) gave the couple "large gold napkin-rings, with the initials of the bride and groom in old English text." Thus, in addition to learning about the latest in wedding attire, readers could find out what wedding gifts were in fashion, at least among those who could afford the expense.

Second on the list of four weddings in the same December 11, 1874, edition of "Weddings" in the *Chicago Daily Tribune* was that of Miss Grace Laflin, "daughter of Mr. George B. Laflin," and Mr. Elisha B. Whitehead, who were married at the bride's father's house before 50 guests. The bride wore "heavy white corded silk with tulle and lace trimmings." Fifty guests were present, but the reception had no dancing. The "collation" included "delicious salads, jellies, and ices," and the room was decorated with "camellias, tuberoses and choice tea-rose buds." The wedding presents were not displayed, "so any idea of them must be left to the imagination."

The other two weddings included in the same article were more subdued, listed under the subheading, "In Brief," and consisted of just one paragraph each. The Weber-Van Keuren wedding was "a very quiet, private affair." However, the bride "looked beautifully" in her "pale apricot-colored silk, with a lace overdress" and garlands of orange blossoms. Within the last paragraph of the article was a brief account of the Kehoe-Murphy wedding, which consisted of a strictly private ceremony for the Hon. Miles Kehoe and Miss Kate Murphy. Although her wedding dress is not mentioned, the writer does tell the reader that she "is a beautiful and highly-accomplished young lady from Hamilton." However, readers were told they would have to wait to find out about their "grand reception," which would not occur until the "close of the session of the Legislature next spring."

All four weddings were described again in the next "The Social World" column in the *Chicago Daily Tribune* just two days later. The December 13, 1874, page 5 column gave the Whitehead-Laflin wedding extra coverage in the form of a lengthy, almost tedious, description about the newly married couple's house, a gift from the bride's father. Readers were treated to a "virtual" tour of the interior, including the closets. A recap of the wedding itself was provided "for those not fortunate enough to obtain a copy of Friday's *Tribune*."

Apart from the society page aspects of these high-profile Chicago weddings during that period, their treatment as news assumes an interest on the part of *Tribune* readers. The emphasis on itemization reflects the increasing mercantilism associated with weddings during the latter part of the 19th century. During the 1870s, merchants began to promote certain products as suitable wedding presents. Weddings became caught up in commercialization which, in turn, raised the expectations and cost surrounding them to the point that, during the late 1800s, social commentators decried the commercialization of weddings by claiming that weddings had become "irreversibly transformed into a vehicle for business interests, class aspirations, and fashion," according to Penner (2004, p. 2). The listing of wedding presents in these newspaper accounts implied how much wedding guests spent on such presents, and also elevated the wedding as a social event associated with money.

Similarly, the emphasis on the bridal gown also implied expenses connected to getting married, at least among the rich. The proper bride was attired not only in her best dress, but one whose cost far surpassed anything she had or would ever wear again. We see this emphasis on the wedding dress continue to the present day, with entire reality television programs—the updated version of published weddings news—devoted to this one costume. Rarely were men's wedding costumes mentioned in these early or even later published wedding news accounts, highlighting again the importance of these events to women. This underscores how unimportant physical appearance is for men. Their worth lies not in how they look, on their wedding day or any other.

For a woman, her appearance was deemed significant enough that room in newspaper reports of weddings had to be made to include descriptions of not only her dress, but her hair and deportment. In the October 23, 1887 issue of *The New York Times*, the "Society Topics of the Week" section told readers about 31 weddings that had occurred. Of these, the third wedding in the column, that of Mr. Howard Henry and Miss Fannie Strong, was a quiet affair. The Strong-Henry wedding ceremony took place on Wednesday afternoon at Zion Church, with a small reception at the home of the bride's aunt. Though the article lacked detail and no description of the bride's gown was included, the writer did note that "Miss Strong made an exceedingly beautiful bride, her rich complexion, fine features, and faultless form being set off by her wedding dress to perfection" (p. 16). Again, there was no mention of the groom's handsomeness or of his attire.

Society weddings on the West Coast during this period received similar treatment in the *Los Angeles Times*. News accounts from the 1880s provide similar details regarding wedding dresses, with several brides dressed in a variety of colors other than white. I found several examples in the *Los Angeles Times* of brides who wore colors that countered the "traditional" version of the white wedding dress. For example, Miss Glenn Fox wore pale blue silk at her 1882 wedding to J. J. Woodsworth ("A Fox Caught," 1882); Miss Eva Bryson "was very richly and tastefully attired in robin's egg blue brocade satin" at her wedding to Mr. James Craik held at her parents' home ("An Elegant Wedding," 1882); and Miss Nellie Cox Barnes "looked charming in plum-colored satin trimmed with lace" when she married N. C. Maher in Pasadena ("Wedding at Pasadena," 1883). Thus, weddings reported in the press reflect that white certainly was not the only color chosen by fashionable brides. These examples, though few among the standard "white weddings," indicate that the idea of the "traditional" white wedding dress, while having become the hegemonic version of wedding attire, certainly was not always adhered to by brides whose weddings nevertheless were worthy of publication.

While newspaper society pages tended to feature large weddings, small, intimate ones also received press attention; these often featured descriptions of bridal attire that eschewed the typical white satin, tulle, and crepe gowns of larger, grander social affairs. Several of these intimate weddings were featured in the *Chicago Daily Tribune* during 1892 and 1893. For example, "Ensnared by Cupid," on page 27 of the September 25, 1892 issue, reported on seven weddings ranging from very large to very small. The headlining wedding of Miss Beatrice Estelle Waterhouse, who wore a white satin gown with train, and William Henry Austin included six ushers, two flower girls, a maid of honor, and 800 guests. In contrast, the last wedding in the column, that of Miss Katherine R. Lavinia to William Gallagher, was a quiet, at-home affair with only 30 guests. The bride was unattended and wore a "traveling costume of gray cloth with hat to match." Similarly, of the three weddings described in "Receptions and Teas" in the *Tribune*'s November 20, 1892 edition, Miss Anna L. Conroy was reported to have worn "a gray traveling gown with trimming of green silk and passementerie and hat to match" when her marriage to J. William Lecky was "quietly solemnized" at their Thursday evening wedding (p. 27).

In the page 26 article, "Many Are Married," from the April 23, 1893 edition of the *Chicago Daily Tribune*, nine weddings were headlined as "the Chief Events in Chicago Society." Among them was that of Miss Bird Buckham to Victor Henry. At their ceremony, held at her parents' home and witnessed only by intimate friends, Miss Buckham wore "a traveling gown of gray cloth and velvet and a hat to match and carried lilies of the valley." Compared to the two large weddings consisting of numerous bridesmaids and ushers that ran at the top of the article, the Buckham-Henry wedding illustrates that not all weddings had to involve some 200 guests or be considered "brilliant" to be included in the wedding news of the day.

Rarely do these early accounts mention the brides' education and even scarcer are any hints that they have occupations. Because they are mentioned in society news, one may assume that they are wealthy and therefore have no other identity than that of heiress. This absence of further description of these women tells us something—either that they were simply rich or that what they did, if anything, was not important. In this form of published gossip, one can ascertain the importance placed on a bride's physical appearance simply by reading the descriptions of her costume and beauty.

Wedding news also gives us a picture of how gender is enacted in everyday life—at least as interpreted by newspaper reporters and editors. We usually don't see stories about what everyday people do or how they enact cultural norms. While we can certainly use advertisements to gauge a culture's treatment of consumerism and social events like weddings, these news accounts of weddings from the past, much like the *acta diurna* of Rome did, capture the goings-on of society. They provide a record of what was and wasn't thought to be important enough to include in reports, or what editors and writers thought their readers ought to know about or would be interested in reading. Most often, the brides in these early wedding announcements and news accounts were described as beautiful, with wedding dress details taking a goodly amount of space. Rarely were their ages or other facts included. On their wedding day, their role and image as bride took center stage.

The inclusion of grooms' occupations highlights the contrast between how brides and grooms were depicted in wedding news of the late 1800s, as illustrated in the society pages of the *Los Angeles Times*. Men's wedding attire appeared to be of little concern or interest, as opposed to bridal costumes. Three examples from this time period reflect gender roles in terms of what information was included in wedding day accounts. The account of the Fisher-Thompson wedding, as related by the *Los Angeles Times'* article "Angelic Angling" on May 9, 1882, included this description of Miss Madie E. Thompson's wedding gown:

> The bride was beautifully attired in ivory moiré antique, and brocaded silk and satin, the font of the skirt of brocaded satin, and the paniers and court train of moiré antique. The bouffant draperies at the back fell from under a large bow of the combined materials. Basque lace down the front, and garnished by rich Spanish lace, which also edged the paniers. She wore long white gloves and the daintiest of French satin slippers. A veil of white illusion completed the costume, falling over the entire figure. (p. 0_3)

This rather lengthy description of the bride's appearance follows introductory information telling readers that the groom, Mr. C. L. Fisher, is "the prominent young merchant." However, Miss Madie E. Thompson is described only by her name; no other information about her is included. What she wore seemed to hold more importance than who she was. The simple fact that this wedding reflected her social standing, and the presumption that readers would be familiar with her identity, seemed to mean that no other facts about Miss Thompson were warranted. However, even a few words would have allowed then and future readers some idea that she was not just the future Mrs. C. L. Fisher.

A high-profile wedding in June of 1883 at the Cathedral of St. Vibiana was reported in the *Los Angeles Times* as gathering "quite a crowd," even though the reception party following the nuptials was intended to be quiet, "and no cards were issued." The wedding was that of Stephen M. White, indicated in the article as the County District Attorney. His wife-to-be, Miss Hortense Saeriste, was described as being "well known in our highest social circles" ("Wedding Bells," 1883, p. 0_6). Thus, while the groom was clearly a prominent person in the community, based on his occupational title, the bride was well known as a socialite. This provides a hint, however minimal, as to what else she was besides the bride for the day. Whether the newsworthiness of this wedding might have been based on the prominence of the groom rather than of the bride is not clear. However, the article does provide an example of the clearly demarcated way in which men and women were written about in this type of news story, at the least.

Not much had changed in the next ten years at the *Los Angeles Times*. The way in which groom and bride were described in the same paper's January 2, 1892 edition of "In Social Spheres" further underscored the difference between the sexes as reflected in wedding news. In its account of the 1892 New Year's Day wedding of Blanche Bonebrake and John V. A. Off, readers are told he is "a popular druggist," while she is described, after another lengthy wedding dress narrative, as "the picture of a sweet, womanly bride" (p. 5).

Conceding that news of weddings might appeal more to female readers than to males, and making allowances for the historical period from which these newspapers date, the portrayal of brides in these articles illustrate a clear difference between them and their grooms. Repeatedly, these women are described as beautiful and their dresses are reported on in great detail, but additional information about them is missing. The inclusion of phrases such as "She made a beautiful bride," in *The New York Times'* account of L. Grovene "Daisy" Vail's wedding to James Converse in 1892, seems innocuous enough ("Miss 'Daisy' Vail Married," 1892, p. 4). After all, on what other day should a woman look her most beautiful and elegant? However, the absence of comparable phrases, such as "He made a handsome bridegroom" when describing men on their wedding day subtly tells us that (a) their appearance is not that important and (b) for men, their wedding day holds nowhere near the significance it holds for women.

These press accounts of weddings from the late 19th century illustrate that the white wedding ideal was not the only way that those in "society" got married. Indeed, as mentioned previously, several of the weddings I found in my sampling of wedding news articles included small, intimate ceremonies and receptions, and varying wedding costumes. Women married in traveling suits, and in colors other than white. Thus, the idea of the "traditional," white wedding gown is countered by these examples.

I must point out that not all wedding announcements during this time period presented a hegemonic version of brides as being one-dimensional or not possessing any other identity on their wedding day. I found some interesting exceptions among brides' descriptions in the March 31, 1895 edition of the "Society" column on page 21 of the *Los Angeles Times*. Among the usual social activities of birthday parties and anniversaries related in this particular column were two very simple weddings. The "pretty wedding" of Sidney J. Doster and Miss Lucy May Phillips was very small and held at the home of a "Mr. Wotton," with a guest list of six. No details were included regarding the bride's dress, nor anything else about the groom or the bride, except that she was "the eldest daughter of Mr. and Mrs. Phillips." The second wedding in the same column, however, included the occupation and former occupation of both the bridegroom and the bride, respectively. The bride, Miss Ada T.

King, was "formerly editor of the Southwest News," and her groom, Will A. Wallis, is described as a "teacher of physical education in this city." The column also mentions that the sister of the bride, Miss Mira King, is "acting as teacher" at the Eagle Rock School, and that her pupils furnished some of the flowers that decorated the church. The bride's current occupation was not mentioned. However, the very fact that her position as editor of the *Southwest News* was included hints that weddings of socialites were not the only ones mentioned in the society page, even if the reader cannot ascertain if Ada King was indeed both a socialite and an editor.

Aside from its accounts of these two weddings and the inclusion of one bride's occupation, this particular edition of the *Los Angeles Times'* "Society" column deserves a little more attention, in that it serves as an example of coexistence between femininity and feminism. Two additional items among the gossip of Los Angeles in early 1895 point to the wider public world in which women lived and worked. One of those items mentions the Woman's Press Club reception held in honor of Mrs. Emma Sechle Marshall, identified as the past president of the Pacific Coast Women's Press Association. Further, among the notices at the end of the column under the heading, "Notes and Personals," appears an announcement for a "woman's suffrage mass convention" to be held the next month. The meeting's purpose is "to organize the county for active, thorough, energetic work, in behalf of the woman suffrage amendment," with First Wave feminism's founding mothers Susan B. Anthony and Rev. Anna Shaw among those scheduled to be present. I find this particular article symbolic of the complexities that mark the negotiation between the feminine and the feminist aspects of women's identity. Indeed, it essentially sums up the premise of this entire book.

Published gossip in the form of wedding announcements thus provides a record of social life that we can examine in terms of the evolution of the treatment of weddings in mass media. The news accounts presented here might come from the society pages of big-city newspapers, but they nevertheless show that weddings in the early days of wedding announcements in the US focused on (a) women, and (b) the physical appearance of women. A "you are there" perspective, evidenced by lengthy descriptions of bridal apparel and ceremony and reception details, gave readers a virtual glimpse into exclusive weddings unlike those the "ordinary" person would have seen. These accounts also likely provided ideas for less-wealthy brides, much as the gowns of royal brides such as Princess Diana and Princess Grace did in later decades. As discussed in the following chapters, this has not changed. The emphasis on bridal appearance still holds true. However, I did find that as the 20th century progressed, wedding announcements began to include more information about brides besides just what they wore.

Searching the same online archives for the *Chicago Tribune* and *Los Angeles Times*, I found two examples of wedding announcements from the 1920s that included photographs of brides in their wedding finery, which resulted in infinitely less detailed and wordy descriptions of their appearance. Such stand-alone accounts, not part of society columns, were much more to the point, listing brides' and grooms' names, parents' names, and wedding locations. For example, the *Chicago Daily Tribune*'s April 6, 1924 "Weddings" column (p. G3) included 12 brief wedding announcements. Some contained more detail than others, but all were brief, about one or two sentences each. As a wedding announcement column unto itself, instructions to submitters topped the article, much like the wedding announcement section of newspapers today. Submissions had to include the "signature, address, and telephone number of a parent" of either the bride or the bridegroom.

The simplest announcement among those included in this edition of "Weddings" in the *Tribune* stated, "Mr. and Mrs. Maurice Taussig of Wilmette announce the marriage of their daughter, Ruth, to John J. Saxleby of New York on Tuesday last." Only one photo of one bride appeared, that of Miss Mabel Laura Melges, who married Arthur Pitann the previous month at the Hotel LaSalle. In her photo captioned "Mrs. Arthur Pitann," she wears a rather heavy-looking headdress, pearls, and a dress with simple scoop neck. The reader must assume that the Melges-Pitann wedding was elaborate, as it took place at the Hotel LaSalle. Even the longest of the 12 announcements, that of the upcoming wedding of Miss Florence Kister to Kyle Runnells Davis, takes up only five sentences. The item also included details about their ceremony, including the minister's name, the fact that the bride's only attendant will be her sister, and where the wedding and following dinner will be held (The Sovereign), as well as where the couple will be spending their honeymoon (Excelsior Springs). If these are society weddings, they pale in comparison to the elaborate write-ups of just a few decades before.

The January 6, 1925 *Los Angeles Times* article "Wedded in Christmas Season" (p. A6) announced the marriage of Miss Margaret Ketas to I. J. Silverman. The report focused on the venue more than on the bride. The article's subheading, "Bride Chooses Clubhouse for Nuptials," referred to the bride's choice of the Hollywood Woman's Clubhouse as the site for her wedding. A full-length photo of Miss Ketas, captioned "Mrs. I. J. Silverman," accompanied the article; in it, she carries a large, flowing bouquet, while wearing a long gown and an elaborate headdress similar to the one worn by "Mrs. Arthur Pitann" in the 1924 *Chicago Daily Tribune* "Weddings" article discussed previously. Also similar to the previous *Chicago Daily Tribune* article, few facts about the Ketas-Silverman wedding were included apart from who officiated, how the Clubhouse was decorated, who served as best man, matron, and maid of honor, and where the couple will live ("here"). As with previous examples of wedding announcements, nothing is mentioned about the groom's attire. There is no other identifying information about the bride (except her mother's name and address) or groom.

Likely reflective of the economically difficult times, the Depression-era weddings described in the *Tribune* contrasted sharply with the intricately detailed narratives of weddings from the late 1800s. The *Chicago Daily Tribune*'s December 10, 1933 "Weddings" column (p. G5) contained a list of recent and future weddings. However, I found this particular article notable in that it lacked any details about wedding gowns or even photographs. Rather, it consisted of a list of weddings with very short descriptions. Brides' and grooms' names, parents' names and addresses, date, and venue were among the minimal facts provided for each of the seven weddings listed.

By the late 1930s, the *Chicago Daily Tribune*'s announcements about the weddings of "everyday" brides also mentioned their educational backgrounds. Two articles in particular highlighted local college women's weddings and engagements. "20 Co-Eds to Be Commencement Wedding Belles," from May 17, 1937, described the weddings and engagements of twenty students from the University of Chicago and Northwestern University. With most of the "pretty coeds" announcing June weddings, sorority affiliations are included among the pertinent facts in this article (p. 22). The dual identities of college graduate and bride combine in this report, illustrating, at the least, an apparent progression from past newspaper announcements that had excluded or likely had not required such information about brides selected to appear in society columns.

The college majors and class rank of co-ed brides-to-be from the University of Chicago and Northwestern University, as well as the occupations of their future husbands, were included in "30 Co-Eds Trade Caps and Gowns for Bridal Veils," on page 3 of the *Chicago Daily Tribune*'s May 9, 1938 edition. For example, the article mentions that Miss June Johnston of Berkeley, California is a journalism graduate of Northwestern University, and that Miss Susanna Laun of St. James, Missouri is a Northwestern commerce graduate whose future husband, Donald Alexander, is a petroleum engineer. As this is a wedding announcement column, however, the impending marriages of the co-eds naturally overshadow their educational achievements. The opening sentence illustrates a continuing focus on the concept of the hegemonic white wedding ideal, which in this article is framed innocuously: "The solemn caps and gowns of commencement week will be replaced by frothy white bridal costumes in the wardrobe of some thirty co-eds at the University of Chicago and Northwestern university."

For some of the women mentioned in "30 Co-Eds Trade Caps and Gowns for Bridal Veils," marriage trumped the completion of their college education: "Two girls, sorority sisters at the Delta Delta Delta house at Northwestern, were married and left school several weeks ago."[7] Moreover, four women from the Alpha Epsilon Phi sorority at Northwestern, the article states, "will become housewives." This article demonstrates that a woman's identity in wedding news can go beyond her role as bride. However, in the end, gender roles become reinstated in that the future occupation of housewife is clearly stated for four of these women, while future plans outside marriage are left out. Whether this is due to the editor's decision or the lack of such information about the other co-eds cannot be determined.

Examples of wedding announcements from the *Los Angeles Times* during World War II also included information about brides' educational attainment, illustrating that even during the 1940s, newspaper accounts of weddings made room for women's achievements in this area. I found three such examples of wartime and post-wartime weddings in 1945 that I consider exceptional in this regard. "Miss Noble Married to Lt. Sheafe," on page C6 of the *Los Angeles Times'* January 7, 1945 edition, told readers of the wedding of Nancy Noble to Charles Milnot Sheafe III, of the Naval Reserve. The bride was described as dressed in "costume brocade and heirloom rosepoint veil" and carrying gladioli. Names of her maid of honor, flower girl, and the ushers are also listed, but reception details and guest list are not. While Lt. Sheafe's educational details are excluded, the article ends with a list of the schools attended by the bride: she was a graduate of Westridge School for Girls, Bradford Junior College in Massachusetts, and the Boston School of Occupation Therapy.

The Hobart-Banta wedding, reported in the January 10, 1945 *Los Angeles Times* ("Patricia Eleanor Hobart," p. A5), was for the marriage of two graduates from "S.C."—which the reader can assume stood for University of Southern California. The bride, Patricia Eleanor Hobart, wore an ivory satin gown at her wedding to former college football player Herbert John Banta, who spent "two years in the Navy lighter-than-air division." The bride is described as a "Pi Beta Phi from S.C." who also had studied at the University of California, Berkeley. In this particular article, descriptions of her wedding attire and her educational background consisted of one sentence each.

Wartime weddings in the US tended to downplay the elaborateness associated with the white wedding. Otnes and Pleck (2003), in *Cinderella Dreams*, noted that wartime scarcity and three-day leaves of military personnel kept the luxury associated with weddings to a minimum. Spending on weddings increased after the end of World War II, with the 1950s "American dream" of the middle class including the white wedding ideal. Examples of weddings news from this time period seemed to reflect this as well. For example, the January 1, 1945 *Los Angeles Times* article "Katherine Dudley Hackstaff Married to Lt. Robert Reis" (p. A5) told of the wedding of Katherine Dudley Hackstaff to Lt. Robert Reis of the U.S. Army Signal Corps on New Year's Eve, 1944. The Hackstaff-Reis nuptials broke from the white wedding ideal: at their church wedding, the bride "wore a gabardine dressmaker suit of aqua blue fashioned of a short peplum and accented with a white blouse and rhinestone buttons. Her tiny flower hat was of white and she wore white orchids." Her only attendant wore a soft blue suit. Both bride and groom's colleges are listed; the bride graduated from both UCLA and Columbia University, and the groom from Lehigh University in Pennsylvania.

Though the couple's specific degrees and areas of study are not listed in these accounts, they do offer evidence that by the mid-1940s, this information was finding its way into a regular part of wedding news of noncelebrities. By the 1930s, the *Chicago Tribune*, as previously noted, had already included the education levels of brides in its wedding announcements. Skipping ahead to the *Tribune*'s August 30, 1945 issue, six marriage announcements were included in the page 19 article titled "Jane Crawford Officer's Bride in New Guinea." Missing from all six announcements were any mention of brides' wedding attire, and all but one included the colleges and universities attended by both the brides and their grooms. All the wedding ceremonies were held either at churches or hotels. Although their ages were not mentioned, I found the inclusion of education and exclusion of apparel notable in that the *Tribune*'s wedding announcement format had evolved from the days of the society weddings of the late 1800s. The replacement of lengthy descriptions of wedding gowns with lists of schools attended by the bride might seem unimportant to the casual, modern reader. When considering the time period, however, it appears that even then, the *Tribune*'s social news editors considered education important enough to include in these very brief accounts of local weddings.

In this particular article, the first wedding listed included particulars that make it even more noteworthy, in light of the story it tells in just a few sentences. The wedding of Jane Crawford to Major Homer Mather, Jr., took place in July of 1945 in New Guinea, where they had served with the same hospital unit that had taken them previously to Sydney and Brisbane, Australia. The bride is described as "connected to the American Red Cross." She was a graduate of Lake Forest College and the University of Colorado, and was on the staff of Ripon College before joining the Red Cross. The groom attended Penn State medical school and was in the Army medical corps. No details on the ceremony itself were mentioned—perhaps due to the difficulty of attaining news from halfway around the globe and the insignificance of such matters, given that the war in the Pacific was not yet concluded. Rather, the long-distance romance that culminated in their wedding and the training that brought them together served as the focus of their wedding story.

Clearly, both bride and groom in this wartime wedding were highly educated professionals, and this was highlighted in their wedding announcement.
The reference to Jane Crawford's new status as "officer's bride" subtly underscores that she is a bride, and an officer's one at that. An alternative headline
reading "Jane Crawford Marries in New Guinea" might have put the attention more on Jane Crawford, who is not described in terms of specific job title
or occupation (such as doctor or nurse). Further, neither is the groom,
although the reader can surmise that he is a medical doctor. Even with these
missing specifics, this particular account of an overseas wedding during WWII
highlights the contrast between how brides were portrayed in 1945 and the
published gossip of earlier decades.

Wedding announcements might seem mundane as sources of biographi-
cal information about women, but they do provide a means by which we can
see how mass media treated not only weddings, but how they portrayed
women in everyday life. The extravagant and highly detailed wedding news of
high society days in late 19th century New York, Chicago, and Los Angeles
rivaled that of royal weddings, providing readers with the minutest, gossipy
details as well as ideas for their own weddings. Other facts about the bride and
groom came to include their educational backgrounds, as this review of several of the articles from the 1930s and 1940s illustrates.

Hatch and Hatch (1947) recognized the usefulness of wedding
announcements as data in their study of ten years' worth of wedding
announcements from *The New York Times*. They examined 413 lead articles
featured by social editors in *The New York Times* from 1932 to 1942 to ascertain common characteristics of "the group assumed to be the top of the social
system" in New York City (p. 396). Wedding announcements, according to
Hatch and Hatch, put the spotlight primarily on the bride and secondarily
on the groom and the couple's families. As one of the most important of family occasions, they contended, the wedding serves as the occasion when families put their most favorable side before the public. Taking this notion
further, the wedding announcement as it appears in print serves as a means
to highlight what "society" would consider the most positive aspects about
the bride, the groom, and their respective families, and, by extension, their
social backgrounds. *The New York Times* announcements analyzed by Hatch
and Hatch contained the basics of wedding news: descriptions of the bridal
party's clothes, ceremony details, brief summaries of the bride and groom's
backgrounds, and facts about their families, including their residences and
social and occupational distinctions.

Among the 413 wedding announcements in their sample, Hatch and
Hatch found that more than a fourth noted brides' college attendance.
However, when compared to grooms, the practice of mentioning occupations

held by the women was uncommon. Specifically, the authors found "only ten women among 413 mention being engaged in any remunerative occupation and those occupations are all rather specialized and possibly the result of personal inclination" (p. 402). Further, the authors noted that membership in clubs appeared to serve as a point of pride in the announcements they studied. Thus, while a quarter of the women were portrayed as highly educated, transferring that education to paid work was extremely rare.

Brides' education appears to have become a regularly, though not always, included item in published wedding news in these newspapers by the 1930s, with several examples from the post-WWII years providing more information about brides than just their wedding clothes. By the 1960s, wedding news in the *Chicago Tribune* ranged from simple announcements of couples' and their parents' names to social column items that mentioned brides' educational backgrounds *and* occupations. For example, in the June 6, 1966 *Chicago Tribune* article by reporter Eleanor Page, "June Brings Nuptial News from Afar" (p. B5), of the two weddings and three engagements listed, all but one included mentions of the educational backgrounds of the brides and brides-to-be. Further, a description of one bride's work experience points to the importance of this aspect of women's identity in wedding news by this time. The account of the Corle-Wheelers wedding in California told readers that the bride, Jean Corle, "made her debut at the Music Academy of the West in 1963," and has been "modeling professionally and working in a bookshop, which delights her mother."

Emphasis on bridal appearance and dress did not wane, however, as demonstrated in Cass's January 15, 1967 article in the *Chicago Tribune* (p. A5), "Lovely Brides Brighten the Midwinter Scene." Of the four wedding announcements in this article, none mentioned the bride's education, but each did include detailed descriptions of the wedding gowns. For example, bride Jeanne Lawlor wore a "gown of silk-faced satin reembroidered at the hem with Alcenon lace and seed pearls and a lace veil held by a satin headpiece." Photos of each bride in her wedding gown and veil were included in the article as well; captions indicated their married names while their maiden names were written in parentheses. For example, the caption, "Mrs. Albert Weiler Wald (Julia Lawrence Pool)," identified one bride, while the caption for another photo of a bride and her groom was worded "Mr. and Mrs. Charles Jardine (Jeanne Lawlor)." The overall presentation evokes an emphasis on femininity, in terms of inclusion of wedding gown details, lack of other identifying information, and photo captions that first identified brides as "Mrs." so-and-so, with their birth names in parentheses, as if tacked on and of secondary importance. While little about the brides (and grooms) themselves was included, aside from who their parents and attendants were, the inclusion of their "real" names in parentheses at least acknowledged their pre-wedding identities.

By 1972, during the midst of the Second Wave of feminism, wedding news in the *Chicago Tribune* appeared to have incorporated a more varied style, with career facts incorporated into published gossip about weddings and engagements. For example, in the May 22, 1972 article "'Country Wife' Gets Updated" (p. B12), three of the ten weddings and all three engagements told readers of brides' occupations. Only one of the wedding announcements, for the Taylor-Birkos nuptials, mentions the bride's wedding gown—with only the fact that the bride wore her mother's wedding gown. Rather, the article focused on "love stories," as reflected in details of how the brides and grooms had met. For example, the headline refers to how the first couple listed, Louise Ehrlich and Anthony Grafton, had met during a production of the play "The Country Wife" at the University of Chicago. Two candid photos from their wedding accompany the description of their wedding day. While readers could see what the bride wore, they did not know the intricate details of her wedding clothes. The Ehrlich-Grafton wedding item ends with a description of their current occupations: the groom was pursuing "graduate study" while the bride continued teach at DePaul University.

Two of the wedding announcements in "'Country Wife' Gets Updated" actually led with the couples' occupations. For example, the Sherrod-Collins wedding item opens with the fact that the bride was "a Playboy bunny" and the groom worked for his father, a funeral director. The Lyden-Hemsworth item leads with the bride and groom's professional status as staff members at the A.C. Nielsen Company. No information about specific occupations appears in the item for the Conway-Fry wedding, however. Rather, their announcement ends with the vague sentence, "The young people are living in Omaha, where both are working."

As for the three engagement announcements in this same article, the Moore-Lloyd item actually begins with the couple's educational backgrounds and occupations. Readers learn immediately that Nora McMahon Moore not only is a "graduate of Centenary College" in New Jersey and the University of Grenoble, France, but an "associate producer of TV commercials." Her fiancé, William J. Lloyd, graduated from Indiana University and is "co owner of a graphic design company." The other two newly engaged couples listed include a medical student (groom) and men's store associate who was unable to find a teaching job after graduating from the University of Illinois (bride), and a reporter for the *Chicago Tribune* (the bride-to-be), whose fiancé's occupation curiously is not mentioned.

The inclusion of such information in half the items in this *Chicago Tribune* article from 1972 further illustrates that wedding news of this sort can and did make room for at least some depth regarding who these women were, aside from their new roles as brides and wives. While one can view this as demonstrating some progress regarding the portrayal of women in this form of media, the accompanying courtesy titles in the photo captions of the brides, in which they are identified as "Mrs."-plus-husband's name, underscore they are still the wife of a man. For example, the photo of new bride Kathleen Hackett in "'Country Wife' Gets Updated" is accompanied by the caption "Mrs. Charles Megan." In contrast, Cass's January 15, 1967 article, "Lovely Brides Brighten the Midwinter Scene," in the same newspaper included brides' maiden names, even though in parentheses. The examples described here did not infer any choice on the part of brides regarding how they were identified in terms of their birth or marital names; one must assume that their photo captions were decided by whomever was in charge of the articles or columns.

A woman's marital name choice has interested researchers because that choice makes a statement about her values and identity; keeping one's birth name serves as an indicator of feminist values, noted Hoffnung (2006). Goldin and Shim (2004) used *The New York Times* wedding announcements as one source of data for their study on "keepers," women who kept their maiden names after marriage.[8] They found that women who tend to keep their maiden names after marriage tend to be highly educated and hold careers in which one's name holds more salience, such as writing and the arts. Hoffnung (2006) also found that brides who kept their birth names tended to have higher education levels. She also found that the number of nontraditional brides did not increase between 1987 and 2002. Hoffnung's content analysis of 480 wedding announcements in *The New York Times* from 1982 to 2002 showed that 71% of the brides chose to use their husband's name, while the remaining 29% chose either to keep their birth name or to hyphenate their birth and married names. Hoffnung noted that *The New York Times* routinely asked brides chosen to appear in its wedding announcements about their name choice preferences and printed such information until the mid-1980s.

If keeping one's surname after marriage indicates feminist values on the part of the bride, then it appears its frequency has not gained enough of a critical mass to reflect significant changes regarding the patriarchal values that underlie the practice of taking one's husband's name. To explain the relatively low numbers of keepers in their samples, both Goldin and Shim (2004) and Hoffnung (2006) suggested that for young women during the Third Wave of feminism, keeping one's birth name as a way of maintaining their identities was, or is, not that important anymore. "Name usage at the end of the 1990s and into this century seems to indicate that feminist values are being maintained at about the same level," Hoffnung concluded (p. 824). She further added: "At the same time, it is disappointing that we are not making progress" (p. 824).

Vows: Allusions to Feminism Within the Wedding Narrative

The examples of wedding news and descriptions of brides from the archives of three major newspapers discussed here reflect an evolution of sorts regarding what information society page and news editors deem important enough to include in such accounts. The socialite weddings of the late 1800s clearly emphasized apparel and wealth, reflected in the details of wedding gowns, decorations, and gift lists. During the 20th century, wedding announcements became shorter and came to include the educational backgrounds of brides as well as that of grooms. By the 1970s, occupational information of both brides and grooms was included as well.

More recently, *The New York Times'* wedding news column, *Vows*, provides readers with not only the current trends in weddings, but goes beyond the stereotypical announcements of the past by focusing on how couples met. Presented more as feature stories than as announcements, *Vows* chronicles how others who know either the bride or groom or both of them view the match, adding an outside perspective that gives insight into the personalities of the wedding couple. *Vows* invites submissions for publication consideration through *The New York Times* web site, asking brides and grooms about their schooling and occupations, how they met, and "noteworthy awards that the couple may have received, as well as their charitable activities, and/or special achievements" ("How to Submit an Announcement," 2009). In addition to wedding day specifics of time, date, and location, submissions also must include parents' residences and occupations.

Published as the book *Vows: Weddings of the Nineties From The New York Times*, a compilation of 98 columns from 1992 through 1996 by Lois Smith Brady serves as a readymade sample for examining media portrayals of weddings during that decade. All the wedding stories in the *Vows* book mention both the ages and occupations of the wedding couples, with occasional inclusion of their educational achievements. Regarding the weddings themselves, ceremony details and wedding dress descriptions appear to take a backseat to narratives of couples' backgrounds and how they met. Although wedding announcements in *The New York Times* evoke an air of high society, Brady also noted that "money alone does not buy heart, style, fun or a great wedding" (1997, p. vii). Supporting this claim, the *Vows* book includes unusual weddings, such as the 1993 elopement of an Australian couple who married at New York City Hall's marriage chapel. The bride, Maryann Blacker, a 34-year-old magazine editor, and the groom, Nicolas Baker, a 32-year-old English teacher, bought their wedding rings from a sidewalk jewelry vendor, and wore street clothes for their city hall ceremony (pp. 44–45).

In the *Vows* book, photographs accompany each of the 98 stories; 75 included editorial, candid-style, black-and-white photos of the bride in some version of a white wedding gown and/or veil. Several wedding stories mentioned wedding gown designers' names, such as the well-known bridal designer Vera Wang, for example. Exceptions to the white wedding gown included descriptions of brides who wore white suits instead of gowns or dressed in colors other than white, such as black or blue. One bride even sewed her own dress.

Another example of an exception to the white gown/tuxedo wedding was the 1992 minimalist wedding of Lucy Shulte, a 32-year-old freelance magazine writer and editor, and 39-year-old James Danziger, a gallery owner. The couple looked more like an "elegant couple on their way to lunch" rather than the typical bride and groom (p. 33). The bride wore a taupe Calvin Klein jacket and skirt over a lace bodysuit, "the one bridal touch" to which she conceded, while the groom wore a gray Armani suit (p. 33). Although their 100-person reception might have denoted high expense, the bride's perspective of her wedding day contrasted with the notion that a woman's wedding day is the most important one in her life: "I wanted to get married in the daytime because I feel like marriage is your daily life. Everybody thinks a wedding should be your fantasy day. I think the opposite. I think a wedding should be a very real reflection of your life" (p. 33). The inclusion of "nontraditional" weddings such as the Shulte-Danziger nuptials as well as the aforementioned Blacker-Baker city hall elopement suggests that the *Vows* column offers more than just wedding news: it provides readers with nonhegemonic versions of celebrations that involve working professionals whose personal stories, rather than their weddings, take center stage.

An underlying feminist thread runs through *Vows: Weddings of the Nineties* as well. In the book's preface, author Brady acknowledged that marriage no longer is vital to women's survival: "Getting married is no longer something you *have* to go through—for your parents, your personal survival or respect from neighbors" (p. ix). Brady further noted that she had met very few brides under the age of 25, denoting the steadily increasing age of first-time brides in recent decades. The requirement that couples selected to appear in the *Vows* column provide their ages *and* occupations, combined with the population of working professionals from which it draws its material, serves as evidence that weddings and feminism need not be viewed as completely incompatible.

Indeed, I found three examples among the 98 weddings in the *Vows* book where the word "feminist" actually appeared in print, which further implies a feminist perspective. In the article about the November 1993 wedding of ordained ministers Felicia Thomas and Walter Parrish, the bride is described as talking about "feminist issues and her own love life" during her sermons (p.

9). An egalitarian-minded pastor, Thomas recounted that in a recent sermon she had said she would never marry a man who does not cook. The reader learns that not only does her new husband cook, but he also rides a motorcycle. Their longer-than-usual wedding ceremony at the chapel of the Union Theological Seminary in Manhattan was followed by a simple reception of coffee, fruit punch, and cake in the seminary's social hall. The couple's decidedly downsized wedding further underscored their nontraditional views.

"Feminist" was how groom Dean Bloch described his bride, Gale Wolfe, in the 1993 *Vows* column that told the story of their "fun and untraditional" wedding in the countryside. Bloch, a 37-year-old chief of obstetrics and gynecology at a New York hospital, and Wolfe, a 27-year-old film and television editor, married outdoors in a short Jewish ceremony at Rokeby Farm, a country estate resembling "a free-spirited commune" where they had been neighbors five years previously. For their "fun and untraditional" wedding, the bride wore a white tank top dress and the groom wore a tuxedo and sneakers. Bloch apparently found his new wife's independence attractive: "When I first got to know Gale, I liked her politics. She was a feminist and ecologically minded and she was her own person," he said (p. 63).

I found the third example of the use of the term "feminist" in the description of the 1992 Lubavitcher (Hasidic Orthodox Jewish) wedding of 29-year-old Shayna Hendel, described as "a Sarah Lawrence graduate, feminist, and former Greenwich Village habitue," and 33-year-old Chaim Meiseles. The Lubavitcher community to which both belonged required married women to wear wigs or hats in public, and prohibited public displays of affection by married couples. The contrast between feminism and strict Hasidic gender roles served as the focus of this *Vows* article. While the wedding reception was segregated by gender, with men and women guests not allowed to interact, the bride did not see her and her new husband's way of life as incompatible with feminism: "My life as a married Lubavitcher woman will be as feminist as any life I can imagine," she said (p. 49).

Although the majority of the weddings in the *Vows* compendium upheld the white wedding ideal, these examples that highlight feminism—whether from the point of view of the writer, Lois Smith Brady, the groom, or the bride herself—demonstrate the potential for this type of published gossip to forward feminist ideals. Even as the wedding as social event serves as the attraction and raison d'être for the *Vows* column itself, two themes permeate the narratives that take it beyond the historical, gossip-style wedding announcement: (a) inclusion of couples' ages and occupations, and (b) emphasis on characteristics of the bride and groom as individuals over the previous importance placed on bridal apparel and ceremony and reception details. Rather than devoting time and space to describe bridal apparel or party decorations, *Vows* appears to be more about the wedding as a celebration in the lives of the couples featured. Especially notable is the effort to include the groom into the picture, as well as his background and the way in which he views his bride.

Though sparse and infrequent, the inclusion of an explicit feminist perspective in the three *Vows* stories discussed here demonstrates that wedding media and those who produce them have the ability to frame the wedding as an important, but not *the* most important, day in a woman's life. By doing so, what the *Vows* column does for bridal media is to present the wedding as an occasion that highlights the accomplishments of both brides and grooms, as well as their views about marriage. In this manner, *Vows* goes beyond the stereotypical wedding announcement by providing a venue for couples to let the newspaper audience, and, in a sense, the wider society, know about their unions. Along with the "news" aspect of wedding announcements, the values and attitudes regarding both gender and love also are conveyed. Thus, one can consider *Vows* as countering a hegemonic ideal of weddings that views them as a solely female-centered means of perpetuating strictly traditional gender roles.

Indeed, one can find *Vows* columns that open with the groom's point of view. Rather than emphasizing the importance of the wedding and marriage for women, such an angle forwards the notion that finding a mate is just as important and significant for a man as for a woman. For example, the April 19, 2009 edition of *The New York Times* included a *Vows* article on the wedding of Christina Matthews and Benjamin Macfarland III that started with the groom's background. While their wedding was large and upscale (they both came from historically wealthy backgrounds), the article emphasized not the opulence or lavishness of the wedding, but the educational and professional aspirations of the couple. Only a short sentence described the bride's attire and décor of the wedding venue: "Under Baccarat crystal chandeliers in the ornate Louis XV-style Grand Ball Room, the bride wore a simple yet elegant Vera Wang gown under her grandmother's lace veil" (Marx, 2009). This expansion of the wedding announcement reflects an egalitarian perspective by telling the stories of both the groom *and* the bride, thereby promoting the wedding as a celebratory event that has meaning for men, who were previously considered unessential in the wedding world save for their appearance at the ceremony itself. Indeed, as noted by Howard (2006), grooms and men (for the most part) remained significantly absent or appeared only marginally in bridal magazines. In terms of the bridal industry, "men were a hindrance to consumption that had to be overcome" (p. 94).[9]

While *Vows* frames wedding news as human interest feature stories, emphasizing the "how-they-met" aspect, the counterpart "regular" wedding announcement in *The New York Times* offers a more factual style. Rather than telling readers intricate details about wedding venues and what everyone wore to the wedding, the typical, non-*Vows* wedding announcement in *The New York Times* focuses more on a couple's educational backgrounds, occupations, and achievements. For example, the wedding announcement of Alison Geraghty and Andrew Bethke in the same April 19, 2009 edition of *The New York Times* included not only the educational backgrounds of the bride and groom, but also brief descriptions of what they did for work. Such descriptions include a fair amount of detail. For example, readers learn that the 28-year-old bride is a graduate of Hamilton College and a planner and distributor for a cosmetics company in New York, who is "responsible for ensuring that product levels are allocated sufficiently domestically and in Canada" ("Alison Geraghty, Andrew Bethke," 2009, p. ST12). The 27-year-old groom is an "Emory graduate" and a senior associate at a real estate company in Miami. Family information included both their mothers' and fathers' names as well as their fathers' previous occupations (in this particular example, mothers' previous occupations were not mentioned, which the reader may assume means they had none). A brief mention of how the couple met (in high school, when they studied Shakespeare in London and Paris) appears at the end of the article, but most of this particular announcement centers on the couple's college education and current careers.

Summary

The appeal of weddings as news finds its origins as far back as written news has existed. In addition to their newsworthiness, accounts of the weddings of the politically important or of popular movie stars have included gossipy details of the most intricate and minute aspects, including apparel—especially the bride's gown—as well as other, seemingly trivial facts. High-profile, high-expense weddings of the rich and famous serve as models for imitation for the less rich and famous, a way to attain some element of luxury and status. The weddings of Princess Diana and Princess Grace further enhanced the fantasy surrounding weddings, bringing to life the fairy tales associated with the feminine achievement of marriage.

The Internet age enhances the "blanket" media coverage of such events, as illustrated by the 2011 wedding of Diana's son William to the commoner Catherine "Kate" Middleton. The pageantry and fanfare of that event, coupled with the media frenzy surrounding the wedding plans and intricacies of the ceremony, wedding attire, and the subsequent reception at Buckingham Palace, impart the notion that fairy tales do exist, even in the 21st century.[10] The portrayal of "Waity Katie" provided a picture of a modern, educated woman who waited some eight years to become William's bride, further underscoring the precedence that her role as wife had over the pursuit of an independent, self-supported existence. The celebrity status she gained was due to her becoming a bride and marrying into *his* world of privilege and prominence rather than making a mark on her own.

Bridal media in the form of wedding announcements allow the non-celebrity woman to achieve fame on "her" day. Wedding announcements thus provide two things: (a) public notice, and (b) a vehicle for brides to reach a level of celebrity. One simply submits the information to the local newspaper, often with a fee, and it becomes news. The convenience of online wedding submissions makes the process even easier, and allows for anyone to become a "newsmaker."

If we take a look back, we see this type of wedding news as evolving over time. Today's wedding announcements include not just a bride's and her parents' names, but also her education and occupation. A comparison of early society page wedding news from the late 1800s through the present provides another historical record of women's progress in the public sphere. I must also note here that my analysis does not consider race as a factor, but rather the way in which brides in general and in these particular news media historically have been portrayed.[11]

While wedding announcements still reflect the femininity personified in the role and image of the bride dressed in "traditional" attire, they also reflect changes regarding women's identity. Today a woman's achievements—educational and occupational—have become required elements. Rather than her wedding apparel or other aspects of the wedding celebration, what these brides do for a living and have accomplished take precedence. When viewed in terms of women's progress outside the traditional role of wife, the juxtaposition of feminine identity and feminist values illustrates conflicting notions of what it means to be a woman in this particular society. Indeed, as Wood (2010) noted, women constantly seem to get mixed messages regarding how they should think and act.

In the case of *The New York Times' Vows* column, the central narrative revolves around the couple's relationship, how it began, and how others view their relationship. When considering these aspects of bridal news, the existence of such information illustrates that "room" can and is made for bridal news to depict women as whole persons, not just a man's new wife. Though, certainly, such announcements uphold the status quo regarding marriage and weddings, they nonetheless give us some insight into how news can eventually come to reflect societal progress.

I find especially noteworthy, and surprising, the explicitly feminist aspect of particular *Vows* columns included in the 1997 book *Vows: Weddings of the*

Nineties From The New York Times. Whether this was an effort by the *Vows* columnist, Lois Smith Brady, during a particular time period, or if any feminist-leaning agenda continues in more recent *Vows* columns deserves further study beyond this discussion. However, the very mention of the word "feminist" in those examples from the *Vows* book by Brady, and descriptions of men who find feminist women appealing, points to the real potential for wedding news to go beyond descriptions of brides in terms of their wedding gowns and physical beauty.

Wedding announcements have evolved to include same-sex weddings. In 2002, *The New York Times* announced that it would publish reports of same-sex commitment ceremonies ("Times Will Begin Reporting," 2002). The section titled "Weddings" became "Weddings/Celebrations," and same-sex weddings had to meet editors' criteria of newsworthiness and accomplishments of the couple and their respective families. In addition, publication of same-sex wedding news also had to meet other requirements; specifically, they had to be public ceremonies of legally recognized unions. *The New York Times'* announcement that it would include same-sex weddings also noted that the *Vows* column would "on occasion" be devoted to same-sex couples ("Times Will Begin Reporting," 2002, p. 30). By 2003, some 70 newspapers across the US published same-sex wedding announcements (Venema, 2003). A more detailed discussion of same-sex weddings appears later in Chapter 6, in terms of how same-sex weddings counter the idea of "traditional" marriage while still manifesting wedding hegemony.

Similar to wedding news, reality television treatments of weddings and wedding planning provide a record of how this event is practiced and about how women who appear in them are portrayed. In the next chapter, I describe the scope of bridal media, which range from the overtly commercial bridal magazine to the covertly consumerist reality television programs that feature brides as they prepare for their wedding day. This chapter illustrated that wedding news need not always focus solely on the feminine dimension of brides. How reality television weddings in particular frame gender—especially in terms of the perpetuation of femininity—and the glimpses of feminism that offer viewers portraits of women beyond their role as bride, serves as the foundation for subsequent chapters.

Notes

1. Several bridal researchers and writers, both popular and scholarly, point to Victoria as the originator of the "traditional" white wedding dress, including Geller (2001) in *Here Comes the Bride*, Baldrige (2000) in *Legendary Brides*, Jellison (2008) in *It's Our Day*, and Schreier (2002) in *Hollywood Gets Married*.

2. Amnéus (2010) noted that elaborate gowns were worn by the wealthiest brides, while brides of lower rank wore their best dress, with flowers in the hair serving as the cue that signaled their bridal identity (p. 17).

3. Allen's (2003) article focused mainly on the inordinate attention paid to Victoria's wedding cake, as it allowed the public to experience in some sense the wedding celebration "in person" simply by reading about the cake and seeing pictures of it. The cake also symbolized the wealth of the British state by its size and complexity.

4. Goffman (1959) defined the personal front as a person's clothing, insignia, size and looks, and other physical aspects presented to others.

5. In the same article, readers also learned about the apparel of other members of the bridal party, including that of the Queen and Queen Mother, Princess Anne, Princess Margaret, as well as the "Lady Diana blue" worn by Diana's mother, stepmother, and Prime Minister Margaret Thatcher (Anderson, 1981, p. A10).

6. Here are examples of programs I found listed on my Cox Communications digital television schedule during the time period of April 29–30, 2011: Lifetime listed several programs under the umbrella title *Royal Weddings of a Lifetime*, including *William and Kate: A Love Story*, *A Tale of Two Princesses*, *Kate's Gown of Renown*, *Feast Fit for a Prince and Princess*, *A Day to Remember*, *The Future King and Queen*; WE tv listed *Charles and Diana: Wedding of the Century*, *Kate: The New Diana?*, *Prince William*, *William and Kate: Wedding of the Century*; TLC listed *Royally Astounding: Defining Days of the Monarchy*, *William and Kate: A Royal Love Story*, *The Making of a Royal Wedding*, *Untold Stories of a Royal Bridesmaid*, *Say Yes to the Dress: The Royal Wedding*, and *The Royal Wedding: Encore and More*; E! Entertainment listed *Will and Kate: Road to the Altar* and *Inside the Royal Wedding*.

7. The practice of female students leaving college to get married was depicted in the 2003 film *Mona Lisa Smile*. Set in the 1950s, it centered on the contrast between an untraditional, feminist art professor (played by Julia Roberts) and her female students at the elite Wellesley College. Even while pursing college degrees, the students were not encouraged to pursue careers but to fulfill their "destinies" as housewives of other elites.

8. The other sources for Goldin and Shim's study were Massachusetts birth records and Harvard alumni records.

9. I recall seeing stories on television news magazine shows about women during the 1990s who "played" at being brides by planning their imaginary weddings and trying on bridal gowns, even though they were single and not in romantic relationships. As an example of wedding "play," the April 16, 1998 episode of the NBC series *Friends*, "The One With All the Wedding Dresses," featured the three female characters, Monica, Rachel, and Phoebe, playing "dress up" with bridal gowns. Captivated by how they looked in wedding dresses as they tried them on in a bridal salon, the women took the dresses home and wore them for fun. The juxtaposition of their drinking beer from bottles while lounging about in the formal white gowns added a further comedic touch.

10. Just as in the time of Queen Victoria's wedding, details about the menu for William and Kate's wedding became the focus of online press reports such as "Eight-Tiered Cake Wows Guests at Wedding Reception" on *Yahoo News* (2011). Not only could one learn that the royal wedding cake was "covered in cream and white icing and dec-

orated with up to 900 delicate sugar-paste flowers," but that 10,000 canapés were prepared for the event, and the champagne served to guests was "Pol Roger NV Brut Reserve."

11. A discussion of race and wedding media appears in Chapter 3 and pertains to how bridal magazines have excluded women of color. Although media coverage of brides based on their race lies beyond the scope of this book, it merits further study. The famed civil rights attorney Morris Dees (2001), in *A Lawyer's Journey: The Morris Dees Story*, described the practice by newspapers, particularly the *Montgomery* (Alabama) *Advertiser*, of segregating wedding announcements by race. Dees described the class action suit *Cook v. Advertiser*, the basis for which was the "shameful practice" of segregated wedding announcements in the newspaper. In 1969, the *Advertiser* refused to print the wedding announcement of a Black couple in its Sunday society page, due to its policy of printing such news in the Thursday "Negro news" edition. The suit did not go to court; by the time the court ruled that civil rights statutes did not cover this type of discrimination, the *Advertiser* had changed its policy (pp. 130–131).

3. The Bridal Media Milieu

AT THE BEGINNING OF THE 21ST CENTURY, THE RANGE OF WEDDING-ORIENTED print and electronic offerings—magazines, Internet web sites, and, most notably, numerous network and cable television programs in the reality genre—demonstrate bridal media's variety, reach, and profitability. These wedding-related media help to fuel not only an entire retail and service industry, but also a growing segment of the media industry itself. Hollywood films and fictional television programs further add to the bridal media milieu.[1] As discussed in the previous chapter, the evolution of the newspaper wedding announcement illustrates that wedding news has come to include information about women beyond their bridal role. Here, I describe the scope and range of bridal media in their print, Internet, and nonfiction television forms.

Bridal magazines mainly address the commodity aspect of weddings, especially those props they, and the manufacturers and retailers of those props, imbue with a sense of "must have" and necessity. Advertising in this specialized media overlaps editorial content; articles considered "editorial" in actuality serve as ads. Like fashion magazines that tell readers about "editor's picks" or "what's new," bridal magazine editorial content promotes specific products, designers, and name brands. Presenting readers with the "dream" wedding, they in essence offer the ideal wedding in which everything and everyone, especially the bride, is perfect. In this manner, bridal magazines provide the wedding fantasy in its final, completed form, with that fantasy presented as being possible as long as one just follows the instructions and purchases the products advertised within them.

Bridal web sites serve as the online counterparts to bridal magazines. These serve mainly as portals to wedding merchandise sites; easy, one-click links lead to not only a magazine's subscription page, but also to sites for bridal products and even sites where couples can apply for credit cards in order to finance their weddings. Online web sites take the bridal magazine to a new level, as would-be brides can literally do their wedding planning from the comfort of their homes or workplaces.

Television documentaries and infotainment specials serve as another type of nonfiction wedding media. Framed as "news," these programs range from stylized and edited portrayals of glamorous, high-price celebrity weddings to blooper-type compendiums of weddings gone awry. As bridal media, they show both the fantasy offered in bridal magazines and web sites, as well as the "dark" side of weddings where what can go wrong does go wrong—all captured on videotape. As entertainment programming, these reality television versions of "real-life" weddings of both the rich and famous and everyday couples provide readily available, relatively inexpensive content, making them easy to edit and then present as appealing, specialty programs. After all, who wouldn't enjoy getting a glimpse into an exclusive Hollywood wedding, or watching the best man faint during the ceremony? These programs, though they show the unusual side of weddings as caught on camera, continue to frame the wedding as a spectacle where anyone can be a star, thus perpetuating the ideal white wedding as desirable and a way couples—but brides especially—can achieve celebrity status, even if for just one day.

Bridal Magazines

Bridal magazines serve as the primary authority on wedding planning. As purveyors of the "correct" and most fashionable way to incorporate wedding trends and bridal apparel, these publications tend to consist of hundreds of pages, most of them advertisements. Essentially catalogs for wedding dresses, accessories, party favors, and honeymoon destinations, bridal magazines present a hegemonic version of the wedding, one that requires a pricey wedding gown and *materiel* for a lavish reception. Today, all three top bridal magazines in the US—*Brides* (formerly *Bride's*; the cover masthead now omits the apostrophe), *Modern Bride*, and *Elegant Bride*—are produced by the same publisher, Condé Nast. Illustrative of media conglomeration, its online outlet, *Brides.com*, offers subscriptions to all three publications (hereafter referred to as The Big Three). The two top bridal magazines, *Brides* and *Modern Bride*, "uphold the traditional status quo ideologically at the same time that they teach readers to purchase numerous commodities," observed McCracken (1993, pp. 269–270).

A prime example of the consumerist origin of bridal magazines, *Brides* was founded in 1934 by Wells Drorbaugh, the advertising manager for the magazine *Home and Garden*. According to McCracken (1993), Drorbaugh realized that even during the Depression, when buying was down and affluent magazines experienced reductions in advertising dollars, women were still getting married—and a magazine about weddings had the potential to persuade them to buy products for their new households. First a local publication in the New York–New Jersey area, then a national publication starting in 1939, *Brides* eventually was sold to Condé Nast in 1959. By 1983, *Brides* became the largest consumer magazine in U.S. history, with its March 1983 issue consisting of 495 pages of advertisements (McCracken, 1993). By 2000, *Brides* had doubled the amount of its advertising; its February–March 2000 issue contained more than 1,000 pages of ads (Kuczynski, 2000). Ingraham (1999), in her overview of bridal magazines, called *Brides* the "standard-bearer of wedding culture" (p. 96). In addition to upholding heterosexuality, contended Ingraham, *Brides* sees its mission as contributing to a healthy economy, through advertising, providing jobs, and helping newlyweds.

Today, one can find a number of bridal magazines at bookstores, mass merchants such as Target and Wal-Mart, supermarkets, and almost any newsstand. Bridal periodicals basically offer the same content. Some of these titles include: *Bridal Guide*, similar in size and scope to each of Condé Nast's Big Three; *For the Bride* (formerly *For the Bride by Demetrios*; Demetrios is a top wedding gown designer); *WeddingBells*, published by the WeddingChannel.com, which has since been bought by The Knot, Inc.; *Wedding Dresses*, from Gerard Bedouk Publishing, with offices in New York, France, and the UK; *Inside Weddings*, which bills itself as the "insider's guide to weddings with style"; *The Bride and Bloom*, a California-based publication; and *Ines Del Mar Weddings*, which provides readers with the "A-list" of preferred vendors on its web site, *Inesdelmar.com*.

Some of the more merchandise-intensive publications play up even more the change in habitus achieved through the purchasing of the perfect items, thus allowing for even more differentiation in wedding elegance. For example, from Elegant Publishing in Rhode Island, the upscale, coffee table–sized *grace ormonde Wedding Style* magazine features designer fashions from New York, Paris, and Milan, and trendy reception ideas. Still featuring white or shades thereof, the avant-garde looking wedding dresses in the Fall–Winter 2009 issue of *grace ormonde* looked more haute couture than the familiar bridal magazine offerings. The same issue included articles on the growing trend of reception "lounges" (which feature low couches, copious amounts of fabric, and dim lighting), and artistic wedding cakes, giving the impression that this particular publication targets the upmarket bride who eschews the do-it-yourself, make-your-own-party-favors approach presented in other bridal magazines. It also offered a "platinum" list of vendors categorized by 29 states and by country, including Mexico, Costa Rica, Fiji, United Kingdom, and Dubai (pp. 153–183).

Several bridal magazines concentrate solely on the items required to throw a successful dream wedding. For example, *Martha Stewart Weddings* began as special wedding issues of her *Living* magazine, first published in 1998 (Ingraham, 1999). Covers of *Martha Stewart Weddings* now typically feature items such as bouquets and wedding cakes, with most of the content concerning decorations, *à la* the "Martha Stewart style" of make-it-yourself, time-intensive home goods. Now its own entity, Stewart herself is listed as founder, although SVP Publishers is the listed publisher, according to the summer 2009 issue of *Martha Stewart Weddings*.

Weddingstar, an online wedding accessories shopping site, also produces a print version. Its November 2008–November 2009 issue consisted of a 416-page catalog of items ranging from cake toppers to party favors and table decorations. A two-page "editorial" article on actual readers' weddings mentions how *Weddingstar* differentiates itself from other bridal magazines; according to one mother of the bride, "other magazines focus more on the dress than anything else," while *Weddingstar* "offers many fabulous products that we know can't be found anywhere else" (Pool, 2009, p. 191). *Weddingstar* not only includes prices of the items it features, but even includes an order form so that readers can directly order the items they like.

Regional bridal magazines further expand the bridal media milieu. These local versions of national magazines contain the same images of white-gowned brides, luscious cakes, flower arrangements, and table settings. Advertisements from area vendors allow for ease of wedding planning, though these regional publications also take advertising from nationwide bridal goods companies as well. Fragmentation illustrated by regional magazines and wedding-themed versions of national publications represents the fastest growing category of magazines. Bridal-themed magazines had nearly doubled between 2002 and 2007, totaling some 135 titles, with localization serving as the most important trend in the bridal magazine world (Snedeker, 2007). Titles such as *Southern Living Weddings*, *Pacific Rim Weddings*, *Manhattan Bride*, *Chicago Bride*, and *Phoenix Bride and Groom* (Arizona), and local magazine special issues, such as *Las Vegas Life Bride*, represent this trend. While other magazines in general have seen downward sales, bridal magazines have a permanent audience because people will always get married. Combine this with the "nesting" trend and interest in home development and interior design of the early 2000s, and bridal magazines appear to have a solid future, observed Snedeker (2007). Online versions of these magazines further increase the scope and variety of media that cater to bridal "needs" through their convenience and ease of use.

Indeed, whole corporations base themselves on promoting and selling the white wedding ideal, notably, the bridal media company called The Knot. *The Knot Weddings Magazine* serves as only one aspect of The Knot, a media company consisting of a web site/portal, books, and a reality television program, Oxygen's *Real Weddings From The Knot*. In addition to a regularly published magazine, one can find special editions of bridal publications from this company, such as *The Knot Wedding Gowns*, whose Fall–Winter 2002 issue consisted of 480 pages featuring what the cover boasted as "1000+ Styles from over 175 Top Designers," in addition to "Trends We Love from Bridal Fashion Week," "Necklines for Your Body," and "Over 3200 Bridal Salon Listings." In 2009, The Knot released the special edition publication *Best of Weddings*, which told readers about "the winners" in cakes, reception venues, photographers, flowers, event planners, bands, and dress shops, as chosen by real brides.

One also can find special wedding issues of "regular" magazines as well, which illustrates the bridal appeal and ready-made aspect of tailoring already specialized magazines toward featuring products suitable for the big event. *Better Homes and Gardens* published its special *Weddings* edition in 2005, which the cover touted as being "back by popular demand." In keeping with *Better Homes'* domestic theme, *Weddings* featured "stunning receptions," specialty foods for the wedding buffet, cakes, boutonnieres, bouquets, and an article on a range of required wedding stationery, including ceremony programs, menus, seating cards, invitations, and thank-you cards (Palkovic, 2005). Other home-interest magazines that have published special bridal versions include *Real Simple* magazine, which published, ironically, a highly detailed, 160-page *Real Simple Weddings* edition in 2009. The special edition promised readers a guide to "planning a beautiful (and stress-free celebration)." The volume consisted of ten chapters addressing various wedding topics and tips, including budget, location, invitations, attire, flowers, vows, photography, food, how to make a planning timeline, and a section titled "scene" that included instructions for reception "essentials" like music, centerpieces, favors, and décor.

Bridal magazines have become even more specialized, with publications that focus on specific wedding-related goods and services. For example, *Destination Weddings & Honeymoons*, published by Bonnier Travel Group, promotes various locales where couples can either get married or spend their honeymoons. The summer 2009 issue included ads for resort wedding packages at hotels and spas mixed in with editorial content on exotic adventures, such as safaris and shark diving excursions. Articles on "real" weddings provide testimonials from couples regarding accommodations and services from vendors both abroad and within the US (such as Hawaii). *Destination Weddings* also includes tips on negotiating the best deals and finding resorts that "match your style," as its summer 2009 cover touted.

Beauty magazines also have published special wedding issues, which is no surprise, given the inherent physical aspects of the bridal appearance. Just as finding the perfect dress is essential for a perfect wedding, the bride also can find the ideal hairstyle to make her special day complete. For example, *Bridal Star Hairstyles*, a version of *Celebrity Hairstyles* magazine produced by Harris Publications, focuses on wedding day coiffures. Issue 28 of *Bridal Star Hairstyles* from 2001 featured articles with titles such as "Elegant Updo's," and "The Looks Men Love." In addition to beauty tips, the magazine also included photos of bridal scenes from popular movies as well as real celebrity weddings. "Over 1500 Ideas and Inspirations" were promised to readers of Issue 67 from 2009, as well as "Sparkle Aplenty! Veils, Tiaras, and Jewels."

Allure magazine, one of Condé Nast's many periodicals, published *Bride Allure* in Spring 2005. As a magazine focusing on cosmetics and women's physical appearance, *Allure* simply added *Bride* to its title and modified its content to frame it in terms of the wedding as a venue where women need to look their best. Articles in *Allure*'s special bridal issue, with titles such as "Wedding Skin," "Wedding Hair," "Wedding Body, "Wedding 911," and "Picture Perfect," provided tips and recommended products by name. To further blur the line between editorial content and advertising, *Bride Allure* included a directory for "the best wedding-day make-up from Broadway to Beverly Hills," with lists of salons, complete with prices and contact information ("Directory: Making Faces," 2005).

Similarly, *Fitness* magazine, whose tagline is "mind, body & spirit," published a special *Fitness Wedding Makeover* edition in Spring 2003. Focusing on weight loss before the wedding, the wedding issue of this fitness-oriented publication included articles telling brides-to-be how to get the body of their dreams in order to fit into the "perfect dress." The article "The Wedding Dress Diet" provided a three-month strategy for brides to lose about a pound a week, based on a 1,500-calorie-a-day diet. The opening sentence of the article normalized weight loss as part of wedding planning: "Dropping a few pounds before your wedding is as much a part of the nuptial rite as the bridal shower or tossing the bouquet" (O'Connor, 2003, p. 56). As previously mentioned in Chapter 2, weight loss became part of the wedding narratives of both Princess Diana and Grace Kelly; their wedding gowns had to be altered to accommodate both women's thinner bodies, their weight loss attributed to the stresses of wedding planning. Today, the connection between body shape and weight has become inexorably linked to having the ideal wedding day, especially the notion of being able to fit into the perfect wedding dress. I explore this aspect of the bridal image in further depth in Chapter 4.

The search for the perfect wedding dress has become elevated to the status of "Holy Grail," with women becoming more concerned about fitting into the princess mold rather than wearing their "best dress," as had been the practice in the past (Amnéus, 2010; Baldrige, 2000). This becomes even more highlighted especially when comparing the importance of one's personal front for women as opposed to men on their wedding day. Bridal magazines address this issue, illustrating the recognition that weddings do involve and reflect differences in how the sexes view weddings as well as themselves as participants in their own wedding narratives. For example, in the June 2008 issue of *Fitness*, the article "Bride-to-Be Confessions" presented results of a survey of 1,000 brides. It reported that 83% of those women wanted to lose weight before their wedding, compared to 34% of men, although the article did not indicate that any men actually took part in the survey (Pevzner, 2008, p. 118). Assuming that the statistics were based on actual responses, whether from the brides themselves or from those who reported responses of their husbands-to-be, the importance of looking good appears to carry more "weight" for weddings than in everyday life.

The same *Fitness* survey also tapped into the "princess syndrome," with 51% of respondents saying they wanted a wedding dress that "makes them feel like Cinderella at the ball." Further, among the proffered statements regarding what these brides-to-be wanted to overhear on their wedding day, 52% said they wanted to hear "she looks so beautiful," compared to "she looks so happy" (46%) or "she looks so thin" (2%) (Pevzner, 2008, p. 121). Thus, even as the women in the *Fitness* survey wanted to look beautiful on their wedding day, the idea of losing weight while not looking "so thin" illustrates the negotiation between the desire to look beautiful in the eyes of others, but not to the point of being considered overly thin. These results, however valid or not, demonstrate an emerging, conflicting message to women in a society that continues to value physical appearance while perhaps also forwarding less severe mandates regarding body weight.

Weddings also serve as a component of the lifestyle genre of magazines focused on consumerism. For example, *InStyle* magazine publishes special wedding issues that feature celebrity brides from television and films. One of the earliest special issues, from Spring 2001, featured actress Courtney Thorne-Smith on the cover. Ironically, Thorne-Smith divorced less than a year after getting married. The cover promised readers "elegant hair," "bridesmaid dresses for every figure," "35 top bridal beauty buys," "perfect weddings for any price," and how they could design their "dream day." The "Love Stories" section gave readers behind-the-scenes photos and narratives of three recent weddings of television celebrities, including Thorne-Smith's "last minute" wedding in Hawaii.

The editorial theme of *InStyle* centers on female-centered consumerism, forwarding the notion that to be stylish one must follow the latest fashion and decorating trends. Its bridal issues similarly promote the superficial, while also providing the dollar amounts required for its readers to obtain a sense of style. For example, the 2001 *InStyle Weddings* article "Buy, Buy Love," whose very title succinctly reflects the overarching theme of bridal magazines, told readers that "affairs to remember are possible—whatever the price tag" (p. 176). However, even with this qualifier, the lowest price to obtain the bridal fantasy started at $5,000 for a "backyard" gathering for 70 guests. The article ended with a $60,000 "seaside fantasy."

While the 2001 issue of *InStyle* focused on the "dream day," the Winter 2005 issue of *InStyle Weddings* concentrated more on the bride herself, with the main cover headline proclaiming, "Beautiful *You*! Hair, makeup & fitness plans for every bride." The cover bride was television actress Mariska Hargitay, who as of 2011 continued to portray the tough police detective Olivia Benson on the long-running NBC series *Law & Order: Special Victims Unit*. The contrast between Hargitay as a "real" bride dressed in white and pearls and her onscreen persona worked well in conveying the cover's message that the issue was for "every bride." One easily could read that Hargitay illustrated that even "tough" women could fit into the bridal mode—even ones portrayed as single and independent like her onscreen character, thus combining the feminist with the feminine. The issue's theme of "beautiful you" featured articles and advertising for bridal gowns, mother-of-the-bride outfits, cosmetics, and jewelry, all in keeping with the theme of bridal beauty conveyed by bridal magazines in general.

The article "Get Ready to Look Great" in the same *InStyle Weddings* issue offered tips on exercise, nutrition, and stress reduction. Normalization of stress as an unquestioned aspect of the bridal role adds to the notion that the bride is expected to bear this burden, not the groom. The article's opening sentence assumes that wedding work falls to the soon-to-be wife: "The morning after she becomes engaged, the typical bride-to-be isn't thinking I do, but to-do: book a venue, interview caterers, design invitations, etc." (Blitzer, 2005, p. 235). The article also listed 10 things to do to stay in shape—including spending even more money by hiring a trainer—as well as 10 things to "keep pounds off" and 10 more things to do to keep "big-day anxiety at bay" (p. 240). *InStyle* reassured its readers that they could achieve not only perfection in terms of the wedding as event, but won ally perfection as well, by staying fit, healthy, and stress free "so you can loo. and feel radiant on that special day" (p. 235). Rather than advising brides to forgo entirely an intricately planned wedding, which one would think would be the logical way to relieve this stress, *InStyle* and other forms of bridal advice instead offer coping strategies that actually create *more* work for brides. Further, the idea that women can have it all—stereotypical of the "superwoman" who can do everything successfully, as well as of postfeminism—becomes attached to the assumption that the bride *must* do it all: look beautiful, plan her wedding, and take care of her body.

Bridal magazine content provides ample evidence not only for the examination of the superficial nature of the wedding business, but also the media-generated notions of the proper wedding, the proper bridal look, and, by extension, the proper way that women should regard themselves as *women*. The superficiality of bridal magazines, though evident from even a casual reading at the newsstand, was the focus of Filak's (2002) study of a year's worth of *Brides* and *Glamour* (both owned by Condé Nast) during 2001 and 2002. Filak's content analysis showed that in addition to containing more advertising than other women's magazines, *Brides* focused more on the party aspects of weddings rather than on relationships or married life. Two-thirds of the ads in *Brides* featured beauty and fashion products, leading Filak to conclude that those ads "focused at externally beautifying women to help them reach a fantasized ideal" (p. 17). Regarding content, 37% of *Glamour*'s content consisted of articles considered as editorial, while less than 17% of *Brides*' content was editorial. *Brides* also contained fewer articles on intrinsic issues and improvements, as compared to *Glamour*. With its focus on the feminine theme of physical appearance, creation of the "princess wedding," and a decidedly cosmetic approach to marriage preparation, Filak concluded that *Brides* ultimately disserves women by telling them how "a type of makeup or dress will solve their problems" (p. 17).

While bridal magazines might emphasize the party planning aspect of weddings, one can find evidence, however scarce, of at least some concern regarding the issues involved in the gathering of two, or more, families at the event. Wedding etiquette does concern this deeper element, but it appears that, for the most part, questions to bridal magazine editors regarding manners relate more to the best ways to handle the ceremony and reception. Questions about the bridal escort, who should sit where, the minimum age for flower girls, invitation wording, and dealing with stepparents largely have to do with making sure the wedding day goes smoothly. These etiquette questions can reflect the importance of keeping family ties strong and cordial, but can also delve into the seemingly trivial and petty. For example, in the "Ask Carley" column of *The Knot* magazine's Fall 2009–Winter 2010 issue, one reader asked how she could let guests know not to wear white to her wedding (the answer: you can't, but no one will mistake a white-wearing guest for the bride).

One can find serious marriage advice among bridal magazine offerings, however, even though it might be buried among the hundreds of pages of advertising and other wedding-item related articles. For example, the July–August 2009, 334-page issue of *Brides* offered a one-page article on marriage tips, "Secret to a Great Marriage" (Dwyer, 2009), in its "Home" section. Already assuming that the reader's own relationship was "effortless," the article presented five basic rules for a successful marriage:

1. Do things together.

2. But also do things separately.

3. Don't diss [disrespect].

4. Maintain a united front.

5. Fight fairly. (p. 182)

The same article also included a call-out textbox that looked almost like a postscript which told readers sex keeps a relationship healthy. The inclusion of such material demonstrates that at least some thought is given to the relationship being publicly acknowledged. However, the brevity of such content disallows a serious treatment of marriage and the essential qualities of healthy, loving relationships. Were bridal magazines to include more material of this type, perhaps readers would reconsider planning a big wedding in favor of bettering their partnerships, or discovering that perhaps they weren't ready for such a commitment in the first place!

McCracken (1993) contended that bridal magazines, namely *Modern Bride* and *Brides*, in addition to upholding the status quo ideologically, provide "cultural leadership" that instructs women to purchase "numerous commodities" necessary for the fulfillment of their gendered roles, notably that of wife and mother (pp. 269–270). The blurring of advertising and editorial content instills in women readers what McCracken termed "pseudo-needs"— needs that suddenly become matters of almost life-and-death importance as women attempt to create the fantasy wedding these magazines promote (p. 268). Further, the various lists and bridal registry "must-haves" that bridal magazines tell readers they need correspond to the very advertising they contain. By listing wedding service businesses and convincing advertisers to market their products as "bridal," bridal magazines essentially invented the bridal market, telling women readers—the nation's consumers—what goods and services they needed for the ideal wedding and for marriage (Howard, 2006, p. 82).

Thus, bridal magazines have the power to create self-generating income by advertising the products featured in "editorial" content. Indeed, the bridal magazine market has seen profits while other publications have lost ad revenue or closed down. Even prior to the economic effects of September 11, the year 2001 was a slow one for magazine publishers. According to Johnson and Prijatel (2007), total advertising pages and revenue across the magazine industry were down, with the exception of only a few magazines. Those few included three of the top bridal titles—*Brides, Modern Bride,* and *Bridal Guide* (Fine, 2001); Johnson and Prijatel noted that these titles were among a handful that "avoided a drop" (p. 103). Indeed, in advertising pages and revenues, *Brides* ranked number one among 100 titles between 2000 and the third quarter of 2001 (Fine, 2001, p. 20). *Brides* was also number one in ad pages during the first quarter of 2007, with *Bridal Guide* at number three and *Modern Bride* at number 16 ("Magazine Ad Page Leaders for January through March 2007," 2007).

McCracken (1993) observed how the "multiple mini-narratives" on women's magazine covers extend to the inner content and advertising, creating a "pleasurable, appealing consensus about the feminine" (p. 3). Regarding bridal magazine covers in particular, "As a 'relay text' that sent advertising messages to readers, the cover was too important a place for capturing the business of brides to feature a groom prominently," explained Howard (2006, p. 94). Because they encapsulate the decidedly female and feminine-oriented role of the bride and only the bride (that is, women), bridal magazine covers *require* the absence of men. Ignored is any mention of what makes the perfect *groom.* Instead, stories inside these publications that tell readers about "real weddings" may include only the most minimal information about grooms/men, such as their name, age, and occupation.[2] Thus, rather than making the wedding a team project, where both marital participants would create a shared celebration, bridal magazines work to create the image that only women can and should make choices regarding how a dream wedding will be handled.

While in reality men can and do participate in wedding planning, the world created by bridal magazines and the larger wedding industry ensures a gendered division of labor. Regarding the groom's financial responsibilities for the wedding, bridal media target this information at the bride for *her* to relay to him (Howard, 2006). This also prepares the bride for the role of consumer in the subsequent marriage. In Chapter 5, I discuss how reality television wedding programs—the television versions of bridal magazines—reflect this sex segregation as well.

By marginalizing men and framing the wedding as a female-centered endeavor, bridal magazines prevent this most important of public events that unites the sexes from becoming a truly egalitarian concern. Marriage as a partnership thus can start out as an unequal state if wedding planning is not shared (Currie, 1993). This irony illustrates how feminist progress becomes hindered when such sex-based responsibilities and desires become normalized. As discussed in the next section, the short-lived publication *For the Groom* attempted to fill the void created by bridal magazines by targeting future husbands. However, that effort was short-lived, though it did offer some alternative versions of the white-wedding ideal so well imaged and perpetuated by bridal magazines.

Bridal magazines historically have excluded minority women as well, with the image of the perfect bride reinforcing white standards of beauty (Ingraham, 1999). In her survey of issues of *Brides* magazine between 1959 and 1998, Ingraham (1999) found only four covers showing women of color; she found that since 1990, an average 2.4% of each issue of *Brides* included African American brides (pp. 93–94). In an updated study of the major bridal magazines *Brides*, *Modern Bride*, and *Elegant Bride*, Frisby and Engstrom (2006) found that from 2000 to 2004, of 6,486 ads, only 70 featured an African American bride. When women of color were included in bridal ads in those magazines, they more often appeared as bridesmaids in a group of bridesmaids. None of the three magazines featured an African American woman on its cover. However, just a year after the sample's cutoff date, *Modern Bride* featured Destiny's Child's singer Kelly Rowland on its April 2005 cover. In another ironic twist reminiscent of Courtney Thorne-Smith's 2001 appearance on the cover of *InStyle*, Rowland's wedding was canceled shortly before publication; her wedding to a Dallas Cowboys football player was called off just before the *Modern Bride* issue featuring her on the cover was published ("Rowland Still Mortified," 2006).

Targeting specific audiences: Further fragmentation

Even while the major national bridal magazines forward the version of the perfect bride as wearing and being white, publications targeting minority women do exist. Notably, the magazines *Signature Bride* and *BridesNoir*, which offer both print and online versions, specifically market themselves to African American women. *BridesNoir* describes itself as the magazine "for the contemporary bride of color," according to its 2005 "Weddings Gone Wild" issue. The *Signature Bride* web site noted that the Signature bride "values her independence, but wants a successful marriage" ("Signature Bride—The Magazine," 2009). Further, the Signature bride combines both ideals of femininity and feminism, as embodied in her valuing of both work and home life: "She is ambitious—career-oriented, success-driven—and a source of stability at home." *Signature Bride*'s mission statement also includes men as vital participants of both wedding planning and marriage: "Designed to help couples through their first 2–3 years of marriage, the publication is about their lives, their needs and issues they face as newlyweds and as a Black couple in today's society" ("Signature Bride—The Magazine," 2009). The notion of tradition remains a focus of *Signature Bride*, as noted by its editor, Linnyette Richardson-Hall: "We give you the guidelines and practices that were established in Europe centuries ago and have been handed down for generations in America" ("Letter from the Editor," 2009). New versions of the same message thus find a comfortable way of not only coexisting, but also becoming subsumed into an image of the "modern" woman/bride of color.

The bridal magazine market has become a prime area for narrowcasting in other ways as well, with several titles in the bridal magazine genre illustrating the various layers of the wedding in terms of audiences and focus. These have included publications that targeted the repeat bride, the mother of the bride, and even the groom. *Bride Again*, "The Only Magazine Designed for Encore Brides," was published in 2001, but ceased publication after several issues. Slim at just 128 pages, the Fall 2001, Volume 3, Issue 3 edition of *Bride Again* featured articles on diamond jewelry, dresses, celebrity "encore" weddings, practical legal advice, including "Attorney Talk" in the magazine's legal issues section, and relationship advice, with "How to Make Your Marriage Last a Lifetime."

The article "Renewing Your Vows" in *Bride Again* acknowledged how the wedding day has come to symbolize the epitome of romance, with newly married couples holding "an often idealized version of married life" (David, 2001, p. 22). The article promoted the idea that renewing vows serves as a means for couples to recommit to their relationship. Even though it appeared to assume that one's actual, original wedding probably followed the white wedding ideal, the article told readers that vow renewals do not require a big party; vow-renewing couples who do not want a "party to end all parties" should "keep it simple and make the vow exchange the highlight of the event" (p. 24). This advice from *Bride Again* points to the very heart of the wedding's purpose, and offers a viewpoint that goes against the focus on merchandise one typically sees in bridal media. Thus, even as this article emphasizes the idea that a couple's vows are more important than the details of the party, it nevertheless only mentions this viewpoint in an article on vow *renewal* ceremonies rather than as an entire article devoted solely to the importance of vows as the most important part of a wedding in the first place. At the least, *Bride Again* told readers that a big party was not necessary for couples to show others how committed they were; the inclusion of such advice in The Big Three bridal magazines would be unthinkable.

Other members of the bridal party have served as the audiences for wedding magazines. The cover of the premiere issue of *Mother of the Bride*, published by Family Creativity Communications in 2000, told its target audience it was "The Only Guide for You: Fashion, Makeup, Travel . . . and More!" In addition to its replacement of ads for wedding gowns with those for mother-of-the-bride dresses, the slim, 71-page issue consisted of editorial articles on the usual wedding-related must-haves: flowers, beauty and makeup, accessories, and cakes. Rounding out this specialized publication were articles on how to budget a wedding and how to reduce stress. *Mother of the Bride* clearly presented a weddings-as-usual approach in "Money Matters," an article on wedding budgets. The article cited that the average wedding costs "between $8,000 and $12,000," but that with careful planning, "it's possible to pay much less" (Taylor, 2000, p. 34). "Your daughter's wedding can—and should—be one of the happiest and most rewarding days of your life," the article proclaimed (p. 34). However, even after a long list of do's and don'ts regarding how much to spend and on what, the article concluded with the reassurance that an ideal wedding need not require a great deal of money: "You don't have to break the bank to have a wonderful wedding. A bride in a homemade dress exchanging vows in her parents' backyard is no less beautiful than a bride wearing Vera Wang at the Plaza" (p. 39). Rather than actually promoting such a subdued, practical wedding, this message instead becomes drowned out amidst the deluge of articles and ads that clearly favor the opposite. In this sense, the idea of a small, backyard wedding with a homemade bridal gown serves as the oppositional, deviant version that further *enhances* the appeal of a big, lavish affair that has come to represent the ideal.

In 2000, Wings Media published the premiere issue of *For the Groom*. It targeted grooms, with articles on tuxedos and men's accessories, including ties and shoes. *For the Groom* contained the usual wedding etiquette and practices, such as the man's responsibility to propose to the woman. However, an article on Las Vegas wedding chapels, "Here and Eloping in Las Vegas," included a call-out box titled "Get Hitched Quick," telling the (assumed) male reader how convenient it is to get married in Vegas. This alternative was framed positively in the form of the question, "where else can you go from the altar to a $6.95 all-you-can-eat buffet and on to a night of shows and slots?" (Belsky, 2000, p. 91).

As a unique form of bridal media, *For the Groom* countered the typical bridal magazine content by focusing on the groom and his interests, even though those interests appear as traditional masculine values. For example, an article titled "Paaaarty!" gave readers advice on what to wear to a bachelor party and featured a photo of several men at a bar with what looked like a stripper (whose clothing is credited with the caption, "Dancer: Victoria's Secret") (Trent, 2000). The magazine's cover headline, "Suite Sex: 10 Moves for Hot Nights," and a double entendre–filled article on manicures, "How to Get

Nailed," reflected a decidedly masculine perspective, illustrating how sexual prowess serves as a key element of men's identity.[3]

At the same time, this masculinity itself was countered in *For the Groom* in "For Better or Worse," an article on marriage advice based on the book *Seven Principles for Making Marriage Work* by University of Washington psychology professor John Gottman. The article's author noted that "most of us simply lack the wiring to feel comfortable" expressing admiration for others, and advised readers to express fondness and admiration and demonstrate respect for their wives, because verbal communication is "important to a happy marriage" (Bechtel, 2000, p. 85).[4] *For the Groom*'s inclusion of articles hinting at the financial advantage of a "quickie" Vegas wedding and providing research-based relationship advice shows at least an effort to widen the established white wedding ideal forwarded by most bridal media to include other forms of weddings.

Both *Mother of the Bride* and *For the Groom* appear to have been rare publications in the bridal media world, and as far as I can tell were single-issue publications. However, even as they existed within the white wedding stereotype, they contained small hints of resistance to the idea that weddings require a high degree of expense. That they did not "catch on" as regularly published periodicals might likely have been an indication that they did not reach their target audiences. Still, they deserve some recognition here as examples of the scope of bridal media, and as evidence that wedding advice can include deeper topics than choosing the right florist, dress, and reception venue.

The overall sameness of bridal magazines regarding the material requirements for today's formal wedding reflects the importance of props to "the smooth functioning of authority" (Allen, 2003, p. 458). Articles on extra-focal content, such as marriage and relationship advice and questions on proper wedding etiquette, serve as informational asides to the primary message of all bridal magazines: one must purchase the proper, socially endorsed items in order to have a "real" wedding. Even as some magazines, such as *Signature Bride*, incorporate shades of feminism via stated notions of women's independence, wedding "traditions" become reified through wedding props. Aside from the monetary profits of the bridal magazine/bridal goods industry, which actually can be thought of as one and the same, the repeated images of white wedding gowns, silver cake servers, and beribboned party favors combine to serve as a concrete, empirical means by which hegemony functions. Bridal magazines serve as the conduit for telling readers about real, palpable objects that symbolize not only matrimony (cake) but also femininity, in the form of bridal "packaging" (wedding dress, headdress as symbolic crown, special cosmetics, special shoes). The online counterparts to the bridal magazine have made attaining the props needed for the smooth functioning of hegemony even easier, as web site visitors need only click on a "buy it now" button and type in a credit card number to procure the items they need for the wedding of their dreams.

Weddings on the Web

Bridal web sites provide not only a platform for brides-to-be to find out about the latest wedding dress styles, makeup tips, and other wedding planning information, but their ability to proffer wedding merchandise so conveniently creates an even more direct way to sell the wedding image. In addition to online versions of print magazines, major bridal web sites have become intricate venues where brides-to-be can find wedding etiquette guidelines, every imaginable item that one can think of for ceremonies and receptions, and even marital advice. In addition, these media spaces expand the bridal media milieu and normalize the consumeristic aspect of not only weddings, but of gender roles. Online versions of bridal print magazines give them a web presence, further expanding the reach of their advertisers. Here I describe three major bridal sites that truly exemplify the blurring of the editorial and the advertisement: *Brides.com*, *TheKnot.com*, and *WeddingChannel.com*.

Brides.com serves as the central web site for Condé Nast's Big Three bridal magazine titles, *Brides*, *Modern Bride*, and *Elegant Bride*. In addition to offering subscriptions to the three magazines, the site's links offer information for every aspect of wedding planning. Visitors can find a gift registry, list of local vendors, and sections on fashion, beauty and fitness, etiquette, and honeymoons. The site also provides visitors with "tools" to manage their own wedding planning, including an electronic budget tracker, interactive seating chart, guest list manager, and task checklist. The "Shopping" pages offer one-click access to jewelry, bridal accessories, party favors, and stationery. The "Engagement" section features links to pages on engagement rings, real-life proposal stories, showers, and parties. The "Essential Guide" link offers tips on how to throw an engagement party and a question-and-answer page for topics related to etiquette, such as the rather crass issue of how to ask wedding guests for cash rather than gifts.

Brides.com's "Groom 101" page lists "must-do" duties for the "dream" groom, starting from the directive to propose, choosing groomsmen, planning the honeymoon, writing vows, greeting guests, and learning how to dance. The gender-based advice also includes ideas for "PG-13" rated bachelor party activities. Reflecting that weddings are ultimately the bride's responsibility, the "Organizing the Men in Your Wedding" page is addressed to the bride, not the groom. Of course, the groom's duties also include some degree of consumerism, illustrated by the links to pages on choosing groomsmen's gifts, how to go tuxedo shopping, and how to shop for an engagement ring.

The "Real Weddings" gallery on *Brides.com* provides brief descriptions of actual weddings, with videos, photographs, and details on wedding themes. Photos illustrate the sameness of weddings, envisioned and framed as desirable, by these magazines: brides in white gowns and grooms in dark suits and tuxedos. Except for differences in themes, such as "rustic wedding" or "seaside wedding," these real weddings appear almost interchangeable. *Brides.com* further eliminates any demarcation between the business of weddings and any semblance of wedding reportage by including links to the vendors who made the real weddings shown in the gallery possible, from the wedding gown designers to florists, photographers, and caterers.

The merging of all three of Condé Nast's bridal magazines and their respective web sites into a single site in 2006 extended the company's "destination-site strategy" (Ives, 2006). Rather than maintaining separate sites for each publication, as has become the practice, the destination site strategy builds web properties around content rather than titles (Ives, 2006). Condé Nast had "watched the circulation of its bridal magazines drained away" by the multi-outlet bridal media company The Knot (Seelye, 2006). The creation of Condé Nast's "powerhouse weddings site," as termed by *Brides.com*'s managing director at the time of the launch, was a response to the success of *TheKnot.com*, the big name in online wedding sites described later in this section (Seelye, 2006).

The destination wedding site *WeddingChannel.com* launched in 1997. The Los Angeles-based company also published *WeddingBells* magazine. The web site's mission was "to help marriage bound women and men through the sometimes challenging but always exciting process of planning a wedding and starting a new home" ("About WeddingChannel.com," 2009). *WeddingChannel.com* features gift registries and one-click shopping pages for every conceivable aspect of wedding planning, including dresses and tuxedos listed by designer, with links to pages for more than 90 designers so as to ease the gown shopping process. Other linked pages let visitors shop for flowers and décor, music, cakes, hairstyles, and honeymoons, and watch videos of wedding gown runway shows. The intricate site allows visitors to search for items by vendor and brand name, as well as purchase wedding items directly. Couples also can create their own wedding web sites, either for free or for a "premium."

Though it primarily serves as an online gift registry, *WeddingChannel.com* also offers newlywed advice, including answers to questions about finances, changing one's name, and taxes. Links to other web sites reflect that *WeddingChannel.com* targets women primarily, despite its mission statement. These links include several motherhood sites, including *TheBump.com*,

Mommyhood.com, and *Breastfeeding.com*. Other wedding sites linked to the *WeddingChannel.com* include *ShopforWeddings.com*, and, most notably, *TheKnot.com*. In fact, *WeddingChannel.com* served as The Knot's largest competitor prior to 2006.

The Knot: Bridal media and more

The web site *TheKnot.com* launched on America Online in September 1996.[5] Founded by "four good friends, two of whom had barely survived their own wedding due to the lack of updated information and real-world resources available," The Knot claims to be the largest online retailer of wedding favors and supplies ("The Knot—About Us," 2005). Brides- (and grooms-) to-be can click on links such as "Wedding Planning," "Wedding Budgeter," "Wedding Fashion," "Bridal Beauty," and "Grooms" (unsurprisingly, grooms only have one link dedicated to them). According to its "The Knot at a Glance" fact sheet, *TheKnot.com* is the only wedding brand on the AOL, MSN, and Yahoo Internet portals. The Knot also established a marketing alliance with May Department Stores Company, the umbrella company of Robinsons-May, Filene's, and Famous-Barr, under which The Knot promotes these stores' wedding registry services ("The May Department Stores," 2002).

In 2002, *The Knot Magazine* debuted with a 500+ page issue priced at $9.99 ("The Knot Magazine Debuts," 2002). In addition to its online and magazine versions, The Knot has published a series of books covering the gamut of wedding-related necessities, with titles such as *The Knot Book of Wedding Gowns*, *The Knot Book of Wedding Flowers*, and *The Knot Guide to Wedding Vows and Traditions*. Specialty publications include *The Knot Weddings*, which features "real" weddings in various regions and major cities, such as DC–Maryland, Ohio, Florida, and New York Metro.

The Knot's print and online outlets cross-promote each other. *The Knot Magazine* includes full-page promotions for these web sites, with directions for readers to consult *TheKnot.com* web site throughout its editorial content. For example, in "Rings & Fine Jewelry," a print spread in the Spring–Summer 2005 issue marked as a "special advertising section," a caption tells readers to "search for more gorgeous jewelry at TheKnot.com/jewelry" (p. 92).

The Knot bought the *WeddingChannel.com* in 2006. The acquisition of its major rival cost The Knot $58 million and some $1.15 million in stock, but the merger allowed The Knot to achieve 80% of wedding-themed web site traffic by 2007 (Hough, 2007; "The Knot and WeddingChannel.com," 2006). Furthering its domination of the bridal media market, The Knot's media holdings continued to expand with the acquisition of *Great Boyfriends.com*, a site where women recommend men to other women, and *TheNest.com*, a site devoted to all the domestic necessities of newlyweds just setting up house. These web sites are advertised in The Knot's print magazine as well.

The June 2006 acquisition of the *WeddingChannel.com* added to The Knot's multiplicity of media and merchandising alliances, cementing a hegemony regarding the marketing of wedding products and etiquette which conveys the idea that in order to get married, people (that is, women) must adhere to the current standards regarding requisite products. The Knot serves this clientele along two levels: by (a) providing information on proper practices, and (b) offering convenient ways to purchase everything needed for the proper wedding on its own web site, and directing visitors to various web-linked retail affiliates. As an entire company built around bridal media and merchandising, The Knot has the ability to enhance a hegemony of femininity in accordance to bridal "rules'—enforcing a mercantilism while at the same time instructing women who buy into, literally, the wedding ideal.

In addition to its various print media holdings, The Knot expanded to the medium of television in 2003, when it collaborated with the Oxygen cable network to produce Oxygen's *Real Weddings From The Knot*, a reality series that followed brides as they prepared for their weddings. As a form of bridal media, it promoted the idea that weddings require a multitude of requisite items, forwarding even more a female-oriented consumerism. However, it also contained subtler messages regarding women, especially in terms of the physical aspect of bridal preparation, and the role of the bride as supervisor of her once-in-a-lifetime spectacle. Though supposedly based in the documentary genre, the "reality" version of The Knot promoted its self-interest through the disguised portrayal of everyday life that endorses traditional gender roles for women and the ideal of the "big, white wedding" it so well promotes in its online and print outlets. I describe *Real Weddings from The Knot* in further detail in Chapters 4 and 5.

Celebrity Weddings as Infotainment

As news, weddings of both the rich and famous and the "ordinary" person have become accepted and expected in print media, whether as front-page stories or wedding announcements in newspapers. The interest in high-profile weddings, as described in Chapter 2, logically extends to human interest gossip magazines. For example, in addition to regular issues that feature high-profile celebrity romances and weddings (and breakups), *People* magazine has produced special issues on celebrity weddings in recent years. Collector's items in book form have included *People's The Greatest Weddings of All Time* in 2002 and *I Do! The Great Celebrity Weddings* in 2005.

Featured on the cover of *The Greatest Weddings of All Time* was a black and white wedding photo of actors Brad Pitt and Jennifer Aniston, who later divorced. Displayed prominently on *I Do! The Great Celebrity Weddings* was a photo of pop music singers Jessica Simpson and Nick Lachey, who also later divorced. Both special editions included weddings of celebrities, such as movie, television, and sports stars, as well as fictional weddings from Hollywood films. *The Greatest Weddings of All Time* also featured famous past weddings such as those of Grace Kelly and Prince Rainier, Princess Diana and Prince Charles, and Jackie and John Kennedy. In addition to more recent notable weddings, *I Do! The Great Celebrity Weddings* also included "Against the Odds," a short, two-page article on same-sex weddings, such as those of celebrities Melissa Etheridge, Rosie O'Donnell, and Elton John, and, as with other bridal media, articles about celebrity weddings gowns, jewelry and rings, cakes, and flowers.

Due to their human-interest appeal, weddings frequently serve as head-lining stories on entertainment news and gossip programs, such as the syndicated show *Entertainment Tonight*. Celebrity weddings not only feature prominently among these television versions of the newspaper society page, but they also have become fodder for cross-over promotions between television and print media. For example, the top story of the November 30, 2000 edition of *Entertainment Tonight* featured the highly publicized wedding of Hollywood notables Michael Douglas and Catherine Zeta-Jones. Relying on "exclusive" photos of the wedding from *People* magazine's upcoming December 11, 2000 issue (thus simultaneously promoting *People*'s issue featuring the wedding as its cover story), *Entertainment Tonight* touted the Douglas–Zeta-Jones event as a "royal wedding." The program gave viewers a peek at the exclusive *People* photos of all the insider details, such as Zeta-Jones's dress by designer Christian LaCroix, and images of the couple feeding each other wedding cake. The Douglas–Zeta-Jones story then segued into a story on prenuptial agreements by mentioning that Zeta-Jones would receive $1.5 million for each year she stayed married to Douglas, in addition to the 10% of his net worth he "gifted" to her as a marriage present (estimated at $22.5 million).[6] By reporting that Zeta-Jones, a Hollywood star in her own right, received a substantial amount of money as a gift from Douglas and would receive more by staying married to him, the story reminded viewers of the gendered aspect of weddings and marriage: her financial gain depended on her continuing role as *his* wife.

Another example of crossover media promotion occurred in 2005. On January 22, 2005, *Entertainment Tonight* offered its viewers a preview of *InStyle* magazine's prime-time television offering *InStyle: Celebrity Weddings*.[7] Of the nine weddings in the upcoming *InStyle: Celebrity Weddings* television special, *Entertainment Tonight* previewed those of Kevin Costner and talk show host Star Jones. Aired on the ABC network on January 27, 2005, the infotainment special's top story featured the wedding of Costner. While Costner was the celebrity, his bride, described as a fashion designer, received most of the attention. That attention centered mostly on her wedding dress, described as a custom-made, "Cinderella fairy-tale gown."

The nine celebrity weddings featured in the same 2005 edition of *InStyle: Celebrity Weddings* included those of actress Mira Sorvino, television stars Mariska Hargitay, Scott Wolf, and Tori Spelling, and pop star Britney Spears. The marriages of Spelling and Spears both ended in divorce. One of the weddings in this program featured a bride who eschewed the traditional white gown; this exception to the white-gown rule was found in the "hip-hop" wedding of rappers Kelis and Nas. Kelis opted for a custom wedding gown in green by designer Matthew Williamson. Consisting of 43 yards of fabric, the bright green dress featured antique embroidery. Nas wore a cream-colored, three-piece suit by designer Yves Saint Laurent. Their lavish reception featured a chocolate-fondue fountain and five-tier wedding cake.

Characterized by large numbers of guests, designer wedding gowns, expensive diamond rings, and theatrical receptions, the weddings featured in infotainment programs like *InStyle: Celebrity Weddings* perpetuate the created need for large weddings as promoted in wedding media in general. Further, the focus on wedding gowns, such as who designed them and the lushness of their construction, and rings received by celebrity brides and brides of celebrities, reinforces the femininity associated with weddings. Though mentions of tuxedo designer names might be included in these versions of bridal media, the intricacy of men's wedding costumes does not receive the same time and attention as that given to wedding gowns, even when the groom is the celebrity.

Entertainment Tonight aired its own prime-time special on celebrity weddings in July 2005. *ET Celebrity Weddings Unveiled* aired on CBS.[8] Putting a twist on infotainment treatments of celebrity weddings, the program took viewers behind the scenes as two Hollywood television stars planned their vow renewal ceremonies at the Wynn Hotel Casino in Las Vegas, Nevada. Cameras followed Melody Thomas, longtime star of the CBS soap opera *The Young and the Restless*, and Holly Robinson Peete, star of the series *Hangin' with Mr. Cooper*, as they prepared for their respective "second weddings" at the Wynn. The resort itself was heavily promoted throughout the program, reflective of the blurring between advertising and information common in the bridal media world. Interspersed with backstage footage of Thomas and Robinson Peete getting ready for their weddings were segments on other celebrity weddings from the past, including the Paris elopement of film stars John Travolta and Kelly Preston, and the weddings of Nia Vardalos, star and writer of *My Big*

Fat Greek Wedding, and *Designing Women* star Delta Burke. Thrown into the mix were segments on professional hairstyling tips and the wedding of an actual noncelebrity couple selected from videotape submissions. The promotion of certain hairstyling products during the wedding day hair tips segment, and that of the Wynn resort as a wedding venue, made *ET Celebrity Weddings Unveiled* more of a blatant advertisement than the usual celebrity gossip show which regularly drops names of designers and jewelers.

The cable channel VH1's forays into the world of celebrity weddings included *VH1's Rock 'n' Roll Weddings* in 1997 and 2001, and *VH1's All Access: Celebrity Weddings* in 2003 and 2004. The *Rock 'n' Roll Weddings* 2001 edition focused on weddings of current and past rock stars as well as film and TV celebrities.[9] Hosted by Marisol Thomas, wife of Matchbox Twenty singer Rob Thomas, the program comprised footage and photographs of rock 'n' roll weddings, with "how-they-met" and proposal stories augmented by details about dresses and receptions. The inclusion of names of well-known designers and merchandisers, such as Vera Wang, Gucci, Versace, and Cartier, and the phrases "princess bride" and "fairy tale" reinforced superficial aspects over any similar importance of the quality of the celebrity marriages in question. The notions of love at first sight and perfection ("The perfect pop star wedding calls for the perfect proposal"—made by the male, of course) further emphasized the magical quality of romance and weddings.[10] As an acknowledgement that "regular" people also get married, viewers got tips on wedding music from Carley Roney, editor in chief of the bridal media company The Knot.com. This intertextuality illustrates The Knot's infiltration of the bridal media world, to the extent that it appears within the content of entertainment programming on other media outlets. The inclusion of wedding tips from The Knot also gives viewers the impression of glamour by association; they, too, can have rock-star weddings—if they buy the appropriate items.

As with other bridal media, VH1's 2001 edition of *Rock 'n' Roll Weddings* emphasized the physical appearance of the celebrity brides it featured with a segment on the gowns of designer Vera Wang. I found notable the difference in how celebrity brides were dressed based on their physical characteristics. For example, singer Carnie Wilson, of the 1990s pop group Wilson Phillips, was overweight and rather heavy-set when she married in 2000; she spent less than $400 for her off-the-rack wedding dress. In contrast, the thin-bodied Victoria Beckham, "Posh Spice" of the British pop group the Spice Girls, wore a custom-made, designer gown with a corset that accentuated her small waist for her wedding to soccer star David Beckham. Whether a reflection of their personal styles or lifestyles as celebrities, the impression given by the program was that thinness equals additional bridal beauty. This focus on bridal wear and beauty in the absence of similar treatment of men's physical appearance and attire further underlines the importance of physical beauty for women.

VH1's *All Access: Celebrity Weddings* expanded the VH1 franchise by including even more gossip on weddings of movie stars, pop musicians, and sports figures.[11] With added emphasis on wedding details and planning aspects rather than on love and proposal stories, the 2003 airing of *All Access: Celebrity Weddings* featured weddings from 2002 and focused on designer labels of wedding dresses and tuxedos, as well as their price tags.[12] Celebrity weddings in the 2002 edition included the nuptials of singers Gwen Stefani and Gavin Rossdale (who had two weddings, one in London and another in Los Angeles). Viewers learned that Stefani's designer wedding gown, though white, had a fuchsia hem to reflect her untraditional style. Even more time was spent explaining the intricacies of the flowers used to transform Stefani's mother's prayer book so that it resembled a bouquet.

The 2003 edition of *All Access: Celebrity Weddings* also included the intricacies of the very traditional 2002 wedding of pop singer Jessica Simpson, who famously made public that she had been "saving herself" for her husband, pop singer Nick Lachey. In addition to details about their 350-guest wedding and five-tier wedding cake that consisted of a top tier made of red velvet cake, the program made room to promote Simpson's wedding advice book. The book supposedly told readers how to have a celebrity wedding on a budget. Ironically, Simpson's marriage to Lachey ended in divorce just four years later.

In the same program, viewers also learned that the 100-guest wedding of actor Russell Crowe cost $600,000 and his wedding suit and his bride's wedding gown were by Armani; basketball star Shaquille O'Neal's wedding reception featured lavender and periwinkle flowers and sterling silver roses; and the 2002 "re-wedding" of pop singer Marc Anthony to Dayanara Torres, a former Miss Universe, was a "blowout" event that treated guests to a seven-course meal and a six-layer wedding cake. Torres's wedding gown was by designer Reem Acra. Anthony and Torres had previously married in a quickie Las Vegas wedding in 2000. Alas, despite the lush second wedding, Anthony and Torres eventually divorced, and Anthony married singer/actress Jennifer Lopez just two years later. In almost-predictable celebrity style, in 2011 Anthony and Lopez announced that their marriage, too, was over (Marikar, 2011).

The Anthony-Lopez wedding was, of course, featured in VH1's *All Access: Celebrity Weddings 2004*.[13] Carrying on the theme of glitz, glamour, and conspicuous consumption, *All Access: Celebrity Weddings 2004* filled in viewers on the usual details about wedding gown designers and styles, wedding cake flavors, and other superficial information. While the previous edition played up the floral designs of celebrity weddings, the 2004 special highlighted the size and cost of featured celebrities' engagement rings. Especially notable were the details on carat size, cut, and cost; rings were emerald cut, square cut, round, and all were, of course, diamonds. The extravagance associated with celebrities' jewelry choices was illustrated by the ring given by music producer Rodney Jerkins to his actress bride, Joy Enriquez: a 17-carat yellow diamond. This emphasis on jewelry was further underscored by the female narrator's concluding statement that celebrity weddings such as these can include "diamonds big enough to sink the Titanic."

However, even as *All Access: Celebrity Weddings 2004* appeared to offer a hegemonic version of the amped-up, celebrity white wedding, it departed from the status quo by including the same-sex weddings of two mainstream female celebrities: talk show host/actress Rosie O'Donnell and musician Melissa Etheridge. These accounts included video footage of O'Donnell speaking out for same-sex marriage while holding up her marriage certificate in San Francisco with her spouse, Kelli Carpenter O'Donnell. Both were shown wearing pantsuits, rather than any apparel associated with weddings. In contrast, footage of the 170-guest wedding of Melissa Etheridge and Tammy Lynn Michaels showed Etheridge wearing a white pantsuit and Michaels, a white gown. Pronounced by the officiant as "beloved wives," the pair was shown dancing during the reception, described as a "huge Mexican feast." Neither of these two unions lasted; the O'Donnells divorced in 2008 and Etheridge and Michaels split up in 2010 ("Melissa Etheridge's Ex," 2010; "Rosie O'Donnell," 2010).

Among the television wedding programs that rely on "real weddings," both celebrities and "ordinary" couples who became celebrities were featured in the Lifetime network's reality series *Weddings of a Lifetime*. This version of weddings of the rich and famous, as well as not so famous, offered its viewers what *TVGuide.com* called "fairy-tale nuptials of celebrities and ordinary folk" that began with the "christening" of Walt Disney World's Wedding Pavilion in 1995 ("*Weddings of a Lifetime* on Lifetime," 2009). Levine (2005) analyzed how this particular reality wedding program reinforced heterosexual romance and marriage ideals that underlie the Disney image, while simultaneously serving as a commercial for the wedding industry. *Weddings of a Lifetime* amplified the fairy-tale, feminine quality of the white wedding ideal, by tying the Disney image (replete with images of Cinderella's castle and other fantasy-related elements) to the infomercial-style promotion of dress designers and tuxedo manufacturers involved in its weddings, Levine concluded.

Weddings of a Lifetime specials included titles such as *Real Weddings Across America, Fantasy Weddings, Dream Weddings on a Budget, Million Dollar Weddings, Brides of All Ages, Hollywood Weddings,* and *Royal Weddings* ("Weddings Special," 2005). The *InStyle: Celebrity Weddings* edition of this series of specials featured weddings of six Hollywood and music celebrities ("Weddings of a Lifetime: Celebrity Weddings InStyle," 1999). The series also included a special on Kennedy weddings, which featured the weddings of "America's royal family," with a tie-in to the book *Kennedy Weddings* ("Kennedy Weddings," 2005).

The special quality of weddings as unique events of a lifetime that *Weddings of a Lifetime* exalted brings into focus the importance of the bridal appearance for women, no matter what their occupations or educational attainment. I offer here a case in point that illustrates a quote from the 1973 feminist novel *Small Changes* by Marge Piercy. Piercy described the character of Beth looking at herself in the mirror on her wedding day: "a dress wearing a girl" (p. 12). This turn of phrase symbolizes how the identity of the woman within becomes subsumed by the gown and its gendered meanings.

As explained in Chapter 1, fairy tales follow a strict narrative that disallows character development and naturalizes traditional gender roles, symbolized by the beautiful princess bride and handsome prince groom. The choice of wedding attire in one episode of *Weddings of a Lifetime* starring a midshipman (bride) and ensign (groom), who wed at the United States Naval Academy, exemplified the meanings imbued in clothing that reflects the power of femininity over other aspects of female identity. The wedding ceremony was performed at the Naval Academy Chapel in Annapolis in May 1996. The groom was dressed in full naval uniform, while his bride opted to forgo her identity as a soon-to-be officer, and instead wore a formal, white wedding gown.[14] In that the bride and groom both would be officers in the United States Navy and share the same public front, the very image of the bride in a white wedding gown negated her role as his professional equal.

In this particular *Weddings of a Lifetime* episode, the bride's choice of apparel reflected postfeminism's central theme of choice: women today can choose their own lifestyles without the burden of feminist consciousness. The bride chose the packaging of femininity—white gown—while her husband opted for his formal naval uniform rather than civilian attire. I see the extent to which this particular bride identified herself as the traditional, white-gowned bride over her role as navy officer, symbolized by her dress uniform, as illustrative of the hegemonic power of the bridal image. As Amnéus (2010) commented in her wedding-dress history book, *Wedded Perfection: Two Centuries of Wedding Gowns*, "Even the most successful and independent women often succumb to the allure of a fairytale-style dress that is the culmination of girlhood fantasies" (p. 15). This has become a familiar theme among bridal industry and feminist commentators such as Wolf (2003), as mentioned in Chapter 1. I explore the creation of the bridal persona in more depth in the next chapter.

Weird Weddings and Game Shows

Unusual weddings garner media attention; one may recall seeing such stories on television newscasts, such as couples whose marriage ceremonies occurred on a roller coaster or underwater.[15] Among these news stories of the weird, I count the perennial story of the Filene's Basement bridal gown sale in Boston, known as the "running of the brides" ("Our World Famous Bridal Event," 2009).[16] In a 2002 newscast on KVBC-TV, Las Vegas, for example, the sale was compared to how men participate in the running of the bulls in Pamplona. The video footage showed women "stampeding" to get their hands on the dresses, all priced at only $249. The appeal of the event as news was confirmed when the co-anchor commented off camera, "We show that every year" ("Filene's Basement Bridal Bargain," 2002).[17] As a news event, the Filene's Basement bridal sale meets the news value criteria of the unusual, with its images of women chaotically grabbing the "bargain basement" white gowns as if their lives depended on it. The significance of the event and its meanings for participants was even a subject of an academic study on consumer behavior (Dobscha & Foxman, 1998).[18]

Unusual weddings have become a familiar theme in news of the weird. Similarly, wedding bloopers provide ample material for the cobbling together of stories of weddings gone wrong. Based on the physical comedy aspect of *America's Funniest Home Videos*, examples of such programs during the early 2000s included *Wild Weddings* and *Wild Weddings II* on The Learning Channel (TLC).[19] *Wild Weddings* consisted of home-video wedding footage and interviews with couples who experienced snafus on their wedding day. Rather than the lighthearted treatment of other blooper programs, the segues in *Wild Weddings* featured ominous-sounding theme music with a foreboding quality. These were weddings with a dark side, such as the British woman who crashed her ex-husband's wedding; she explained her side of the story by saying that she was glad to have appeared uninvited and to interrupt the ceremony in order to object to her ex's new marriage. Also included in the same program was footage of a hung-over groom fainting at the altar, and weddings ruined by bad weather in the form of blizzards, floods, and rain. Other wedding day disasters in *Wild Weddings* included the story of the groom who was arrested in church during his wedding ceremony (he was an armed robbery suspect).

As the follow-up to *Wild Weddings*, *Wild Weddings II* gave viewers more wedding-day mishaps, but with a slightly lighter tone. Except for the best man who was injured while parachuting to the wedding site, compared to the first *Wild Weddings*, the "wildness" in the second edition tended to look more like mildness. The weddings selected for this second compilation included an outdoor ceremony ruined by a hail storm, a bride and groom who got married in a hot tub outdoors during wintertime in a snow-covered backyard, and the church wedding that was interrupted by a faulty fire alarm. Wacky weddings also found a spot amongst the weirdness, with a Wizard of Oz-themed wedding in which the bride played Dorothy, wearing a white dress with ruby slippers, and the groom was dressed as the Scarecrow.

The weird, wacky, and definitely tacky found an outlet in the Fox Reality channel's 2008 offering *America's Trashiest Weddings*.[20] The one-hour special featured four decidedly downscale weddings. Indeed, one groom declared on camera, "I am white trash." Weddings of dubious taste in this compilation included a Halloween-themed wedding held at a drive-in, the porta potty wedding of a groom who worked for a portable toilet company, a hunting-themed wedding held outdoors with bride and groom dressed in camouflage, and a wedding reception held in the strip club where the bride worked. Video footage of wedding guests drinking alcohol and holding beer-chugging contests also gave evidence of the trashy quality of these weddings. Among myriad television wedding programs in the reality genre, I found *America's Trashiest Weddings* unique in that it included an advisory in the middle of the program: "Due to some sexual content and coarse language, viewer discretion is advised." Although some elements of the traditional white wedding did appear in *America's Trashiest Weddings*, the wacky weddings included in this program illustrate the constant potential for counterhegemony, in that they definitely did not exude the elegance or expense typical of bridal media portrayals.

Offbeat weddings served as the focus of a reality television series on the Arts and Entertainment network in 2005. *Married in Vegas* showed viewers the inner workings of a Las Vegas wedding chapel that churned out 455 weddings per month.[21] The Viva Las Vegas Wedding Chapel and Villa offers traditional and theme weddings; those mentioned in the program included the following themes: Austin Powers, James Bond, Star Wars, Camelot, "goth," and "gangster." This behind-the-scenes look at the wedding chapel business featured the fiascoes and snafus associated with operating a high-volume venue, including the tardy bride who threw off an entire day's schedule, and a faulty fog machine. The chapel also offers live Internet ceremonies for family and friends who cannot attend the weddings. Highlighting bizarre and weird weddings, *Married in Vegas* framed the chapel operation in a comical tone, emphasizing a sense of otherness associated with the stereotypical Vegas "quickie" wedding.

As gimmicks, weddings have served as game show prizes since the early days of television. In the 1950s, the 15-minute daytime program *Bride and Groom* aired live from New York and featured couples who got married in front of a studio audience (McNeil, 1991; Roddy, 2000). Some fifty years later, the ill-fated 2000 Fox network special *Who Wants to Marry a Multi-Millionaire?* created a media frenzy in the wake of domestic violence allegations against the "millionaire" groom.[22] Even with that debacle, instant, reality weddings became the premise of another Fox prime-time special, *Surprise Wedding*, in November of 2000. Set in Las Vegas, all-expenses-paid weddings were performed on the spot in front of a large studio audience for five women who proposed to their boyfriends "live" on the show.[23] Dressed in white wedding splendor, the women each had lured their boyfriends to Las Vegas under the guise of appearing on a makeover show. They each then had their turn at convincing their altar-shy boyfriends to marry them. All five men said yes, and later reappeared in tuxedos to say their vows on stage. One of the five men at first appeared to reject his bride's proposal, but turned the tables (back to "tradition") by getting down on one knee and proposing to *her.*

As bridal media, *Surprise Wedding* gave a twist to the traditional notion of male proposals and female acceptance while also playing up the feminine aspect of wedding planning. Footage of the female "contestants" trying on wedding gowns prior to the show was accompanied by voice-over narration telling viewers that these women's most emotional moments came "when they saw themselves transformed into princess brides." In *Surprise Wedding II*, aired on May 10, 2001, I watched as one man actually rejected his would-be-bride's proposal, fulfilling the potential for these seemingly desperate women to be humiliated and embarrassed on national television. The interplay between media forms was illustrated when the wedding announcement of one of the featured couples in *Surprise Wedding II* appeared in the *Topeka Capital-Journal* ("Thompson-Swarts," 2002).

The Fox network's foray into the world of reality television weddings in 2003 included the short-run series *Married by America*.[24] Described as "reality TV's first venture into arranged marriage," the program paired five couples who became engaged after being selected from a group of suitors, first by family and friends and then by the viewing audience. After the selection process, they became "engaged" and were sent to live in a mansion as engaged couples, which meant sharing a bed. Each week, a panel of relationship experts decided whether or not the couples should continue their engagements. By the end of the show's run, only two couples remained. If either couple actually got married, they would receive a $500,000 wedding "gift" from the show. During the two-hour finale, the last two couples prepared for their respective weddings. Adding to the drama was the stipulation that any of the participants could call off their impending marriage during the vows portion of their respective ceremonies. Despite the enticement of the cash prize, neither couple decided to go through with their weddings, much to the relief of some tense family members.

In the summer of 2003, NBC aired *Race to the Altar*, a reality competition program featuring engaged couples who competed in various physical stunts and trivia games to win a "spectacular dream wedding."[25] Eight couples were whittled down to one, who would be married in a free wedding during the show's finale. Viewers were not shown any dollar amounts associated with the prize wedding, just a "ka-ching, ka-ching" (mimicking a cash register) sound effect uttered by cohost and wedding "guru" Colin Cowie. All the vendors who provided the wedding accoutrements, including the diamond wedding rings, fine crystal and china place settings, flowers, linen, and Italian-themed dinner, received prominent mention during the reception portion of the final episode.

Other programs in this wedding-as-a-game subgenre of reality television have centered on wedding budgets; the object of these games was to plan a wedding with a given amount of money and time. During the early 2000s, these programs included TLC's *For Better or for Worse*, a show in which friends and family members of engaged couples were given limited budgets to plan their weddings for them. In 2002, the Pax TV cable network (as of 2009 known as the ION network) made wedding planning a competition with *48 Hour Wedding*. In that program, three contestant-couples, selected from "thousands" who auditioned, had to plan the wedding of their dreams with a budget of $10,000 within 48 hours ("48 Hour Wedding," 2002). While a countdown clock and countdown "budget" clock ticked down the hours and dollars, the couples also took on special challenges to earn extra cash. The couple who won the competition also won an all-expenses-paid honeymoon.

As part of its *Weddings of a Lifetime* series mentioned previously, the Lifetime channel offered *The I Do Diaries: Instant Wedding* in 2003.[26] In that program, an engaged couple won a wedding that had to be put together in one day. The program followed the couple during the four hours prior to their surprise wedding, which unsuspecting guests believed was an engagement party. Cameras followed the bride as she chose her wedding gown and jewelry, wedding cake, and wedding night lingerie. Viewers watched as she underwent a complete bridal transformation, with the help of a makeup artist and a hair stylist. In between these scenes, footage showed wedding preparations at the outdoor venue, a resort-style ranch in California. An inflatable wedding chapel was put up, and the wedding's caterer was shown preparing the food for the reception buffet. The program ended with a lavish reception featuring a dinner buffet and dancing. The couple was then treated to a complimentary honeymoon in Tahiti. With plenty of vendor promotion, *Instant Wedding* focused mainly on the bride as she found her "Cinderella" wedding gown and other seemingly essential "must-haves" for the perfect, instant wedding.

The combination of wedding as news and wedding as a game has become a staple of NBC's *Today* show, with its "*Today* Throws a Wedding." Each year since 2000, *Today* has given away a wedding for an "ordinary" couple chosen by viewers. Viewers also vote on the "must-have" items for the lucky couple's free wedding, including the bride's gown, the groom's attire, attire for all attendants, the wedding rings, and the honeymoon (Inbar, 2009). Archived on the *Today* show web site, these weddings represent the accepted form of the wedding as stipulated by bridal media. By furthering the commonsense ideal of what weddings in the US should (and do) look like, they provide models after which "regular" couples should pattern their own nuptials ("Today: Weddings," 2010).

Summary

Taken together, the composite picture of today's nonfictional bridal media, in the form of magazines, celebrity news, and reality television programs, emphasizes the superficial qualities of the wedding and offers the promise of fantasy, fun, and romance without delving too deeply into the intangibles that make for lasting relationships. Bridal magazines, while promoting the role of bride as perfect-looking princess, serve more to promote the items required for weddings, in turn ensuring the health of the wedding industry and reaffirming women's roles as consumers. As purveyors of the white wedding ideal, they not only provide an economic role in the continued success of the bridal industry, but the very items they advertise and indirectly advertise in their editorial content serve, as Allen (2003) observed, as "props to the smooth functioning of authority" (p. 458). Just as Queen Victoria's wedding cake symbolized the wealth and prosperity associated with the state, these contemporary symbols of prosperity validate the weddings that incorporate them. In this sense, wedding accessories become literal stamps of approval, and bridal magazines tell women that they need these objects to legitimize their own weddings. In turn, these media illustrate how hegemony functions within civil society—not through coercion, but through a subtler persuasion that offers a certain prestige associated with wedding expenditure.

Beyond this, the "need" for material goods ensures women's roles as buyers, shoppers, and decision makers for the home; the acquisition of goods remains a feminine trait. One could say that bridal magazines not only ensure that weddings remain a consumeristic endeavor, but that weddings remain a gendered task. Taking this a step further, bridal magazines cement the relationship between happiness and materialism by telling their (assumed) female readers how to create the perfect wedding and realize their dreams, thereby perpetuating the unquestioned notion that it is not you that will make you happy, but the items you will obtain. Bridal magazines use adjectives such as "elegant," "stunning," "dazzling," and the standbys "perfect" and "dream" to instill in women that the fantasy is a realistic goal, if only they have the correct props.

As discussed in Chapter 2, the human interest appeal and opulence of celebrity weddings provide ample material for infotainment. Weddings of Hollywood film and television stars as well as figures from popular music have become part of the entertainment "news" business. As bridal media, these accounts of over-the-top weddings enhance to an even greater extent the fantasy and fairy tale associated with the white wedding. Typically offering viewers the "inside" look at the celebrations of well-known stars of film, television, and popular music, this type of special programming reinforces wedding practices by offering repeated images of something familiar, albeit a more lush and opulent version.

Reality television programs that treat fantasy weddings as achievable and as backdrops for competition uphold the hegemonic notion of weddings as displays of consumerism associated with a change of habitus, the practices surrounding everyday life that meet necessity and embodying tastes and behaviors associated with one's social class (Herr, 2005).[27] Documentary, slice-of-life treatments and game-show type programs, in which competitors vie for the prize of a wedding, offer examples of how couples (in essence, brides) try to go beyond their habitus. Reality television programs like Lifetime's *Weddings of a Lifetime* teach viewers how to escape their own habitus "to create the perfect, lavish, elegant wedding" (Herr, 2005, p. 17). They also imbue in viewer/participants the notion that only versions of the wedding that are like those most often presented in bridal media "count." In contrast, the weird and wacky weddings presented in *Wild Weddings* and *America's Trashiest Weddings* provide examples of otherness that reinforce the properness of the weddings depicted in the majority of bridal media.

A special subgroup of reality television wedding programs offers viewers a behind-the-scenes perspective of brides as they prepare for their big day. Rather than featuring over-the-top celebrity weddings or the "wacky" weddings of blooper shows, they feature everyday women as they go about the everyday tasks required for the creation of their own perfect weddings, such as visiting bridal salons, trying on dresses, choosing party favors and floral arrangements, addressing invitations, and dealing with snafus without end. These slice-of-life programs differ from other bridal media by showing viewers the process of wedding planning rather than only the end result seen in accounts of real weddings in bridal magazines. Whereas the celebrity and game-show style reality programs focus on the wedding itself, bride-focused programs give viewers a backstage look at the process of becoming a bride. In the next two chapters, I analyze the content of reality-based, wedding planning programs to determine how their narratives reaffirm ideals of femininity even as the brides featured in them represent feminist progress within American society.

Notes

1. For a longer treatment of wedding portrayals in the movies, see Jellison (2008). Jellison devoted an entire chapter to movie weddings, tracing the depiction of weddings from the 1946 classic *The Best Years of Our Lives* to popular films of the late 1990s and early 2000s when weddings were used as settings for romantic comedies such as *My Best Friend's Wedding* and *The Wedding Planner*.
2. These accounts of real weddings in bridal magazines tend to highlight wedding ceremony and reception details, such as locale, party favors, colors, table settings, cakes, and party themes. Information about these real couples rarely goes beyond their names and occupations. Photos of actual weddings reflect the magazines' recurrent version of weddings, with brides dressed in formal wedding gowns, grooms in tuxedos, numerous bridesmaids, and lavish-looking wedding receptions with many guests. Examples of these treatments include "America Gets Married," in the July–August 2009 issue of *Brides*; "Real Weddings" and "Real Wedding Award Winners," in *The Knot* magazine (Fall 2009–Winter 2010); and "The Wedding Album" in *Brides* (March–April 2005).
3. Kim et al. (2007) noted that essential to masculine identity, the accumulation of sexual experience has become an important aspect of mass media's socialization of men and boys.
4. Indirectly addressed in this article was the concept of normative male alexithymia, which refers to a mild form of alexithymia, the inability to express emotions, common among males. Theorized as originating in socialization that prohibits boys from expressing feelings of fear or sadness, emotions labeled as showing weakness and vulnerability, this nonclinical condition is considered "normative," in that it does not require clinical intervention. In everyday life, men in North American culture are not expected or encouraged to express emotions, in accordance with gender norms of masculinity. For more, see Levant et al. (2006).
5. Portions of this section come from my article "Unraveling The Knot: Political Economy and Cultural Hegemony in Wedding Media" (Engstrom, 2008), available from http://jci.sagepub.com. The final, definitive version of this paper has been published in *Journal of Communication Inquiry*, Vol. 32, Issue 1, January 2008, pp. 60–82, by SAGE Publications Ltd./SAGE Publications, Inc. All rights reserved. ©2008 by Sage Publications.
6. This episode of *Entertainment Tonight* aired on November 30, 2000.
7. *InStyle: Celebrity Weddings* was recorded on January 22, 2005.
8 *ET Celebrity Weddings Unveiled*, airdate and recorded July 5, 2005.
9. The 2001 edition of *VH1's Rock 'n' Roll Weddings* was recorded March 12, 2001.

10. Galician (2004) expounded on these media-created love myths. The love-at-first sight myth celebrates the notion of instant attraction, while the idea of perfection relates to the myth of the one-and-only perfect partner who is cosmically predestined.

11. The VH1 *All Access* series also included programs on the aftermath of high-profile celebrity relationships and marriages, such as *Celebrity Breakups 1* and *Celebrity Breakups 2* and *Shortest Celebrity Marriages.* A total of 103 episodes of *All Access* had been produced as of 2007 ("All Access: Episodes," 2009).

12. The 2003 edition of *All Access: Celebrity Weddings* was recorded September 28, 2003.

13. VH1's *All Access: Celebrity Weddings 2004* was recorded February 11, 2005.

14. "Episode Detail: Weddings of a Lifetime" (2009); E. Levine, personal communication, March 4, 2005. According to the Lifetime web page featuring their wedding, the bride was a midshipman first class set to graduate from the Naval Academy in May 1996, and then attend flight school in Pensacola, Florida, for training to become an aviator. The groom was a 1994 graduate of the Naval Academy ("Weddings of a Lifetime: D'Earcy Paul Davis & Tracy Lynn Hoyte," 1997).

15. An underwater, scuba wedding ceremony was among those featured in TLC's *A Wedding Story.* The unusualness of that ceremony in terms of its counterhegemonic version of the bridal appearance is discussed in Chapter 4.

16. "Our World Famous Bridal Event" (2009) on the Filene's Basement web site touts how the sale garnered so much press attention that it became known as the "running of the brides," similar to the running of the bulls in Pamplona. The web page even lists frequently-asked questions for customers, giving them tips on how to get ready for the sale.

17. This was a short, voice-over story on the 4 P.M. newscast of my local NBC affiliate, KVBC-TV, Las Vegas. The newscaster's comment reminds one of how familiar this story has become over the years, as it provides interesting video and has a somewhat comedic appeal that makes it conducive as a "kicker" story to end a newscast or close out a block of stories.

18. Dobscha and Foxman (1998) studied the meaning of the event by interviewing 11 women who bought or helped others buy dresses during the sale. The authors explained how they were "drawn to study the event from a consumer behavior perspective by the paradoxical juxtaposition of perfection with chaos, royalty with bargain hunting" (p. 131). They concluded that the attainment of a Filene's gown "is like bearing the scars of wounds ritually inflicted in some rite of passage: it signifies achievement, braving a chaotic buying environment and obtaining the prize of value, beauty, and frugality" (p. 140).

19. *Wild Weddings,* recorded July 21, 2001; *Wild Weddings II,* recorded July 27, 2003.

20. *America's Trashiest Weddings* was recorded October 4, 2008.

21. *Married in Vegas* was recorded July 16, 2005.

22. The program's ill-conceived premise served as a topic for network talk/news programs, including CNN's *Newsstand* on February 20, 2000; NBC's *Dateline* on February 22, 2000; MSNBC's *Newsfront* on February 22, 2000; and ABC's *20/20* on February 24, 2000. Due to the negative publicity, Fox cancelled a scheduled rebroadcast of the original airing.

23. *Surprise Wedding,* airdate and recorded November 2, 2000.

24. *Married by America* premiered on March 3, 2003. The finale aired on April 14, 2003.

25. *Race to the Altar* aired from July 30, 2003 to September 13, 2003 (Rogers, 2003, "NBC's *Race to the Altar*").

26. The Lifetime channel's *The I Do Diaries: Instant Wedding* aired on August 14, 2003.

27. Herr (2005) explained that one's habitus involves practices associated with meals and their preparation, the style and function of one's clothing, and other ways of addressing the needs of daily life. Herr gave the example of how the wedding meal departs from one's habitus: rather than eating one's meal on mismatched plates one might use in everyday life, wedding guests enjoy delicacies served on fine bone china.

*4. Creating the Perfect Bride**

NOTHING IN THE BRIDAL WORLD HOLDS MORE IMPORTANCE THAN THE appearance of the bride herself. As the center of attention in the wedding play, she becomes a spectacle—all eyes follow her. In her 1975 *Screen* article on the male gaze, Mulvey asserted that the male-created, traditional cinema frames women as objects for display, with their appearance coded for strong visual impact. In that she receives the gaze of those around her, the surveyed female turns herself "into an object," a "sight," as Berger (1998, p. 98) explained: "Her own sense of being in herself is supplanted by a sense of being appreciated as herself by another" (p. 97). Similarly, the bride is an object for display, and her entrance at the wedding ceremony itself becomes a spectacle upon which all the attendees focus their attention. Indeed, only with her entrance can the ceremony begin, often when the audience members greet her by standing and acknowledging her special status as the wedding's main attraction. Thus, the bride becomes a "visual production of celebrity" (Freeman, 2002, p. 31).

In the context of media weddings, the bride becomes a display to be appreciated by others often after a transformative process in which she is adorned in artifacts associated with the "correct" way a bride should look. Bridal magazines offer plenty of content to analyze regarding the bride's "after" appearance, often in the form of professional models in editorial or advertising content. The wedding industry revolves around the manufacturing and advertising of bridal products, including those that it deems necessary to create the personal front of the bride, including apparel, cosmetics, and jewelry.

this chapter, I examine how reality television programs reveal the cre-
of the bridal appearance and the practices in which women participate
"make" themselves appear as brides to others. I find highly relevant Berger's
(1998) assertion that "men act and women appear" (p. 98). This notion, in
turn, becomes even more relevant in the context of the wedding as a social and
mediated event. Rarely, if ever, does this star status accompany the images of
the bridegroom in wedding media, which further underscores the visual
importance of women within the world of weddings and in larger society.

In the previous chapter, I described the diversity of bridal media today. In
this chapter, I draw upon the narratives and images contained in reality television programs that offer a slice-of-life approach to the wedding planning
process. Rather than providing accounts of celebrity or weird and wacky weddings, these programs center on how "real-life" brides prepare for their wedding appearance. The content of these reality television wedding planning
programs relies on the video vérité technique, offering outsiders that fly-on-
the-wall, behind-the-curtain perspective that brings credibility to the scenes
on view.

In *The Presentation of Self in Everyday Life*, Goffman (1959) described
this area as the back region, the place where one's "front"—the image of oneself created for presentation to others—is scrutinized and adjusted for flaws.
The reality television genre allows glimpses into the "back region" where,
Goffman observed, "the suppressed facts make an appearance" (p. 112).
These programs frame certain back region activities, to which wedding guests
do not have access but viewers of these series do, as being important simply
by including them in the final edited and presented product. Indeed, it is what
the wedding guests in these programs do not see that gives glimpses of the
hidden backstage activities a certain voyeuristic appeal, and provides television viewers who do get to see them a sense of privilege. Even though these
programs present the back region as the front region to the at-home viewer,
access to the suppressed facts surrounding the creation of the bridal image
gives viewers of these programs a sense that they are getting a sneak peek into
the beauty "secrets" of the bridal image.

I describe the five reality television wedding planning programs that
serve as data for the analyses presented in this chapter. I then follow these
descriptions with an examination of the creation of the successful bridal
appearance along four major themes regarding the portrayal of the bridal
appearance: the importance of the wedding gown, the disciplining of the
female body, the emphasis on female physical beauty, and the perfection
embodied in the ideal bridal appearance. To this end, I first examine how these
programs in particular emphasize the tremendous importance placed on the
wedding gown, which serves as both costume and additional enforcer of the

rules of beauty. In the world of weddings, the wedding gown commands a magical and almost holy status. Indeed, for reality brides, the wedding gown serves as a central character in their stories; it far eclipses all other bridal party members, including the bridegroom. Among the themes addressed here, the wedding gown and the physical and psychological work required to attain the perfect one thus receives the most attention and therefore constitutes the lengthiest discussion.

Second, I discuss the notions of the disciplined and docile female body, in that the body must conform to the wedding dress. I base my analysis on Bartky's (1990) work regarding women's adherence to the "rules of beauty," which tell them how to meet current standards of the feminine ideal. Third, I describe how these programs forward the notion that the successful bridal appearance also requires that she be physically beautiful, with this beauty achieved only through specialized application of cosmetics and an elaborate coiffure. Last, the bridal appearance requires perfection. Indeed, the very use of the term "perfect" appears repeatedly not only in the reality television programs I analyze here, but it has become a familiar rhetorical motif in bridal media in general. I conclude this chapter by addressing how these themes combine to create the perfect bridal appearance/image/persona.

Reality Television Wedding Planning Programs

Reality television wedding planning programs not only follow the wedding planning process as couples create their wedding day, but they also provide true-to-life accounts of the creation of the bridal appearance. I find especially useful these programs' reliance on "everyday" couples, rather than celebrities, and the way they approach the day-to-day creation of not only the bridal appearance, but the wedding as an event. The vérité approach documents the back region activities of brides in particular, thereby offering a sort of guide-book for viewers regarding what actually happens when the "normal" woman sets about planning her wedding.

My past research on these programs allowed for a "big picture" summary of their content, in the form of images and text that combine to uphold the themes regarding the various aspects of the bridal image. I use examples from the content of five reality television wedding planning programs and the common images and narratives among them that relay the importance of a bride's physical appearance in creating the ideal wedding: The Learning Channel's (TLC) *A Wedding Story* and *Say Yes to the Dress*, Oxygen's *Real Weddings From The Knot*, WE tv's *Bridezillas*, and FitTV's *Buff Brides*.

A Wedding Story

One of the most popular programs on The Learning Channel, *A Wedding Story* debuted in 1996. Inspired by the 1986 royal wedding of Britain's Prince Andrew and Sarah Ferguson, and created to establish a strong female audience, it provided reality fare for the "pedagogical mission" of the cable outlet, now called TLC (Barovick, 1999). Using first-person narrative and natural sound of its participants, including the bride, groom, in-laws, and other family and friends involved in the weddings, *A Wedding Story* provided viewers with half-hour episodes of couples as they prepared for their weddings (Brown, 1999). Couples featured on the program went through a selection process, including submitting videotapes and a 12-page questionnaire (Noxon, 1999); producers sought out couples with "genuine love stories" (Brown, 1999).[1]

Episodes of *A Wedding Story* follow a certain progression, starting with couples recounting how they met, when they knew they were in love, and how and where the marriage proposal occurred. The show followed the bride and groom in the days and hours before their wedding; episodes concluded with footage of the ceremony itself followed by a montage of the reception, including cake cutting, toasts, and dancing. Noted for its upbeat portrayal of the stressful process of wedding planning, the program leaned "toward the saccharin," as viewers never saw brides and grooms arguing or having second thoughts in the hours before the ceremony (Acosta, 1999). While some weddings featured themes, such as Halloween, or replicated historical eras, such as colonial, U.S. Civil War, or medieval, the weddings on the series followed the same, basic, white-wedding format. As noted in *The New York Times*, "Despite the variety of the people, places and outfits, the series cannot escape the sameness of the marriage ritual" (Noxon, 1999).

A Wedding Story also served as a how-to guide for weddings, with fans admitting they watched it to get ideas for their own weddings (Weiss, 2000). While the episodes always ended with successful weddings, some observers noted that the show did not follow couples' *marriage* stories (Brown, 1999). After 436 episodes, the last episode of *A Wedding Story* was shown in November 2007, according to archives kept by *TVGuide.com* ("Wedding Story on TLC," 2009). However, as of 2010, the TLC online "fan site" continued to maintain a web page where couples featured on the show posted updates about their marriages and families.[2]

Say Yes to the Dress

Say Yes to the Dress premiered on TLC in October 2007. The 30-minute episodes feature two or three brides as they search for the perfect wedding dress at Kleinfeld Bridal in Manhattan, dubbed "the world's premier bridal salon" on the show's web site ("About *Say Yes to the Dress*," 2008). Brides introduce themselves on camera by name, with accompanying full-screen graphic indicating dress budget, wedding date, and fiancé's name, along with a photo of the couple. Men generally are absent in this program, except for the occasional father of the bride and rare instances when fiancés visit the salon with their future wives. The only males who do consistently appear include the salon's co-owner and fashion director.

Described as "part docusoap surrounding the shop, but more the fascinating tales of the women who are in search of the most important dress they'll ever buy," *Say Yes to the Dress* centers on problem resolution as staff work to ensure customer satisfaction, an especially important part of the bridal salon business ("About Say Yes to the Dress," 2008). The wedding dress, rather than the bride herself, serves as the star of this program, as well as the star of the wedding. Rarely are a bride's age, occupation, or income mentioned, which is typical of other bridal reality programs. Brides rarely visit the store alone: mothers, sisters, mothers-in-law, and friends usually accompany these women on their quest. Occasionally, members of the bride's party cause conflict by getting out of control and choosing dresses for her, while store consultants try to wrangle them in order to regain their own authority as the dress experts.

Dollar figures have a prominent place in *Say Yes to the Dress*, with wedding dress price tags in the episodes I viewed ranging from $1,400 (lowest) to "unlimited'; the average dress budget was $4,620. In one episode, a bride bought an $11,000 ball gown, then came back to buy a second gown for her reception. Staff members use persuasion and reassurance not only to close the sale, but to "make each bride completely satisfied on what may be the single most important day of their lives" ("About Say Yes to the Dress," 2008). Sometimes brides want dresses that are beyond their budget, or cannot find the perfect dress they seek, and end up leaving without making a purchase from Kleinfeld's. Indeed, even if brides choose not to purchase a dress from the salon, *Say Yes to the Dress* nevertheless follows up their stories to reassure viewers that those women did eventually find the "perfect" dress elsewhere. As of 2011, *Say Yes to the Dress* remained on TLC's schedule.

Real Weddings From The Knot

Real Weddings From The Knot debuted in 2003 as a joint venture between The Knot and the Oxygen cable network. Cofounded by Oprah Winfrey, Oxygen is available to 52 million cable households ("About Oxygen," 2007). Its mission, according to its web site, is "to bring women (and the men who love them) the edgiest, most innovative entertainment on television" ("About Oxygen," 2007). Presented on Oxygen during cross-promoted "Wedding Weeks" about twice a year, the program featured couples from "all walks of life with all kinds of weddings" ("Oxygen Proposes to the Knot," 2004).[3]

Each 30-minute episode followed the wedding couple as they prepared for their wedding, often weeks in advance.

In this program, brides provide the voice-over narration during the introduction and conclusion of each episode, with other audio coming from both natural sound and other participants such as the groom, parents, family members, and wedding coordinators who speak directly into the camera. Couples write their own vows, choose flowers, put together party favors, and perform other wedding-related activities. *Real Weddings From The Knot* was not a regular series. Rather, for each season of *Real Weddings From The Knot*, episodes were presented in weekend marathons, ending with a special "wedding gown" fashion show. Episodes during the marathon were interspersed with short segments on wedding tips from The Knot's editor in chief. As of January 2005, a total of 21 episodes had aired on Oxygen since the series' debut in 2003.

Bridezillas

WE tv's *Bridezillas* centers on a new bridal identity that has emerged within the bridal media milieu, one that takes the role of bride in a new direction by encouraging women to assert themselves and take explicit control over what a gendered society tells them is their special day. Defined as the out-of-control bride, the "bridezilla," a combination of the words "bride" and "Godzilla," has become a commonplace term used in news headlines.[4] In their 2002 book *Bridezilla: True Tales From Etiquette Hell*, Spaemme and Hamilton refer to the bridezilla as "a subspecies of a bride-to-be who believes her wedding day is 'her day,' that she is a princess for the day, that the world owes her" (p. x).

Bridezillas originated as *Manhattan Brides*, an eight-part documentary series produced by September Films. The series chronicled "the pre-wedding lives of couples living in high-priced, high-octane, high-strung New York City," and first aired on local New York cable stations and in Australia, England, and Hong Kong (Traister, 2004). Online summaries of this initial season of the series include wedding details and cursory information about each couple, such as where they met ("Bridezillas' Wedding Details," 2007). Edited into a one-hour special retitled *Bridezillas*, it aired on the Fox network in January 2003, as a precursor to its appearance as a regular series on the WE network (Rogers, 2003).

A subsidiary of Rainbow Media Holdings, WE tv calls itself "the premier source for women looking to satisfy their curiosity with fascinating, original stories and entertaining, fresh content that is relevant to key stages of their lives," its programming offers viewers "compelling perspectives on women's lives ranging from the ordinary to the extraordinary, presented in a nonjudgmental voice" ("About WE tv," 2009).[5] While the first season of eight episodes concentrated on New York brides and featured high-priced weddings, the second season went cross-country, featuring weddings in Chicago and Los Angeles. As of 2011, *Bridezillas* served as one of the WE tv channel's showcase programs.

Buff Brides

Buff Brides premiered in 2003 on the Discovery Health Channel. Its run of ten episodes later became a regular offering on FitTV, the Discovery Health Channel's fitness outlet. Programming on FitTV centers on fitness instruction programs; shows on the network range from "in-home" workout sessions, such as *Namaste Yoga* and *Gilad's Bodies in Motion* (a long-running aerobics/calisthenics program), to lifestyle programs about how to get one's home "fit" (with *neat*, a program that transforms messy homes).

Each *Buff Brides* episode opens with a voiceover by an anonymous female narrator introducing two brides. Shot on videotape, the footage features separate, chronological story lines that go back and forth between the two brides, giving the viewer a sense of the progress of each woman. Narrative comes from on-camera interviews with the women and their fiancés, in addition to natural sound of the women as they work out with their personal trainers, participate in wedding planning (such as shopping or rehearsal dinners), try on their wedding gowns either at home or at bridal salons, and engage in other nonexercise-oriented activities.

Episodes feature weigh-ins that show brides' beginning, midpoint, and final weights. Close-ups appear prominently when personal trainers measure these women's thighs, arms, and hips, and when the women are doing push ups or using exercise machines. Brides admit cheating on their diets and complain about working out on the "Bride Cam" in confessional-style, black-and-white segments. Wide shots of the hustle and bustle of New York City feature the women themselves scurrying to or from work or the gym. Each episode ends with footage of the wedding ceremony itself as well as the reception. As of 2010, FitTV still offered *Buff Brides* as reruns.

The Wedding Dress

The "perfect" dress serves as the foremost element in the creation of the perfect bride. In the world of bridal magazines, ads for wedding gowns and dresses for bridesmaids and mothers of the bride constitute the bulk of their content. Indeed, some magazines devote their entire content to the wedding dress, as illustrated by the periodical *Bridal Gown Guide*, and *The Knot Weddings Magazine*'s 785-page Spring/Summer issue 2005, which proclaimed on its cover "Over 900 weddings gowns." Among its continuum of myriad bridal media products, The Knot also offers a regularly published volume, *The Knot Wedding Gowns*. Its Fall/Winter 2002 issue, for example, featured "1000+ styles from over 175 top designers." Because wedding gowns serve as the focus of both editorial and advertising content in these gown-only issues, they in essence serve as one big advertisement that tells women their one and only choice regarding wedding apparel is the formal, white gown, with a "good" one often costing thousands of dollars. More so than the bride herself, her *dress*—her "packaging"—serves as the center of attention (Goldstein-Gidoni, 1997).

The significance of the wedding dress as costume and its function as a symbol of wealth and status throughout history becomes even more apparent when museums create entire exhibitions around this particular article of clothing. For example, Amnéus's 2010 book, *Wedded Perfection: Two Centuries of Wedding Gowns*, documented the Cincinnati Art Museum's exhibit that featured a variety of wedding costumes from various decades, including a second-marriage suit and haute couture, "mod" versions of wedding dresses. As discussed in Chapter 2, the special attention paid to the wedding dress of actress/Princess Grace Kelly illustrated the near-mystical aura surrounding the "perfect" wedding dress, and provided enough material to warrant Haugland's (2006) book documenting the museum exhibit featuring Kelly's gown.

Aside from overwhelming amounts of bridal gown advertisements in magazines, journalistic accounts of celebrity weddings and magazine editorial photographs of actual weddings focus on the bride already "in costume." Compared to these images, the backstage access offered by reality television programs allows for a glimpse into the process of "staging" the bride, similar to the staging of homes to impress potential buyers. The performance of getting ready, from choosing the costume to the creation of the entire bridal visage, invites the gaze of viewers as brides get dressed on the wedding day, often assisted by others due to the elaborateness and complexity of the "costuming."

The wedding dress holds a magical aura, or "hierophany," a term used by Lowrey and Otnes (1994) in their study of perceptions of wedding artifacts. For example, brides acquire their "perfect" wedding dress through hierophany: the "right" dress appears almost magically, and the bride knows somehow that "this is the one." Jellison (2008) noted that finding the perfect dress has become a "magical process," and the quest for it has assumed mythic proportions (pp. 64–65). In contrast to the perfect wedding dress, one never hears a groom exclaim how he found the "perfect tuxedo," or that he had been searching for the ideal suit for months, years, or even a lifetime.

Regarding the wedding dress as an important, if not *the* most important, item of the bride's personal front, I organize the following discussion along three lines: wedding dress as a source of angst, the hierophany involved in finding the perfect wedding dress, and the sameness that permeates the variety of wedding dress as brides try to imbue their own personalities and tastes into their weddings. As an item of almost mythical proportions, the wedding dress requires, according to these wedding planning programs, a great deal of effort and emotional trauma in order to (a) find it, and (b) make the bride happy. This quest in turn requires some kind of supernatural indication that the dress in question is indeed "the one"—the one dress that will fulfill the bride's dreams and create a sense of well-being and "rightness" that validates the perfection of the wedding day. Hierophany becomes an essential component of the bridal image, and these programs reflect this through the reactions of brides and others during the dress selection process/quest. Finally, in that hegemony requires opposition to some degree, bridal media do allow, to some extent, diversions from the white-gown requirement. I discuss how *A Wedding Story*, due to the sheer number of episodes, serves as an example of both a hegemonic portrayal of this all-important piece of clothing, while also allowing for variations in wedding apparel.

Wedding dress angst

In Season 1 of WE tv's *Bridezillas*, wedding gown designer Henry Roth, of the upscale New York City fashion salon Michelle Roth, called the wedding dress the bride's "ground zero."[6] The importance of the bridal gown, especially in this reality series, becomes a central theme as the bridezillas constantly deal with gown-associated worries and anxiety. The most common problem depicted in the two seasons' worth of episodes of *Bridezillas* I viewed involved the wedding gown, either its fit, state of cleanliness, or availability.

Season 1 of *Bridezillas* established the bridezilla persona within the context of the type-A personalities of New York City brides. The quest for the perfect wedding dress ran through each bridezilla's wedding story; wedding gowns among this group of brides ranged from custom-made, designer gowns to one found off the rack at a discount bridal store. Of the examples of high-maintenance brides, the story line of Manhattan bride Karen highlighted just how important a role the wedding dress plays in the world of the bridezilla. Karen's narrative centered on the multiple fittings she required for her $4,000 custom-made gown. Viewers follow her as she visits the salon six times until she is happy with the dress. The pricey gown even came with a dress consultant who attended to Karen on her wedding day, ensuring that the ever-picky bride looked fabulous.

The quest for the perfect wedding dress played a part in the story of 30-year-old New York actress Cynthia in Season 1 as well. This bridezilla decided on a custom-made, $2,800 "alternative" wedding dress. The viewer watches as Cynthia eschews visiting mainstream bridal shops but instead chooses designer Christine Kara's funky designs and deconstructed garments created in the designer's East Village dress shop. Cynthia beams with excitement about her nontraditional dress and explains on camera how well it fits her realistic body shape. Indeed, throughout Cynthia's narrative, she repeatedly acknowledges that she wants to go against the hegemonic (not her words) bridal image, and how different she is from the stereotypically thin models in bridal magazines. The drama of her story line comes just three days before her wedding, when she suddenly decides she "wasn't meant to be a bride." Unable to articulate just what she sees wrong with the funky dress she had specially made for her, Cynthia begins to cry as she tells her mother how unhappy she is with it, even though she was almost ecstatic when she first tried it on. After an extended scene at the designer's studio, Cynthia decides to have the designer create an entirely new wedding gown for her, which she picks up just hours before her wedding. In the end, Cynthia got what she wanted, even if it took extra time and money. This upholds the idea that the wedding dress is so special that one cannot find happiness without making sure it is *exactly* what one wants.

In *Bridezillas*, even when the bridal gown does not cost thousands of dollars, it still holds vital importance; no wedding can occur without it, or its required perfection in terms of appearance and fit. For example, in Season 2 of *Bridezillas*, Thuy, a 27-year-old Vietnamese business planner living in Orange County, California, undergoes several fittings until her $800 dress fits correctly; her problem is that she needs a special bra in order for the dress to look "right" on her.

Thuy's story line illustrates the back region access given to viewers of this type of program; viewers see footage taken in dressing rooms or other areas where bridal "staging" takes place. Often, brides are shown in moderate stages of undress. These otherwise private locales thus become open to viewer scrutiny, and serve as a reflection of the permeable ego boundary of the feminine identity, as noted by Wood (2010) in *Gendered Lives*. This access in a way illustrates the acceptance of a lack of modesty by and given to women in these programs, that is, they are open to further scrutiny—and the gaze of viewers—in a manner we do not see with men in these programs. As an example of the willingness to forego privacy or sense of modesty on the part of these brides, the viewer gains backstage access to these brides' comments about their "boobs" (Karen) and small chest (Thuy). In this sense, the backstage views of these women indicate that they have little concern about allowing cameras, and thus viewers, to see them this way, nor are they shy about criticizing their own bodies.

In other *Bridezillas* episodes from Season 2 that I analyzed, brides must deal with delays and poor service from their bridal shops. These accounts tell the viewer to expect similar problems as a normal part of their own quest for the perfect wedding dress. For instance, Chicago bride Antonella must visit her bridal shop several times before being able to pick up her dress. She unleashes a tirade at the shop when she discovers her veil still does not have a detachable clip, calling the staff "a bunch of morons." The dress's small tear and dirty hem become the subject of her final tirade against the store on her wedding day. Other examples of wedding gown woes included bridezilla Korliss visiting her bridal gown shop to pick up her dress only to find it closed, and discovering that her reception dress has the wrong train. This results in a confrontation with the dress shop manager, who refuses to allow cameras in his store.

Other Season 2 bridezillas face equally frustrating snafus with their wedding dresses. For example, Jada stresses over her still-unmade custom-designed gown, which is in pieces one week before her wedding; Gretchen discovers a yellow stain on her pricey veil, which the saleswoman states "smells like pee"; and Magdalena tries on several wedding dresses in an extended scene at a Los Angeles designer's wedding dress boutique, only to say one is a "nightmare" and the other is "hideous." In keeping with the *Bridezillas* theme of playing up conflicts and highlighting the perfection-seeking nature of the bridezilla, wedding gown problems and worries further imbue this all-important piece of clothing with almost supernatural qualities. These depictions of wedding dress angst in *Bridezillas* tell viewers that the quest for the perfect gown is not and should not be easy.

In Season 2, not all the bridezillas have a terrible time with their wedding gowns. The story line of the exuberant, and rather overbearing, 43-year-old first-time bride Julia stands out as the exception to the rule. A self-described "princess," Julia appears to be genuinely happy when she finds her dream dress at a bridal outlet store offering off-the-rack gowns. Julia admires herself in the mirror, saying, "This dress will stop the show. I'm so happy." The outlet store where Julia finds her dream dress serves as a stark contrast to the high-end, pricey wedding gown salons of the other New York bridezillas.

When viewed in the context of the other bridezillas' search for the perfect gown, the apparent ease with which Julia chooses her long-sleeved, heavily appliquéd and beaded white gown—at a bridal outlet store, no less—implies that low-ticket gowns are easy to find, while truly exceptional wedding gowns require much more angst, time, and, of course, money. While Julia expresses happiness with her outlet dress, Karen spends thousands of dollars on her boutique gown and never appears happy with her choice. In this sense, *Bridezillas* frames the quest for the "proper" dress as requiring extra time, emotional work, and price.

Hierophany and the quest for "The One"

In the 20 episodes of Oxygen's *Real Weddings From The Knot* I analyzed, brides wear some type of formal, white dress.[7] The "magic" surrounding the perfect dress holds significance for many of the brides in *Real Weddings From The Knot*. Several seek that perfection by hiring designers to make a one-of-a-kind gown. For example, bride Amy started looking for dresses a year before her wedding. After trying on "a hundred" dresses and not finding the "right one," she finally had a couturier make one for her. High style also surrounds the wedding dress quest of bride Tiffany, a public relations executive who oversees every detail of her New York-Harlem Renaissance wedding. Tiffany is shown being fitted in a Vera Wang gown, and prominent *Vogue* editor Andre Leon Talley gives her a lesson in how to walk properly in it. However, for Cara, a New York stockbroker who claims in her voice-over introduction, "Every bride dreams of being a princess on her wedding day," her dream dress serves as a source of unhappiness. As she tries on her ill-fitting, custom-made gown, she comments in a disappointed tone: "I don't love it. It's not what I imagined." Her words point to the significance this piece of apparel holds—her happiness hinges on how her "dream" dress looks and feels.

Hierophany also plays an important part in the 1997 "Lisa and David" episode of TLC's *A Wedding Story*.[8] Lisa, a 20-something bride, met police officer David when he responded to her fender-bender accident. The prominence of the gown and its "journey" to the wedding make this particular episode outstanding among those examined here. Lisa and David's episode revolves around the dress itself; an accident with the dress perpetrated by Lisa's own mother threatens the entire wedding. The drama portrayed in this episode heightens the importance of the wedding dress, and serves to reify the hierophany surrounding it. The following narrative demonstrates the overarching significance placed on the wedding dress not only in *A Wedding Story* or this particular episode, but also in bridal media in general.

On the day before the wedding, Lisa visits the bridal salon with her mother and a friend to pick up her gown and veil. The dress has custom appliqués on it, sewn on by the bride's own seamstress. Lisa makes a point of showing the dress's detail on camera, and practically screams with delight upon seeing it in its completed form. Her friend asks where she will hang up the dress until the wedding day. Lisa then asks her mother if they will need special hardware to hang the dress properly, illustrating the gown's special significance as well as practical considerations regarding its heavy material, shape, and bulk; this is no mere dress that one can hang in a closet. Little do they know how prominently the dress will figure on the wedding day.

Hierophany also plays a role in Lisa's quest for her headpiece, which held almost as much importance to her as her gown. As Lisa tries on a veil at the bridal salon, she recalls the moment she found her "perfect" headpiece. Her mother's on-camera recollection augments the story:

Lisa (voice-over):   I found my headpiece in an antique shop.

Mother (on camera): And all of a sudden I hear, 'Oh, my God! I found it!' and she's screaming and I said, 'Lees, what's the matter?' and she said, 'I found my headpiece!'

Lisa (voice-over):   So I bought this tiara and I didn't have a dress and so everywhere I went I had to bring the tiara with me to make sure that I could find a dress to match it. And when I found my dress I knew that was the dress.

As she leaves the bridal salon, Lisa holds up the garment-bagged dress for the camera and yells, "I got it!"

The real drama of the episode begins on the wedding day. It starts with Lisa and her bridal party having their hair done at a beauty salon. The bride receives a greeting card from David and begins to cry. "I really feel nervous today," she says between tears. Unbeknownst to her, her nervousness actually serves as a foreshadowing of what is to come. Interspersed with the beauty salon scene are shots of David and his male companions enjoying themselves at a restaurant.

Viewers next see Lisa's mother talking on the phone. A graphic that reads "90 Minutes to Wedding" appears onscreen. "John, what am I going to do?" she asks worriedly. Clearly, she is panicked, as the fate of her daughter's wedding depends on her now. She explains what happened:

Mother (on camera): I went to pick up the gown—it is so heavy—and it, uh, fell towards me and lipstick brushed on the front right here (motioning to the upper right side of her dress).

The viewer then sees a bridesmaid speaking on the phone: "It's a good splotch of makeup—you can definitely see it—it's a white dress." Then the mother says, on camera: "I called my brother who has a dry cleaning business to see if he can spot it out." While all the commotion occurs onscreen, the viewer neither sees nor hears Lisa during this portion of the episode.

The drama heightens as Lisa's father takes the damaged dress to the dry cleaning store. An unidentified man, most likely the bride's uncle, brushes the stain out of the dress. I found notable that the stain is never shown; instead, the viewer must only imagine just how bad it is. The man then says, "Well, that didn't work." The scene cuts to a shot of the bride's father looking pensive. All the while, happy "working" music, reminiscent of 1950s housecleaning films, plays on the soundtrack. Next, the words "75 Minutes Before Wedding" appear onscreen while the man still works to remove the stain. He asks, "What time is it?" Finally, Lisa's father carries the train of the dress out of the dry cleaning store as "55 Minutes to Wedding" appears over the video.

Notably, Lisa remains absent during this part of the program as well. This leaves the viewer to wonder where she is and what she is doing—with only an imagined picture of her visibly upset, or worse. Finally, the lipstick stain successfully removed, we see Lisa putting on her wedding gown. The bridal party then poses for photographs before leaving for the ceremony in limousines. With the tragedy averted, we see the bride and her father making small talk as they ride to the wedding site. Right before the ceremony begins, a remarkably composed Lisa says on camera, "I feel very calm. I feel very fine. I feel very ready. I'm excited. I gotta make sure everyone does their job." The wedding takes place with no further problems. The drama of the day seems forgotten as the bride and groom enjoy themselves at the reception hosted by a Benjamin Franklin look-a-like where the famous Philadelphia Mummers String Band makes an appearance.

Although everything works out in the end, as do all episodes of *A Wedding Story*, the hierophany and drama of Lisa's lipstick-stained wedding dress underscores the monumental importance of the wedding gown as the central feature of the wedding itself. It is not necessarily Lisa that is required for the wedding ceremony—it is her *dress*. The drama is created only because the dress holds so much importance. Indeed, the viewer understands that if the stain is not removed, no other alternatives regarding Lisa's attire are available. In short, there will be no wedding if there is no wedding dress. The requirement of the wedding gown, as emphasized in this particular episode of the show, further perpetuates the hegemonic, commonsense knowledge that says the bride must wear a wedding gown: it is the required "uniform." Lisa's concern that "everyone does their job" also underscores the bride's responsibility for managing her "special" day.

While Lisa's wedding dress drama clearly stands out as a unique circumstance, the emphasis she and her mother, and the entire episode in general, give to "the perfect dress" illustrates the importance and symbolism of the wedding gown as a special, magical article of clothing: it serves as the bride's one chance to truly stand out and be appreciated by onlookers, especially her husband, as she reveals herself in all her splendor. I must note that it was cosmetics in the form of the mother of the bride's red lipstick that threatened to derail Lisa's wedding. Ironically, artifacts designed and used to improve a woman's appearance had a hand in affecting the creation of the bride's appearance, with only the miracle of modern cleaning products and the intervention of a male savior standing between success and disaster.

The wedding dress serves as the raison d'être for the TLC series *Say Yes to the Dress.*[9] Most of the program focuses on the hierophany surrounding the quest for the perfect, dream dress. Indeed, the phrases "perfect" and "dream" appear consistently in the voice-over narration and by brides on camera. The notion of knowing a particular dress is "the one" further enhances the magical qualities associated with the wedding gown as perpetuated by bridal media.

The mythology surrounding the quest for "the dress" becomes reified when sales associates explain on camera the importance and significance of the wedding gown. For example, in Episode 2, Elise, Kleinfeld's director of sales, explained that the purchasing of a wedding gown distinguishes itself from any other consumer transaction in that it serves as the culmination of women's dreams: "Bridal is completely different than selling a car or a house. This is a very personal, personal purchase. These girls had been waiting to buy this dress since they were three years old."[10] Elise's observation points to how childhood dreams of little girls become reified by this particular article of clothing, thus reaffirming the notions of femininity associated with the bridal persona.

In this reality-based program, the added aura of fantasy becomes manifest in the change in habitus wherein apparel of the everyday and even special occasions becomes completely overshadowed by the wedding dress, further enhancing the notions of magic and perfection required by the idealized image of the wedding day. After all, the wedding day serves as the one day when a female of noncelebrity status becomes the sole object of the gaze. *Say Yes to the Dress* frames the drama surrounding the wedding dress quest in terms of its overwhelming importance, as the voice-over narrator tells viewers that when "dealing with the most important purchase" of a woman's life, "emotions are bound to run high."[11]

Say Yes to the Dress emphasizes the fantasy of the wedding dress, but also contrasts the idealized image of "the" dress with the reality of the fitting room. Thus, the conflict between fantasy and reality serves as a means by which the finding of the perfect dress that fits perfectly (after alterations) becomes paramount—and reifies the mystical quality surrounding the wedding dress. Often brides are shown coming in for their first post-purchase fittings and saying it's the wrong dress. The ensuing conflict resolution, wherein mistakes are remedied and any second doubts are allayed, leaves the viewer with the impression that all's well that ends well. In the end, all the dresses turn out perfectly. Even when no sale is made at Kleinfeld's, the program reassures viewers that the brides featured on the show do obtain their dream dresses elsewhere; every bride is shown as having a successful wedding.

The quest for the perfect dress comes relatively easily for the brides at Kleinfeld's, thanks to the well-versed bridal consultants who choose dresses based on which ones they think work best for each bride. "The" dress might be the first one tried on; sometimes it takes three tries, sometimes even nine, to find it. Family members often express overwhelming emotions and cry at seeing the bride in "the" dress, which confirms the choice and increases the "magic" and fairy-tale ideal of the wedding. The tears and gasps of the family members and friends who accompany the brides and witness the finding of "the one"—a term repeatedly used in this series—adds to the drama. "I knew that this was the one and I put it on and I started to cry," exclaimed a bride whose perfect dress exceeded her budget (the sales staff took pity on her and gave her a discount).[12]

In *Say Yes to the Dress*, comments regarding the hierophany that characterizes the quest for "the" dress often come from brides' mothers. The impression on the viewer becomes one of assigning credibility and validation to the mothers, whose reactions to seeing their daughters in "the one" seals the deal. Comments such as "I felt like this was the one" by one mother of the bride[13] and "Magnificent. I knew it was the dress" by another mother[14] confirm for viewers that the perfect dress at last has been found.

The following exchange between bride Kim and her mother serves as a typical example of how the women decide if a dress is "the one."[15] Kim tries on dress number three as her appointment time comes to a close, and says, "I think this is it." Her mother gasps as she sees Kim walk out of the dressing room, and starts crying as she puts her hands to her mouth. "The minute she walked out, I just knew this was the dress," the mother says on camera. As she looks at her daughter in "the one," she says, "Oh, Kim, it's gorgeous." As she continues crying, she says on camera: "I am beyond excited. This is the day every mother waits for." Regarding the price tag, Kim's mother notes, "There is no budget for Kim." Kim reaffirms the choice: "I had that moment everyone says, 'You'll know, you'll know.' I love it." When Kim returns for alterations and tries on her veil, her mother cries again. This confirmation is reestablished and finalized at the end of the episode when the narrator tells viewers, "Kim is every bit the perfect bride." The episode concludes with footage of her wedding and her new husband's comment, "She took my breath away. Just an angel. The dress was outrageous."

In *Say Yes to the Dress*, Kleinfeld's in essence serves as a bridal factory, churning out essentially the same bride dressed in white, formal dresses that cost thousands of dollars. While backstories might differ, the interchangeability of these women results in the overall portrayal of brides as generic, identity-less women who wear a specific uniform considered legitimate and acceptable for today's American wedding. The dress, rather than the bride herself, serves as the star of this program, and the star of the wedding. Of the episodes I viewed, nearly all the brides chose a strapless gown, which further created a sense of uniformity—and conformity. Several brides mentioned the importance of the dress as being the "key" to the perfect wedding, further illustrating the notion of bridal packaging described by Goldstein-Gidoni (1997). Among the 47 brides featured in the 14 episodes I viewed, only one steered slightly away from the white dress: a Halloween bride chose a white dress trimmed with black lace. Because no alternatives to the white gown are offered—even when no sale is made at Kleinfeld's—*Say Yes to the Dress* reinforces the hegemonic frame presented by bridal media that says only a white, formal gown of some type can be considered legitimate wedding apparel.

Hierophany thus becomes reified and demonstrated when "the one" is finally found; I found this process illustrated in Oxygen's *Real Weddings From The Knot*, as well, as brides are often shown being fitted for their dresses, many times with female onlookers. Not only does the finding of "the one" become validated by others' approval, such as when these women's mothers tearfully express how beautiful their daughters look, but through the frequency of the term "princess." Self-gaze becomes another means of validation, as brides in this series repeatedly use the term "princess" as they see their reflection in fitting room mirrors.

In *Real Weddings From The Knot*, phrases that assess one's state of being and the comparison to royalty, an appeal of Brideland described by Wolf (2003), denote the power of the wedding dress as the cue essential to creating one's identity as a bride. "I feel really pretty. I feel like a princess," comments 23-year-old Jen, a former recording artist who gave up her career in favor of marriage. "It's starting to hit home, the whole reason why we're here is this dress. . . . Oh, my god, I feel like a princess," says Orisha, whose marriage to John comes after they have already been living together and have a daughter.

The identity-changing power of the wedding dress was illustrated most pointedly in the *Real Weddings* episode featuring Cara, the self-imaged princess bride, who in "real life" is a Wall Street broker who has earned a seat on the New York Stock Exchange. However, even as women like Cara serve as examples of egalitarianism, and seemingly promote feminism in terms of creating equality in the sphere of business, they still symbolize the feminine values embodied in the self-image of beautiful, finely dressed "princess." The very use of the term "princess" denotes a secondary status of royalty (as opposed to, for example, "queen"), an ideal embraced by the idealized portrait of the princess bride so common in bridal media.

Variations on the white wedding gown theme

Whatever its price or impracticality, the white wedding dress serves as the mandatory costume, however modified, for the brides in TLC's *A Wedding Story*. In my study of 100 episodes, nearly all of the brides wore some version of a white bridal gown and veil.[16] Early episodes of the program, during its initial few seasons, featured a number of alternative wedding gowns. Notable episodes included the American Revolutionary War wedding in which bride Rhonda wore a replica of an 18th century dress in white, and the Civil War reenactment wedding of Nancy and Jeff, for which Nancy wore a 19th century white dress and Jeff wore a replica army uniform.[17] Other alternative wedding dresses included Shannon's medieval-style gown worn for her and Bruce's 1996 medieval-themed wedding, Amy's all-white, "Old West" frontier costume complete with cowboy hat worn for her wedding held at an Old West theme park in 2000, and Katherine's traditional German bridal costume worn during her and Roland's German-themed wedding in 1997.[18] Except for Katherine's costume, these "reproductions" were actually some modified form of the white wedding gown that serves as the familiar bridal costume of today.

In a very rare exception to the requisite dress, one episode of *A Wedding Story* stood out from the others. It underscored, by its exception, the strength of wedding hegemony. The 2000 episode of scuba divers Kerri and Mike, who met through the online dating service *Match.com*, departed from the familiar big, church wedding.[19] Their Florida coast wedding ceremony was held underwater and attended by two other couples and Kerri's mother. The wedding couple wore appropriate clothing for their chosen venue—bathing suits. The bride did not wear a white bathing suit, which at least would conform to the custom of wearing white. Instead, her special French-braid hairdo with tiny, white silk flowers, created at a local bridal salon, served as the only cue to her role as bride.

For the most part, however, even the more unusual weddings in *A Wedding Story*, such as Raquel and Lance's 2000 Halloween-themed wedding in Salem, Massachusetts, invariably featured some version of the white dress.[20] In their episode, the wedding guests all wore some kind of Halloween costume. Lance's father dressed up as the Phantom of the Opera, complete with mask and tuxedo, and his groomsmen all wore Halloween "ghoul" makeup and sported long, black fingernails and fake fangs. The bridesmaids wore black dresses, complete with witches' hats. Raquel, however, wore a white gown and veil. Taking the central roles within the apparent macabre, out-of-the-ordinary Halloween trappings of this particular wedding, the bride in her "regular" white wedding apparel and her bridegroom in a tuxedo made the juxtaposition even more visually exceptional. Rather than assuming the roles of witch bride and ghoul groom, Raquel and Lance appeared as a normal-looking wedding couple.

Even as "untraditional" brides in *A Wedding Story* attempted to personalize and create a unique bridal persona within a fantasy theme, such as

Shannon and Bruce's medieval wedding, they still conformed to the white gown ideal. Thus, attempts at the carnivalesque never truly defy contemporary versions of the white wedding dress. However, within the bridal media milieu, this program serves as a venue that allows for such alternatives. While the sheer number of *A Wedding Story* episodes produced certainly provided potential for a wider range of couples and personalization of weddings, this program at least made room for counterhegemonic depictions.[21] Thus, this program to some degree told viewers that one need not explicitly follow the bridal rules as enforced in bridal magazines and other bridal media in order to have a "legitimate" wedding, or at least one that would be shown on television. In this manner, *A Wedding Story* departed from other wedding-related programming and media by encompassing a variety of wedding styles that served as alternatives to the ideal.[22]

The Disciplined Body/Bride

As a metaphor for culture, the body serves as the text of culture. As such, it becomes a practical and direct locus of social control, with the norms of cultural life controlling and regulating the docile body (Bordo, 1993). Thus, the body, the female body in particular, can be considered "docile," as it is subject to social norms and habituated to self-improvement and transformation to meet those norms (Bordo, 1993). Related to this concept, the disciplined body invokes the idea of control—over both one's (female) body and over the (female) sex as a whole. Disciplinary practices, such as dieting and exercise, comprise the process by which the ideal (or hegemonic) feminine body is constructed (Bartky, 1990).

Regarding what "society" considers ideal, hegemonic femininity today "has a strong emphasis on appearance with the dominant notion of an ideal feminine body as thin and toned" (Krane, Choi, Baird, Aimar, & Kauer, 2004, p. 316). Advertising especially perpetuates the mandate that the female shape be unnaturally thin. The ultimate result, said Kilbourne (2002), tells women not to take up too much space or use their physical weight as power, but rather to be quiet, submissive, and invisible. As the star of the big day, invisible a bride is not. But the trappings of the bridal metamorphosis create an identity which erases the individual within, so that no matter her place in myriad public and private interactional strata, in the worlds of work, social networks, education, and the home, her uniqueness becomes erased and replaced by the resplendent bridal persona. To achieve it, the beauty standard becomes even more strict, with the media products to which women turn for advice reinforcing these rules.

In her study of weight loss as spectacle, Lockford (1996) observed that women's bodies constantly are scrutinized by the self and others. In the context of the wedding as a more overt spectacle, one in which gazing upon the "centerpiece"/bride is eagerly anticipated and women's bodies become even more scrutinized, virtually dissected by the gaze of self and others. The bride's disciplined body, noted Boden (2003), is defined, indeed, literally shaped, through control, denial, and anticipation; this stands in contrast to the abundance of choice and sumptuousness appearing in the form of food at the wedding occasion. Because bridal magazines emphasize the female body, this focus on physical presentation devalues women by telling them that their outer appearance holds the utmost importance (Boden, 2003; Filak, 2002). Bridal gown ads feature thin, young models. The bridal role has become so important an exemplar of hegemonic ideals of physical beauty for women that even magazines in other genres glorify it. For example, in spring 2003, *Fitness* magazine published a special bridal issue. The cover headline told readers to "Get the body of your dreams!" and offered 30-, 60-, and 90-day plans to get in shape for the wedding day.

Clothes usually are used to cover and conceal the body, especially the overweight body (Lockford, 1996). However, the wedding gown's form-fitting construction and heavy, white material disallows any concealment. The restrictive nature of the formal wedding gown's construction further underscores the restrictive nature of clothing for women. Formal women's apparel, made to outline and emphasize the female shape, reflects societal expectations for women to serve as objects of the gaze (Wood, 2010). As the absolute ultimate in women's formalwear, the bridal gown serves as a metaphor for women's continued relegation as objects of the gaze; their value lies in their ability to be admired, to be still.

Akin to Wolf's (2002) metaphor of the beauty myth as "Iron Maiden" (p. 17), the bridal gown, perpetuated in bridal advertisements and media as the only acceptable costume for women who marry, creates a similar three-dimensional mold into which women are "trapped" or, more correctly, trap themselves. In her study of bridal salons, Corrado (2002) confirmed the aesthetics-over-comfort requirement for the bridal appearance: "The gown must look a certain way, so the bride must push and squeeze her body to conform to this ideal" (p. 51). So rigid are the bridal rules, noted Corrado, that some bridal salons require brides to sign a contract promising they will not gain weight prior to the wedding. Indeed, any alterations cost additional money and can delay delivery of the gown.

Thus, the bridal gown serves as the impetus for obtaining the disciplined body, in that the bride must conform to the gown, rather than it conforming to her. Because the bridal gown dictates the body within, brides should not be heavy or "plus-size," noted Patterson in her 2005 essay, "Why Are All the Fat Brides Smiling?" As a recent bride herself, Patterson observed that the wedding gown "wreaks havoc" on a bride's self-esteem; shopping for it is "depressing," as one wants to "shrink" into a tiny size (p. 243). Patterson also found manifestations of a thin-bride standard in her casual surveillance of bridal magazines. She noticed that plus-size brides appeared only in bridal gown ads, not in editorial/fashion spread content. Additionally, she noticed that plus-size bridal models in the ads she viewed smiled openly, a departure from the "haughty," unsmiling, or demure facial expressions of fashion models. This suggested to Patterson that the heavier brides were portrayed as being joyous in the fact that they, too, were able to marry, despite their nonconformity to the thin ideal: the fat brides were smiling because they achieved the same goal as their slender counterparts.

Because the bridal appearance serves as an ideal example of self-gaze, this self-scrutiny combines with the concern for how one appears to others, reflective of a "feminine narcissism," which Bartky (1990) viewed as being rooted in the original psychoanalytic definition of narcissism: "an infatuation with one's bodily being" (p. 37). This becomes problematic if a woman is overweight or thinks of herself as falling short of the perfect bridal image. If the hegemonic ideal of femininity is to be thin and toned, as noted by Krane et al. (2004), the dissonance between the actual body and the idealized body results in what Bartky (1990) called a "permanent posture of disapproval" (p. 40). This disapproval becomes the impetus for the various weight loss and shape-up tips offered in bridal media—a highly feminized form of media—that, when coupled with images of the ideal female form in advertisements, further endorses and enforces the rules of femininity.

Buff Brides: Weight loss as spectacle

The reality program *Buff Brides*, first presented on the Discovery Health Channel and later renamed *Buff Brides: The Bridal Challenge* on the cable channel FitTV, combines hegemonic notions of physical fitness and weddings to provide an ideal venue upon which to examine how the docile body becomes disciplined under the rules of bridal beauty. In that this program specifically features the female body—its imperfections, its owner's desire to become physically fit in order to wear a garment that physically and symbolically restricts her, but is importance to a woman's self image—it provides an example of the significance of female outward appearance.

The term *buff* provides a counter to past representations of the feminine, demure bride. Rather than the blushing, petite bride, buff, as its slang definition implies, denotes a strong, well-toned physique. Among the numerous references to this term I found in the online Urban Dictionary (a user-contributed web dictionary), the definitions "very strong and well built," "having well-defined muscles," and "good looking" denote that *Buff Brides* intends to transform formerly out-of-shape women into toned, physically fit brides.[23] While one might question the term *buff bride* as almost oxymoronic, taking into consideration the contradiction between the decidedly feminine aspect of bridal appearance and the almost-masculine implications of a strong, well-built body, it provides at least a semantic space where women can be strong as well as feminine. The buff bride thus allows a "strong" woman to pursue the decidedly "girly" pursuit of creating her bridal appearance. In other words, it's okay to be buff *and* a bride.

Although on the surface this program appears to be about women wanting to become buff and fit for their weddings, *Buff Brides* reveals as much about the hegemony of femininity as it does the requirements of the successful bridal appearance. Just as Lockford (1996) compared women's weight loss in the Weight Watchers' program to a "spectacle," this televised version of weight loss opened these women up to view; their stories became even more of a spectacle through use of the camera lens and subsequent airing of the program. I base my analysis on a sample of five one-hour episodes featuring 10 brides.[24] Several themes emerged from my reading of these episodes, based on the voice-over narration and comments by the brides themselves. Not surprisingly, the major recurrent issue was that all the brides expressed dissatisfaction with their bodies. Other themes included the wedding gown as motivation for losing weight, food as enemy, and the discipline and pain necessary to transform one's (self-perceived) unacceptable body into one befitting a bride. Together, these narrative themes combined to form a picture of these brides as being controlled by and trying to control their bodies in order to meet the hegemonic ideals of femininity—and the bridal appearance.

The issue of brides' body image and unhappiness with their current shape and weight serves as the prominent theme of *Buff Brides*. Brides' "before" weights are given at the start of each episode in graphics superimposed on screen next to their full-length image, but their heights are not. The only exception was for Jessica, who stands 5 feet 2 inches and wants to return to her former size 2 figure. In that "normal" weight ranges are determined by height and weight, such as in the National Heart, Lung, and Blood Institute's *Body Mass Index Table* (2007), the program bypasses the notion of healthy weight and uses each bride's own assessment of how much weight she would like to lose, rather than how much she needs to lose in order to be considered medically healthy. Other indications of health are solely based on body fat percentages, calculated by the brides' personal trainers.

The voice-over narrative by an anonymous female announcer adds to the visual elements of the program to create a negative impression of aging, which for women apparently begins as early as one's late twenties or early thirties. Both the narrator and some of the brides mention that metabolism starts to slow when a woman hits her mid-twenties. This, combined with mention of the type of work these women do, hints at the unacceptability of aging for women. In short, deskwork plus age equals the less-than-perfect body. For example, Madhu, who is Indian and "works for a New York-based women's organization," comments, "Somewhere around my mid to late 20s, my metabolism fell." Her goal is to lose 10 to 15 pounds and "fit into the size 4 red suit that I love." The notion of returning to one's youthful and thin past is expressed repeatedly in brides' voice-overs, as old photos of them in their skinny past appear onscreen. Justine, a twenty-something nonprofit worker, used to be thin and slender with flat abs when she was younger. Now, she says, "I think my body is ready to be back to the way it was." Jessica, a bank worker who is 5 feet 2 inches tall and used to be a size 2, says in her voiceover: "I was so skinny all through high school." Now in her twenties, she weighs 140 pounds and wants to lose 20 pounds.

In addition to wanting to return to one's former size, all the brides express an intense dissatisfaction with specific body parts. They explain their target "problem" areas while pinching their fat on camera. For instance, Colleen, a public affairs manager, wants to lose 20 pounds. She identifies her arms and back as target areas to the viewer: "Nobody likes flabby arms for a wedding gown." Greta, a cosmetics company public relations executive, weighs 141 pounds and wants to lose 20 pounds for her wedding. On camera, she points to areas she dislikes: "I hate this extra butt that I have here," pinching her hip. "This nice little 'grandma' arm," she says, pinching the skin on the underside of her (rather unchubby) arm. "I have my little tummy I have here," she continues. For this bride, however, the issue of being overweight is coupled with her work as a beauty industry insider: "There is in today's world an intense pressure on women and I'm in that world: size 0, size 2 if you're heavy. And if you're a size 12 or 14, you just don't feel good in the company that you keep." In addition, Greta has a history of anorexia, further underscoring her concerns about losing weight.

The issue of bodily disapproval becomes significant when ideals clash with physical features related to race. For example, both of the Asian brides comment on their fattened up, "Americanized" bodies. Margaret, who wants lose the "cushioning" in her middle torso, went to high school in Taiwan, where all the girls were smaller than her: "The Chinese people by nature are very slender and shorter, more petite size. And I was kind of this, like, milk-fed girl from New Jersey and I was definitely bigger" (according to her *Buff Brides* web site bio, Margaret is 5 feet 7 inches tall). Linxiu, a bookkeeper who came to the US from China when she was a child, comments that her face is too round and chubby: "Just more of the fat went to my face" (her beginning weight was 146 pounds).

Cultural ideals of health and beauty also collided in the case of Nadege, an executive assistant who is of Haitian descent. Nadege's desire to lose weight, especially around her lower body, contrasts with her native culture's ideal of the perfect body: "Black women are supposed to be thick on the bottom. We come from a mentality the thicker you are, the healthier you are." Nadege's Haitian mother cannot understand why she wants to lose weight. Even Nadege's personal trainer scolds her: "I really sometimes feel that you have a little distorted perception of your body. . . . So you need to stop all this nonsense." Eventually, Nadege does lose 13 pounds, but falls short of her 20-pound goal. The disconnect between what Nadege sees as an acceptable body shape, reflective of current hegemonic femininity, and what her mother thinks is acceptable illustrates the strength of hegemony and its effects on women's self image.

Bodily disapproval becomes even more reified as brides undergo weigh-ins and measurements. Each bride is shown being weighed by her personal trainer on a medical scale, having her arms, waist, hips, and thighs measured either with a measuring tape or body fat calipers. Most of the brides fall within the range of 20% to 30% body fat, with high percentages nearing unhealthy levels. However, no medical experts appear on the program to provide more information for viewers about what exactly constitutes the danger zone for fat levels.

As noted previously, the bridal gown requires the bride within to conform to it, rather than it concealing any imperfections of the body. In *Buff Brides*, all brides had chosen a formal, white gown except for Madhu, who instead chose several traditional Indian costumes for her three-day wedding. Her form-fitting costumes, which showed her midriff, became her motivation for continuing her weight loss program. After seeing all the "sexy" outfits, she says, "I'm glad I'm working out." Madhu's final weigh-in shows she lost 11.5 pounds, trimming 11 total inches from her waist, abdomen, and hips.

Several of the brides in *Buff Brides* had chosen a strapless gown, which required them to have bare arms for their weddings. The arms then became a site not only of initial disapproval, but also for others' gaze. Colleen, for example, goes on a shopping trip with her mother and female entourage at Kleinfeld's, New York's largest and oldest bridal salon. "I cannot believe my bridal gown is going to be strapless," she says. She then pinches the lower part of her arms, explaining, "This has gotta go." Pinching her back fat, she says, "This has gotta go. It's all gotta come off." Finally having chosen a gown, she concludes, "I feel like now I have to get in it. I gotta look my best." Similarly, Justine, who had purchased an off-the-shoulder dress, says, "I can't believe my dress is sleeveless. I don't want to be self-conscious about mushy arms. I want not to be worrying about how my arms are looking to everyone and how they're going to look in the pictures."

Already-purchased gowns of other brides served as the impetus for their weight loss and toning programs as well. At the home she shares with her fiancé, buff bride Linxiu takes her strapless wedding gown out and shows it on camera, a "Carolina Herrera" tag, denoting the high price tag of this designer gown, peeks from underneath the inside neckline in a close up. Her wedding dress is a size 8, but Linxiu finds it difficult to put it on without holding her breath. Clearly ill fitting, the gown, or rather its numerical size, serves as a definer of Linxiu's self-image: "I don't think I'm a size 10. I refuse to even go to a size 10. I think I'm a tight 8." Eventually, Linxiu loses 17 pounds. As a sign of her accomplishment, her new husband pinches her buff and toned bare arm during their limousine ride after their wedding.

Borrowing from Frye's (2000) rubric of the quest, in *Buff Brides*, bridal perfection serves as the goal of the protagonist bride with the role of "enemy" played by food. The female narrator's voice-over repeatedly includes phrases such as "Temptation is everywhere," and the word "weakness." This program consistently portrays food as "indulgence" rather than vital, with brides' appetites and "cheating" constantly threatening to derail their efforts. Talk of favorite foods also illustrates the badness of food and the will and discipline the women will need in order to achieve their target weight. For example, Justine, who wants to regain the flat abs she had before she hit her mid-twenties and gained weight, says, "I found that I couldn't indulge and stay thin . . . I love ice cream. Chips. I love chips. I love the combination of ice cream and chips." Her on-camera sound bite is followed by the narrator voice-over, which admonishes this errant bride: "For the next 16 weeks, Justine will have to abandon the ice cream. Indulgence will give way to discipline."

Close-up shots of food in general appear prominently in this program; the event for which these women are preparing involves food at receptions, rehearsal dinners, and other pre-wedding parties. Close-up images of food actually being eaten by these women instruct viewers that food—especially its appreciation—demarcates the "good" buff bride from the "bad" buff bride. The weakness for food plays a prominent role in Nadege's story line, for example. During her bridal shower, for which she chose the food and is shown eating it, the viewer is treated to close-ups of the luncheon buffet comprised of evil carbohydrates: macaroni and cheese, rice with lima beans (a Haitian dish), vegetable lasagna, potato salad. Nadege acknowledges her menu goes against her training regimen, but rationalizes her choices: "I knew that I was going to blow my diet today." Similarly, Margaret, the "milk-fed" Chinese-American bride, also consistently ignores her strict diet, indulging at a pre-wedding party. Margaret falls well short of her target weight, but nevertheless has her dream wedding, where she enjoys "one more piece" of wedding cake.

The Bridal Cam, which features black-and-white video segments during which brides make confessions directly to the viewer, becomes the site for brides to describe in detail the forbidden foods they have allowed themselves to eat. Often, these transgressions are accompanied by admissions of guilt. For example, Linxiu, who clearly takes pleasure in enjoying her favorite "bad" foods, describes the "toasted almond soufflé" with heavy cream she had for dessert at a French restaurant. After a day of indulging in the various tempting foods in her refrigerator in the absence of her fiancé's watchful eye, she tells the viewer via the Bridal Cam: "I gave myself a treat. I didn't work out today, either . . . I have a guilty conscience." During Christmas, a time when food becomes plentiful and eating almost mandatory, Justine admits to eating *zepola*, fried dough in powdered sugar. She planned to eat during the holiday, but kept herself in check: "I had a little bit of everything and didn't go overboard." In the case of Tiffany, the medical resident who succeeds in meeting her weight goal, eating is termed as a reward by the narrator: "After all her hard work, she's earned the right to indulge and enjoy an ice cream sundae and just be a bride."

Related to the portrayal of food as enemy, the denial of food also appears in several brides' story lines. The juxtaposition of the buff bride on her quest and the abundance of "evil" food offered at these pre-wedding events further emphasizes that only through denial will the bride achieve her ideal image. Greta, whose history of unhealthy dieting and anorexia serves as a concern for her and her family, demonstrates an iron will during pre-wedding festivities and on the job. At a company event she oversees, she waves off a tray of food being served by the caterer, saying, "Not for me, not for Greta." Footage of her bridal shower features a close-up shot of what looks like hot garlic bread being passed around, followed by a close up of her lunch plate: simple salad greens and some kind of folded tortilla. Other brides show similar discipline. For example, at Colleen's surprise bridal shower luncheon at a large restaurant, a big cake is shown, but she does not partake. Emphasizing her weight loss "quest," one of the bridal shower gifts she receives is a scale.

The denial of food and the portrayal of eating certain foods, or eating at all, as indulgent relates to another common theme in these episodes: the requirement of discipline. The notions of pain and hard work permeate these episodes, both via the narrator's voice-over and brides' confessions via the Bridal Cam. Specific words and phrases used by the narrator that denote these ideas, such as "punishing," "stays on track," "battle carbs at the table," "there's a long road ahead," and "grueling," add to an impression that losing weight is, and must be, a trying and taxing ordeal. Control over one's body and over one's need to eat is constantly emphasized in *Buff Brides*, especially for those undisciplined brides who surrender to their weakness for food.

The visual images of these women being weighed and measured enhance the notion of the docile body/object in need of discipline. Almost as if they were being tortured, brides tend to grimace and groan as their personal trainers weigh and measure them. Comments like "I'm a little nervous" (Justine, being weighed at the midpoint of her program); "I'm too nervous to face the scale" and "it sucks" (Nadege); and "It's never fun to step on the scale, but at least now it's not so horrifying" (Greta, after losing 12 pounds) illustrate the fear of their own weight. The resulting message to female viewers, to whom this program is targeted, points to the idea that women are and should be afraid of violating current expectations of body weight and shape. Further, one can take this to signify the underlying fear of women to weigh anything, to be substantial, to take up space, as noted by Kilbourne (2002).

Pain and discipline are needed in the gym and at the dinner table; they are the price these brides must pay in order to get their perfect bodies. In that these brides try to lose at least one pound a week before their weddings, their workout programs are designed for maximum effect, which requires not only strict dieting, but exercises that work muscles long dormant. As a smiling Madhu leaves the gym after her first session with her personal trainer, the narrator says, "Madhu is smiling now, but the pain should kick in soon." Later in her episode, Madhu says on the Bridal Cam, "I am in perpetual pain. I don't see a lot of progress. All I feel is very, very sore right now." The ever-present narrator reminds viewers that brides have only so many weeks to achieve their goals. For Margaret to lose her weight, "It'll take diet, discipline, and dedication," announces the narrator. After Linxiu's first workout session, the narrator previews the coming weeks: Linxiu will have "about 50 more punishing workouts ahead of her. While they will get easier in time, for now it's pain over pleasure."

However, in the case of some of these brides, even if they do not achieve a buff physique, termed the "Holy Grail" by the iron-willed bride Greta, they still get their dream weddings. It seems that all these brides, whether they have lost 20 pounds or just 7 pounds, are still considered beautiful by their onlookers; success or failure appears to be a moot point in the end. In this manner, the denouement of each *Buff Brides* episode tells viewers that a successful bridal appearance will result if they just follow the bridal rule of white gown, big wedding. This implies that although a bride might not reach her desired weight at the end of her training program, the fact that she has put forth the effort to create the stereotypical big, white wedding is enough to ensure her status.

Physical Beauty: The Docile Body, Made (Up) Better

The creation of the bridal image requires special application of cosmetics for maintaining a fresh visage through what for many women becomes a marathon day of activities. In addition to offering women an incentive to lose weight, bridal media provide new secrets for attaining what the cover of the 2003 special bridal issue of *Fitness* magazine promised to give its readers: "radiant skin, romantic hair, and glowing makeup." Every aspect of the bride's person, from gown to lipstick, from hair to shoes, must adhere to an idealized portrait—one that exemplifies the meaning of woman. As Peiss (1996) observed, making up has become a tangible way for women to confirm their feminine identities: "The legitimation of visible cosmetics occurred first in contexts where women were consciously representing themselves to others, performing a role, or creating themselves as spectacles to be viewed" (p. 320).

Makeup's transformative power becomes more so on a woman's wedding day; through the use of cosmetics and hairstyling, brides become "transformed" from mere woman to bride. Magazine articles tell women to "Get ready to look great" (from the cover of the winter 2005 issue of *InStyle Weddings*), and instruct them on how to be "fabulous!" with "glowing skin and beautiful makeup" (from the cover of the spring 2005 issue of *For the Bride*). We see these well-established norms everywhere in mass media, ones that create harsh penalties for women who are not thin, unblemished, or wrinkle free. The creation of the bridal role—an exception to the everyday application of the "everyday" front—requires more than just the usual cosmetics.[25] It requires special *bridal* makeup, often applied by a professional other.

Oxygen's *Real Weddings From The Knot*, TLC's *A Wedding Story*, WE tv's *Bridezillas*, and FitTV's *Buff Brides* all offer some aspect of the backstage preparations on the wedding day. Of these, *A Wedding Story* gives a substantial amount of time to this aspect of the bridal appearance; brides have their hair elaborately coiffed at either a beauty salon, at home, or in a hotel room, and often have makeup applied by a makeup artist. Obviously, it takes hours for a bride to become presentable. Often these scenes of the bride "getting ready" are interspersed with footage of the groom engaged in some kind of athletic activity, or getting dressed with other men in the wedding party, all at a leisurely pace.

Similarly, in *Real Weddings From The Knot*, brides and their female attendants are shown at beauty salons on the wedding day, and/or having their cosmetics applied by either a makeup artist or themselves. In one episode of *Real Weddings*, bride Katie, who happens to be a model in addition to her occupation as dental hygienist, insists on doing her sisters' makeup and hair herself because she wants them to "look perfect." The importance of brides' physical beauty become further underscored when viewers get even more visual details of the backstage, such as in *Real Weddings From The Knot* when pre-made-up brides appear on camera "performing" beauty routines. For example, Orisha is shown with a facial mud mask and Kaijsa is shown taking a bath with cold cream on her face and cucumber slices over her eyes.

In contrast, while *Real Weddings* groom John has his braids done by a female family member at home and Todd has his hairdresser brother coif his hair, men are never seen shaving or applying beauty products. The absence of such images of men attending to their visage makes these exceptions even more jarring, as in the case of Catina and Todd's episode. In addition to doing his hair, his hairdresser brother applies facial makeup to Todd, explaining that doing so will prevent Todd's face from being too shiny for the wedding photographs. Todd's other brothers laugh as they look on, which further emphasizes that such treatment is inappropriate for men.

While the brides in these programs all undergo beauty regimens of some sort, the notion that beauty requires pain was especially noteworthy in *Real Weddings*. Twenty-something Kaijsa has her hair done in an "updo" at a beauty salon, and says, "I don't like pain, but if it makes me look good, I don't care," while wincing as her tiara and veil are positioned into her coiffure. Especially telling is how this idea of pain equaling beauty extends to younger female bridal party members. For example, one of bride Lori's two young step-daughters-to-be cries in pain because her hairpins hurt, as the other child (no more than ten years old) comments on camera, "Beauty is pain." Thus, not only do brides expect to experience some kind of pain or discomfort, this example illustrates that young girls already understand that beauty involves some amount of sacrifice, sometimes to the point of crying. As with *Buff Brides*' emphasis on the aches and pains required for weight loss, women are told that looking beautiful requires pain. When considered within the wider realm of beauty advertising for plastic surgery and other invasive treatments, the message that beauty literally means pain becomes an expected and accepted part of the feminine identity.

Repeated images of brides having cosmetics applied, hair coiffed, and being dressed by others supports Bartky's (1988) description of the "docile" female body that becomes disciplined by self-enforcement, through dieting, body shaping, and the transformative power of cosmetics. One can consider the process of the wedding, that is, the "making" of the bride, as a disciplinary practice that creates ideal feminine beauty. Bartky noted that "the media images of perfect female beauty that bombard us daily leave no doubt in the minds of most women that they fail to measure up" (p. 71). The special attention given to the application of makeup on the female face thus further emphasizes the unpainted female face as "defective" and in need of correction, as opposed to a male's face. When a male is subjected to similar treatment, as in the case of Todd, he is apt to be ridiculed. For women, the application of makeup is "natural"; it creates feminine identity (Hall & Hebert, 2004). In this sense, women are not truly women without it, or the accompanying discomfort required to look beautiful.

Taken together, these backstage glimpses of brides undergoing special treatment to make them ready for the big "reveal" at the wedding result in a pattern similar to what one might see in a factory. Add to these scenes of their bridesmaids undergoing similar treatments as groups in hair salons, and one gets the sense that these women appear as items on an assembly line. The repetition of the beautification process further enhances our view of the bride as an object of beauty, similar to a doll or mannequin. Indeed, some brides literally are compared to their doll counterparts, as during the wedding reception that ends the *Buff Brides* episode featuring Colleen, a bride who chose a strapless gown and worked to ensure her body would fit into it. Regarding how she looks on her wedding day, her new husband Chris says on camera, "She looks like a Barbie doll or a china doll. Just so perfect and so amazing. So beautiful. Absolutely beautiful." When considered as a whole, these programs depict the brides they feature as essentially the same object—all wearing white, all receiving the same makeover, all adhering to the overarching and all-important requirement of the feminine/bridal appearance: to look beautiful, as a true woman should.

Bridal Perfection

"Overwhelmingly, femininity is conceptualized as 'picture-perfect,' triggering visual pleasure for the bride as well as her audience for conforming to the cultural requirements of a successful bridal appearance," observed Boden (2003, p. 62). I found this idea of perfection repeatedly mentioned in the reality programs examined here. For example, in *Buff Brides* the female narrator repeatedly uses the word "perfect," further instilling the notion that the bridal appearance requires that everything about the bride be just so, with the perfect accoutrements, the perfect look, the perfect spectacle: "Jessica has only seven weeks to become the perfect bride"; "In spite of the weather, this has turned out to be the perfect wedding that Greta was dreaming of"; "The dress is a perfect fit, and Margaret is every inch the perfect bride." This repetition, in turn, further pushes the idea that a woman must attend to every aspect of her outer person in order to fulfill not only the supposedly once-in-a-lifetime role of bride, but, in an extended fashion, every aspect of her everyday life.

This desire for perfection and the association of perfection with the bridal appearance emanates from the buff brides themselves. For instance, Melanie, who wanted to lose 30 pounds but had to settle for 12 pounds, summarized this desire: "Everyone wants to look their best on their wedding day. You know, you always dream about the perfect dress. With the perfect dress goes the perfect hair, the perfect smile, and, naturally, the perfect body." The hegemonic aspect of Melanie's comment—"everyone wants"—reflects the unquestioned acceptance that *everyone*—all brides, that is—want to look their best on their wedding day. If a woman chooses not to follow the bridal rules, and pays no attention to her outward appearance when she marries, she obviously cannot be considered a "real" bride: this appellation is reserved only for those who adhere to the requirements of the successful bridal appearance.

At the bridal factory disguised as Kleinfeld's salon in TLC's *Say Yes to the Dress*, the use of the terms "dream," as in "dream dress," and "princess" are used liberally, but not nearly as much as the word "perfect." I noted that this term, whether heard in the voice-over narration, from brides, mothers, friends, family, or sales staff, was uttered some 26 times in 14 episodes. I present here just a few of the sound bites from the series that invoke the notion of perfection:

> This is the first time the dress has to be done to perfection. . . . The first time they're going to be the star of the show and 250 or 150 or how many people are going to look at no one except the bride. It has to be so perfect, it's got to be a lot of stress and pressure. (Mara Erschel, Kleinfeld's co-owner)

> I tried on the perfect dress and it's the one I fell in love with. (Caryn, bride)

> This is the day most girls dream of, and if they haven't dreamt of it, they want it to be perfect. (Elise, Kleinfeld's director of sales)

> And on a spring day in New York City, 240 people saw Gayle walk down the aisle in her perfectly fitted and beautiful gown. (Narrator)

> Me and 500 people are looking for the perfect dress. (Unidentified bride at sample sale)

> Kim is every bit the perfect bride. (Narrator)

> The perfect dress is important to me. (Jillian, bride)

> It's just perfect. (Mother of the bride)

> Her dream dress made her the picture perfect bride. (Narrator)

> I'm here to hopefully find the perfect wedding dress. (Diana, bride)

> On the day of her wedding, she walked down the aisle in her perfect dress. (Narrator)

You only have one day that you're going to be wearing this beautiful dress and everyone's going to be looking at you, and you're the center of attention. So, I feel that you have to be happy and look perfect on your wedding. (Lynn, bride)[26]

"Perfect" refers to the appearance of the bride, but more importantly, it is her dress that must be perfect: perfect in terms of appropriateness, perfect in terms of her body fitting into it, perfect in terms of it fitting her. The perfect dress *creates* the perfect bride: her mind, her accomplishments, her thoughts, her spirit, are of no consequence. It is the packaging that is valued. Without the perfect dress, there can be no perfect wedding or perfect marriage. A woman must again "wow" her man, in essence make herself attractive to him even at their wedding, when essentially the deal is done.

The requirement of perfection on her wedding day further emphasizes that a woman must continually attend to her physical appearance in order to keep a man interested in her. If we take this further, the wedding day really calls for female submission to not only compulsory heterosexuality and the hegemonic expectation that she takes great pains to look the part of perfect bride, but to an article of *clothing*. Thus, even as she becomes the object of the gaze on this one day, she is still subservient to an object.

The perfection promised by these reality versions of the bridal magazine concerns a woman's outer appearance, but nothing that has to do with her as a person. In the world of bridal media, the wedding day serves as the one time that the ordinary woman will have all eyes on her, and her only. No one will be looking at the groom, no one cares what he wears. The wedding day is the one time that a male serves an ancillary purpose, an accessory to the bride. Rather than the most important day for him to look good, to pay attention to grooming, to pay attention to the fit of his clothing, to spend *his* time in quest of the perfect suit or the perfect tuxedo, it is the *woman* who willingly subjects herself to the notion of perfection, because this is what she is told she must do to successfully fulfill the bridal role.

The created desire for perfection fueled by bridal media further strengthens the notion of the female as object—some*thing* we, the audience, whether in person or as television spectator, gaze upon, rather than someone who acts. The mantra of *Say Yes to the Dress* requires that in order for a woman to be the perfect bride, she must have the perfect dress. Ideals of perfection become intertwined with magic; hierophany in the world of weddings refers to the mystical qualities associated with the bridal gown, rather than the bride's partner. Finding "the one" person to marry becomes replaced by "the one perfect dress." When all eyes are on her in the perfect dress, the bride literally becomes an object of the gaze, *an object within an object*. And therein lies the impetus for desiring the perfect dress: the bride is there to be gazed upon, not to converse with, or to learn about or from, but to receive the attention earned by successfully attaining the perfection required by her one-day performance as the star of her own show.

Summary

Hegemonic femininity has been "formed through mass production and mass reproduction, disseminated through endless images of female glamour and female domesticity," asserted Felski (2000, p. 83). It requires the "tacit approval" of those who adhere to or unquestioningly follow its rules (Dow, 1990, p. 262). While unlikely aware or conscious of the implications of these rules on their progress within the already firmly entrenched society in which they exist, the brides described here have become complicit with the self-enforced rules of femininity. The media described in this chapter provide a picture of how women obtain that feminine glamour and celebrity status associated with their role as bride.

The overarching importance of the wedding gown becomes the central means by which the bride as object becomes the site of the gaze. In turn, a successful front depends on her ability to obtain the perfect dress to draw all attention to her. Although the most common, i.e., hegemonic, portrayals featured a specific form of wedding dress, namely, the white gown, however modified, *A Wedding Story* provided token instances of variations from the common theme. Inclusion of instances where bridal costumes actually *were* costumes illustrates the possibility for not following the norm; hegemony is always "leaking," not monolithic but always challenged. While these leaks might appear occasionally, the most common image of the bride found in these specific media—reality television and magazines—still promotes the white dress in some form.

Bartky (1988) described beauty practices related to the formation of the feminine persona as constituting "a disciplinary power that inscribes femininity in the female body" (p. 74). The importance of the bride's physical appearance in reality television treatments of the creation of the bridal persona, and in bridal media in general, illustrates the wedding's significance as the ultimate "disciplinary" power. While Bartky contended that this power exists everywhere and yet nowhere, clearly the contemporary wedding and its practices as depicted in bridal media provide certain "rules" that women must follow in order to play the part of bride. One of these mandates is that brides must present a "flawless, beautiful image" (Corrado, 2002, p. 51).

The reality television programs described here allow the viewer access to the back region, where that image is created and where we see these women plain and unpainted, or in unflattering poses, squatting, huffing, puffing, and groaning during their workouts, as in *Buff Brides*. This behind-the-curtain view opens up the women who appear in these reality programs to further scrutiny. In this form of bridal media, we see much more of the brides than the bridegrooms in the backstage area. Women appear in various forms of undress, express unhappiness about their bodies, or confess weakness such as giving in to the temptations of junk food. Repeated images of such brides in programs like the ones discussed here normalize such behaviors; femininity becomes even more associated with physical appearance and bodily disapproval. The enactment of the beauty myth thus becomes real—we see how much time and effort it takes to become a beautiful bride. At the same time, we see in concrete terms the larger story of women's self-imposed pressure to meet current beauty standards.

In Oxygen's *Real Weddings From The Knot* and TLC's *A Wedding Story*, the emphasis on female beauty becomes even more heightened with the juxtaposition of images of brides and grooms getting dressed and ready for the wedding day. The most common image among these episodes features the groom visiting a tuxedo shop a day or two prior to the wedding for a final fitting, or getting dressed on the wedding day. In *Real Weddings From The Knot*, I found that even this aspect is implied to be controlled by the bride, as the men on the program are not shown actually *selecting* their attire. For example, in Orisha and John's episode, John and his attendants make their requisite visit to the tuxedo shop to have a last-minute fitting, with Orisha and other female family members supervising. Speaking into the camera, Orisha reminds viewers, "*I* picked the color for the tux. It's my theme here." Typically, however, attention to men's apparel is confined to brief visits to the tuxedo shop or making last-minute adjustments to neckties on the wedding day itself.

While throughout this chapter identities of the brides mentioned in specific examples are included, one might notice that, with the exception of the buff brides, the viewer does not learn much about each individual woman. I found most noteworthy the exclusion of any mention of these women's educational attainment. In addition, these programs' narratives rarely include mention of their stars' occupations. If they do, such as in *Buff Brides*, the women's occupations are described in general terms, such as "public relations manager," "executive assistant," and "medical resident." One never truly gets any sense of the *careers* of these women. While certainly the focus of these programs centers around these women's role as brides, a short bio would at least acknowledge the depth and breadth of these women's lives aside from their one-day role of bride. Even television game shows provide more background information about their contestants.

Thus, however resplendent she might appear, the bride's packaging obscures the individual human being within—she is just another bride whose package is wearing *her*. While certainly nearly all roles in society "wear" the person fulfilling them, the role of bride brings with it numerous requirements beyond the standard "uniform"—requirements that embody only certain dimensions of the feminine identity. Doane (1989) noted that feminist theory "tends to envisage women's relation to the commodity" in terms of "being" rather than "having," the "object of exchange rather than its subject" (p. 23). If one views "the bride" as a commodity, a "thing" of exchange (within patriarchy), then as an object of exchange *she* becomes an object, a thing in need of discipline, to be worked out and over, through diet and exercise, and worked on, through the application of special cosmetics and hairstyle, in order to create the successful, picture-perfect spectacle. Individual identities cast aside, the value of the product of the bride factory—the bride—lies in her/its physical appeal and perfection. The feminine ideal forwarded in these programs thus underscores and amplifies the importance of women's physical appearance in the wider picture of U.S. society today. Even though the reality television programs examined here feature "real" women who have established successful careers for themselves, achieved high levels of education, and attained status and competed with men in the working world, the wedding demands of them to play roles that remain decidedly feminine, thus reestablishing the gender binary and, in that process, patriarchy.

The additional self-enforcement of the disciplined bridal body provides evidence for Bartky's (1988) assertion that "normative femininity" has become more and more centered on women's appearance, even as older forms of patriarchal domination erode (p. 81). In that the bride takes on the role of "marquee," yet generic, player/item in the wedding script, the application of the metaphor of commodity is appropriate and provides a foundation for examining how portrayals of various, individual women morph into one identity: "The Bride."

These programs all normalize the required time commitment of becoming a perfect bride; the real bride takes her "job" seriously and puts in overtime in order to achieve the bridal front. However, once the wedding day concludes, the bride once again becomes another ordinary woman, though now afforded a higher status as *married* woman, her celebrity status negated and replaced with the secondary status bestowed her by a patriarchal society. In this manner, woman as bride becomes a commodity to be created, viewed, and then forgotten once the wedding day passes. Leonard (2006) spoke to the role of wedding media as preservers of the bridal image when she noted how brides later return to their wedding photos and videos to "memorialize themselves" (p. 47). Thus, the work that women do to create the perfect bridal appearance, though ephemeral, can be "memorialized" in photographs and, in the case of these reality programs, on videotape.

The effort and time they dedicate to their one-day appearance as bride reflects the everyday effort and time it takes for women to create the personal front of "woman." In the next chapter, I examine the transient role of bride. Though the wedding itself lasts a few hours, it requires months, even years, of planning and preparation. The minimal contribution of bridegrooms to wedding work underscores the feminine nature of wedding planning, and, by extension, the perceived triviality of women's work in general.

Notes

* Portions of this chapter were published as the followi￼ articles and appear here with permission: "*Buff Brides: Disciplining the Female Ec ly,*" *Popular Culture Review*, 2008, Vol. 20, No. 1, pp. 35–44; "Creation of a New 'Empowered' Female Identity: WE tv's *Bridezillas,*" *Media Report to Women*, 2009, Vol. 37, No. 1, pp. 6–12; "Hegemony in Reality-Based TV Programming: The World According to *A Wedding Story,*" *Media Report to Women*, 2003, Vol. 31, Issue 1, pp. 10–14. Portions also appeared in "Unraveling The Knot: Political Economy and Cultural Hegemony in Wedding Media," available from http://jci.sagepub.com; the final, definitive version of this paper has been published in *Journal of Communication Inquiry*, Vol. 32, Issue 1, January 2008, pp. 60–82, by SAGE Publications Ltd./SAGE Publications, Inc. All rights reserved. ©2008 by Sage Publications

1. Noxon (1999) quoted executive producer Barbara Alfano-White of Banyan Productions, the series' production company: "We're not looking for the most outrageous couple. We're looking for genuine love stories. The best episodes are those where you really feel their love."

2. The latest updates on the web page "Couple Updates: *A Wedding Story*" on *TLC.com* appeared to have been posted in 2003.

3. In this press release, Oxygen claimed that viewership of *Real Weddings From The Knot* increased by 100% to 2.7 million between the show's premiere in 2003 and the June 2004 "Weddings Week," termed a "ratings hit" by The Knot's editor in chief, though actual ratings are unclear.

4. News stories that use the term bridezilla have included "Beware of the 'Bridezilla Syndrome'" (Morales, 2002), "Eva Longoria: I'm No Bridezilla" (2007), and "Kate Walsh's Bridezilla Moment" (2007).

5. The WE network, launched as Romance Classics in 1997, was rebranded as WE: Women's Entertainment, and finally renamed itself as WE tv in 2006.

6. *Bridezillas*, copyright dates of 2003 (Season 1) and 2005 (Season 2); both seasons available on DVD, produced by the Weinstein Company. Story lines for the brides in *Bridezillas* run concurrently, rather than in separately titled episodes. I introduce brides and quoted material as from either Season 1 or Season 2.

7. *Real Weddings From The Knot* episode copyright dates 2003–2005. Air and recorded dates were as follows: Jessa and Jeff, Danielle and John, Catina and Todd, Whitney

and Jeff, Susan and John—June, 2003; Orisha and John, Kaijsa and Ryan, Cara and Aaron, Lori and Mark, Sarah and Mark—January, 2004; Katie and Gus, Amy and Bill, Sarah-Jane and Nate, Jen and Jeff, Amy and Mark—October, 2004; Christin and Michael, Tiffany and Calvin, Allison and Tommy, Alem and Johannes, Xylina and Eric—January, 2005.

8. "Lisa and David," copyright date 1996; recorded circa 1998, month and date not documented. Because of their high rotation, episodes can have multiple airdates. This particular episode was unique in that in a subsequent episode of the show, one bride actually referred to it on camera.

9. I analyzed a convenience sample of 14 episodes of *Say Yes to the Dress* recorded in October 2007, November and December 2008, and March 2009. Copyright dates were 2007–2009. Episodes could include as few as just two brides or up to six. In one episode, in addition to the "serious" brides, two women came into Kleinfeld's who obviously were just looking with no intent to buy a dress (episode title and airdate: "To Have and to Hold . . . the Dress," November 28, 2008).

10. "Bridal Breakdown," airdate and recorded October 27, 2007.

11. "That's Not My Dress," airdate and recorded October 27, 2007.

12. "That's My Dress!," airdate and recorded December 19, 2008. The bride's sad story involved an overseas wedding to take place in her native Slovakia; she was doing the wedding for her deceased mother. Whether genuine or for the camera, the sales associate negotiated the price so that the bride could obtain her dream dress for a discount.

13. "Emotions Run Wild," airdate and recorded December 12, 2008.

14. "Daddy Knows Best," airdate and recorded December 26, 2008.

15. "It's My Wedding, but Don't Tell the Bridesmaid," airdate and recorded November 21, 2008.

16. *A Wedding Story*, episode copyright dates 1996–2000, recorded April and October 1998 and June 2001. See my article, "Hegemony in Reality-Based TV Programming: The World According to *A Wedding Story*," in *Media Report to Women* (Engstrom, 2003).

17. "Rhonda and Paul," copyright and airdates: 1998; November 27, 1999. "Nancy and Jeff" was episode #25 in the show's first season, copyright date *circa* 1996; airdate July 15, 1998.

18. Episode titles, copyright and airdates for these particular examples were: "Shannon and Bruce," 1996, June 26, 2001; "Amy and Nick," 2000, June 4, 2001; "Katherine and Roland," 1997, June 25, 2001.

19. "Kerri and Mike," copyright date 2000, recorded June 5, 2000.

20. "Lance and Raquel," copyright date 2000, recorded June 4, 2001.

21. Episodes of *A Wedding Story* continued to run on TLC as of early 2008; *TVguide.com* listed a total of 400 episodes as of February 29, 2008.

22. For more on *A Wedding Story* and my early research regarding its content, see Jellison's (2008) chapter on reality weddings in *It's Our Day* (pp. 211–218).

23. Urban Dictionary (http://www.urbandictionary.com) serves in a similar capacity as Wikipedia, in that it provides an online, ever-changing source for slang terms. Users contribute their own definitions of terms, as well as examples. "Buff" as an adjective refers to well toned and strong. Among other definitions of "buff" found in my search

of the site as of February 2008, in addition to references to bodily physique was "buff" as a verb, as in to erase graffiti.

24. I recorded at random during early 2007 five one-hour episodes featuring the stories of 10 brides on FitTV. Episodes were repeated once every several weeks, with the series taking months to recycle. Thus, this sample can be considered one of convenience. Episode titles and dates recorded are as follows: "Margaret and Tiffany," February 14, 2007; "Colleen and Nadege," February 21, 2007; "Linxiu and Melanie," March 2, 2007; "Jessica and Madhu," March 21, 2007; "Greta and Justine," March 21, 2007. Episode copyright dates were either 2003 or 2004.

25. For a discussion on the politics of makeup and its nonuse as protest against patriarchal societal norms, see Bartky (1990).

26. Sound bite sources, episode titles and air and recorded dates are as follows: Mara Erschel, Kleinfeld's co-owner, "Bridal Breakdown," October 27, 2007; Caryn, bride, "That's Not My Dress," October 27, 2007; Elise, Kleinfeld's director of sales, "Bridal Breakdown," November 21, 2008; Narrator, "It's My Wedding, but Don't Tell the Bridesmaid," November 21, 2008; Unidentified bride, "It's My Wedding, but Don't Tell the Bridesmaid," November 21, 2008; Narrator, "It's My Wedding, but Don't Tell the Bridesmaid," November 21, 2008; Jillian, bride, "Emotions Run Wild," December 12, 2008; Mother of the bride, "Emotions Run Wild," December 12, 2008; Narrator, "Daddy Knows Best," December 26, 2008; Diana, bride, "Time to Cut the Cord," December 26, 2008; Narrator, "Time to Cut the Cord," December 26, 2008; Lynn, bride, "Changes and Challenges," March 6, 2009.

5. Working the Part*

Bride as Actor

IN ADDITION TO THOSE OF FEMALE GLAMOUR, NOTED FELSKI (2000), IMAGES of "female domesticity" contribute to the ideal of femininity (pp. 82–83). In the previous chapter, I explored how the bridal image creates an *über*-femininity through the costuming and disciplining of the female body. Here, I look at how reality television wedding programs provide repeated images of female domesticity that reaffirm wedding work as women's work. This unpaid work by brides is made to look desirable; the taking on of wedding chores in addition to paid work and the work required to create the bridal image reflects just how much time and effort women depicted in bridal media put into the creation of their perfect day.

The wedding serves as a microcosm in which its participants either follow traditional gendered divisions of labor, or in some rare cases, create their own. As "the bride's day," the wedding requires consumption of material goods, an activity typed as feminine (Boden 2003; Lowrey & Otnes, 1994). The work involved in the planning and execution of weddings, when they follow the format requiring a formal ceremony and reception, has been ignored because, according to Sniezek (2005), the male-dominated field of sociology has overlooked these activities. The seemingly mundane tasks required to create a wedding—choosing clothing, deciding on food and decorations, and shopping—relegated the study of such work to the domestic realm, unworthy of serious examination.

However, several studies have used the wedding as a venue to analyze gender roles and their performance. Published research on wedding work includes mostly small, interview-based studies involving pre-wedded couples. For example, in their research on weddings, Lowrey and Otnes (1994) found gender differences concerning the way their sample of 19 brides and four grooms from the Midwestern U.S. perceived certain wedding-related artifacts. Grooms saw the reception and the feeling of communion it conveyed as a highly important aspect, while brides considered the wedding dress as highly important.[1] These findings infer that for men, weddings signify a time to get together with family and friends, while women see weddings as a means to realize the feminine glamour associated with the wedding gown.

Reflective of the notion of perfection surrounding the wedding as discussed in the previous chapter, Currie (1993) conducted an exploratory study of 13 brides and three grooms in Canada who had traditional-style white weddings and found that a desire to have things picture perfect determined the amount of expense and work they had anticipated. Consequently, the brides and grooms in her study reported spending more money than they considered reasonable, with some even saying their weddings turned out to be a waste of money.

"As a ritual symbol," wrote Currie (1993), "the wedding signifies commitment and shared love" (p. 415). This shared love did not necessarily carry over to shared wedding chores. Currie found, not surprisingly, that brides did far more work in wedding planning than did grooms: "Because respondents expected—or even claimed—to have egalitarian domestic relations, it is perhaps ironic that the couple's first public act already begins to establish a traditional, unequal pattern of domestic labour" (p. 419). Thus, the work involved in planning the picture-perfect wedding appears to set the stage for the subsequent division of household labor in the marriage.

Sniezek (2005) also looked at the gendered labor divisions regarding "wedding work" by approaching such work as a form of unpaid labor performed by women. She interviewed 20 couples from southern California to uncover divisions of labor involved in planning their weddings. The average age of the participants was 26; all worked either full- or part-time, and more than half of them were cohabiting at the time. While participants reported and persisted in their belief that wedding planning is a joint effort, Sniezek found that the women devoted a disproportionate amount of time to wedding work when compared to their male partners. Sniezek noted that wedding planning prepares women for subsequent family work, known as "kin work"; kin work refers to the development of and maintenance required for family-related ritual celebrations, wherein women usually are the ones who communicate and coordinate family gatherings. As a family-centered event, then, weddings become one of the major events involving female-based kin work.

One may see kin work as yet another responsibility borne by women, one that excuses men from such tasks because of their assigned role as financial provider. But Sniezek (2005) concluded that it actually might benefit women. First, the women in her study did not view the work they did in planning their weddings as unfair; indeed, they saw taking responsibility for wedding details as a means of keeping their relationships harmonious. Second, the planning of the wedding serves as a way for a bride to "construct her identity and for family to celebrate and cement the good relationships with in-laws" (p. 215). Third, traditional wedding gender roles might positively affect women by providing them with status and power they do not ordinarily have. Thus, the bride, "by managing and completing wedding work, gains control over it and a degree of status and attention from it" (p. 230).

The status either earned or bestowed on women by the wedding and its corresponding requirement of time, energy, and emotional investment may indeed allow them to enjoy some modicum of attention. However, this status is temporary. Once the wedding day is over, the bride—who is now a wife—is relegated back to a world in which she takes a subordinate position in the realms of business, politics, education, science, and, if traditional gender roles prevail, in her own newly created marriage. One can make the argument that weddings are harmless, and do not really affect the progress of women who already have careers that challenge a gendered history within male-dominated fields. However, I find this argument less than compelling, in that wedding work is still unpaid and unequal. Because kin work still falls to women, men continue to enjoy their privileged place and are allowed to concentrate on economic gain while women still must find the time and energy to maintain family and other social ties. This becomes even more significant when women *voluntarily* take on the planning of their weddings—and in some cases find it easier to do it alone rather than to involve their male partners.

Wedding work has received national media attention in recent years. In a 2006 *Newsweek* article, "Weddings: A Veil of Sadness," Balz told readers about the postwedding letdown experienced by some brides, as evidenced by visitor contributions to message boards on the *Nest.com* web site, part of The Knot media company. As Balz described it, the letdown "usually comes when out-of-control bridezillas wrap themselves up with planning for the big day—and don't plan for the day after" (p. 13). The editor in chief of *Nest.com* (and also of *TheKnot.com*) called the phenomenon "post wedding blues," the letdown of everyday life following a wedding. Balz also cited a psychologist who reported that postwedding blues tended to come up during couples' counseling six to 12 months after a couple's wedding: "Getting married is a party. Being married isn't so glamorous. You don't get to be a star all the time" (p.

13).[2] "Weddings: A Veil of Sadness" highlighted what bridal media tend to ignore: that the wedding serves only as a celebration of the marriage to come, with the focus on the subsequent relationship seen as secondary to the fancy party and change of habitus promised by the white wedding ideal.

While weddings have been the domain of women and women's interest, the contribution of grooms has received some positive press. Trends that showed increased groom involvement served as the subject of a 2006 article in *USA Today*. "Grooms Are Getting More Engaged in Wedding Planning" listed three signs of "guy power" that evidenced a degree of involvement by men in the planning of their own weddings. The article cited as evidence for men's participation in wedding work several then-recent books for grooms and the popularity of guy-friendly party favors such as hand-rolled cigars and customized wedding day ties (dellaCava, 2006). The article also cited a 2005 survey in *Bridal Guide* magazine that reported 38% of couples said that they were planning their wedding together. The reporter also noted that grooms' interest tended to relate mainly to reception details and gift registries. This interest by grooms in reception planning reflected Lowrey and Otnes's (1994) findings that men are more interested in the party aspects of the wedding, especially details regarding the celebratory side of the reception.

Clearly, research on wedding work and news reports on wedding trends illustrate gendered divisions of labor and differences in how men and women see their own weddings in terms of what is or isn't important to them. In this chapter, I examine reality television portrayals of the bride as actor, and the agency she gains as the director/producer of the wedding production process. This female agency stands in contrast to the past chapter's examination of the bride as object. Using the same content of reality television programs that document wedding preparation, namely, FitTV's *Buff Brides*, TLC's *A Wedding Story* and *Say Yes to the Dress*, Oxygen's *Real Weddings From The Knot*, and WE tv's *Bridezillas*, I look at how these programs portray women and men as actually "doing" things prior to and on their wedding day. Just as these programs show viewers how brides prepare the packaging that surrounds them in order to create the perfect bridal persona, they also provide a glimpse of how wedding work is done.

What gender roles are portrayed in these programs? More importantly, in addition to their identities as brides, how are the women featured in these programs presented to viewers? Can these forms of bridal media provide alternate identities of the women who are shown planning their weddings? These questions bring to the fore the notion that these programs, because they find their inspiration in "real life," have the potential to present viewers with different images of women—especially women who represent feminist values in some way through their identities beyond that of bride.

My investigation into this aspect of the backstage region starts with a look at the way these reality bridal media identify the women taking on the bridal role. I then delve into the actual wedding work done by these women, and sometimes by the men, such as the various tasks they must complete in order to create the perfect wedding. The taking on of the additional role of manager of her special day requires the woman who seeks to create her perfect wedding to take on additional work. I examine how wedding work becomes normalized in reality television wedding programs, and then look at the exceptions to the bridal rules and roles related to kin work, particularly those instances where men break away from traditionally "masculine" gendered labor and venture into "feminine" work associated with weddings and domesticity.

Identities Beyond the Bride

Of the reality television wedding programs I examine in this chapter, I explore the way women are identified in three of them, based on their consistent inclusion of information (however scant) in the episodes themselves so as to allow for a feasible discussion of nonbridal identities: FitTV's *Buff Brides*, WE tv's *Bridezillas*, and TLC's *Say Yes to the Dress*.[3] Demographic information about the "real" brides featured in these reality television wedding programs usually appears at the start of each show; some type of graphic or short descriptors in the voice-over narration give viewers an idea of the identity of the women they will be following in the wedding preparation story line. These descriptors often include women's names, but any other demographic information such as race and ethnicity must be derived from their physical appearance. Regarding their educational levels, the programs discussed here generally do not include this type of information. I find most telling the lack of any mention of income or finances of these women; their power as wage earners is ignored totally.

In FitTV's *Buff Brides*, ages are not mentioned in the episodes, but brides appear to be in their early 20s to early 30s.[4] The program reflects a degree of racial diversity even within a convenience sample of five episodes featuring 10 brides: five were Caucasian; two were African American (with one of these brides of Haitian descent); two were Chinese American, and one was Indian. Brides' and grooms' occupations are announced in the female narrator's voice-over at the beginning of each episode. While husbands-to-be are not the subject of the program, their occupations are given nevertheless. Brides came mostly from business-related or professional fields; one could surmise based on the brief job descriptions that they held desk jobs. Occupational descriptions ranged from specific titles (such as for Nadege, an executive assistant, and Margaret, a promotions manager for *Town and Country* magazine) to general (for example, Jessica "works in banking in New York," and Justine "works for a nonprofit that helps low-income women enter the workforce"). While some information is given about what these brides do for work, no information is given about education levels of the brides except for some hints. For example, Justine met her fiancé Tom in journalism grad school, though whether or not she holds an advanced degree is not clear.

Based on my reading of *Buff Brides*, the dismissive attitude of the program toward these brides' careers and status in the working world reflects an overall perspective that also trivializes feminism. The portrayal of brides as the epitome of femininity, which this program frames in terms of creating the perfect bridal body, comes to the fore when one takes a critical look at the way in which this program paints the non-bridal identity of these women. For example, bride Tiffany is described simply as a "medical resident in pathology" rather than as holding a medical degree. Her achievement is further downplayed when the female narrator says Tiffany's residency in pathology is "not what most people think of as a glamorous, high-profile branch of medicine." The lack of mention of Tiffany's high educational level becomes more noticeable when juxtaposed with her fiancé's occupation: he "has law school plans." The discounting of Tiffany's achievement as a medical school graduate underscores that her more significant achievement is having been asked to marry a man. The trivialization of Tiffany's career becomes even more apparent when she can finally enjoy an ice cream sundae after having achieved her weight loss goal at the end of the episode. What one might consider a child's treat—an ice cream sundae—serves as the reward for Tiffany's hard work; the image implies that rather than a medical doctor, Tiffany is a child who is "allowed" to enjoy a special reward for completing a chore. I view this portrayal as not only associating women with juvenility, but as thoroughly ignoring Tiffany's real-world identity in favor of her role as bride.

In the first two seasons of WE tv's *Bridezillas*, brides' ages ranged from 19 to 43, with most brides in their 20s or early 30s.[5] Grooms' ages ranged from 20 to 49. Regarding the racial/ethnic composition of the couples, of the nine featured in Season 1, six were both White, one was both African American, and two were White and Asian/Asian American. In Season 2, of the nine couples, one couple was Asian American, three were both African American, and five were both White (with one of the five couples' weddings incorporating the bride's Latino heritage).

For the most part, occupations of both brides and grooms in *Bridezillas* are mentioned in the narrator's voice-over. These are worded in generic terms, such as "fashion publicist," "advertising executive/senior vice president," "beauty consultant," "interior design student," and "field events coordinator."

For example, high-powered ad executive Tricia's husband-to-be Jeff is only described as "freelance." Information lacking in the narrative appears on the *Bridezillas* web site, where one can find additional information regarding bride and groom occupations.

Updated by season, the *Bridezillas* web site provides more details about the bridezillas and their grooms.[6] From Season 1, visitors to the online "Bridezillas' Wedding Details" page found out that 43-year-old bride Julia, described in the program as a beauty consultant, also works as a drug counselor at New York's Albert Einstein College.[7] Season 2's "About the Brides" web page told visitors that 31-year-old Gretchen is actually a "sales associate" and that her groom, Norman, is a plumber, 20-year-old Jason is a Navy firefighter, Peter is a "rail engineer," and Erez owns a locksmith shop.[8] Educational levels of the bridezillas are not mentioned at all. This, coupled with only basic information about what these women and men do for a living, glosses over their other roles, bringing the focus to their temporary roles of "bride" and "groom."

TLC's *Say Yes to the Dress* centers primarily on the search for the "perfect" dress and frames this quest as work. Brides are introduced to viewers both by the voice-over narration and video footage; these are augmented by a full-screen graphic with the following information: full name, dress budget in dollars (often in the thousands), wedding date, and fiancé's full name. Missing from these descriptors are her age, occupation, and education. While one certainly could argue that these latter three items really have no bearing on her role as bride, the inclusion of these simple facts would take little screen space and narration time. Rarely were brides' job titles or occupations mentioned in the sample of episodes I viewed.[9] Of the 45 brides introduced on camera, only four were identified by their occupation: "singer," "teacher," "first grade teacher," and one who worked "for an IT company." Of the three brides whose ages were mentioned, all were in their twenties. Of these 45 brides, 42 were White, one was African American, one was Egyptian, and one was Indian.

In *Say Yes to the Dress*, fiancés' first and last names are included in these introductory graphics, even when they themselves do not appear during the footage taken at the salon. This implies that the men are important enough to include in this introductory material, even when they are not part of the wedding work. While only four of 45 brides' occupations were mentioned, the occupations of the fiancés of six brides were mentioned. And of those six brides whose fiancés' occupations were mentioned, only one also was identified by her own occupation: the bride was a teacher, her fiancé, a computer consultant.[10] In short, more of the men were identified by their occupations than were the brides—on this show about *women*.

Female identity in financial dependency

TLC's *Say Yes to the Dress* features dress budgets as part of bridal identity, and who is paying for those wedding gowns serves as another way to frame that identity. Dress budgets of the women in this sample of episodes ranged from $1,500 to "unlimited." If brides are paying for their own dresses, the narrative does not make it clear. Indeed, in the absence of knowing a bride's income or occupation, the viewer is left to assume that someone else, most likely the bride's family, is footing the bill for her dress—and her wedding as well.

I found especially notable that several of the brides with "unlimited" dress budgets had parents who clearly stated that they were buying their daughters' dresses. For example, bride Kim, who appears to be in her early thirties and identifies herself as a singer (in a rare case of career title accompanying a bride in this program), had just a month to plan her wedding.[11] Accompanying Kim is her mother, who acknowledges on camera that she would pay any price for her daughter's wedding dress: "There is no budget for Kim." Similarly, the dress budget for bride Melissa, who "works for an IT (information technology) company" but whose career title is not given, is unlimited; her upcoming wedding is described as "very formal" and Italian oriented.[12] Both Melissa's mother and grandmother accompany her to Kleinfeld's to find her wedding gown. Referring to the fact that there is no budget for Melissa's dress, her mother says on camera, "Whatever she wants, she will get." In another example, 25-year-old Diana, whose occupation is unknown, also had an unlimited dress budget. In a rare instance, this bride's fiancé and mother both accompany her on her dress-buying visit to the salon. When Diana tries on "the" dress, her mother cries, exclaiming, "My heart is beating so fast." The price of Diana's dress is never mentioned during this episode, but her mother does say that she "can't put a price on my daughter."[13]

I did find episodes of *Say Yes to the Dress* that did specify who was paying for what regarding the wedding expenses. In the case of bride Dana, the $10,000 budget for her wedding gown is covered by her parents, who are buying her dress as a gift since Dana and her fiancé are paying for their wedding. After trying on four dresses, Dana finally found the perfect dress; her mother says it is "breathtaking," and that Dana looks like "Scarlett O'Hara from *Gone with the Wind*."[14] In another episode, bride Katherine expresses her guilt over the amount of money her mother is spending on her wedding gown—$5,000—then goes on to say that she felt "grateful and ecstatic."[15]

Price tags of wedding essentials are highlighted in these programs, but the issue of who exactly is paying for these items or footing the bill for the entire event is spotty. Sometimes, such as in TLC's *Say Yes to the Dress*, parents actually say they are paying for their daughter's dress. However, the vagueness regarding the identifying information about these women results in an incomplete picture of the bride as a person independent of her relationship to her future husband or to her family, upon whom she might, to varying degrees, still depend to fund her dream day.

When brides are young and financially dependent on their parents, the vagueness of their identities becomes even more problematic. I found especially notable one particular episode of *Say Yes to the Dress* that highlighted the power of the bridal role to negate all other identities. This was combined with a palpable tone that put into stark relief the status of women in patriarchy. In the episode "Daddy Knows Best," father of the bride Tony played a feature role in the wedding dress quest of Guistina, his twenty-something daughter.[16] With no mention of her age, occupation, or education, viewers only see that she is young and dependent on her father. For Tony, the wedding of his only daughter, his "princess," required the best, including a $6,500 designer gown; indeed, he says on camera that the "best day of my life" was when Guistina tried on the gown a year earlier.

During this particular episode, Guistina is shown coming to the salon for a fitting. Unfortunately, Tony points out emphatically, the dress is not the same as the one they purchased; the fit and design are wrong. This results in several alterations in order to correct the errors, with the perfect dress finally achieved for Guistina's 400-guest wedding. The interest taken by Tony in his daughter's dress serves as an exception to the other rare appearances by fathers and fiancés, in that Tony actually physically handles the still-to-be-altered dress while Guistina is wearing it to show the sales consultant exactly how it should be corrected. The interest and insistence on Tony's part that his daughter's dress be perfect for her wedding illustrates Guistina's status within the family—she is Daddy's little girl, rather than a grown woman capable of making her own decisions. In addition, the implied expense of her wedding furthers her identity as a "princess."

Say Yes to the Dress tells viewers that in order to fulfill the image of perfect bride, a woman must look beautiful—in a beautiful gown that costs a good deal of money. The viewer gets no clear idea of these women's potential for purchasing this high-ticket article of clothing. Only vague descriptions of these brides' occupations are provided, if at all, which furthers the murkiness surrounding who pays for what. When a woman's parents say that they will pay whatever price to create their daughter's perfect bridal image, and she accepts their monetary support in order to follow this particular bridal rule, the connection between financial dependence and femininity becomes apparent. If one views feminism as a means by which women can achieve financial self-sufficiency and independence, the repeated scenarios in which parents buy a dress for their adult daughters resist such notions. The adherence to "tradition" undoubtedly comes into play here, in that "etiquette" dictates that a bride's family pays for the wedding.[17] Indeed, the guise of the wedding allows parents to buy their grown daughter something to wear—and her acceptance of such a gift may seem polite, even an act of gratitude. However, it also conveys the notion that she is still a child, relying on her mother and father to clothe her. This continued, acceptable dependency prevents a true break from such financial support.[18]

Whether or not brides have a college degree becomes something the viewer must surmise based on any additional information gleaned from brides' job titles. Certainly the argument could be forwarded that the age, occupation, and educational level of the brides shown on these programs are not essential to the narratives, since these programs are about their wedding day only and not about their lives in general. However, to not include or emphasize the identifying information about these "real life" women implies the insignificance of their status outside the world of the wedding. Several of the women included in these programs hold advanced degrees and have high-status and high-paying careers. These achievements are ignored, and, thus, nullified, when compared to their status as brides. These reality programs have the potential to show viewers that women can and do hold careers and have personal lives, as it takes only a few seconds to include such information in voice-over narration.

What results from these vague descriptions of brides is the message that what they do in "real life" takes secondary importance to their role as brides. The generic, temporary label of "bride" becomes their primary identity, leaving viewers to not care so much about these women's real (read: boring and everyday) lives. In other words, the status of celebrity for a day becomes pertinent and significant for the woman as opposed to the man. The amount of time, material goods, expense, and stress expected and required for a woman to take on the bridal role should, after all, mean something. Whatever else she is, has accomplished, or does is set aside: her *real* accomplishment and the thing she should be recognized for is that she is a bride.

Wedding Work as Women's Work

"Planning a wedding is still mostly women's work," announces the male narrator in Season 1 of *Bridezillas*.[19] The amount of time and effort required to plan the perfect wedding is framed as equaling a second job. Comments from the Manhattan brides in the initial season of the program all reiterate this idea. Says 27-year-old stock broker/bridezilla, Vanessa: "It's tough. It's really tough. Working full-time, going to school part-time at night and squeeze in the gym and wedding preparations." Michelle, the 26-year-old events manager and demanding bridezilla who already is familiar with the wedding industry, adds, "Nobody knows what to do so I have to do everything myself....It's like a full-time job." Miho, whose husband-to-be, Joe, has been planning their wedding while she has been in Japan for the previous four months, says, "I'm lucky 'cause I don't work. It's like another job or a job." Miho's comment becomes even more significant, given that she had not done any wedding work for several months and yet still sees wedding planning as a "regular" job even after Joe has handled things for them both.

In *Bridezillas*, wedding work is taken very seriously, and does not equate to enjoyment at all. Says the highly demanding Jada from Season 2, "I'm not able to have fun with it right now. It's work. It's not fun." She adds, "This has been a lot more work than I ever imagined." The nature of wedding planning emphasizes attention to detail, in that the perfect wedding requires the bride to take care of everything, as noted by fellow Season 2 bride Antonella, who claims her hair is falling out due to the stress: "I knew there was a lot of work but not all these detail things. . . . The things that, like, nobody gives a sh— about, nobody pays two cents to. And these are like the most important things." Time becomes a factor, even for those brides who have hired wedding planners, like Korliss, who repeatedly states on camera how hectic her life has become: "I have so many things to do and not enough time." Taken together, these comments reaffirm not only the importance of the wedding to the bridezilla, but their accompanying stress levels indicate just how serious these women take their wedding planning responsibilities.

In FitTV's *Buff Brides* the women take on additional "shifts" in addition to their regular jobs and their personal lives. The first shift involves their job, another shift is devoted to working out and going to the gym, and a third shift is spent planning their weddings. The notion of increased labor and work is mentioned at the start of every *Buff Brides* episode by the narrator, who reminds viewers that not only are these brides trying to get buff, they also have big weddings to plan and "a million" or "a thousand" details to take care of. The narrator describes wedding plans as "chores," and brides must fit this aspect into their already hectic lives. Images of these women scurrying from place to place on the busy streets of New York add to the impression that their lives are in constant motion.

Stress becomes another enemy in *Buff Brides*, as the women express their frustration with not only trying to lose weight, but also having to deal with (self-imposed) wedding chores—often by themselves. The program does show a few brides doing wedding-related things with their fiancés, such as shopping, going to food tastings, or even working out together. However, these depictions of couples are so few as to create the impression that the planning of their special day is really a one-woman operation. For example, brides Nadege and Greta complain that their fiancés don't understand the amount of time and worry it takes to handle the tiniest wedding and reception details. "I think brides are put under pressure that grooms would never, ever, ever get it. Grooms just couldn't pull it off," says Greta. "I don't think anyone else understands how tough it is to plan a wedding and do anything else," vents Nadege.

The added stress taken on by these brides becomes even more normalized by the voice-over narration of *Buff Brides*. Viewers learn that planning a wedding, trying to lose weight, and holding a steady job requires a monumental amount of time and effort. In the case of buff bride Jessica, voice-over narration from both the narrator and Jessica herself enhances the video footage of her riding the subway, weary from a long day. Prior to the footage of her on the train, the camera followed her as she left the gym and walked to the subway. The narrator tells viewers that Jessica's days "have gotten longer and longer: an early morning commute into the city, a full day at the office juggling numbers for a financial services company, then, finally, her strenuous workouts." Jessica's voice then is heard over the footage of herself on the train: "After a long day, I'm exhausted. It's hard to do anything but work, work out, eat, sleep. And then every day the cycle starts all over again." Comments such as these remind viewers that to become a buff bride, women have a dedication above and beyond what one would expect from the "normal" bride, who simply must deal with the extra time and frustration associated with wedding planning. In this manner, *Buff Brides* makes the stress associated with wedding planning depicted in other reality wedding programs seem a matter of course, even minimal.

Throughout *Buff Brides*, voice-over statements like these reiterate to viewers the difficulty of wedding work: "Like many brides, Margaret is busy and exhausted most of the time, so it's hard to find the time and enthusiasm for exercise"; "Most brides find outside activities to alleviate stress"; and "It's all work and no play—a relentless schedule that can trigger frustration and bridal burnout."[20] *Buff Brides*, by adding the additional element of weight loss, overtly and clearly instructs the potential buff brides watching at home about the daunting work they'll have waiting for them every day once they finish their paying jobs. In addition to the brides themselves expressing frustration as they try to meet their wedding deadlines, this program makes clear that weddings are *work*, and women who want to fulfill the ideal of femininity by losing weight need to do a lot more work than other brides.

At the same time, one can consider *Buff Brides* as incorporating feminist ideals by way of including at least some mention of these women's occupations—some are executives and managers—and portraying these women as being able to manage several roles at once. Just as the supermom image idealized in magazine advertising cultivates the notion that women can do it all— have a career and a family, and perform both roles successfully—the repeated images of busy women in *Buff Brides* promotes a similar ideal.[21] The amalgam of examples from *Bridezillas* and *Buff Brides* illustrates the expectation that wedding planning not only stays within the purview of the female world, but also that brides must devote all their free time prior to their weddings to planning them. Grooms, on the other hand, need not be bothered with, think about, or worry over details concerning their upcoming weddings; they can carry on with their day-to-day routines as their future wives take care of the wedding details.

So natural has wedding planning become a "woman's thing" that The Knot's web site even posted an article on tips for women to work on their weddings at their *place* of work. "Wedding Planning: How to Plan Your Wedding at Work (Without Getting Fired)" (Wood, 2009) encouraged (indeed instructed) brides to use every available minute at work to complete wedding tasks.[22] Some tips on planning one's wedding on the job included: using the Internet as much as possible to research vendors, and making sure to know your employer's policy on computer use at work. Familiarity with company policy on the monitoring of computer use becomes an especially important factor when doing wedding work *at* work: "If it seems like Big Brother is watching, you may need to scale back your at-work wedding planning—but don't worry, you'll still find a way to get it all done," the article's author reassured the reader. A woman can do her wedding chores at work if she follows the three tips for "not getting caught":

1. "Stay on Task."

2. "Go Online" rather than "bring [a] wedding binder to work."

3. "Watch Your Back" by making sure to "close or minimize" wedding web sites "if you have to step away from your desk."

As if to close the lid on any possibility that a bride can actually enjoy her time away from work, "Wedding Planning: How to Plan Your Wedding at Work (Without Getting Fired)" also instructed the bride on "ways to max out your free time" by: making use of commuting time, including using one's cell phone *while driving* "to record any sudden bursts of inspiration," using the lunch hour to call vendors, and reading wedding materials during exercise and while "waiting for the oven to preheat or . . . while your fiancé" cooks for you. This last tip assumes an egalitarian-style relationship of cohabiting couples, but contradicts it at the same time: a man can cook for his woman, but she must deal with their upcoming wedding on her own.

The Superbride

According to the bridal rules, brides must always maintain control of their wedding (Corrado, 2002). As the "producer" of this major event, the bride directs all the action and ensures the high quality of all aspects of the wedding ceremony and reception. Boden's (2003) concept of the "superbride" described the type-A woman who approaches her wedding as if it were a monumental event. While brides certainly take charge of their wedding day by making decisions about the most detailed aspects of the apparel, ceremony, and reception, some take this responsibility to the extreme. The notion of femininity becomes subsumed by the domineering bride, and this in turn can create a negative portrayal of all brides. Yet somehow this aspect of bridal behavior is overlooked and at times, even exalted. In this way, Boden's superbride identity allows for the incorporation of behaviors associated with masculinity (and, taken to its logical conclusion, leadership) into the feminine identity of the bride.

I found several examples of the superbride in Oxygen's *Real Weddings From The Knot*.[23] While this particular reality series views wedding planning as mainly about shopping and the attainment of material goods, a few of the brides in the episodes I analyze here serve as exemplars of the superbride; these brides wield a certain power over their wedding planning, but do not delve too far into bridezilla territory. As they decide every detail of what is supposed to be their "special day," superbrides on *Real Weddings From The Knot* frantically make arrangements, run errands, and ensure everything from wedding rings to bouquets are accounted for, all the while commenting to the viewer that they don't mind being frazzled because it is worth it.

Superbrides in *Real Weddings From The Knot* direct ceremony rehearsals, tell people what to do and how to act, and oversee catering, decorating, and their own and others' apparel, even when they hire wedding coordinators. While their grooms do participate at times, such as making party favors or going to food tastings to choose their reception menus, final decisions are nearly always made by the brides alone. Aside from these "normal" duties, several brides on this program also took on additional responsibilities to ensure the smooth execution of their wedding day; such skills were added to their repertoire of typical bridal duties. For example, bride Catina choreographs the dance numbers for her elaborate, big church wedding, and bride Katie, the model/dental assistant, orders her bridesmaid sisters to "stand up straight" just as they are to walk into the ceremony. Katie's stage managing deftly defines the superbride: she is both the star of the show and its director/producer.

I found an especially illustrative example of the extreme superbride in the *Real Weddings From The Knot* episode "Amy and Mark," featuring the controlling Amy. In this episode, I see a form of the bridezilla play out even though the term "bridezilla" is never used. Superbride Amy's constant bossiness, penchant for tirades, and verbal abuse of her parents, which includes constant profanity and directives for them to "shut up," may seem over-the-top, but somehow these antics are portrayed in such a manner as to make them "okay." Indeed, her parents seem to take Amy's behavior in stride; they never react in kind, leaving the impression that they have become used to Amy's domineering personality.

Amy oversees every minute aspect of her wedding at a mansion in the New York countryside, including the coordination and assemblage of gift baskets for guests, which includes gluing artificial flowers to guests' flip-flops. Her mother comments, "She's a girl with a mind of her own, she knows what she wants." Her future husband Mark even acknowledges her controlling nature when he explains to the viewer that "Amy wears the pants. She's the boss of the family." Indeed, Mark mainly stays out of Amy's way; he goes off-road motor biking just hours before the wedding.

On the wedding day, Amy becomes upset to find her bouquet is the wrong color, and her parents nag her about being late to the ceremony as she calmly smokes a cigarette. Ironically, this "superbride" is 45 minutes late to her own wedding. However, Amy's controlling nature apparently doesn't bother Mark, as he tells her in front of the wedding audience, "You are my sunshine, my angel." Amy's seemingly stressful wedding preparations all work out in the end, as she says in her voice-over conclusion: "In the future, I'll forget all the worry and stress that went into planning this wedding."

While one might expect the visible effects of stress on superbrides to create an undesirable image of their experiences, the serious, video vérité treatment that *Real Weddings From The Knot* gives these brides seems to negate any ill effects. For example, even as superbride Amy treats those around her poorly and arrives late to her wedding ceremony, images of her tearfully reciting her vows to Mark while dressed in bridal splendor erase the previous images of her bad behavior. In that each episode of *Real Weddings From The Knot* concludes with a successful wedding despite numerous snafus and near disasters, viewers repeatedly get the message that all's well that ends well.

Even as Amy serves as the extreme superbride, all the brides in the episodes that I examined illustrate superbride behavior in one form or another. In contrast, the grooms generally serve either as companions or assistants to their future wives. For example, Bill accompanies his bride Amy (a different Amy) to a meeting with their cake designer, John and Danielle visit their florist, and Kaijsa and Ryan go food tasting together. Or grooms stay out of the planning altogether, as in the case of Lori and Mark. Lori does all the planning for her and Mark's destination wedding. "It doesn't bother me that I'm doing most of the planning by myself because Mark does all the work when we're at home all week long," Lori explains.[24] Her remarks imply an uneven division of labor that helps her justify why she has done all the planning for their wedding.

Just as stress and worry characterize the "superbride," potential disasters and real disasters mark the weddings themselves in *Real Weddings From The Knot* before or on the wedding day. These range from rather big problems, such as inclement weather and fear of parental fights, to smaller ones that might ruin the bride's perfect day. Almost as if to warn viewers to avoid outdoor weddings, bad weather serves as the villain of several episodes, and clashing personalities and divorced parents serve as possible derailments for several weddings. However, in the end, these problems all work out, somehow, and fail to mar the beautiful wedding that concludes each episode. Commentaries by the brides on how well things went and how it was all worth it in the end reaffirm the appeal of the wedding as a worthwhile endeavor.

The Bridezilla Persona and Requisites of Role Performance

Beyond the superbride, the bridezilla takes the image and persona of the controlling bride to the extreme. As first described in Chapter 4, the program *Bridezillas* features the bride-Godzilla "monster" as she battles her way through incompetent vendors, uninterested grooms, and any other obstacles that threaten her vision of the idealized, perfect wedding. Viewers learn what constitutes the bridezilla through voice-over narration and on-camera comments by brides, grooms, and other participants in the series. In Season 1's introductory episode, the male narrator defines this new bridal image: "A bridezilla is a bride who mutates from being a normal human being to being an obsessive control freak when it comes to planning her perfect day. . . . A bridezilla believes a wedding is her day."

In Season 2 of *Bridezillas*, the female narrator's inflection is noticeably more varied and emphatic than the flat delivery of Season 1's male narrator. Season 2's bridezillas are introduced separately, with emphasis placed on the enunciation of "bridezilla," almost as if to warn the viewer of the impending doom awaiting those who cross their paths. For example, 31-year-old Gretchen, a self-described "aggressive person," is introduced as "Gretchen: Control freak. Worry wart. Self-confessed—Bridezilla!" The teenaged Adrianna, a "piano teacher" who lives with her parents, is described as "Adrianna: Loving fiancée. Hopeless romantic. Potential—Bridezilla!" Twenty-nine-year-old Magdalena is described as a former "high-powered talent agent" who has become "a high-maintenance, high-handed, high-decibel—

Bridezilla!" The emphasis in the enunciation of "Bridezilla!" in the narration becomes a vocalic means to overstate the power the term supposedly implies.[25]

The narrative in the first two seasons of *Bridezillas* established two elemental qualities of the bridezilla in addition to the visual characterization of the "princess" and "perfect" bride, as described in Chapter 4. Beyond the physical attributes of beauty and loveliness, the bridezilla strives for and insists on perfection and high standards concerning every detail of her wedding. This, coupled with the visual image of perfection, further emphasizes the importance of the wedding day as "hers" and hers only; any obstacles that stand in the way of this goal must be eliminated by whatever means possible.

In Chapter 4, I described how the bridal persona relies on perfection. The repetitive use of the word "perfect" in the *Bridezilla* episodes I viewed underscores to viewers that the bridezilla will settle for nothing less when it comes to her special day. For example, in Season 1, the voice-over narration tells viewers, "Preparations for the perfect look start months in advance," as 29-year-old publicist Karen has her hair done in an updo during a hairstylist "audition." Unhappy with the result, Karen then goes to another stylist before making a decision about her wedding day hairstyle. Other comments in the narration reflecting the "perfect" aspect of weddings include: "Just how far will a New York bride go to get her perfect day?" and, referring to Cynthia, Karen, and Julia, three of the Manhattan brides, "These three brides have made a huge investment in making their big day perfect." In Season 2, Antonella, the hairstylist with the big Italian wedding, says on camera: "My wedding day will be perfect. I will make sure that it is perfect. Whatever isn't perfect, I will make sure somebody makes it perfect."

The need for perfection serves as the bridezilla's raison d'être; her every move is powered by the need to create the perfect wedding, and allows the "monster" within her to come out, as the narrator in Season 2 says of 31-year-old publicist Jada: "Making her wedding day perfect has made Jada more of a tyrant than ever." Jada's story line features her almost-militant approach to ensuring her six bridesmaids all look alike; not only do they all wear the same dresses, but they also have the same hairstyle, same makeup, and same fingernail polish. Indeed, in one scene, Jada has them line up and inspects them as if readying them for a military procession.

Not only does the bridezilla demand perfection on *her* day, but she sees her wedding day as something that is owed her. This sense of entitlement in turn allows for her bad behavior. In *Bridezillas*, this additional element manifested itself in Season 2, with the use of the word *bitch* repeatedly uttered by bridezillas to describe women who did not conform to their demands for perfection or who irritated them in some way. The word *bitch* also is used by others in their descriptions of the bridezilla herself. As used in the narrative of

Season 2, the term *bitch* reflected a retooling of the program from simple documentary about upscale weddings of women in Manhattan to a more vivid and "realistic" treatment of the middle-class weddings across "real" America (represented by the locales of Chicago and Los Angeles).

Bridezillas' use of the word *bitch* in several episodes of Season 2 in self-descriptions or when describing other women addresses the underlying—and perhaps truer—nature of the bridezilla as the demanding, aggressive female. Examples of the close association between bridezilla and bitch from Season 2 include groom John referring to his wife-to-be Thuy as a "bridezilla, a total bee-atch (bitch)," and a description of Adrianna by her own mother: "She *is* a bridezilla. She can be a bitch sometimes, let me tell you." Foul-mouthed Antonella (whose many tirades include numerous bleeps to block out profanity) is called a bitch and calls other women "bitch." Season 2's Magdalena refers to a manicurist who didn't do a good enough job as "I was, like, bee-atch (bitch)." In turn, Magdalena's best friend jokingly says that others might see Magdalena herself as "that bridezilla bitch!"

The use of the word *bitch* adds to the bridezilla's aura of power and respect—knowing that others fear her thus fortifies the image of a competent woman. In this sense, the program's inclusion of such scenes might steer the bridezilla image away from the femininity associated with the bride, and support a seemingly feminist-based reimaging of the bride as assertive and strong. Unfortunately, when used against other women, the use of the word *bitch* becomes a means by which women allow themselves to treat other women badly. Thus, what appears as a way for women to become empowered by the role of the bridezilla ultimately also becomes a way for women themselves to normalize misogyny.[26] It also fosters the drama associated with conflict, which serves as a motif for the reality television genre in general.

In *Bridezillas*, battles over wedding details are given ample screen time as the brides deal with last-minute snafus and complain about incompetent wedding planners and vendors. Because the bridezilla demands perfection, she gets more and more out of control as her wedding approaches. Other reality wedding programs, such as Oxygen's *Real Weddings From The Knot*, tell viewers that the planning of weddings involves unexpected problems and that snafus are inevitable. *Bridezillas* feeds on the anxiety and angst faced by these already stressed-out women as they deal with seemingly life-and-death problems that crop up as they desperately work toward perfection. The sheer difficulty of planning a wedding that meets the bridezilla's exceedingly high standards becomes even more emphasized when described in the narrative. For example, in the voice-over narration about bridezilla Jada in Season 2, viewers are told, "Planning this event has been the most hellish experience of her life."

Brides' reactions to wedding-related problems range from simple complaints to all-out tirades, complete with hysterical crying or profanity. Complaints made directly into the camera include those by Korliss, a 31-year-old real estate investor, who says she's unhappy with her wedding planner's unavailability, and 22-year-old Patricia, who claims her wedding planning is a "total joke" and that she wants to fire her wedding planner (she never does). Other times, wedding planners shoulder the panic of unexpected problems. When the flowers for Joe and Miho's Tavern on the Green wedding arrive just two minutes before the start of the ceremony, wedding planner Lynn begins to think of ways to improvise, and nearly cries with relief when the florist finally arrives. Other minor wedding day problems take on monumental proportions when depicted onscreen. For example, Season 2 bridezilla Korliss becomes irate when she finds out she'll have no recorded music for her bridal entrance at her ceremony because the venue won't accommodate a CD player. She also expresses unhappiness with her bouquet because it did not match her florist's description.

Complaints just minutes before or after the wedding ceremony mark these episodes, illustrating just how demanding the bridezilla can be. In Season 2 for example, bridezilla Noelle rejects her wedding bouquet because the red roses are not the right shade even though she is an hour and a half late for her big church wedding (she carries them anyway). Noelle is further miffed because her tardiness has caused the monsignor officiating her wedding to trim parts of the ceremony in order to accommodate the next scheduled wedding. Noelle then keeps complaining about it on camera at her reception. The finicky Karen from Season 1 meticulously planned her $90,000 Manhattan wedding, and then makes a scene by complaining to the catering manager during her wedding reception at the upscale W Hotel. Karen expresses her dissatisfaction and unhappiness because the cocktail hour actually turns out to be only 20 minutes long—even though this is stipulated in the catering contract. These two examples demonstrate that problems occur even as these brides are supposed to enjoy "their" day: the bridezilla's need for perfection leads her to continue to find something to complain about, even during her wedding reception.

The backstage access viewers get from *Bridezillas* allows them to witness bridezillas' emotional meltdowns with vendors and others. In Season 2, tantrums and tirades become a regular part of the bridezilla experience. For example, Jada berates her interior designer by telling him to "man up" to his errors after she sees the still-unfinished decorations of her New Orleans-style reception. Just one hour before her big church wedding, Antonella uses profanity when calling the bridal salon to complain about a tiny tear in her dress, declaring, "You guys f—n' suck!"

The video vérité treatments of the minutes prior to the weddings of 19-year-old Adrianna and 22-year-old Patricia allow viewers to see the hysterics that can accompany stressed-out younger brides as they try to cope with the pressure of getting married and ensuring all the wedding details are attended to. For example, teenage bridezilla Adrianna suddenly has cold feet just as she is about to marry, crying, "I'm nervous, I'm scared!" (her father calms her down and she makes it through her wedding). Patricia has crying jags on her wedding day, first when she discovers she does not have the marriage license (blaming the snafu on her wedding planner, but then smiling with relief and chagrin when she discovers she had it all the while) and then again right before the ceremony, crying because she's afraid "something will go wrong!" (her mother and wedding planner manage to calm her down).

Even as some bridezillas appear to "lose it" just as their weddings are about to commence, others offer a more controlled image of the frazzled bride/manager. For example, just hours before her wedding, bride Gretchen gets involved in a confrontation with her mother's rental car company, and calls the police. She then calmly talks to a police officer as she steam presses her wedding gown.

In *Bridezillas*, conflict between bridezillas and their future husbands become commonplace as well; scenes of couples bickering and fighting prior to these "perfect" weddings betray the romance-imbued elegance presented during the "front" of the wedding play. These scenes further normalize the work and frustration that supposedly accompany wedding planning. In Season 1, viewers witness several on-camera squabbles concerning wedding costs, especially when those costs were to be shared by the couple. For example, Karen and Emmett bicker over the cost for the hotel room Karen "needs" in order to prepare for their wedding. Emmett sees it as a waste of money, since they already live together. In another example of unhidden premarital conflict, "princess" bride Julia goes wedding ring shopping with future husband Allen. During their visit to a jewelry store, we watch him become visibly miffed as Julia insists that they purchase more-than-budgeted-for platinum rings; indeed, he practically fumes as he takes out his wallet to pay for them.

In Season 2 of *Bridezillas*, viewers see conflicts connected to the wedding that also hint at other conflicts within the relationships. Some of the arguments have to do with actual wedding details, such as when Jada and Julius argue about the increasing size of their wedding party; Jada perceives an imbalance of groomsmen and bridesmaids, which she says will ruin the wedding photos. Also in Season 2, stress by osmosis becomes a complaint of groom John when he talks about his upcoming wedding to Thuy. "I'm tired," he admits to a wedding shower guest. "All the stress that Thuy goes through, she just unloads it on me," he says. Thuy and John also bicker as they pack their belongings on moving day; Thuy complains that John has too much junk.

Grooms' faults become the subject of other arguments between couples; errors in judgment on the part of the men result in the bridezillas' anger. It seems the men are always doing *something* wrong in the eyes of these demanding women. Examples of confrontations that address grooms' wrongdoing include Magdelena's "huge fight" with her husband-to-be, Justin, over his lying about going to a strip club. Bride Antonella gets angry with Michael after he skips going to a florist's appointment with her and instead has dinner with his buddies—at Hooters, no less.

The conflict theme becomes especially evident in the Noelle and Dan storyline in Season 2, as the narrator tells viewers, "Lately the couple has been fighting nonstop." Indeed, during an interview about how they met, Dan actually walks out of the room when Noelle says that she didn't think much of him when they first met. The inclusion of these arguments, especially those concerning *grooms'* wishes (such as Julius' insistence that he and Jada "jump the broom" during their ceremony) normalizes the idea that wives should expect constant disagreements with their husbands. In the end, each of these bickering couples finally do get their successful wedding, thus glossing over the obvious conflicts that indicate deeper problems. However, because most of the arguments between brides and grooms in *Bridezillas* revolve around wedding details, what results is the impression that once the wedding is over, the conflicts will end.

When viewers take the role of bystander and watch these women throw tantrums and generally misbehave, it allows them to take pleasure in seeing out-of-control women not get what they want. In this sense, the entertainment value of *Bridezillas* finds its origins in the enjoyment of seeing another suffer, known as schadenfreude.[27] Indeed, even as they pursue their perfect wedding, several of the bridezillas still cannot find satisfaction on their wedding day; indeed, the smallest problems become magnified by the bridezilla, who sees even the most minor problems as threats to her perfect wedding. Taken together, these scenes create a negative image of demanding brides and, by extension, ambitious, competent women. Images of bridezillas having to constantly field wedding-related problems contrast sharply with the overall absence of grooms. Indeed, the involved groom becomes an exception to the rule, further underlining the gendered nature of wedding work.

Where Are the Men?

Although bridal media in general target women and show women as being responsible for planning and overseeing the wedding, images of grooms involved with wedding work do appear on occasion in these reality television programs. As women's work, wedding dress shopping practically always disallows the presence of men. For example, of the 45 vignettes featuring brides by name in my sample of *Say Yes to the Dress* episodes, three brought their fiancés with them to Kleinfeld's. One of the grooms stated on camera that he felt that he shouldn't have been there; his bride thought he should because, as she explained on camera, "It's our wedding."[28] Four of the 45 brides also had their fathers accompany them along with their mothers and other family members. For the most part, men tend to remain absent from *Say Yes to the Dress*, and when they do appear, they clearly stand out as exceptions to the rule.

The creation of men's space within the wedding world warrants attention, even if their presence is rare, because these accounts of "real people's" weddings do, to some extent, reflect actual practices. I find especially important that even though they may constitute the exception to the wedding-as-women's-work rule as reflected in the general absence of men depicted in bridal magazines, the backstage view of grooms in these reality programs shows at a minimum that (a) men do care about their own weddings, and (b) examples of egalitarian attitudes regarding this form of domestic labor do exist. Overall, brides assume most of the wedding planning, details, and errand running. However, I found several couples featured in these reality television programs who shared wedding chores.

Indeed, some grooms actually took on the entire responsibility for planning their weddings, demonstrating reverse gender roles. One of the more notable examples of a groom actually making wedding reception decisions occurred in the 2003 *Real Weddings From The Knot* episode featuring millionaire John and his bride Danielle, a model. Viewers see them visiting their florist together, and discussing wedding and reception details on camera. John appears intricately involved with every aspect of their glamorous Newport, Rhode Island wedding, which involves two reception sites, one for cocktails at the Tennis Hall of Fame and another for the "real" reception at a mansion that John had chosen as a wedding site when he was a boy. That John reveals he had picked the mansion for his wedding venue during childhood serves as a counter to the numerous accounts of brides in these programs who relate the "princess" vision they had since they were little girls. John's interest in his and Danielle's wedding illustrates that men can and do, however rarely, contribute to the planning of their own weddings.

Despite John's egalitarian-like approach to the wedding preparations, he ultimately downplays his involvement. He makes it a point to explain to their guests at their rehearsal dinner that Danielle has made most of the wedding decisions, and he does so again at their wedding reception: "We've put—she's put—a lot of planning into this for the last two years," he says during his toast.[29] John's public acknowledgement that Danielle really has been the one in charge negates his work, "correcting" any appearance that a man has inter-jected himself into the female realm of the wedding. Thus, even as John and Danielle's story incorporates a level of equality regarding the wedding as an event created for and by the couple, the narrative reverts to the hegemonic, familiar notion that Danielle planned their big day. Overall, then, grooms may participate in various ways in the wedding planning, but the main credit for the event is still given to the brides.

In *Bridezillas*, women clearly and explicitly reinforce the gendered bound-ary of the wedding world several times on camera. In both seasons I analyzed, men remained largely absent from any purchasing or planning decisions. If they did participate, or offered their opinion, their input was dismissed and they were treated as incompetents. Indeed, several grooms during Season 1 state on camera how they would rather leave the wedding plans to their brides. This acquiescence to their future wives not only underlines the expectation that grooms stay out of wedding planning, but also further emphasizes the con-trolling nature of the bridezilla.

On the other hand, when brides verbalize their status by saying their weddings are for "*me*," rather than for "*us*," they deny the possibility for an egalitarian or team effort. For example, in Season 1, Tim (whose fiancée, Amy, was doing most of the work with the help of her mother and wedding plan-ner) says, "It's easier for her to get things done without my input . . . the less I get involved the better off I am." Similarly, Amy acknowledges that their wed-ding is not about them as a couple, but "for my mom and me," adding, "Tim has a very small role."

The implicit, commonsense "knowledge" that weddings belong to women becomes explicit and almost advantageous for the grooms involved in the pro-gram. By letting their brides do all the work, they then don't have to do much of anything. Season 1 groom Jeff, the "freelance" husband-to-be of 33-year-old Tricia, a Los Angeles advertising executive senior vice president who is foot-ing most of the bill for their high-end, trendy wedding, says, "She's got the whole thing planned out. Like with the ceremony, I couldn't give a sh—." The honesty with which Jeff expresses indifference to his wedding, or more accu-rately, Tricia's wedding, clarifies his role as a bystander who's happy to stay out of it altogether. The fact that Tricia alone is paying for the wedding implies her dominant role as financial provider in the relationship, as well as a rever-sal of traditional gender roles. In this instance, one could view a bride like Tricia who truly takes charge of her wedding in all regards as an indication of a fem-inist aspect of the bridezilla persona. How this role plays out in the subsequent marriage brings into question whether or not one can view the bridezilla per-sona as empowering, or as another way in which women willingly subject them-selves to an unequal power/labor division within romantic relationships.

In contrast, when gender role reversal in the opposite direction occurs, such as when "the man" takes on the majority of the wedding planning tasks, his masculinity comes into question. The Season 1 *Bridezillas* episode featuring groom Joe further distinguishes what is supposed to be women's wedding work and what men are *not* supposed to do. His future wife Miho is out of the country, so Joe must take on the wedding planning and attend to all the details. Lynn, their wedding planner, repeatedly refers to Joe as "the bride." Further, Joe's ideas are met with skepticism by the wedding industry professionals who are hired to help with his and Miho's wedding. This was evident when Joe and Miho finally met with Lynn and their reception deejay. Joe suggests that at their reception, he and Miho skip their first dance in favor of sitting down for the first course of the meal. He also wants to have a child ring a bell to signal that dinner is served. Lynn and the deejay respond to Joe's ideas for the reception at the legendary Tavern on the Green with incredulity and laughter. Later, the deejay comments into the camera about how ludicrous Joe's suggestions were, implying that Joe is an ignorant clod, unaware of the locale's classy reputation.

The reaction to Joe's suggestions portrays him and men in general as wedding ignoramuses. It illustrates another running theme throughout *Bridezillas* regarding the male-female role boundary: Even when men try to contribute, their ideas are shot down by the women, thereby implying men's obvious incompetence at creating the ideal wedding. I found another example of the uselessness of men in Season 1 during the story line of bride Cynthia. Cynthia's stepfather, Chuck, is paying for her $90,000 wedding. When Chuck says that he wants to have a New York Police Department singer perform at her wedding ceremony to add "local color," Cynthia finds the suggestion ludicrous, saying it would be like a memorial, not a wedding. Cynthia accepts her stepfather's money, but dismisses his opinions outright. Added to this rejection of her stepfather's suggestion is the voice-over narration during a scene in which Cynthia decides on the upholstery material for a custom-made chair to be used at her reception. As Cynthia and her entourage visit the furniture maker's gallery, her future husband nonverbally expresses his puzzlement over why the fabric for this chair/prop has been given so much importance: "Fiancé Matt isn't necessarily all that interested in the minutest details of his wedding," says the narrator. Close-ups of Matt's face show him bemused, with a half smirk. The combination of these images forwards the notion that weddings might be paid for by men and lead to marriage to a man, but the wedding itself is clearly all about the woman, who is also the only person capable of making the final decisions.

As noted by Howard (2006), bridal magazines have portrayed the groom as an obstacle that brides need to remove in order to create their weddings. I found support for this observation in *Bridezillas*. Indeed, several brides emphatically vocalize the uselessness of their grooms. For example, in Season 1, Karen makes no bones about how unhelpful she finds Emmett, her future husband. Apparently replying to an off-camera question regarding his where-abouts, Karen says, "What's my fiancé doing? Uh, aggravating me, com-plaining about how much money I'm spending." Replying to another question about what she sees as the hardest part of wedding planning, Karen answers with a laugh, "Dealing with the ignorance of the groom." Emmett, a banker, constantly comments on how much his and Karen's wedding is costing (the eventual price: $90,000, according to the narrator). Emmett wants just two things at their reception: a sushi station and a Guinness (ale) bar. Emmett's focus on the refreshments for his wedding reception reflects what Lowrey and Otnes (1994) found regarding grooms' concern that guests have a good time at their receptions. But Emmett's requests, like those of "bride" Joe, are treated with disdain.

When brides do ask their grooms to handle specific tasks, it usually means the grooms are to serve in a secondary capacity. In Oxygen's *Real Weddings From The Knot*, for example, several of the grooms are depicted as their brides' "assistants." For example, Ryan helps Kaijsa with seating assignments for their reception; Jeff goes shopping with Jessa at Wal-Mart; Gus runs errands based on Katie's "to-do" list to "help relieve some of Katie's stress."[30]

Even as some grooms try to be helpful, brides often become frustrated when their men fall short of completing even the simplest of tasks. For exam-ple, Sarah-Jane does all the planning for her and Nate's wedding; she constantly makes to-do lists every day and stresses out over the "68 things" she must do. Nate's major task is to learn how to dance for their reception. Sarah-Jane becomes upset when Nate still can't remember the dance steps after eight months of lessons. At their wedding rehearsal, Kaijsa asks Ryan to help her direct the intricate Jewish ceremony. After it becomes clear that nobody is lis-tening to her instructions, she finally throws her hands up in frustration. These backstage glimpses provide examples of grooms doing wedding work and helping their future wives with the big day. Even as some of these men do help, however enthusiastically, reluctantly, or incompetently, the self-created stress of the brides who work to meet the perfect-wedding ideal appears to negate whatever possible contributions their male "helpers" provide.

I see this treatment of grooms as incompetent wedding helpers as a man-ifestation of a "gender territoriality" wherein brides see the wedding as theirs, a way to protect what could be seen as one of the last areas of social life where women are in charge and where they display their competence in matters of the domestic. Similar to the cook who bans others from the kitchen, the bride becomes the expert who bans incompetent males from her wedding "workspace." The only male persons seen as having expertise are those who get paid to be wedding experts, such as wedding planners, caterers, florists, wedding gown designers, and salon owners. And even then, the bridezilla may deride them with gendered directives, as in the previously mentioned case of Jada, who told her interior designer to "man up."

In short, weddings provides an interactive space wherein women make all the decisions, and, in the case of *Bridezillas*, are allowed a justifiable excuse for breaking any of the "rules" of femininity, those that define the womanly woman as kind and nurturing. The idea of letting the bride have whatever she wants becomes an excuse for her to indulge in this activity because, after all, it is *her* wedding day—the one day just for her. Thus, if one looks at the wedding world with a wider perspective, it constitutes a place and space where women rule and have their own special day. Therein lies the betrayal of the wedding as the "bride's day"—she has only one day to enjoy the power given to her. After that day, she must rejoin the still-patriarchal world where she returns to the secondary status her gender still holds.

Wedding day roles: Separate lives

With few exceptions, women clearly assume wedding planning responsibilities. However, what brides and grooms actually do on the wedding day itself also reflects the demarcation of gender roles. For example, in my analysis of 100 episodes of TLC's *A Wedding Story*, I found that of the 100 brides in my sample, all but one were shown at a beauty salon, at home, or at a hotel getting dressed on their wedding day.[31] Having their hair and makeup applied or getting dressed, usually with the help of others, comprised most brides' wedding day activities prior to the ceremony. On the other hand, in addition to getting ready for their weddings, the grooms went golfing on their wedding day or the day before the wedding, played some other kind of sport, such as football, shooting at a rifle range, swimming or exercising, or went out for breakfast or lunch at a restaurant with their groomsmen and/or male friends. Of the more exceptional male activities I saw the grooms in this program doing prior to the wedding, one groom went shopping for a gift for his bride, one shopped at a comic book store, and one took part in an American Civil War reenactment, then got married in a reenactment wedding.

In *A Wedding Story*, the images of brides dedicating most of their wedding day to physical preparation contrasted with the variety of activities that their grooms engaged in prior to their wedding ceremonies. This comparison reflected a marked gender difference regarding wedding work: women worked to look the part of bride, while grooms still found time to play—literally. Indeed, prior to conducting research on this program, I had watched the program as a casual viewer and noticed a pattern of men shown golfing while their brides were at the salon or otherwise busy with wedding preparations. While a few brides also were shown doing other things in addition to getting ready physically for their weddings, such as jogging or having a meal with female bridal party members, these examples were far outweighed by footage of grooms doing more non-wedding-related things.

A notable 1996 episode of *A Wedding Story* in particular demonstrates the gendered aspect of wedding work on the wedding day itself.[32] The sharp contrast between the wedding day preparations of divorced mother of two Lynne and her groom, Jim, illustrates the work versus play theme that characterizes my observations of the way the wedding day unfolds for men and women on *A Wedding Story*. Lynne and Jim met on a blind date arranged by mutual friends. They began a long-distance phone courtship soon afterward. He proposed at her family home in Idaho. Jim, a bachelor, was not used to being around children, but, says Lynne, "they took to him like glue." Jim admits that after 37 years of waiting, he's found the right woman and "instant family" that is "perfect" for him." The couple will marry on the yacht once owned by legendary actor John Wayne, with Jim's friend officiating.

On the day of their wedding, gender roles play out as Lynne and Jim each get ready for the big event. Lynne and the children get dressed at what appears to be Lynne's home. The entire bridal party is there getting ready, along with Jim's officiant friend and Lynne's parents. There are other children there as well. It seems a very crowded house where, as Lynne's father comments, "Confusion reigns supreme." Scenes of Lynne getting her hair done, making sure her children are dressed properly, and searching for various items are juxtaposed with scenes of Jim serenely playing golf with his friends. Lynne drives herself and two of the bridesmaids to the yacht, all the while talking about how she must buy a necklace for one of her daughters, saying that "she needs a gift from her mother." Lynne is obviously stressed as she drives her small, stick-shift car to the yacht for the first time. She says while driving and looking at the clock on the dashboard, "I don't have a good feeling about this."

The scene then cuts to Jim as he asks his friends for the time, laughing and joking about getting to the ceremony on time. Meanwhile, still on their way to the yacht, one of the bridesmaids sitting in the back seat asks Lynne how she is doing. "I'm on high overdrive," Lynne replies. Once at the yacht, Lynne, still not dressed for the ceremony, continues to coordinate things. She must also contend with her son, who appears unhappy about not getting a gift for the day and asks her for his present. As Lynn attends to last-minute preparations, such as the delivery of flowers by the florist, she narrates over the video: "Initially I wanted a real simple wedding, with it being my second wedding. Later I realized that Jim had never been married before. I wanted him to have a wedding ceremony, so it's turned into a full-scale wedding with all the trimmings."

Jim finally arrives, and is next shown tying Lynne's son's tie. Finally the ceremony begins. Lynne wears a formal white wedding gown and is escorted by her father. The wedding goes without a hitch. The reception then takes place, with guests and the bride and groom watching Fourth of July fireworks over the bay. The romantic music accompanying slow-motion footage of Lynne and Jim smiling and dancing with each other erases all the stress Lynne had to endure, giving viewers the happy ending that always concluded every episode of *A Wedding Story*. If the wedding day served as any indication of the playing out of gender roles in their subsequent marriage, Lynne and Jim likely followed a traditional gender role pattern, with Lynne assuming responsibility for household work and childcare, and Jim likely being the financial provider.

Exceptions to the rule: When men do wedding work

Even as hegemonic versions of the wedding and domestic labor play out in these reality programs, the existence of exceptional grooms who undertake wedding chores provides counterpoints that illustrate counterhegemony. The 1998 episode of *A Wedding Story* featuring twenty-something couple Jessica and Michael serves as an example.[33] Their untraditional wedding ceremony reversed the best man and maid of honor roles; Jessica instead chose to have a "man of honor" and Michael had a "best woman." Video footage of their episode reflected the hands-on aspect of their wedding, with the couple and family members shown helping with wedding tasks; Jessica and her mother assemble party favors, and Jessica, Michael, and other family members put together the simple flower arrangements for the reception.

Unlike other grooms depicted in *A Wedding Story* and other wedding reality programs I have examined, this one stands out due to Michael's contribution of designing the bridesmaids' dresses for his and Jessica's wedding. Jessica explains that they went shopping for the dresses together, but found nothing to their liking. As a result, Michael sketched out a dress, and subsequently designed it. Jessica tells the viewer this didn't shock her at all, indicating Michael has no problem with either contributing to their wedding in a real way nor with doing "women's work." In addition to drawing the sketches for the dresses, Michael's mother points out that he also designed the intricate folds for the dresses' back panels.

The viewer then sees Michael, with his mother watching over his shoulder, using a sewing machine, which he says he had never touched before. His foray into the previously unknown world of fashion design adds a touch of "cuteness" to the scene. Images of Michael's sketch and his working with the fabric complement footage of Jessica creating the flowers for their wedding cake. Prior to the wedding itself, Michael washes and details the vintage automobile that will serve as his and Jessica's wedding transportation. Michael is seen in a variety of chore-related situations, resulting in the impression that he does not follow the same gender norms as other grooms in the series (no golfing in this episode!).

Michael and Jessica's episode of *A Wedding Story* illustrates the potential for counterhegemony amidst the certain sameness of weddings presented in bridal media. Not only does the groom design the bridesmaids' dresses, but Jessica sees no problem with his doing so, indicative of the egalitarian relationship they share. That she depends on Michael to help equally with the task of putting together this significant event provides evidence for the ability of bridal media, especially reality programs that take viewers behind the scenes, to include a wide range of couples and ways of "doing" gender. The imagery of Michael actually sewing the dresses he has designed adds to the counterhegemony. That no one questions Michael's talent, but rather sees it as expected, serves as a contrast to the portrayal of incompetent, unhelpful grooms in WE tv's *Bridezillas* and Oxygen's *Real Weddings From The Knot*. Because *A Wedding Story* forwarded a decidedly more romantic tone that separates it from these other reality programs, viewers rarely see conflicts or arguments. However, even with the qualification that perhaps any disagreements had been edited out, it appears that Jessica and Michael might actually have had a relationship that eschewed traditional gender roles, even though their wedding followed the stereotypical white wedding, church ceremony format.

So, where are the men in these bridal-focused reality television versions of today's American wedding? Grooms tend to stay out of the way, especially in WE tv's *Bridezillas* and TLC's *Say Yes to the Dress*. They played secondary roles in Oxygen's *Real Weddings From The Knot*, and some even were "fired" by their brides. Although grooms rarely are shown doing wedding work at all in these programs, the example of Michael in TLC's *A Wedding Story* also illustrates that men can and do take part in wedding chores. When men do break away from traditional gender roles, such as in the case of *A Wedding Story's* Michael, the groom who designed the bridesmaids' dresses, one clearly sees there is a possibility to let go of any gender-based labor "rules"—even within the bridal-focused cultural space defined by these television programs.

The positively framed depictions of men like Michael doing "women's work" parallel news portrayals of stay-at-home dads examined by Vavrus (2002). Among the network television news treatments of stay-at-home dads in her sample, Vavrus found that even while the men were shown engaged in domestic tasks, their masculine identities were never in doubt because "effeminate associations" were avoided, replaced with a framing of feminine qualities like nurturance as a desired quality in "real" men; these qualities then became folded into the identity of the "new" man (p. 361). Vavrus noted that in television news stories of stay-at-home dads one of the discursive tools that helped to reestablish these men's masculinity was the inclusion of admiring statements by women who viewed the domestically-inclined male as being even more manly. Such statements by women also appeared in the story of Michael's sewing abilities in *A Wedding Story*. However, Vavrus concluded that the gendered binary of masculine and feminine identities and roles was reaffirmed in the news portrayals of stay-at-home dads she examined because of the gender differentiation expressed by the dads themselves or by images of them playing sports. This reaffirmation of "manliness" among the examples of "wedding-involved" men in my samples of reality television programs did not appear to the extent that warranted study as a pattern, but in the next chapter I do discuss one such instance that echoed Vavrus's findings.[34]

Though sparse, I see the examples of men doing "women's work" presented in this chapter as evidencing the possibility for these programs to include progressive couples, those who eschew traditional norms and/or embrace an androgynous, egalitarian approach to domestic labor. These snippets of real life within recognizable versions of white weddings allow for counterhegemony to infiltrate the wedding media world. Thus, the inclusion of these backstage accounts of noncelebrity weddings provides a venue for counterhegemonic versions of wedding work to become part of the bridal media milieu.

Summary

Donald and Hall (1986) characterized ideology as consisting of "often fragmentary, episodic, internally contradictory, and incomplete chains of thought" that we use in everyday life to figure out our social world (p. xii). Every wedding depicted in these reality programs consists of unique pairs of people and variations regarding décor and problems encountered. These individual episodes eventually do make up a cohesive image of weddings as they are "supposed" to look. Brides handle the details of the event, sometimes with the help of their soon-to-be husbands, but more often without. The sameness of these weddings becomes common sense, and results in a "practical social consciousness," to use Donald and Hall's words, regarding the way men and women get married (p. xii).

The wedding day may last only a day, but the work one must put into it takes months. Wedding etiquette guides and bridal magazines recommend that wedding planning start a year in advance, adding to the expectation that brides devote at least some part of their everyday lives to attending to myriad decision-making tasks. Tips from wedding "resources" like Kate Wood's 2009 article at *The Knot.com* tell brides to spend every spare minute working on their weddings. The fleeting nature of the resulting product points to the ephemeral nature of women's work in general. As Felski (2000) noted, women's activities within the domestic sphere are associated with cycles, and "repetitive tasks of social production" (p. 82). Similarly, one can view wedding preparations as both repetitive and mundane, illustrative of women's relegation to the everyday. Wedding work by women stands in opposition to the work of men in the public world where, according to Felski, progress and history are made: "Women, like everyday life, have often been defined as negation. Their realm has not been that of war, art, philosophy, scientific endeavor, high office" (p. 80).

Though certainly the women who appear in reality bridal programs can and do hold high-paying, high-status occupations, these become downplayed, as in the case of medical doctor Tiffany in FitTV's *Buff Brides*, or mentioned only briefly. I see that when the public identities of these highly competent women are ignored in these accounts of "real life," the alternative portrayal becomes that of the superbride, who applies her talents of organization and leadership to the creation of the perfect wedding. Portrayals of superbrides such as Amy in Oxygen's *Real Weddings From The Knot* open the portrayal of the feminine bride to a wider characterization that includes decisiveness, direct communication, and the explicit expression of wants and desires. In this way, the notion of the superbride moves beyond the femininity associated with the role of bride, and one can view it as a means of progress toward a fuller portrayal of women.

When the superbride identity morphs into the bridezilla persona, we see even more of a break from those gender expectations associated with the blushing, demure bride. The bridezilla knows what she wants, demands what she wants, and gets what she wants. If she does not get what she wants, she makes her unhappiness clear to everyone around her. Rather than acquiescing to others, the bridezilla tells others what to do—including her future husband. The bridezilla thus achieves a status and power that further removes her from any connection to submissiveness. In the world of the bridezilla, men are seen as useless, incompetent, and a hindrance. Conflicts, poor treatment of others, and emotional tirades mark the bridezilla's performance, with grown women allowed to berate other women. However, the power they hold is illusory: they have power only within the confines of the wedding, which, ironically, returns them to the feminine realm.

In reality, the bridezilla's power stops at the border of the wedding world. WE tv's description of *Bridezillas* as "a comedic look at how brides-to-be go from sweet to certifiable while planning their big day" dismisses the bridezilla as a comical figure ("WE Corporate," 2007). She is the out-of-control woman whose hysteria stems from the trivialities of a social event and minor inconveniences such as a torn dress hem, uneven numbers of men and women in photographs, and manicurists who give her attitude. In the scheme of the larger world, in which life-and-death decisions remain the responsibility of men, the bridezilla betrays women by offering them a false sense of importance. Thus, gender territoriality, manifested in the deriding of grooms and their fashion sense and taste, becomes a way for women to protect their "turf" and ensure that the wedding stays within women's control.

Unlike in bridal magazines, grooms are included in the reality television wedding programs examined here, although their roles take secondary status to those of the brides. In Oxygen's *Real Weddings From The Knot* and TLC's *A Wedding Story*, I found several grooms who helped with wedding planning, especially when those weddings had a "do-it-yourself" approach. In FitTV's *Buff Brides*, the bulk of the wedding work was shown as the bride's responsibility. In addition to working out and working at a job, the brides on that particular program must also deal with the chores related to the big day. Indeed, the stress of juggling all the roles a bride must fulfill serves as a voice-over motif in the series. In the case of *Real Weddings From The Knot* and especially in WE tv's *Bridezillas*, the men tend to either opt out of wedding planning or are told to leave things to the bride; some even admitted they were perfectly content to be left out of the wedding planning altogether. However, when men did help or tried to help in *Bridezillas,* they were dismissed and in a real sense subjected to male bashing by the brides. Here again, the "strong woman"/bridezilla persona prevents a true equality between the sexes.

The voluntary nature of this kind of work, amounting to a second shift similar to that borne by working mothers, thus becor s a self-created source of what Hochschild (1989) in *The Second Shift* term :d a "stalled revolution" regarding the progress of women outside the home. "The influx of women into the economy has not been accompanied by a cultural understanding of marriage and work that would make this transition smooth," she wrote (p. 12). Changes in the workforce and in women, Hochschild asserted, had not been accompanied by changes in the workplace or the attitudes of most men within the household environment. The strain between the change in women and the absence of change elsewhere thus resulted in the stalled revolution she described some 20 years ago.

Similarly, I contend that the absence of change regarding the gendered nature of wedding work—work supposedly required and portrayed as desirable and desired—also contributes to the stalled revolution. In other words, wedding work serves as a voluntary means by which women *themselves* continue to do domestic, unpaid work that prevents their own progress in the wider world, that outside the realm of the feminine. Here is where I see hegemony's strength: it draws not only on its acceptance by the subaltern, "but also the subaltern's desire of it," as observed by Zompetti (1997, p. 73). Creation of a culture with "illusory benefits," continued Zompetti, allows hegemony to co-opt any resistance or to incorporate it into a universal philosophy through the use of common sense (p. 73). By creating the dominant image of the beautiful, perfect bride and her beautiful, perfect wedding, bridal media similarly disguise an ideology of gender that remains unquestioned.

In order for that ideology to remain dominant, alternatives and deviations must be seen so that we can determine what is "abnormal." As I pointed out in this chapter, aberrations regarding who does the wedding work concerned grooms, not brides. Although the bridezilla certainly counters ideals of femininity—especially traits such as submissiveness and deference to others (especially men)—she still adheres to the requirements of physical appearance, never eschewing the bridal preparation involving cosmetics and elaborate, feminine attire. On the other hand, images of grooms breaking the rules of masculinity, especially the caveat "Don't Be Female" (Wood, 2010, p. 171), demonstrate that this form of bridal media can and does include instances of men doing women's work without any fear of being labeled unmanly.[35]

As rare as they are, the inclusion of instances of men doing women's work illustrates at the very least the openness required for hegemony to exist. The potential exists for reality wedding programs to show viewers more grooms such as Michael in the example from TLC's *A Wedding Story* who take equal responsibility for wedding planning, and in turn open the door for changes in social consciousness. Such incursions into the accepted common sense must reach critical mass before material changes can occur. These instances of uncommon sense already have made a presence in wedding news of unusual ceremonies and elopements, as recounted in Chapter 3, and the counter-hegemonic versions of unusual grooms here. In the next chapter, I examine reality television portrayals that specifically challenge the wedding status quo.

Notes

* Portions of this chapter were published as the following articles and appear here with permission: "*Buff Brides*: Disciplining the Female Body," *Popular Culture Review*, 2008, Vol. 20, No. 1, pp. 35–44; "Creation of a New 'Empowered' Female Identity: WE tv's *Bridezillas*," *Media Report to Women*, 2009, Vol. 37, No. 1, pp. 6–12; "Hegemony in Reality-Based TV Programming: The World According to *A Wedding Story*," *Media Report to Women*, 2003, Vol. 31, Issue 1, pp. 10–14; "Unraveling *The Knot*: Political Economy and Cultural Hegemony in Wedding Media," available from http://jci.sagepub.com; the final, definitive version of this paper has been published

in *Journal of Communication Inquiry*, Vol. 32, Issue 1, January 2008, pp. 60–82, by Sage Publications, Inc. All rights reserved. ©2008 by Sage Publications.

1. Lowrey and Otnes's (1994) sample included graduates and undergraduates from a Midwest university and working adults.
2. This quote came from Lee Madden, a psychologist from Oak Park, Illinois.
3. TLC's *A Wedding Story* did not regularly provide background information on brides or grooms. I would characterize that program as the most vague regarding this aspect. Oxygen's *Real Weddings From The Knot* did not consistently mention brides' and grooms' ages and occupations; rather, one had to visit corresponding web pages for the episodes to find such information, and therefore I do not include this program in this section.
4. Episode titles and dates recorded are as follows: "Margaret and Tiffany," February 14, 2007; "Colleen and Nadege," February 21, 2007; "Linxiu and Melanie," March 2, 2007; "Jessica and Madhu," March 21, 2007; "Greta and Justine," March 21, 2007. Episode copyright dates were 2003–2004.
5. *Bridezillas*, copyright dates of 2003 (Season 1) and 2005 (Season 2); both seasons available on DVD, produced by the Weinstein Company.
6. The "*Bridezillas*: About the Brides" (2010) web page provides details on only the current season's brides.
7. Season 1 information from the web page "Bridezillas' Wedding Details" (2007).
8. Season 2 information from the web page "Bridezillas: About the Brides, Adrianna-Korliss" (2007; no longer available).
9. I analyzed a convenience sample of 14 episodes of *Say Yes to the Dress* recorded in October 2007, November and December 2008, and March 2009. Copyright dates were 2007–2009.
10. The occupations of the six men were "fashion buyer," "Episcopal priest," "U.S. Marine," "computer consultant," "hairdresser," and "nurse."
11. Episode title and airdate: "It's My Wedding, but Don't Tell the Bridesmaid," November 21, 2008.
12. Episode title and airdate: "Daddy Knows Best," December 26, 2008.
13. Episode title and airdate: "Time to Cut the Cord," December 26, 2008.
14. Episode title and airdate: "Time to Cut the Cord," December 26, 2008
15. Episode title and airdate: "Emotions Run Wild," December 12, 2008.
16. Episode title and airdate: "Daddy Knows Best," December 26, 2008.
17. The 1988 edition of *Etiquette: Charlotte Ford's Guide to Modern Manners*, for example, noted that traditionally, the bride's family paid for the expenses for the wedding and reception, and the groom was responsible for such items as the marriage license, bride's ring and gifts from him to her, the officiant's fees, and the honeymoon. However, Ford also noted, "Weddings are expensive today, and therefore wedding costs are often shared more equally between the families of the bride and the groom" (p. 229). Ford also mentioned that working brides and grooms "may pay some of the wedding costs" (p. 229). Some 20 years later, the rules hadn't changed much. Bridal magazine web sites such as *Brides.com* have sections on budget and etiquette, with guides for who pays for what. The *Brides.com* web page "Budget Etiquette" as of 2011 still cited the tradition of the bride's family paying for pretty much everything, with the groom's family paying for the rings and their own formalwear.

However, it also noted: "Today, the rules are looser and couples and their families are coming up with a plan that works for all involved, with the groom's family often contributing as much as half of the cost of the reception" ("Budget Etiquette," 2011).

18. I have witnessed how the dependence of females on others for financial support can manifest itself in everyday objects. A few years ago, I was shopping at my local Target retail store and saw a t-shirt in the girls' section that read, "Buy me something." I found this rather disturbing, in that even a seemingly harmless message on a child's t-shirt socializes girls into thinking they are owed something and to depend on others to provide for them. The 2008 film *Sex and the City: The Movie* provided an example of gift-giving gone awry when the fiercely independent-minded Samantha is outbid for a piece of jewelry at an auction, only to find out her boyfriend, Jerrod, is the winning bidder. Rather than the gratitude he expected, Samantha explained to him that she wanted to buy it for herself, because she never wanted to depend on a man for anything.

19. Story lines for the brides in *Bridezillas* ran concurrently, rather than in separately titled episodes. I introduce brides and quoted material as from either Season 1 or Season 2.

20. Comments were drawn from the following episodes, in order listed: "Margaret and Tiffany," "Linxiu and Melanie," "Jessica and Madhu."

21. Robinson and Hunter (2008), "Is Mom Still Doing It All? Reexamining Depictions of Family Work in Popular Advertising." In their study of magazine advertising of family consumer products, the authors reviewed, citing others, the depiction of mothers during the 1980s as the "supermom." The supermom served as the "stereotypical/ideological family woman," the competent, confident working mother. Even as she made her way through a man's world in her career, she held onto her femininity. Robinson and Hunter cited advertising scholar Jean Kilbourne, who noted that the supermom image reinforced traditional gender roles because women still were shown as taking responsibility for domestic chores and child care.

22. I thank Sandra Donovan for providing this source on gendered wedding work. As part of a project on gender portrayals on the Internet in my course Communication Between the Sexes during the Fall 2009 semester, Donovan analyzed The Knot and used this article to illustrate how The Knot endorses a gendered division of labor.

23. Based on my analysis of 20 episodes of *Real Weddings From The Knot* with copyright dates of 2003–2005. Air and recorded month and year were as follows: "Jessa and Jeff," "Danielle and John," "Catina and Todd," "Whitney and Jeff," "Susan and John"—June, 2003; "Orisha and John," "Kaijsa and Ryan," "Cara and Aaron," "Lori and Mark," "Sarah and Mark"—January, 2004; "Katie and Gus," "Amy and Bill," "Sarah-Jane and Nate," "Jen and Jeff," "Amy and Mark"—October, 2004; "Christin and Michael," "Tiffany and Calvin," "Allison and Tommy," "Alem and Johannes," "Xylina and Eric"—January, 2005.

24. Episodes and recorded dates: "Amy and Bill," October 22, 2004; "Danielle and John," June 8, 2003; "Kaijsa and Ryan," January 19, 2004; "Lori and Mark," January 22, 2004.

25. Story lines for the brides in *Bridezillas* ran concurrently, rather than in separately titled episodes. I introduce brides and quoted material as from either Season 1 or Season 2.

26. Behm-Morawitz and Mastro (2008) examined the "mean girl" stereotype of socially

aggressive teenage girls as depicted in films such as 2004's *Mean Girls*. They conducted a content analysis of teen movies from 1995 through 2004 and found that the image of the sweet teenage girl had been replaced by a dominant image of the mean teenage girl. A survey of undergraduates found that exposure to teen movies was associated with unfavorable attitudes toward women. Though qualifying their findings as tentative, the authors concluded, "Exposure to teen films seems to send the message that success in the female social world can be obtained through duplicitous means" (p. 141). Whether or not viewing *Bridezillas* correlates with similarly negative opinions of women serves as a subject for future research. One can surmise, however, that such portrayals certainly do not help the cause of feminism.

27. Cassidy (2005) described the "misery shows" of the 1950s, like *Queen for a Day*, that featured women and were aimed at female audiences. These programs centered on finding the most pathetic woman to reward with prizes. I used the term schadenfreude to describe the appeal of these and similar, more recent reality programs in my review of the book (Engstrom, 2006).

28. Bride Diana, in the episode "Time to Cut the Cord," airdate December 26, 2008.

29. Episode of "Danielle and John," recorded June 2003.

30. Episodes and recorded dates: "Jessa and Jeff," June 5, 2003; "Kaijsa and Ryan," January 19, 2004; "Katie and Gus," October 22, 2004.

31. Over the course of my research on this program I recorded a total of 141 episodes of *A Wedding Story*. 77 in 1998 and another 64 in 2001. Copyright dates ranged from 1996 to 2001; 41 episodes were repeats. For more on my take on this show, see my article "Hegemony in Reality-Based TV Programming" in *Media Report to Women* (Engstrom, 2003).

32. "Lynne and Jim," copyright 1996, airdate July 3, 1998.

33. "Jessica and Michael," copyright 1998, recorded June 4, 2001.

34. In Chapter 6, I point out an instance of this when discussing Clementine's dilemma in the 1997 "Clementine and Paul" episode of TLC's *A Wedding Story*.

35. Wood (2010) reviewed themes of masculinity based on the work of J. A. Doyle in *The Male Experience* (3rd ed., 1995, Madison, WI: Brown & Benchmark). Additional rules of masculinity articulated by Wood in *Gendered Lives* (2010) were: be successful, be aggressive, be sexual, be self-reliant (pp. 171–176).

6. Alternative Brides and Grooms*

CULTURAL HEGEMONY AS THEORY DEPENDS ON THE ACCEPTANCE OF COMMONSENSE ideas about the world. Regarding the way people enact the wedding ritual and the way in which institutions like the media produce cultural work, the majority of the wedding portrayals in bridal magazines and reality television programs present a largely uniform picture. Bridal media in those forms examined in previous chapters forward a standard with which one may compare weddings that appear "appropriate" with those that do not. In terms of hegemony, this acceptance becomes the basis for common sense, which, Landy (1994) noted, "eradicates the possibility of alternatives, presenting as natural, inevitable, and intelligible the present state of affairs" (p. 16).

However, even as the creation, dissemination through media, and realization of the dominant cultural order becomes the normal, unquestioned, and uncritical way of enacting common sense, Gramscian hegemony allows for deviations from the natural state of affairs. Indeed, deviations become necessary for the reestablishment and validation of common sense. As described in Chapter 2, examples of difference appeared among the published descriptions of society weddings during the late 19th and early 20th centuries, when the occasional bride replaced the lush, white wedding gown with traveling apparel. More recently, published accounts of ceremonies that eschewed "tradition," such as elopements and city hall weddings, were documented by the *Vows* column in *The New York Times* (Brady, 1997).

Lears (1985) pointed to cultural power as a means of defining the boundaries of commonsense "reality"—with the resultant hegemonic viewpoint keeping those lines of propriety intact by "ignoring views outside those boundaries or by labeling deviant opinions 'tasteless' or 'irresponsible'" (p. 572). Reality television compilations of wild, wacky, and unusual weddings such as those described in Chapter 3 serve as examples of such difference. The weirdness and "low class" tastes manifested in reality television specials like *Wild Weddings* and *America's Trashiest Weddings*, with its beer-chugging contests and strip-club receptions, create a space in which participants challenge the norms of the proper wedding as forwarded by stylized images of weddings in bridal magazines. To term such weddings as the "trashiest" demonstrates that deviant weddings are not only deviations from the norm, but also tasteless and undesirable. Instances of overt resistance in the bridal media milieu demonstrate that even within the overwhelmingly similar weddings we see in magazines and on reality television wedding programs, there are examples of brides and bridegrooms that serve as exceptions to the rule.

Breaks from traditional gender roles and wedding traditions also appear in reality-based television programs that show us "regular" weddings. In the previous chapter, for example, the wedding of Jessica and Michael on TLC's *A Wedding Story* illustrated departures from common sense regarding who does what in today's wedding. Michael designed the gowns for his brides' attendants, and both he and Jessica decided to have persons of the other sex in the form of a man of honor and best woman stand up for each of them during their ceremony. These departures from the currently accepted ideal, not only in media portrayals of weddings but also those we experience firsthand, offer venues for examining Hall's (1996) assertion that "cultural hegemony is never about pure victory or pure domination," but is "always about shifting the balance of power in the relations of culture" (p. 468).

Gramscian hegemony as a process does not mean a static, closed, or complete system; "the creation of counterhegemonies remains a live option," wrote Lears (1985, p. 571). Mumby (1997) interpreted hegemony as "embodying simultaneously (and in a tension-filled and contradictory manner) the dynamic of power and resistance" (p. 346). Just as "real" couples tailor their own ceremonies to their own tastes, or reject the social norms surrounding the expected version of the wedding, media accounts of real weddings also include exceptions to the rule. Hegemony becomes even more useful when interpreting the presence of similarity and difference among myriad versions of the wedding; even as they tend to look alike, there exists opposition within the sameness.

Though few and far between, the inclusion of exceptions to the rule allow for challenges to the dominant viewpoint; this tension between dominance and resistance creates the possibility for change once that resistance reaches a point where deviations become acceptable and even desirable. Portrayals of a social practice such as the wedding offer a sameness that characterizes hegemony yet make room for nonconformist examples. Gitlin (1987) noted how media deal with deviations from the dominant viewpoint:

> Hegemony in news as in entertainment takes notice of alternatives to the dominant values, descriptions, and ideals, and frames them so that some alternative features get assimilated into the dominant ideological system, while most of that which is potentially subversive of the dominant value system is driven to the ideological margins. (p. 244)

In this chapter, I examine instances of resistance and difference within the world of the white wedding. I discuss notably different episodes of TLC's *A Wedding Story* and Oxygen's *Real Weddings From The Knot* that illustrate challenges to both the overall hegemonic notions associated with weddings and within the programs specifically. The example I discuss from *A Wedding Story* centers on one bride's open discussion about her misgivings about her formal wedding. From *Real Weddings From The Knot*, a series that I found overall to promote the materialistic aspects of weddings, one particular episode breaks away from the others by offering viewers a way to have a wedding without a high price tag.[1] I find these two examples worthy of further examination because they challenge the dominant versions of weddings presented in reality television, without being so different as to be labeled "trashy," "wild," or "wacky." Instead, these two episodes align with the white wedding ideal enough to be included in these mainstream versions of real weddings, but offer enough difference to illustrate the inclusiveness of alternatives within the hegemonic wedding format.

The underlying assumption that marriage and weddings are reserved for heterosexual couples signifies another aspect of hegemony within civil society (as well as the legal system); one can see that Rich's (1980) concept of compulsory heterosexuality also serves as a manifestation of hegemony in everyday life. One can find evidence to support this and evidence that counters it. Regarding how this "hetero-only" rule appears on television, Maher (2004), in her observations of the reality based programming line-up of TLC, including *A Wedding Story* and its subsequent ratings hit, *A Baby Story*, characterized the near-uniformity of demographics and the total absence of gay weddings as compulsory heterosexuality at its most uniform. "There are no single parents and no gay weddings or commitment ceremonies despite TLC's website claim that the shows 'spotlight the wonderful diversity expressed by modern couples,'" she contended (p. 200).

Same-sex weddings inherently and obviously counter the status quo.

However, the inclusion of same-sex weddings in reality television specials of celebrity weddings, such as those discussed in Chapter 3, and same-sex wedding announcements in newspapers discussed in Chapter 2, provide evidence that these versions of marriage no longer occupy the ideological margins. Wedding web sites that target same-sex couples, notably *GayWeddings.com*, also counter the compulsory heterosexuality that Ingraham (2008) asserted is inherent in and perpetuated by weddings.

The 2002 reality television series *Gay Weddings* on the Bravo cable network featured weddings of lesbian and gay couples, and serves as another example of the incorporation of alternatives into the dominant value system. I examine how *Gay Weddings* compares to other reality-based wedding programs in terms of its treatment of same-sex couples who created their own versions of the familiar, traditional wedding, replete with the same artifacts and practices forwarded in the wider bridal media milieu. Later in this chapter, I examine bridal media that claim to offer alternatives to the white wedding stereotype, ones that evoke feminism either explicitly or implicitly.

Questioning Tradition on *A Wedding Story*: Clementine's Wedding Dilemma

Hegemony as a means to explain how the majority view becomes the dominant way and perspective of participating in social life allows for individuals to challenge common sense. However, as Lears (1985) explained, "most people find it difficult, if not impossible, to translate the outlook implicit in their experience into a conception of the world that will directly challenge the hegemonic culture" (p. 569). Thus, even if and when one sees a problem with the way things have always been done and comes to criticize hegemonic culture, the ability and willpower to actually take an active role in either changing or questioning common sense becomes problematic. To reject the common sense associated with certain practices required of the wedding (ceremony details, expense, and the like) becomes a matter of deciding if the battle is worthwhile, especially when considering the pressure of family desires. One may wish to forego the time, effort, and symbolism connected with the white wedding ideal purported by various sources (media, common sense, relatives' wishes), but to actually do so becomes another matter.

Such was the case of Clementine, the reluctant bride in a 1997 episode of TLC's *A Wedding Story*, who expressed misgivings about her own wedding.[2] I find Clementine's dilemma as significant because it presents a departure from the "feel good" aura of *A Wedding Story*, an aura that evoked the "rightness" of couples' love and of weddings in general. Each episode of *A Wedding*

Story required that a wedding occur, despite, and in spite of, any dramatic elements such as getting to the church on time or a lipstick stain on the wedding dress. Indeed, the show's producers cited as the series' strengths its uniformity and predictability (Noxon, 1999).

In *A Wedding Story*, we never see the bride and groom bickering in the final hours before the wedding, and rarely, if ever, see either the bride or groom admit any misgivings or second thoughts (the cliché of "cold feet") about getting married (Acosta, 1999). The inclusion of an on-camera discussion with her bridesmaids prior to her wedding makes Clementine's story unusual enough for me to discuss as an example of a counterhegemonic bride (although I realize the oxymoronic nature of this term). Among the many episodes of *A Wedding Story* I have seen either as part of systematic research or as a casual viewer, she was the only bride that verbalized her reluctance to follow the white wedding ideal. Though short and fleeting, this particular scene, which I will describe shortly, brilliantly captures the essence of hegemony and how it functions even among "modern" women to marginalize and discount alternative voices that question the dominant ideology.

In this episode, Clementine's wedding story begins innocuously enough. Clementine and Paul, her future husband, had met at their place of work, the United States Naval Academy in Annapolis, Maryland, when Paul found Clementine's dog wandering about and brought it back to her office. Although they do not mention their specific job titles or occupations, Paul is obviously a naval officer. Clementine's occupation as an instructor or professor is implied only; she mentions she "does anthropology." Their interaction at work included conversations about political science and Clementine's area of expertise. As I mentioned in the previous chapter when discussing the identities of brides in reality wedding programs, the nonbridal identities in reality television wedding programs tend to be vague. Whether Clementine holds an advanced degree is not clear in this episode; however, one can assume that she does if she serves as an instructor or professor at one of the U.S. military service academies. One can surmise, however, that both she and Paul are highly educated career professionals who have common intellectual interests.

The episode shows footage of both Paul and Clementine engaged in several activities on the day before their wedding. Paul prepares his dress uniform as he explains on camera the meaning of each medal he earned. He and Clementine then go shopping at a supermarket for a family welcome party to be held at what appears to be their shared home. Then Paul, who is Asian-American, is shown folding origami cranes that will serve as wedding favors that incorporate Japanese tradition into the celebration. He says, "It's something for us—and for Clem." Paul's hands-on involvement in the making of party favors reflects to a degree an egalitarian perspective, or at least that he sees this aspect of the wedding as important enough to do himself. Footage of the ceremony rehearsal and rehearsal dinner follow.

On the wedding day, Clementine and three of her female friends gather and chat about the wedding. This kind of backstage footage tends to be rare among the episodes of *A Wedding Story* I have viewed over the years. Rather than showing a frantic bride putting on her gown and having her makeup done or rushing to get to the church on time while having to take care of last-minute details, this bride appears to have enough time to have a leisurely conversation with her female attendants. One of her female friends (Friend #1) casually comments that Paul and Clementine could have eloped and had a party afterwards. Clementine admits that she had hoped to do just that. However, as the following interaction reveals, her desires had become secondary to those of others, illustrating the power of "common sense" associated with the importance of the wedding as a symbolic requisite for marriage:

Clementine:	Well, that [the elopement] was what I was sort of thinking and hoping, but it kind of happened that Paul really wanted a wedding, and my mom really wanted a wedding, and my grandmother really wanted a wedding. And they wanted to have, they wanted to see their little girl—(Laughter). And I really didn't want to see myself like that. I figured, here I am—I'm an adult, I'm a 32-year-old professional. But you know, what is this with a wedding? But Paul really wanted a wedding, so—
Friend #1:	Why did he want it?
Friend #2:	(Jokingly) Yeah, what's the matter with him? (Laughter)
Clementine:	He likes tradition. When it comes to family, this is really important to him and he wants everyone—he wants to mark the event, the moment, and the ceremony. He wants a ceremony and everyone to come together for it, and that's the part that I like—is getting all my friends together. I—but I—you know—
Friend #2:	Oh, just admit it—you just caved to social pressure. (Laughter)
Friend #1:	And you just wanted a really excellent dress. (Laughter)

The revelation that Paul is the one who wanted a wedding contrasts with Clementine's wish to elope. Here we learn of the counterhegemonic views she held before her wedding day and still appears to hold on her wedding day.

Video then cuts to a scene of Paul and his brothers at a shooting range. They shoot skeet, a pastime they shared with their father when they were younger. Similar to the pattern of sports and outdoor-related activities I found in my analysis of *A Wedding Story*, the shooting range footage returns Paul to the male gender role. The juxtaposition of Clementine talking with her female companions and Paul and his brothers engaged in a manly activity reaffirms gender roles: she is interacting with her female friends through face-to-face conversation; he is interacting side-by-side with his brothers firing guns.[3] While Paul previously was shown making party favors, the images of him with guns reassure viewers of his masculinity. The episode then cuts back to Clementine being made up by a makeup artist. "We'll have to see what Paul thinks," says Clementine. She says that if he looks "chipper" when he sees her walking down the aisle, she'll consider wearing cosmetics regularly. Though subtle, Clementine's comments further indicate that she does not follow the "regular" feminine role. The enactment of femininity via the bridal role and use of cosmetics appears to counter Clementine's self-image and attitude. One can interpret her self-description as a "32-year-old professional" rather than "32-year-old woman" as reflective of an androgynous or even feminist perspective. Clementine's beliefs, illustrated by her comments about the wedding and about herself, clearly go against hegemonic notions connected to the feminine persona embodied in the bridal role.

In the next scene, Paul tells his relatives about the now-defunct elopement idea as they accompany him to the ceremony site: "I kind of insisted that we get married in a *wedding*," he says. "We were going to elope." Clementine then arrives in a white gown and veil at the ceremony site and says, "I feel really old." This comment further implies a reluctance on her part to take on the bridal role and new status as wife.

Paul and Clementine repeat vows in a nonreligious ceremony before about 30 guests in a small reception hall. At the reception itself, held on a boat, Paul presents Clementine with a necklace he had purchased in 1991 when he was on an overseas assignment, before they had even met each other. Paul and Clementine are then shown cutting the wedding cake with the sword from his dress uniform; she throws the bridal bouquet. The episode ends with Clementine and Paul talking to each other about how happy they are. "Can I kiss you?" Paul asks his bride. "Yeah," she replies. The music swells as the credits roll, and viewers experience another perfect ending to another perfect wedding.

This particular episode thus presents a portrayal of a reluctant bride unable to extricate herself from the wedding hoopla. Rather, her wishes become subsumed by her husband-to-be, indicated by his comments on camera that the wedding was his wish, rather than theirs as a couple. The opposing voice, the resistance to the wedding itself that Clementine expresses seems to be discarded, as if her questioning of tradition is irrelevant. Indeed, her opposition to the whole idea is swept away, as she is seen acquiescing to everything she may have stood against. Notably, the viewer sees that Clementine is uncomfortable with makeup, and will only wear it if her husband-to-be "approves." That is, Clementine obviously does not wear makeup regularly, but will consider it if Paul's reaction to her wedding maquillage is positive. Also, Clementine wanted to elope, rather than cast herself as the star of her (initially unwanted) wedding; she relented because everyone *else* around her wanted "a wedding." Clementine sees herself as an independent, modern woman, who is free (she thought) to make her own decisions, and to commit to Paul on her own terms. What the viewer does not see is how or if Clementine even tried to negotiate a compromise between the wedding her husband and her family wanted and the simple elopement she had envisioned.

Throughout this exceptional episode and even up to the moment of her wedding, Clementine expresses on camera her misgivings about almost every aspect of the wedding and its preparations: she tells her friends that she wanted to elope but that everyone else wanted a wedding; she allows herself to be made up only because it is her wedding day; she says she feels "really old" as her father escorts her to the wedding ceremony. In the end, the viewer sees that such resistance cannot stand up to social expectations, or even the wishes of Clementine's life partner; it seems her concerns carry little weight, and she goes along with everyone else's desires, as women become socialized to do.

"Enlightened" women such as Clementine obviously have the ability to question rituals that contradict their worldview. But questioning and contradicting the deeply embedded core values based in patriarchy pose a more formidable challenge, especially in a society in which women are socialized to please others as they take on their gendered life roles. Even up to the point when she arrives at the wedding site, Clementine reveals that this was not what she wanted. Rather, it is the desires of her husband and her female family members that she follows.

Within the context of *A Wedding Story*, and other reality television wedding programs as well as bridal media in general, Clementine's dilemma serves as a counterpoint to the themes regarding the bridal appearance discussed previously in Chapter 4. However, even as this particular episode offers viewers an alternative to the feminine bridal role, hegemony in the form of pressure from her husband-to-be and her female family members and friends eventually silences her protestations. Clementine's opposing voice represents deviation from common sense, but the idea of eloping becomes negated as the episode concludes with another wedding, thereby fulfilling *A Wedding Story*'s purpose of giving viewers yet another happy ending.

A Real Wedding from *Real Weddings From The Knot*: Jessa and Jeff's DIY Affair

As discussed in Chapter 5, wedding work falls mainly to brides, along with the stress associated with creating the perfect event. The distinction between Oxygen's *Real Weddings From The Knot* and other reality wedding programs discussed throughout this book lies in the online details on *TheKnot.com* web site that accompanied each episode. Viewers of the program who were interested in the dresses, flowers, cakes, and reception and ceremony sites could simply log on to the Internet and find vendor contact information for the weddings they liked.

Among the episodes of Oxygen's reality wedding program *Real Weddings From The Knot* in 2003, one stood out as an exception to the pricier weddings that featured designer wedding gowns, high-price venues, and lavish receptions. The "Handmade Christmas Wedding in Maryland" of Jessa, a research scientist, and Jeff, a medical student, gave viewers a look at how to create a wedding on a tight budget.[4] In the episode, viewers are told simply that the couple must put together their wedding while on a budget, and watch them shop for wedding items at Wal-Mart. Nearly everything for their wedding is made by the couple and their family and friends. The handcrafted wedding items included the invitations, wedding cake (baked by Jessa), corsages (handmade by Jessa), bridesmaids' dresses (sewn by Jessa), and specially made platforms for the lanterns used in their ceremony (built by Jeff).

While the television version of Jessa and Jeff's story emphasizes their tight budget and the amount of work they put into creating their version of the dream wedding, the online synopsis of their episode describes their wedding as being on "a graduate student budget of only $6,000."[5] This frugal couple makes the most of their money, and finds ways to save on nearly everything needed for their wedding. Because they married at Christmas time, the church in which they were married already was decorated with holiday décor. Jessa bought her wedding gown by designer Alfred Angelo online "and at a discount."[6] The bridesmaids sewed their own dresses at a "sewing party" at Jessa's house.

Further savings come from making their own or reusing items from Jessa's family. Jessa repurposes her sister's bridal veil by sewing it to a headpiece bought from an arts and crafts chain retailer. She decorates her home-baked wedding cake and she tops it with the same cake topper used in her parents' wedding. Jessa's mother had died the year before the wedding, adding further significance to the cake topper and enhancing the episode's emotional appeal.

Five days before Jessa and Jeff's wedding, the graphic "Doing It Our Own Way" appears onscreen. Footage of the couple shopping at Wal-Mart for last-minute accessories underscores the theme of thriftiness. Jeff comments that some people might use the term "cheap bastards" to describe the couple. "We prefer 'thrifty,'" he says. The implication is that because the couple is paying for the entire wedding themselves with "only" $6,000 to spend creating it, it is different from other white-wedding portrayals, as Jessa and Jeff work to stay within their budget. By emphasizing the "homemade" quality of their wedding, the message conveyed suggests that Jessa and Jeff cannot do much with their money, and couples with similarly "small" budgets should expect to bake their own cakes as well. Footage of Jessa breaking out a box of Betty Crocker cake mix to make the wedding cake adds a visual emphasis to this decidedly downsized approach. When considered within the context of bridal magazine spreads featuring designer wedding cakes, and other images from reality television wedding programs of ordinary and celebrity couples, the out-of-a-box wedding cake made by this thrifty bride further illustrates deviance from the "regular" wedding.

The low-budget wedding of Jessa and Jeff also counters the common depictions of the big, white wedding in *Real Weddings from The Knot*. As they work around their self-described thriftiness, the viewer gets the sense that planning a wedding on this relatively small amount of funds—when compared to the average wedding's price tag of approximately $20,000 or more—would require even more time, effort, and skill than that associated with the stereotypical wedding forwarded in bridal media. The title of the episode, "A Handmade Christmas Wedding," also contrasts with other *Real Wedding From The Knot* episode titles provided online that denote flashier, more expensive weddings, such as "A Tropic Garden Wedding in Jamaica," "An Exotic Beach Wedding in Mexico," "A Global Gathering in DC," "Silver and Snowflakes in New Jersey," and "Gatsby Style in Newport, RI."[7]

Another episode in the series followed a similar, low-budget theme, but did not highlight it to the degree as was done in Jessa and Jeff's story. The episode "A Handcrafted Celebration Near Dallas" of Whitney and Jeff (a different Jeff), featured a "down home" wedding put together with the help of family and friends, but there was no mention of budget or dollars in their episode.[8] Rather than the bride doing most of the work, Whitney's grandmother and sister-in-law helped her with bridesmaids' dresses and the wedding cake, respectively. The term "handcrafted" denotes a custom-made aspect, compared to the word "homemade," which infers less expense and labor.

Juxtaposed with the more sumptuous weddings featured in *Real Weddings From The Knot*, Jessa and Jeff's "Handmade Christmas Wedding" looks shabby, even more so when compared to the "handcrafted" country wedding of Whitney and Jeff. Jessa and Jeff's low-budget, DIY affair leaves the viewer with the impression that $6,000 does not go a long way, unless one is willing to shop at Wal-Mart and make wedding clothes and accessories by hand. Especially notable regarding Jessa's wedding work was that *she* made her *own* wedding cake; Jessa's wedding was truly a do-it-yourself endeavor.

The inclusion of low-budget alternatives among the more costly white weddings as portrayed in bridal magazines illustrates the potential of reality television programs that rely on the lives of "regular folks" to reflect everyday life. In this sense, the title *Real Weddings From The Knot* is accurate, as it includes *real* weddings. Thus, the inclusion of less-expensive, alternative weddings conveys some sense of authenticity and a sincere desire on the part of The Knot and Oxygen to show their female audiences that they care about them. However, to include more aberrations from the white wedding and its requisite expenses would threaten the financial purpose of both media entities. In this sense, the wedding industry and its media counterparts continue to "sell" a specific ideal regarding weddings, in turn ensuring the reproduction of certain ideologies that tell women what they need to do and spend to have their dream wedding.

I have presented examples of how counterhegemony may appear within the "mainstream" bridal media; these examples from two reality television wedding programs illustrate how this form of bridal media allows for deviations from common sense. Clementine's counterhegemonic views of weddings and of her self-image as an independent, professional woman rather than blushing bride serves as only a short, eventually glossed-over "blip" in the years-long continuum of *A Wedding Story* episodes. The low-budget, homemade wedding of Jessa and Jeff similarly serves as a deviation from the more obviously costly weddings featured in *Real Wedding From The Knot*.

Although certainly counterhegemonic, these two examples serve only as deviations rather than complete departures from heterosexual weddings as presented on television. The counterhegemony represented by same-sex couples who only recently have been afforded the chance to legally validate their unions challenges the common sense of marriage itself, and, consequently, the wedding as currently practiced. Next, I examine how the portrayal of same-sex weddings within the reality television genre creates an additional cultural space where hegemonic notions surrounding today's wedding are both challenged and followed.

Hegemony and Counterhegemony of Same-Sex Weddings

"Our society privileges heterosexual marriage, and thus weddings also link the personal decision to marry with an institutional heterosexual privilege carrying profound social, legal, financial, and religious benefits," wrote Oswald (2000, p. 349).[9] However, wedding rites do not limit themselves to heterosexual unions, in that traditional prayers, blessings, and vows can embrace both different-sex and same-sex unions (Jung & Smith, 1993, p. 164). In *Same-Sex Unions in Premodern Europe*, Boswell (1994) traced same-sex unions to as far back as 400 B.C.E. to 400 C.E.; an 11th century treatise of Byzantine law provides evidence for the legality of same-sex unions in early medieval Byzantine society (p. 53). In ancient Rome, such formal unions were even publicly acknowledged: "One might view these unions as 'imitative of' heterosexual marriage, but it would be more cautious to see them as modes of 'participating in' the majority culture," he explained (p. 82). Boswell examined in particular an early Christian "ceremony of union" for passionate friendships, which he saw as functioning as a marriage ceremony. Regarding its purpose and similarity to today's notion of marriage as sanctioning heterosexual relationships, Boswell noted: "In almost every age and place the ceremony fulfilled what most people today regard as the essence of marriage: a permanent romantic commitment between two people, witnessed and recognized by the community" (p. 281).[10]

In *Recognizing Ourselves: Ceremonies of Lesbian and Gay Commitment*, Lewin (1998) conducted ethnographic research of same-sex weddings, by witnessing the commitment ceremonies of and interviewing gay and lesbian couples. Observed Lewin, "Lesbian and gay commitment ceremonies offer symbolic resistance to heterosexist domination" (p. 234). However, they at the same time reaffirm the symbolism of marriage and the need to have a public means by which to signify these relationships.

Same-sex wedding announcements had been published in "mainstream" newspapers long before *The New York Times* announced that it would publish announcements for same-sex weddings and changed the title of its "Weddings" page to "Weddings/Celebrations" ("Times Will Begin Reporting," 2002). Indeed, Jensen (1996) noted that the Austin, Texas *American Statesman* ran a same-sex wedding announcement of a lesbian couple in 1992. The alternative weddings that appear in *The New York Times* likely represent same-sex couples from an elite segment of society, and the paper's "notoriously secretive" editorial policies (Mundy, 2008, p. 12) may prevent the readers from knowing if there are many more or much fewer same-sex wedding submissions than appear in print. Nevertheless, the very appearance of same-sex weddings in mass media opens the way for further ideological reproduction reflective of "real life," especially in terms of how counterhegemony eventually can become folded into common sense. The acknowledgement by newspapers that gay and lesbian couples warranted the same treatment as heterosexual couples regarding ceremonies of commitment illustrates Hall's (1996) observation about hegemony as a shift in "the balance of power" (p. 468).

Wedding announcements of same-sex couples become a means to give visibility through the mundane. In a 2008 analysis of *The New York Times*' same-sex wedding announcements, Mundy explained that the "commonplace content" of the mundane information in heterosexual wedding announcements holds special meaning for gay and lesbian couples (p. 25). Perfunctory and brief, often consisting of a few lines with minimal detail, the newspaper wedding announcement nonetheless provides validation and proof of existence. In addition, noted Jensen (1996), they "have the potential to counter stereotypes of lesbians and gays that heterosexuals may hold," and at the same time allow lesbians and gays "to see representations of a wider variety of their community" (p. 15).

Simultaneously representing assimilation and distinction, announcements for same-sex weddings and commitment ceremonies allow for a counterhegemony within hegemony—a means to acknowledge and celebrate genuine love and commitment between two people. This form of wedding news provides a venue for what Mundy (2008) saw as an intersection between the label of being a same-sex couple (via their individual names), the image of a same-sex couple (via photographs), and the narrative of their wedding story. Of these, the issue of "how to play the kiss," that is, the composition of the accompanying photograph of the couple, becomes important in creating the "appropriate visibility" of the couple (p. 2).

In the end, even as same-sex wedding stories become normalized, the distinction from heterosexual marriage remains. Therefore, Mundy (2008) suggested, editors and those who serve a gatekeeping function regarding what does and does not appear in the final media product must focus on creating "a *sincere* representation of love and not a reliance on heteronormative tradition" (p. 15). Similarly, Lewin (1998) explained the significance of the sincerity of same-sex ceremonies based on a lack of acknowledgement and legitimacy: "Celebrants struggle to overcome the limitations that accompany the statutory invisibility of their unions, but it is that lack of status that also makes the rituals as emotionally compelling as they are" (p. 250).

Whereas same-sex wedding news has become somewhat commonplace since the early 2000s, the retail side had recognized the potential for a new market since the 1990s. In *Brides, Inc.*, Howard (2006) noted that the market for same-sex weddings began with commercial wedding guides at that time.

The flexibility of the Internet, in contrast to "tradition-bound" older retailers, allowed online entrepreneurs to cater to this formerly ignored audience (p. 223). For example, *TheKnot.com* had acknowledged and covered same-sex weddings since 1997 (Howard, 2006); in 1999 it featured a lesbian couple in a contest asking its web site visitors to vote for the "Millennial Couple" (Werde, 2003). The web site *GayWeddings.com* has a link to *GayWeddingStore.com*, a site featuring the typical items one finds at the traditional, heterosexual wedding: personalized champagne flutes, cake toppers (groom-groom and bride-bride), invitations, and guestbooks. The 2004 Massachusetts ruling allowing gay marriages saw even more growth in the gay wedding industry (Howard, 2006).[11]

In terms of print media, counterhegemony became folded into the common sense of bridal magazines with the publication of "Outward Bound," an article in the September–October 2003 issue of *Brides*, written by David Toussaint. "Outward Bound" made news in Bill Werde's July 28, 2003 article in *The New York Times*, "A First at Bride's Magazine: A Report on Same-Sex Unions." Werde reported that "Outward Bound" was the first feature article on same-sex weddings to appear among the top five bridal magazines. As reported in Werde's article, "Outward Bound" told readers why gay and lesbian couples wanted to have their commitment ceremonies recognized publicly and also gave advice to guests, telling them "'not to panic'" (p. C6). As for why *Brides* decided to include an article on same-sex weddings, Werde cited *Brides* editor in chief Millie Martini Bratten, who gave two reasons: "same-sex couples had become an important part of [retailers'] gift registries," and the magazine was finding itself answering more questions from readers asking for guidance on the "appropriate attire" for lesbian ceremonies. Bratten "also noted that *The New York Times* and other newspapers had begun publishing notices of same-sex ceremonies" (p. C6).

As a media artifact of a media artifact, the *Times* article not only illustrated the news value of "Outward Bound" as a sign that bridal print magazines finally acknowledged same-sex unions as being a segment of the wedding market, but it also included a wider discussion of the history of gay weddings in bridal media in general, both in terms of the Internet and other bridal media. For example, it mentioned that Internet wedding web sites already had been catering to same-sex couples, and included a quote from *TheKnot.com*'s editor in chief, Carley Roney, regarding the *Brides* article: "Wow, they [*Brides*] finally caught up," she said, alluding to The Knot's already-established coverage of same-sex weddings that began in the late 1990s (Werde, 2003, p. C6). The *Times* article concluded with reaction to *Brides*' acknowledgement of same-sex weddings by quoting David Toussaint, who said that he was "overwhelmed" by the response to his reportage. The people involved with his article were "thrilled," he said. "One gay couple, two men I interviewed, said they would buy every issue of *Bride's* on the newsstand," Toussaint said (Werde, 2003, p. C6). The response by the gay community to these incursions into the hegemonic wedding mediascape also denotes the sincerity and depth of meaning associated with same-sex commitment ceremonies, as noted by Lewin (1998) and Mundy (2008).

Popular culture as presented in mass media serves as a platform upon which "the terms of hegemony are affirmed and negotiated" (Gitlin, 1987, p. 242). As a conveyor of popular culture and popular practices, *Brides* (which the *Times* article mentioned had been publishing for 70 years at the time of "Outward Bound") and other bridal media serve as venues for both affirming hegemony and negotiating the inculcation of alternative views. Entrepreneurs on the Internet had already recognized a potential new market for selling wedding wares to an alternate audience. The eventual recognition of same-sex weddings in "traditional" bridal media like *Brides* became newsworthy enough for another medium, *The New York Times*, to tell its readers about, thus completing the circle of media coverage.

Bravo's *Gay Weddings*

Though gay characters have appeared on television in a wide array of genres since the 1950s, portrayals of gays and lesbians have historically marginalized this segment of the population (Tropiano, 2002). Story lines typically treated homosexuality as abnormal, stereotyped, or a problem to be fixed (Dow, 2001; Gross, 1989; Harrington, 2003). Gay characters were rarely shown as "just plain folks" in roles that did not center on "their deviance as a threat to the moral order which must be countered through ridicule or physical violence," according to Gross (1989, p. 137). Network television followed specific "rules" when portraying gay characters: theirs was a one-time appearance; story lines emphasized their effect on heterosexual characters; and they were rarely shown in the community, their own homes, or in same-sex relationships (Dow, 2001). In some 50 prime-time network series that included lesbian, gay, or bisexual characters whose homosexuality was incidental rather than a problem, characters more often than not appeared in comedies in which their erotic desires were largely absent (Harrington, 2003). Daytime soap operas through the 1990s continued to follow the same rules as prime-time programs (Harrington, 2003).

Gay weddings on prime-time television fiction began to appear around 1991, according to Capsuto (2000); until that time, the wedding story "was the one arena into which it was assumed same-sex couples could never enter"

(p. 352). Prime-time episodes of sitcoms such as *The Golden Girls, Dear John, Roc, Roseanne*, and *Friends* focused on the planning of gay wedding ceremonies and their effects on straight regulars. Network programs tended to omit mentioning issues surrounding the legal status of same-sex partners, but late 1990s episodes of *Spin City, Ellen*, and *The Practice* did provide insights into the more practical day-to-day benefits of marriage for gay characters (Capsuto, 2000).

Gay weddings on network TV followed the "rules" for portraying gays and lesbians in general. For example, same-sex marriages on television usually concerned either characters portrayed by guest actors or by regulars in peripheral roles (Capsuto, 2000; Dow, 2001). Additionally, gay weddings served either as catalysts for the examination of other issues or as centers of controversy, until one episode of the CBS drama-comedy *Northern Exposure* showed characters treating same-sex weddings as essentially uncontroversial, noted Capsuto (2000). Capsuto asserted that media's images of homosexuals have become mainstream, with TV episodes involving gay weddings becoming "almost cliché" (pp. 352–353).

In 2002, the Bravo channel's reality television program *Gay Weddings* joined the milieu of reality television wedding programs. I see *Gay Weddings* as an example of counterhegemony that illustrates the inherent changeability of hegemonic ideology within a liberal capitalist society, as described by Gitlin (1987, p. 242). As a media artifact, *Gay Weddings* offers a dual significance. First, it provides a next step in the continuum of television portrayals of gay and lesbian persons, historically framed as outside the norm, via the reality genre that features real people rather than fictional characters. Second, its focus on the weddings of same-sex couples challenges the notion that marriage and commitment are, or were, reserved for heterosexual relationships only.

The Bravo cable channel was looking for a reality series with a gay theme, targeted at adult audiences, after having had success with previous gay-themed reality programs ("Gay Weddings Go Prime Time," 2002; Shister, 2002).[12] Bravo approached Evolution Film and Tape in Los Angeles, a production company specializing in reality programming, to create a new show. Evolution founder Douglas Ross was also the executive producer of *Big Brother* on CBS and *Fear Factor* on NBC. Kirk Marcolina, who would become cocreator of the new reality show, recalled the wedding of two male friends as an "elaborate production, very theatrical and dramatic. And a lot of drama led up to the day" (Shister, 2002). Marcolina, who is gay, wanted the new show to demonstrate and validate the commitment of same-sex couples ("Gay Weddings Go Prime Time," 2002).

Recruitment for couples began in 2001. Budget considerations limited the series to the Los Angeles area. Ads in the local gay press, e-mails, ads in coffee shops in gay areas, and personal contacts were used to find couples who were planning their weddings. Casting began in May 2001, and all weddings had to take place by May 2002 ("Gay Weddings Go Prime Time," 2002; Shister, 2002). Of the 25 couples who responded, four couples, two gay and two lesbian, appear in the final production (Shister, 2002). Three of the couples were both Caucasian, one of the lesbian couples consisted of Sonja, who is African-American, and Lupe, who is Hispanic. Some 2,000 hours of footage resulted in eight episodes that followed the four selected couples as they planned their ceremonies (Lin-Eftekhar, 2002).

Gay Weddings premiered on September 2, 2002 as an eight-part series of half-hour episodes that followed the four couples as they planned their commitment ceremonies and ultimately "tied the knot." The show's debut coincided with *The New York Times'* announcement that its Sunday editions would begin publishing notices of gay and lesbian unions ("Gay Weddings Go Prime Time," 2002). In addition to its initial presentation, Bravo promoted the entire series of eight episodes as the "*Gay Weddings* Marathon" in early 2003. *Gay Weddings* drew largely positive reaction from media critics and reviewers from both the mainstream and gay press.[13] The rerun of the series opposite the 2003 Super Bowl resulted in Bravo's highest ratings, a success which eventually led to the gay relationship series *Boy Meets Boy* (Cook, 2003). As reality programming, *Gay Weddings* provides a groundbreaking portrayal of gays and lesbians in television by tackling the controversial issue of same-sex marriage that even prime-time, "gay friendly" programs such as *Will and Grace* had not been able to do (Piepenburg, 2002).

Gay Weddings follows the same format as other reality television wedding programs like TLC's *A Wedding Story* and Oxygen's *Real Weddings From The Knot*. Using the video vérité perspective, the series gives viewers a glimpse of the backstage activities of the four couples as they scout for ceremony venues, try on wedding apparel, and assemble party favors. The couples, their families, and friends provide voice-over narration. Occasionally, participants speak directly to the camera during a "video diary" segment. Even though none of the weddings featured in *Gay Weddings* held legal status, the term "wedding" is used throughout to denote the similarity of their ceremonies to "regular" weddings.

Each couple's wedding story unfolds within the context of how others, especially their families, view their relationship. As the following synopses illustrate, the four story lines address the unique characteristics of each relationship and the challenges faced by same-sex couples putting together a wedding. Following descriptions of the couples' individual narratives, I discuss themes in *Gay Weddings* that reflect previous and more current research of mass media portrayals of same-sex weddings.

The weddings

Scott and Harley. Scott, a 32-year-old consultant, and Harley, a 29-year-old who works in sales, have been together for two years. One of the story lines in their wedding reflects their seeming incompatibility, with episodes highlighting their recurring differences of opinion and the fact that they are seeing a couples' counselor. Scott even sees a counselor of his own. The viewer sees them constantly disagreeing about the details of their wedding, from the location of the ceremony to the centerpieces for their reception. Harley especially expresses concern over Scott's desire to include a strongly religious element into the ceremony (Scott had once studied to be a Catholic priest).

Differences between Harley and Scott also lie in how their families have accepted or not accepted their decision to have a wedding. Harley's mother is shown as very supportive and accepting of their relationship, and is involved with wedding preparations, as she is providing financial support. Scott, on the other hand, admits he has never actually come out to his parents, who are very conservative. Another story line in the narrative of this couple's wedding focuses on how Scott's parents, while saying on camera they don't fully understand his sexuality and commitment to Harley, do attend the wedding and demonstrate their support for Scott. Thus, in Scott and Harley's story, family approval plays a central part, and viewers see that Scott's parents do come around and show their acceptance for his gay wedding. Indeed, during the wedding reception, Scott's father gives his son a kiss and tells him he loves him.

Scott and Harley have their wedding in Puerto Vallarta, Mexico, the place where they first met. They have some 40 guests, and throw a pre-wedding dinner where drag queens hired by Harley perform because he wanted everyone to "see more gay life." The casual ceremony is held on the beach, with all the guests dressed in casual, tropical-themed clothing. Harley and Scott wear tropical shirts with slacks, and they appear barefoot. Harley is escorted by his mother, Scott by his parents. The officiant appears to be a male friend. The ceremony includes the exchanging of rings, and some hint of religion as the officiant mentions "God" and ask guests to pray. Scott and Harley read vows they have written themselves. The couple poses for photographs and then joins the reception with dinner and dancing. Their wedding day ends with everyone watching a fireworks display.

Dan and Gregg. Of the couples who appear in *Gay Weddings*, Dan and Gregg are clearly the most affluent. Together for several years, Dan is a 37-year-old Hollywood movie executive and Gregg, 35, is vice president of a travel company specializing in gay vacations. One of the recurring themes in their narrative is the way they demonstrate affection through gifts and surprise trips. For example, Gregg surprises Dan with a helicopter ride on Valentine's Day and Dan makes a last-minute surprise visit to Gregg while he is working on a gay-themed ocean cruise in Hawaii.

The other major story line for Dan and Gregg revolves around how each man's family regards his sexual orientation and decision to marry. Gregg's family is very supportive; his parents and siblings attend the wedding and some of the pre-wedding events, while Dan struggles to gain the acceptance of his mother and sister. "The journey with my family has been a bumpy one," Dan comments. Dan receives numerous Christmas gifts from them, but they decide not to attend his wedding. Dan says they think "it's odd" for him to be living with a man and to want to commit to Gregg. Gregg consistently offers Dan support and reassures him that he is loved and appreciated. While Dan admits to being jealous of the support Gregg has from his family, Dan's three cousins do show him their support by attending the pre-wedding dinner and the ceremony itself. "It meant the world to me," says Dan. Dan and Gregg attend a "bridal" shower thrown by their friends, and host a pre-wedding dinner at which Gregg's mother makes a toast to her "two favorite sons."

The couple hires Merv Griffin Productions to put together their wedding at the luxurious Park Plaza hotel in Los Angeles; they have about 200 guests. Several times they refer to their wedding by saying, "Showtime!" At the outdoor ceremony, Dan and Gregg wear identical suits and ties and walk in together. A gospel choir provides music. Their officiant is Phil, who apparently is a close friend. They read vows they have written to each other, and exchange "eternity bands" which are brought into the ceremony by their pet dog. The ceremony evokes a somewhat religious nature, with Phil mentioning the word "God" several times. Phil mentions that some people have chosen not to be at the ceremony, referring to the absence of Dan's mother and sister. The ceremony ends with the traditional Jewish breaking of glass.

A Scottish bagpipe ensemble then greets guests into the indoor reception, which includes a lavish sit-down dinner, wedding cake (actually consisting of a tower of individual cupcakes), a live band and dancing, and traditional Jewish wedding music and chair dance. The atmosphere inside the large reception hall evokes images of a glamorous, "movie-star" wedding similar to celebrity weddings featured in the reality programs described in Chapter 3. As Gregg's brother-in-law and father each make toasts to the couple, we see Dan's emotional reaction as they welcome him into their family.

Dale and Eve. Together for four years, Dale, a 32-year-old entertainment lawyer, and Eve, a 30-year-old film student, are shown throughout their story line dealing with their somewhat controlling, New Age wedding officiant. Eve's parents, though supportive of her relationship with Dale, renege on their financial contribution to the wedding. Eve's mother, however, is clearly enthusiastic about the wedding itself. Eve's grandfather is also supportive. In contrast, the reaction of Dale's family was "tepid," and she is not sure if any of her family will attend. She comments that her wedding to Eve does not seem to hold the same status as that of her siblings' heterosexual weddings. Despite Dale and Eve's concerns about their families' attendance, their families meet each other for the first time at a "rehearsal" lunch at Eve's parents' home. Both families eventually do attend and participate in the wedding.

Dale and Eve's wedding ceremony and reception are held in a high-end hotel with about 50 guests. At their ceremony, they are each escorted separately by their parents, and both have a maid of honor. An acoustic ensemble with vocalist provides the music; the officiant blows a conch shell to cue each woman into the ceremony. Eve and Dale say their own vows, and exchange rings reciting more traditional vows ("With this ring, I thee wed"). Both wear similar white designer gowns and carry a bouquet of red roses.

The officiant causes some minor mishaps during the ceremony, such as saying that Dale's family came from Albania, rather than Armenia, and dropping and picking up small pieces of paper from the book she uses. Shots of Dale and Eve looking concerned are interspersed as the ceremony progresses. After the ceremony, Dale comments, "Well, that was a comedy of errors." The following reception consists of a sit-down dinner, music provided by a deejay, dancing, and a wedding cake. Dale and Eve then cut the cake and feed pieces to each other. Eve's mother makes a toast to the couple, after which Dale and Eve toss their bouquets. Their reception ends with them slow dancing in the almost-empty reception hall.

Sonja and Lupe. Of the four couples, Sonja and Lupe seem to experience the most stress, as their plans are met with obstacles at almost every step. Sonja, 39, is an emergency room supervisor and Lupe, 32, is in marketing. Their parents are not mentioned, but Sonja does have a teenage son. Though he is accepting and supportive of her, Sonja worries about his reaction to their wedding. When Sonja tells him, he reacts very positively, and tells her that he assumes he will give her away at the ceremony.

As Sonja and Lupe scout for ceremony sites, they experience discrimination; on the phone, one hotel manager seems welcoming, but when Sonja and Lupe visit the site together, they encounter the cold shoulder, with the manager saying they cannot be accommodated. They get an outright "absolutely not" when they visit another site and say they are having a lesbian commitment ceremony. They finally decide to hold their ceremony and reception at the home of a lesbian couple they know, even though Lupe expresses unhappiness with the location. Another obstacle involves the fear that their wedding cake will not be ready in time, but disaster is averted, much to Lupe's relief.

Of the four weddings featured, theirs is the least lavish. The ceremony takes place in the backyard of their friends' modest home with about 40 guests. Sonja's son escorts her in first; Lupe's sister escorts her in next. There are no others in the bridal party. Their apparel denotes a gender-based element in their relationship; Sonja liked feminine women, and Lupe had changed her "butch" appearance and mannerisms after she met Sonja. At their wedding, Sonja wears a dressy, flowing white pantsuit and does not carry any flowers, while Lupe wears a white, formal, cocktail-length gown with matching headdress and carries a bouquet. The female officiant appears to be a minister; she refers to the Church of Jesus Christ, although there is no mention of "God" or any other religious reference. Sonja and Lupe repeat gender-neutral vows spoken by the officiant, which are based loosely on traditional vows. They exchange rings, reciting, "With this ring, I thee wed."

After Sonja and Lupe are declared "spouse and spouse," guests mingle outside for the reception. However, the weather turns too cold for comfort and the party is moved indoors, causing more consternation for Lupe. Everything is rearranged and the reception goes smoothly. No dancing is shown. Sonja's son makes a toast to the happy couple. Their wedding day ends as Sonja and Lupe leave in a limousine. As an epilogue, the viewer sees them enjoying a trip to the beach during their honeymoon.

Common themes in Gay Weddings

Taken together, all four weddings described here share the familiar wedding elements commonly present in heterosexual wedding ceremonies. They all closely followed some kind of traditional "wedding" script: a formalized public ceremony incorporating an exchanging of rings and vows followed by a reception. The two lesbian weddings looked like the "stereotypical white wedding" as described by Ingraham (1999): "a spectacle featuring a bride in a formal white wedding gown, combined with some combination of attendants and witnesses, religious ceremony, wedding reception, and honeymoon" (p. 3).

However, some elements are noticeably missing in *Gay Weddings*. Except for passing mentions of religious reference, clearly identified clergy are absent, except at Sonja and Lupe's wedding, and none of the ceremonies were held in a church or religious site. Although there is some mention in the first episode of *Gay Weddings* that same-sex marriages are not legally recognized, there is no mention of religious sanctioning of gay and lesbian weddings. Mundy (2008) found a similar pattern in his study of same-sex wedding announcements in *The New York Times*, with friends serving as celebrants for most of the same-sex couples in his sample.[14]

The "packaging" of *Gay Weddings* reflects the message that these formalized events in which gay and lesbian couples publicly declare their commitment and love to each other are the same as those of heterosexual couples. Even its title illustrates the program's intent to mainstream same-sex unions; the title *Gay Weddings* certainly has a more traditional-sounding ring than one like *Same-Sex Commitment Ceremonies*, for example. This is further manifested by the series' opening credits: a wedding cake serves as the background for the show's title and the names of the couples are written in frosting. The cake toppers, a bride and a groom, are knocked off the cake and replaced with figures of two grooms standing together and two brides standing together.

In the four total hours of programming, I found several themes common to each couple's story that distinguished these weddings from those of heterosexual couples. First, as found in previous research on same-sex unions, the approval and participation of family members had a high level of significance for each couple. Second, in contrast to the way in which heterosexual couples in other wedding reality programs prepared and worked for their weddings, couples appeared to have an equal division of labor. Third, couples in *Gay Weddings* regularly and overtly express their stress and nervousness on camera. Last, these couples saw their weddings as validating their relationships. In the following discussion, I explain how their stories illustrated these themes.

"The few interpretive studies of heterosexual weddings and related rituals that have been published have not questioned the heterosexist social context in which family relations are negotiated," noted Oswald in 2000 (p. 350). In that our ideas of the wedding are implicitly heterosexist, the additional pressures faced by gay and lesbian couples, such as their families' (not to mention society's) acceptance, present themselves in *Gay Weddings*. Indeed, the Bravo channel's own program description of the series points to the additional factors faced by same-sex couples as they plan their commitment ceremonies: "One of the most stressful events any couple can undertake is compounded for these couples by social and political pressures" ("Bravo Fact Sheet," n.d.). Among these pressures is the importance placed on family members' validation, a recurrent theme noted by *Gay Weddings* cocreator Kirk Marcolina ("Gay Weddings Go Prime Time," 2002).

The angst and concern over whether family members would attend or even accept their sexual orientation and decision to commit publicly to their partner was especially evident for two of the gay men, Scott and Dan. Scott's parents eventually come to accept his decision to marry Harley, while Dan's mother and sister remain absent from his wedding to Gregg. Sonja expressed concern about her son's reaction to her wedding to Lupe, and Eve and Dale experience ups and downs regarding their families' actions. However, for these two lesbian couples, their initial worries dissipate. Perhaps the acceptance of their unions reflects a society-wide tolerance for lesbian couples, while homosexuality among men might not be as accepted.

Because same-sex unions generally fall outside legal boundaries and lack the same "credibility" that accompany heterosexual weddings, "couples who have commitment ceremonies understand these occasions to be about their relationship to their families," noted Lewin (1998, p. 250). Though one's "family" may constitute close friends, "the absence of relatives may be as marked and emotionally intense as their presence; in either case, both are taken note of and interpreted at length after the fact" (Lewin, 1998, p. 250). Lewin's observation appeared to be validated in *Gay Weddings*. Although they were surrounded by supportive and close friends, each couple expressed how significant it was for their families to be involved in their weddings. The emphasis on family participation illustrates the need for the same approval and recognition given to heterosexual weddings.

Unlike the traditional gender roles that mark heterosexual weddings, the way in which these same-sex couples approached the planning of their weddings illustrated an equal division of labor. While planning and decision-making often fall on the bride-to-be in the typical heterosexual wedding, the couples in *Gay Weddings* made decisions about the most detailed elements of their ceremonies as a team. This egalitarianism appeared as couples did all the things associated with "regular" wedding planning, such as visiting sites, choosing clothing, deciding on flower arrangements, and assembling party favors. For example, Gregg and Dan assemble party favors together, with Dan even quipping, "I feel like I'm in a sweat shop." Eve and Dale go wedding dress shopping together, and Sonja and Lupe attend a bridal show.

These depictions reflect the egalitarian nature of same-sex couples, as compared to heterosexual couples, in which the woman most often does the work in planning what is supposedly "her day" (Currie, 1993; Geller, 2001; Lowrey & Otnes, 1994). When compared to other reality wedding programs discussed in Chapter 5, the images of these couples planning their weddings and doing wedding chores together creates the impression not only of cooperation, but also illustrates the importance the wedding itself holds for them. In short, these scenes further add to the authenticity and meaningfulness with which same-sex couples approach their weddings and commitment ceremonies. In this sense, *Gay Weddings* provides a pictorial argument in support of same-sex marriage as well as evidence that same-sex weddings are just like everyone else's and require the same preparations and decisions.

The honesty of the couples as they talked about the problems they experienced marked all four couples' story lines as well. All admitted to being stressed and worried about their weddings and to having misgivings and being nervous on the wedding day itself. Of the four couples, Sonja and Lupe experienced overt discrimination, adding to their wedding planning woes. In this regard, *Gay Weddings* offers viewers a realistic portrayal of the unique challenges faced by same-sex couples, and the prejudice they may face in a society that still considers such relationships as illegitimate, and, indeed, wrong.

Regarding the theme of open expression of stress and nervousness, *Gay Weddings* stands apart from other wedding reality programs by revealing points of contention between couples. For example, Dan and Gregg have differing opinions about having children, and Scott and Harley admit to relationship problems that require counseling. Rather than framing these couples as having ideal romantic relationships, which served as a hallmark of TLC's *A Wedding Story*, viewers witness the backstage issues that these couples deal with on a daily basis. The willingness of the couples to have their real lives included for all to see on the one hand illustrates how the reality genre may exploit the people who appear in these programs and feeds into the schadenfreude appeal of watching arguments and learning about others' problems. On the other hand, these revelations serve as "reality checks" to show the multiple layers of complexity involved not only with (a) romantic relationships in general, but (b) planning a wedding that (c) counters a society that is only now starting to accept and legalize same-sex marriage. Thus, by showing the additional challenges faced by couples of the same sex, *Gay Weddings* conveys to viewers just how much strength is needed for these couples to accomplish what heterosexual couples may take for granted. In this sense, the issues of family acceptance and relationship validation become highlighted, with the real stories of real gay and lesbian couples serving as a means to enlighten viewers about the significance of the wedding as a means to give legitimacy to this version of committed relationships.

In addition to the desire for family validation, relationship validation serves as another theme of *Gay Weddings*. In the first episode, Dan explains that even though same-sex marriages are not legal (in California), "It's really no more complicated than two people who love each other and they want to make a commitment to each other in front of their friends and family." By agreeing to appear in the program, the couples obviously share the same view. For the couples in *Gay Weddings*, having a wedding ceremony helped to strengthen their bond, as the following comments illustrate:

> Eve (married to Dale): I think that if we hadn't had a ceremony and we hadn't gone through the whole process, you know, then there wouldn't have been any milestone or major moment to signify the change in our relationship.

> Sonja (married to Lupe): . . . it *is* the whole hoopla. It is, you know, getting everything together and just the planning everything and have the whole ceremony. Definitely a different feeling. I feel so differently about Lupe now.

Dale (married to Eve): I think the ceremony has created a shift in our relationship and I feel like it's given people that know us [the chance] to see how special our union is.

Harley (married to Scott): It's not 'I' or 'me' anymore. It's an 'us.'

Thus, having a formal ceremony served as a way for these couples to strengthen their relationships and to attain the public recognition they felt gave their relationship an elevated status as a "married" couple. That the couples featured in this program all wanted a wedding/commitment ceremony attests to the special status given by society to heterosexual marriages.

In that *Gay Weddings* featured what one could certainly call "mainstream" weddings modeled after heterosexual weddings, it supports Condit's (1994) interpretation of hegemony as concordance.[15] Rather than ideology forced upon a subordinate class by a ruling, dominant class, as hegemony is defined, concordance emerges from among all the viewpoints and voices considered within pluralism, with those having the most universal appeal "rising to the top," so to speak. The gay and lesbian couples included here share and express these universally appealing, commonsensical, accepted views regarding love, marriage, and weddings. They all go about putting the tremendous amount of time, energy, and emotional investment into the planning and execution of their wedding ceremonies and receptions. Additionally, the use of the term "wedding" pointedly illustrates how deeply inculcated and ingrained these societal ideals and expectations are. Thus, *Gay Weddings* offers something "natural," with just a minor twist.

"As it is, 'Gay Weddings' is a sweet, enjoyable program, but it could have made more of a statement," wrote Alter (2002) in his critique of the show. Alter asserted that rather than approaching the subject as reality TV, the producers could have used a traditional documentary format to give viewers a history behind gay weddings and a background on current marriage laws in the US. Padget (2002) criticized the series for its production values, which mimicked MTV's *The Real World*, and its focus on materialistic concerns of wedding planning that reflect the "money-sucking straight marriage-industrial complex" wedding norm. Similarly, I see *Gay Weddings* as demonstrating the presence and importance the couples placed on familiar, traditional wedding elements promoted in bridal media.

However, unlike the more "mainstream" versions of reality wedding shows described in previous chapters, *Gay Weddings* provides more insight into the dynamics of romantic relationships by including participants' second thoughts, arguments, and doubts. In the context of hegemony, a traditional documentary treatment would have further demarcated these weddings as gay, versus straight. Throughout the eight episodes, the viewer is reminded repeatedly that these are gay weddings. Footage of Gregg on the gay cruise, Sonja and Lupe being turned away from potential wedding sites, drag queens performing at Scott and Harley's rehearsal dinner, and Dan and Scott's emotional turmoil as they yearn for their parents' acceptance all remind the viewer that these couples face a set of challenges they otherwise might not if they were straight. Thus, while Alter (2002) suggested that a more educational, informational background would have helped viewers appreciate the obstacles same-sex couples face, those struggles are interwoven into their stories anyway.

All the traditional bridal elements are present in both of the female couples' weddings, which illustrates the hegemonic aspects of the bridal appearance. Of particular note is the wedding apparel of Sonia and Lupe, with Lupe taking on a decidedly feminine look with elaborate wedding gown and veil while her partner Sonia wears a non-traditional—but white—pantsuit. However, the other three couples wore similar outfits for their weddings, indicating an absence, at least appearance-wise, of identities regarding "masculine" or "feminine" roles. This issue of differentiation within same-sex couples, such as the different wedding apparel of other same-sex weddings, could be studied further.[16]

Gay Weddings as entertainment programming manages to illustrate both hegemony and counterhegemony: the hegemony surrounding the belief that relationships need to be formalized by a public ceremony and a counterhegemony that questions heterosexuality as a requisite for romantic love. According to Lewin (1998), "even as conventions are overturned in these ceremonial occasions, they are reinscribed and reinvented; by arguing that they don't need the trappings of legal marriage, couples simultaneously demand access to analogous symbolic resources" (p. 232). Thus, Lewin asserted, "lesbian and gay commitment ceremonies offer symbolic resistance to heterosexist domination, but they often do so by exalting the very values they might claim to challenge" (p. 234). *Gay Weddings* provides a certain degree of support for Lewin's observation regarding the dichotomy of convention and subversion these ceremonies embody. However, the wedding, and thus any commitment *ceremony*, by nature finds its basis in tradition that in turn originates in some socially historical endorsement of accepted practice and values. In other words, weddings are inherently based on tradition (Geller, 2001).

Venues for Change: Anti-, Offbeat, and Feminist Brides

Media examples of resistance to wedding hegemony include books advising women to create stress-free weddings that reflect their own tastes and individuality. However, even as they claim to challenge the white wedding ideal, they tend to look pretty much like the standard wedding guides one might consider "traditional." The wedding becomes a way to have it both ways: (a) one can be individualistic, and (b) one can achieve this individualism without deviating too much from the accepted way of doing things. One book in particular acknowledges the appeal of the wedding as a feminine endeavor while encouraging women to do things their own way.

Published in 2002, Gerin and Rosenbaum's *Anti-Bride Guide: Tying the Knot Outside of the Box* implies a counterhegemonic attitude. "Out of the box," a catchphrase for questioning authority now overused to denote uniqueness, infers an alternative to the "regular" wedding. As an example of Third Wave feminism, wherein personal choices and definitions of feminism have replaced the active changing of gender expectations and the challenging of patriarchy in the Second Wave, *Anti-Bride Guide* forwards the notion that women can be feminine while asserting their own identities free from the stress of mothers and others. The authors, Carolyn Gerin and Stephanie Rosenbaum, overtly endorse femininity in their introduction and acknowledge the appeal of the wedding as a means of achieving temporary celebrity by asking, "At what other time do you get to plan, stage-manage, and then (wearing a really fabulous outfit) star in your very own show?" (p. 9).

Thus, right at the start of this anti-wedding book, Gerin, Rosenbaum, and the reader already accept the inherent work involved and the common sense associated with the production aspect of weddings. The enjoyment of preparing one's person for the bridal role and materialism associated with the wedding are also assumed, further endorsing the femininity embodied in creating the perfect bridal appearance: "After all, we love pedicures, presents, and Champagne. . . . And unless you're Miss America or Madonna, you'll probably never have so many people dedicated to making you beautiful as you will for this one day" (p. 9). The authors of *Anti-Bride Guide* balanced this aspect of the bridal role with an indirect nod to feminism by noting that the reader/bride is a modern woman in modern times: "You're not living the same kind of life your mother or grandmother had," they wrote, establishing that the anti-bride they describe breaks from traditional gender roles (p. 10).

In this form of bridal media, the underlying symbolism and common sense of the wedding—its rituals, ceremony, and "fabulous dress"—still exist, but the anti-bride does things her own way. The creation of new traditions deemed appropriate and meaningful for women (and their partners) who see themselves as individualists articulates resistance to hegemonic portrayals still firmly entrenched among myriad bridal media examined here. Indeed, emphasis on alternative weddings and brides become underscored, in that Gerin and Rosenbaum specifically included lesbian brides under the anti-bride umbrella, stating, "maybe you'll be making your lifetime commitment to another woman" (p. 10).

Invoking the language of the beat generation that espoused anti-establishment messages during the mid-20th century, Gerin and Rosenbaum defined their anti-bride as "a cool chick who gets to have (and eat) her cake, work her style to the max, and dance the night away" (p. 10). They go on to tell readers that the wedding "is not an end in itself," but the beginning of marriage, a point rarely made in "traditional" bridal media (p. 12). The clarity of the counterhegemonic theme of the anti-bride and her desire to be her own person deviates enough from common sense but not enough to reject completely the concept of the wedding. Hence, the subsequent chapters of *Anti-Bride Guide* mimic the planning rubric of other wedding guide books and bridal magazines, with information and advice on subjects such as how to find a venue, incorporating one's own style into the wedding, ceremony details, dress-buying tips, "beauty notes," checklists and timeline for completing tasks, and a resource guide listing vendors for invitations, jewelry, discount bridal apparel, and vintage clothing. The anti-bride may do things her own way, but apparently there are enough things for her to still do that *Anti-Bride Guide* was followed in 2004 by *Anti-Bride Wedding Planner: Hip Tools and Tips for Getting Hitched* (Gerin, Hughes, Hornick, & Tubkam).

In popular media, humor has become a way of questioning hegemony without invoking an explicitly feminist stance. For example, a series of books by a group humorously titled the Cambridge Women's Pornography Cooperative (CWPC) offers readers a comical take on the concept of "pornography" by offering readers a glimpse of "what really turns women on"—in the form of men depicted doing housework, cleaning, and taking care of children.[17] The turning of the tables regarding the second shift and domestic work serves as the basis for these books, with titles such as *Porn for Women* and *Porn for New Moms*. Photos featuring young, handsome men holding babies and doing housework or cooking serve as the "porn" women seek. These small novelty books offer women "porn" via an image of the ideal man as both good-looking and taking on household chores with glee.

In 2009, the CWPC added *Porn for the Bride* to the series of these humorous books. The questioning of the gendered division of labor that marks wedding planning becomes the basis for photos and captions that offer brides the "dream groom," as the blurb on the book's back cover attests: "Prepare to meet the groom of your wildest dreams. These hotties write thank-you notes, insist their fiancées put on some weight before the wedding, and best of all, take over the cooking and cleaning so their blushing brides can rest up before the big day." Giving acknowledgement to the pursuit of perfection that has become part of the common sense of wedding planning, the book tells readers to raise their standards, and provides a quiz for the bride to see how her man rates on a series of items testing his wedding etiquette and regard for her. Captions that accompany the "porn" photos include: "Baby, I can't wait to look at china patterns this weekend" (p. 17), "You don't need to exercise before the wedding" (p. 27), and "I feel it will be much more meaningful if we write our own vows" (p. 32). The reader finds the essence of *Porn for the Bride* captured in the caption accompanying a photo of a shirtless man in jeans running a vacuum cleaner while spraying glass cleaner on a window: "Is there anything else I can do around here, so you can just totally relax and focus on our big day?" (p. 25).

One may easily dismiss these books as comical novelties, good for a laugh as inside jokes aimed at women. Because it only encourages brides to persuade their men to share—or wish for a man who would share—the burden of wedding planning, *Porn for the Bride* on the surface continues the mindset that weddings must involve the amount of planning and unpaid labor dictated by mainstream bridal media. However, a deeper reading reveals a critique of current gender norms not only regarding weddings, but in general. The use of humor allows for counterhegemonic commentary that creates awareness of gender inequities while not threatening the status quo.

The Internet has become an equalizing medium allowing diverse opinions to reach a wide audience. The wedding industry took advantage of the "portal" format of linking customers to vendors, and it was the Internet that foresaw catering to same-sex couples wanting weddings. One bridal web site that explicitly uses the term "feminism" and extends the boundaries of the wedding world is *Indiebride.com*. Rather than a destination or wedding planning site, *Indiebride.com* serves as a blog where visitors can post questions, receive advice, and vent. To demarcate it from other bridal media, the "Our Vow" page states the purpose of the site is to not only fill a void in the hegemonic world of wedding media, but to serve as "a place for would-be brides who have more on their minds than planning a reception, women who never for a second believed in Prince Charming and who have not, despite all of the cultural cues, been breathlessly awaiting their wedding day for their whole life" ("Indiebride: Our Vow," 2008).

Despite *Indiebride.com*'s self-stated separation from the bridal media milieu, the usual suspects of wedding planning do make an appearance. For example, the "Indieetiquette" page authored by "Elise" serves as an advice column on various wedding-related questions. The "Kvetch" link, however, does offer critical observations, advice, and "kvetching" from visitors. The "Kvetch" title itself reflects the creation of a cultural space where women (and men, one assumes) can vent their ideas, feelings, and self-reflections as they contemplate the wedding process, or choose to forego it altogether. A discussion board for a variety of threads on wedding advice, preparation, and reception planning, the "Kvetch" link takes visitors to ongoing conversations on "Showers," "Cutting Costs," "Vows," "Veils," "Makeup on Wedding Day," and "Invitations." *Indiebride.com* also fosters discussions about wedding stress ("Second Thoughts," "Anxiety," "Horror Stories") and questions about what comes after the wedding, with discussion board titles like "Life After Marriage" and "Second Marriages."

However, I found more telling the subversion and consciousness-raising aspects of this site regarding wedding traditions and how to change them. These appear in the titles of discussion threads such as "Eloping" and "Commitment Ceremonies." The thread "Same Sex Marriage" originated from a post by a bride who asked for suggestions of film clips showing respectful portrayals of gay weddings. She wanted to use the clips in a montage of wedding images at her heterosexual reception. These particular threads all point to counterhegemonic perspectives. Eloping offers an alternative way to get married that avoids the wedding altogether. Threads on commitment ceremonies and same-sex marriage offer clear counterpoints to the compulsory heterosexuality assumed by the institution of marriage.

Explicitly feminist viewpoints also make an appearance on *Indiebride.com*. The "Marriage and Feminism" discussion thread and "Ridiculous Bridal Ads and Articles," which even includes a critique of the "ridiculous" prices of bridal gowns in the TLC program *Say Yes to the Dress*—discussed in Chapter 4—demonstrate that scholars aren't the only ones questioning the authority of wedding etiquette experts or the media-created ideals of femininity. Indeed, the March 29, 2007 posting on the "Marriage and Feminism" thread by one visitor named Lauraska (2007) asked, "Am I being too uber-feminist, here?" because she found it insulting to be called her live-in boyfriend's wife rather than by her own name. What becomes clear on the discussion boards on *Indiebride.com* is how the adage "the personal is political" surfaces from narratives of the mundane.

As if to symbolize the shrugging off of gendered traditions associated with the wedding, the site's "The Bouquet Toss and Other Antiquated Traditions" discussion thread provides a virtual place where visitors can ask for alternatives to the culturally scripted rituals and artifacts associated with engagement proposals, ceremony escort, rings, in addition to the b quet toss and other antiquated rituals. A visitor named Garnet (2004) asked, "Anyone else feel icky about bouquet/garter toss?" This question reveals how some women see such practices as uncomfortable and "icky" (for example, one might see persons actually trying to avoid contact with the bouquet as revealing their aversion to the ritual and its meaning). Additionally, one could view a literal throwing off of the bridal role as being represented on *Indiebride.com*'s "Trousseau—Indiebride Gear and Clothes Swap" section. This section of the site gives visitors the opportunity to "unload all of the bridalware taking up your closet space," or to find bargains on designer gowns worn, of course, only once ("Indiebride: Trousseau," 2008). In an eBay style format, "Trousseau" features photos and descriptions of used wedding gowns at discount prices, for a listing fee of $10.

Indiebride.com was mentioned in the acknowledgements of the book *Offbeat Bride: Taffeta-Free Alternatives for Independent Brides* by Ariel Meadow Stallings (2006), who cited the web site as helping her to plan her own wedding as well as with writing her book. Wrote Stallings, "I must also bow down at the altar of the almighty Indiebride.com" (p. 209). In the introduction to *Offbeat Bride*, Stallings explained how she was "amazed by how many freaks, feminists, and freethinkers find themselves getting married at a ceremony that looks like it belongs to someone else" (p. 1). As a bride who could not relate to the traditional bridal identity requiring interest in floral arrangements and "decorative bows for the backs of rented chairs," Stallings's purpose addressed the implicit counterhegemonic perspective of those for whom she wrote her book: couples who sought to create their own weddings on their own terms (p. 1). Subsequent chapters in *Offbeat Bride* offer wedding planning hints, with one on the issue of changing one's name.

Created to promote Stallings's book, the web site *Offbeatbride.com* serves as a blog for "couples who dare to walk off the beaten aisle" ("Offbeat Bride: Altar Your Thinking," 2003–2010). Claiming visits by more than 150,000 "nontraditional brides" a month, *Offbeatbride.com* serves as a venue where one can find details about the nontraditional weddings of couples as well as tips and links to vendors who specialize in goods and services catering to unique weddings ("Offbeat Bride: Advertise," 2003–2010). *Offbeatbride.com* supports "couples all along the nontraditional spectrum from beautiful hardcore freaks and geeks all the way to what we affectionately call 'Offbeat Lite'" ("Offbeat Bride: About," 2003–2010). Although certainly not anti-wedding, the site nevertheless aims to provide "positive encouragement" for couples, and further distinguishes itself from other wedding web sites by showing that such sites "don't have to be snarky, bitchy places where women decree each other tacky" ("Offbeat Bride: About," 2003–2010).

The counterhegemonic overtones of *Offbeatbride.com* become evident by the photos posted on its comically titled "Wedding Porn" section. A quick look-see evidences the offbeat nature of the weddings featured on this site; one can read about "Trish & Patrick's Tattooed, Gothic Rockabilly, Metal Funfest," "Danae & Dougie's 50s Style Lego and Candy Wedding," and "Danielle & Dave's Geeky, Puzzle-Laden, Brooklyn Wedding" ("Offbeat Bride: Wedding Porn," 2003–2010). Wedding photos reflect what I consider a quirky retro look—brides in colorful dresses reminiscent of the 1940s and 50s (as well as colorful hair) and grooms in variations on the tuxedo. Weddings based on literary and popular culture themes also reflect the personal style and interests of the couples, such as the "*Moulin Rouge* Meets *Dr. Who*" wedding and one wedding based on the classic children's book *Where the Wild Things Are*.

While white wedding gowns and formal tuxes do appear among *Offbeatbride.com*'s "Wedding Porn" offerings, the emphasis on alternative comes not only from the site's statement of purpose, but follows through to its offerings for wedding-related products. For example, "The Name Changer Kit," priced at $24, contains forms and directions for changing one's name upon marriage, including "women taking their husband's name, men taking their wife's name, gay and lesbian couples changing their last name(s), and het [heterosexual] couples taking a new shared last name" ("Offbeat Name-Changing Kit," n.d.). *Offbeatbride.com* celebrates difference by flouting the rules, not only through its text and visuals, but the products it features that challenge the common sense of cultural norms and expectations associated with the change in status of couples who do marry, regardless of sexual orientation.

Aimed at the offbeat *bride*, the site's title still assumes a female target audience, and thus remains within the gendered world of weddings, preventing it from being truly counterhegemonic (as with other alternative wedding media, of course). It works both within and outside the boundaries of what Lears (1985) termed "common-sense 'reality'"(p. 572) by including a wide gamut of weddings and personal styles ignored by "mainstream" bridal media as represented by print magazines and web sites that still present uniform versions of the white wedding.

The web site *FeministWedding.com* presents a decidedly more overt feminist leaning while also reflecting an expressed consciousness that offers its visitors ways to negotiate the wedding while holding onto their feminist ideals. On its home page, the site's statement of purpose includes the acknowledgement of "Western patriarchal culture"; the site "exists to reiterate that fact and provide information and resources for those who are wondering if it is possible to have a feminist wedding and what it might look like" ("FeministWedding.com," 2010). This negotiation between one's self-identification as a feminist and one's participation in wedding practices that originate in patriarchy becomes key to how *FeministWedding.com* serves as an example of a platform for escaping without leaving, as de Certeau termed it (1984, p. xiii).

On its "FAQ" (frequently asked questions) page, site creator "Casey" explains she developed *FeministWedding.com* because "there was no central place on the internet for me to discuss various aspects of the traditional 'white weddings' I was attending." "As a feminist," she states, "I wanted to know how other women have subverted patriarchal traditions in their weddings and where those traditions came from in the first place. I also wanted a site where I could point my non-feminist friends to in order to show them some of what I envisioned for a feminist wedding" ("FAQ, FeministWedding.com," 2011). On the same page, Casey points out that the term "choice feminism" is really a misnomer: a woman who makes the "wrong choice" faces opposition and social censure, such as when she must explain and defend her "choice" not to take her husband's name after marriage.

In lieu of the expected wedding tips presented on other "alternative" wedding sites, the links on *FeministWedding.com*'s "Topics" page actually take visitors to individual pages featuring information and histories of various wedding rituals and artifacts. The links "White Dress & Symbolism," "Accessories," "Ceremony," "Invitations," and "Changing Names" take visitors to pages that feature informational content rather than wedding planning ideas or, as with other sites, more links to merchandisers. The site's "Resources" page offers reviews of scholarly books and articles on weddings, such as *Here Comes the Bride: Women, Weddings, and the Marriage Mystique* by Geller (2001), *White Weddings: Romancing Heterosexuality in Popular Culture* by Ingraham (1999), and *Cinderella Dreams: The Allure of the Lavish Wedding* by Otnes and Pleck (2003). In a review of Naomi Wolf's (2003) "Brideland," the writer admits being disappointed that the article was only a few pages long but tells readers that it provided "a refreshingly open" look at the bridal industry through feminist eyes ("Resources, FeministWedding.com," 2011).

At the bottom of *FeministWedding.com*'s "Resources" page, visitors can click on links to other sites for more feminist-oriented information. One is for *Offbeatbride.com*, which demonstrates the degree of intertextuality that characterizes bridal media in general, at both the "popular" and "alternative" levels. Other links take visitors to: *LucyStoneLeague.org*, a site named for the 19th century suffragist Lucy Stone, who kept her maiden name after marriage; *RosieWedding.com*, a personal web site created by feminist bride "Rosie"; and *Unmarried.org*, the site for the Alternatives to Marriage Project. These links reflect a truly alternative nature that other sites I found in this vein did not, in that the *Unmarried.org* site's counterhegemonic nature stands against marriage altogether. I discuss that particular site in more detail as an example of counterhegemony in the next chapter.

Both *FeministWeddings.com* and *RosieWedding.com* serve as examples of the openness of access provided by the Internet that allows for the circumvention of Gramsci's functionaries, the group of intellectuals whom he described as organizing and conveying already accumulated intellectual wealth (Gramsci, 1999). Instead, these two sites originate in the creative efforts of individuals, whom, it appears, do not represent media organizations or profit financially from their sites. Also, I see no mention of any credentials that would hint at a formal, intellectually based background (such as that of an academic or published author) for these web site creators. In this sense, they would be defined by Gramsci (1999) as "organic intellectuals" who direct "the ideas and aspirations of the class to which they organically belong" (p. 131).

Based on Gramsci's description of hegemony, the creators of these sites come from the subaltern, rather than the dominant class, and thus evidence hegemony's allowance for "leakage," as described in Chapter 1. In this manner, the ability for such organic intellectuals to access the means for disseminating counterideologies further stresses "the democratic character of the intellectual function," wrote Gramsci (1999, p. 131). Thus, these examples support Gramsci's contention that all persons (his actual word was "men") "are potentially intellectuals in the sense of having an intellect and using it," and, in turn, can parlay that ability into creating a new philosophy (p. 131).

Summary

As cultural work, the content of wedding media inherently embodies a certain ideology concerning how this public expression of private emotions becomes realized. In conveying a stylized, idealized picture of the white wedding—formal apparel, public ceremony, reception—the gatekeeping function of media workers logically involves a sense of the appropriate as well as the acceptable. The editing of video footage and natural sound of reality television programs that document noncelebrity weddings requires a sense of narrative as well as aesthetic appeal. To attract viewers, and, in turn, sponsors, the producers of such programs must consider these elements of storytelling. When considering the wedding, then, appealing visuals and a sense of romance become requisite elements of any television treatment, fictional or real.

However, the reality television genre not only depends on the expected and familiar, but also the drama of "real" events. Also, the dependence on the willingness of real people to have their lives documented and made public to viewers means that program producers must collect as many wedding stories as possible in order to have enough material to create a program or series. For example, in the long-running TLC program *A Wedding Story*, the gamut of weddings came to include several that departed from the typical white wedding, including weddings with holiday and historical themes. As a whole, however, they all followed the same basic format. Thus, slight modifications created visual appeal and novelty, but did not create such distinctions as to be excluded from the central purpose of showing happy couples and happy weddings.

To question wedding practices is to question the common sense of the wedding. As hegemony and the dominant viewpoint become part of our everyday way of thinking, the very notion of challenging that viewpoint illustrates that not all the social participants hold the same views. Such was the case of Clementine in the episode of *A Wedding Story* discussed in this chapter. Her reluctance to fulfill the hegemonic bridal role and even to participate in a wedding offers a concrete example of how hegemony can be questioned—even within a template narrative that exalted the sameness of weddings. The inclusion of her interaction with her bridesmaids in which she admitted she did not want a wedding but would rather have eloped suggests that the producers and editors either needed the footage to fill time or saw that it held enough value to be included in the final product. Regardless of whether or not this portion of the episode was vital, it illustrates Hall's (1977) point that "'ideological reproduction'" cannot be accomplished without reproducing contradictions and "counteracting tendencies" of those ideologies (p. 346).

Although vocal and authentic, Clementine's resistance to the common sense held by her husband and her family was not enough to reverse the course of the day's events. Indeed, while her episode of *A Wedding Story* ended with a successful wedding, one wonders if it was a truly happy ending. I see the symbolism of Clementine's protestations as even more relevant when considering the implied feminism of her stance. Clementine saw herself as a professional; the transformation required to turn her into a bride did not match her self-image and created a discomfort that hinted she was only going through the motions in order to get the wedding over with. In the end, the feminist-based "power" that Clementine thought she had could not overcome the hegemonic notions held by others.

The programs examined here appeared on cable television channels, media outlets that assume their audiences have the economic ability to acquire them. The version of the white wedding offered by them also assumes a level of expense commensurate to meeting the production values, visuals, and interest needed to produce a show about weddings which in turn has enough appeal for those same audiences to watch. In other words, no one (it is assumed) really wants to watch a cheap wedding in which the bride and groom wear street clothes and go home right after the ceremony. Oxygen's *Real Weddings From The Knot* may have centered on real weddings, but one must consider the additional economic benefit gained by The Knot and the Oxygen channel as a result of producing that series. The additional facet of The Knot web site pages that gave viewers specific details about the products and services shown in the series further underscores The Knot's purpose of connecting viewers with vendors. After all, The Knot serves as the portal for wedding retailers to reach a wider range of customers. Therefore, the more lavish the wedding, the more opportunity for retailers to gain clients, thus resulting in a healthy wedding industry. In turn, The Knot's continued financial health becomes assured.

The inclusion of slight deviations from the mercantile-based, white wedding ideal forwarded by The Knot's television counterpart offers novelty, but just enough so as to reaffirm the familiar. The "handmade Christmas wedding" created by the budget-minded Jessa and Jeff gave viewers a look into a low-cost wedding that still embodied a white gown, tuxedo, church, and reception. What makes Jessa and Jeff's episode different is the extent to which this couple actually *hand*made the requisite wedding items: Jessa bakes her own wedding cake with store-bought cake mix and makes her own veil. The footage of other couples in the *Real Weddings* series shows them visiting custom cake bakers and choosing various items for their celebrations directly from wedding vendors. In contrast, Jessa and Jeff visit Wal-Mart, a discount retailer. One can see the inclusion of this version of the white wedding as reflecting "real life" and real people who actually must watch their money and care about the expense associated with formal weddings. In this manner, The Knot allows for a "cheap" wedding as a token acknowledgement, but to include more examples of such small-ticket weddings would undermine its very purpose of promoting wedding goods and services.

Bravo's *Gay Weddings* offered a backstage view of the unique challenges faced by same-sex couples as they planned their weddings. Simultaneously countering hegemony and adhering to common sense, the weddings of *Gay Weddings* reflect the paradox of difference and assimilation posed by same-sex weddings, previously noted by Lewin (1998) and Mundy (2008). Its debut came at a time when same-sex weddings began to gain more visibility, especially in the form of wedding announcements in major newspapers. As a reality television program, it, too, received a fair amount of press coverage, a case of media covering other media. What makes *Gay Weddings* different from other wedding media is its focus on gay and lesbian couples, historically denied the same rights as heterosexuals who wish to make their unions both public and legal. Aside from the (then) nonlegality of the marriages resulting from these weddings, the open expression of doubt, stress, and worries regarding family acceptance further demarcates it from other reality television programs. What makes it the same as other programs is that the couples followed the typical, white wedding format.

Alternative bridal media offer ways to specifically put aside the trappings of "regular" white weddings while still retaining some semblance of normalcy. The ones described in this chapter fold in tenets of feminism—such as female independence and rejection of traditional gender roles—into contemporary femininity that still allows for and encourages the taking on of the bridal role and taking pleasure in the wedding's celebratory aspects. Neither the anti-bride nor the offbeat bride advocates an anti-wedding/anti-marriage stance. Nor do they completely reject the idea of expenditure to attain one's dream wedding. Indeed, romance, love, commitment, and the wedding itself are all unquestioned here. As sites forwarding varying degrees of resistance to traditional bridal media, these examples at the very least illustrate that what has become the prototype for the proper wedding in U.S. society during the late 20th and early 21st centuries does not resonate with all its participants. Rather than completely foregoing the wedding altogether, these examples of "new" bridal media focus on the creation of celebrations that reflect a bride's/couple's personality; the basic format still exists, but with a few tweaks to distinguish it from the standard, dominant version.

Counterhegemonic examples such as these demonstrate that while media tend to reproduce ideology, hegemony need not be thought of as monolithic or unbending. Rather, these slight deviations and challenges show there is room for otherness within the overall common sense associated with weddings today. The very existence of publicly accessible media that directly challenge the status quo, such as *FeministWedding.com* and *Unmarried.org*, points to the openness of civil society and the potential for changing, in whatever slightest way, the dominant viewpoints about weddings, their traditions, and marriage.

I do not consider the examples presented here as representative of the totality of resistance against wedding hegemony. However, they do illustrate the flexibility allowed within the hegemonic perspective that makes room for alternative viewpoints. In the case of Bravo's *Gay Weddings*, the drama of real events that reality television so well relies upon to catch the attention of viewers makes almost necessary the inclusion of the unusual, as conflict serves as a main staple of storytelling in general. That the people who appear in *Gay Weddings* are shown preparing for and participating in an important and personal life event while dealing with family disapproval and even discrimination (as in the case of brides Sonja and Lupe) makes the authenticity of the content even more salient. In short, the real stories of real people challenging hegemonic ideals concerning marriage, gender roles, and basic civil rights provide valuable insight into how counterhegemonies are portrayed in mass media.

The dichotomy of familiarity and difference within the framework of the wedding—two people making their commitment to each other in a public setting—evidences Hall's (1977) observation that the "ideological reproduction" performed by mass media constantly manifests "counteracting tendencies" (p. 346). Hall cited what Gramsci termed "unstable equilibria," which we can view as the de facto contradictions within common sense. That is, even as reality television versions of actual people's weddings convey a commonality regarding structure, style, performance, and other indicators of uniformity, the inclusion of alternative weddings naturally becomes part of the mix. Examples of "nontraditional" bridal roles, though few and far between, evidence that hegemony is always challenged by those who find the prevailing worldview incompatible with their own, and support interpretations of Gramsci's original theory that contend hegemony need not always refer to a monolithic force (Hall, 1996). Indeed, once counterhegemony reaches a critical mass, wherein enough participants in a society desire a change in current practices and values, it, too, eventually becomes common sense.

The question then becomes to what degree alternatives become both visible and incorporated into common sense. Individuals or even groups and alternative social movements certainly may challenge the dominant viewpoint that results from common sense and popular knowledge. Bridal media provide a cultural space that illustrates both Gramsci's take on common sense as a means to sustain the status quo *and* the openness of hegemony that allows for efforts to oppose and resist the "natural state of affairs" regarding marriage and weddings. The universe of bridal media may continue to expand with more offerings of glamorous events that promote materialism and the appeal of the bridal identity, but there do exist additional modes of resistance and opposition that overtly and covertly challenge popular knowledge regarding weddings and marriage. In the next chapter, I summarize my findings from previous chapters to offer a sense of the "state of the art" of bridal media today.

Notes

* Portions of this chapter were published as the following articles and appear here with permission: "Hegemony and Counterhegemony in Bravo's *Gay Weddings*," *Popular Culture Review*, 2004, Vol. 15, No. 1, pp. 33–45, and "Unraveling The Knot: Political Economy and Cultural Hegemony in Wedding Media," available from http://jci.sagepub.com; the final, definitive version of this paper has been published in *Journal of Communication Inquiry*, Vol. 32, Issue 1, January 2008, pp. 60–82, by SAGE Publications Ltd./SAGE Publications, Inc. All rights reserved. ©2008 by Sage Publications.

1. In "Unraveling The Knot: Political Economy and Cultural Hegemony in Wedding Media" (Engstrom, 2008), I concluded that *Real Weddings From the Knot* promoted wedding expenditure and consumerism.

2. Episode title: "Clementine and Paul," copyright 1997, airdate July 20, 1998. Due to high rotation, episodes of *A Wedding Story* may have multiple airdates.

3. In *Gendered Lives*, Wood (2010) summarized feminine and masculine communication and interaction styles, which this episode illustrates extremely well.

4. Episode of Jessa and Jeff, copyright 2003, airdate and recorded June 5, 2003.

5. The synopsis of Jessa and Jeff's wedding from the web site http://www.the knot.com/oxygen_main.html (retrieved January 20, 2005, copyright 1992–2003) included the dollar amount of their wedding; other episode synopses did not mention budgets or prices.

6. Augmenting the television version of *Real Weddings From the Knot*, The Knot web site featured each wedding, with additional details not included in the television episodes, such as full names, ages, and occupations. The story of Jessa and Jeff's wedding appeared as a separate web page, "Jessa and Jeff: A Handmade Christmas Wedding in Maryland," retrieved from http://www.theknot.com/ch_article _local.html?Object=A21230144003&keyword=DC&MsdVisit=1.

7. Web sites for each couple's episodes available at *TheKnot.com* (http://www.the-knot.com): Katie and Gus, "A Tropic Garden Wedding in Jamaica"; Xylina and Eric, "An Exotic Beach Wedding in Mexico"; Alem and Yohannes, "A Global Gathering in DC"; Catina and Todd, "Silver and Snowflakes in New Jersey"; and Danielle and John, "Gatsby Style in Newport, RI." All downloaded 2004–2005.

8. Episode of "Whitney and Jeff," copyright 2003; recorded June 8, 2003.

9. The decision for same-sex couples to marry becomes even more of a challenge, given the U.S. legal system's general consideration (suspicion) of the recognition of such unions, as observed by Stoddard (1992), and endorsement of the belief that marriage should be codified and reserved for man-woman relationships, such as that by President George W. Bush in 2003 ("Bush Wants Marriage Reserved for Heterosexuals").

10. Boswell (1994) provided more in-depth descriptions of the various types of same-sex unions from ancient times to pre-modern Europe.

11. See Howard (2006), pp. 223 and 233–234, for a fuller discussion on the growth of the same-sex wedding market. Manifestations of counterhegemony within the wedding industry include web sites catering to gay couples and same-sex wedding expos, and wedding-items created especially for gay and lesbian couples, such as cake toppers. Howard also included a photograph from her own collection of boy-boy and girl-girl cake toppers on p. 234.

12. Shister (2002) noted Bravo's success with the niche-reality programs *Gay Riviera* and *Fire Island*.

13. Press coverage included articles online and in print news, both in the gay press and mainstream outlets: Piepenburg (2002), Mansfield (2002), Alter (2002), "Gay Weddings Go Prime Time" (2002), and Shister (2002).

14. Mundy (2008) found that only two of the 20 same-sex wedding announcements he analyzed in detail indicated celebrants with religious affiliations.

15. Rather than a purposive, dominant worldview, Condit (1994) perceived hegemony as a manifestation of something universal that naturally becomes the most common viewpoint. The creators of media products and of cultural work can be seen in this perspective as simply reflecting a commonality among a society's participants rather than deliberately excluding alternative voices.

16. For example, in Chapter 3, I described the wedding of singer Melissa Etheridge and how she wore a white pantsuit while her partner wore a traditional white wedding gown.

17. The "Porn for Women" home page plays on the reversing of traditional gender roles and the household and childcare tasks associated with the second shift. Offering to divulge the results of a quest to find out what turns women on, the web site tells visitors: "Prepare to enter a fantasy world. A world where clothes get folded just so, men insist on changing diapers, delicious dinners await, and flatulence is just not that funny" ("Porn for Women," n.d.).

7. Modern Women, Traditional Brides

BRIDAL MEDIA OFFER RICH AND VARIED WAYS TO LOOK AT FEMINISM, HEGEMONY, counterhegemony, and femininity. Once considered mundane and relegated to the female realm, weddings are now acknowledged as useful and meaningful cultural artifacts. Media portrayals of both women and the generic wedding now so common among the middle and upper class point to a continued tension between feminism and femininity. This book has shown how bridal media in its different forms communicate certain commonsense beliefs regarding women's roles and, especially, the requirements of the bridal appearance.

Artz and Murphy (2000) explained that media function in relation to social practices and the conditions of capitalistic hegemony. Thus, bridal media serve the interests not of their readers, but of their advertisers. As communicative products, they perpetuate and magnify the materialism associated with social practices and operate within the system of capitalism—which in turn needs cultural hegemony to sustain itself. Media as businesses themselves depend on people spending money on things "needed" for the temporary change in habitus provided by the wedding. And those people, it turns out, are mainly women who see the wedding as a necessary affirmation of their status (Geller, 2001).[1] The fact that so many bridal media feature so many modern women who have bought into the wedding ideal illustrates the importance of hegemony as a tool that we can use to discover how cultural production defines meanings and values, and from whence these meanings and values originate (Carragee, 1993).

Just as news media present their versions of social and political realities through news stories, as Carragee (1993) contended, bridal media present a certain version of social reality. Carragee asserted that the "reality" presented in news largely upholds the "meanings, values, and interests of powerful institutions and groups in society" (p. 331). Similarly, wedding "news" by its very nature ensures the dissemination of particular values associated with not only marriage, but also gender roles and expectations for women and men.

In Chapter 2, I focused on how weddings of the rich and famous embody the news values of prominence and the unusual. Emphasis on the appearance of brides more so than on grooms coupled with the detailed descriptions of wedding dresses, flowers, and jewelry reflect that the world of weddings revolves around women. Weddings of royalty not only provided and continue to offer news media an easy story to tell, but they also perpetuate their fantasy and fairy-tale aspects, especially the mythic ideals of handsome prince and beautiful princess who find true love. Indeed, this notion of true love persists to the modern day; in 2011 it was promoted and highlighted by news accounts of the years-long romance and subsequent marriage of William, the elder son of Princess Diana, one of the most famous brides in modern history, and Kate Middleton, a commoner.

Published gossip in the form of newspaper accounts of big-city society weddings in 19th century and early 20th century America allowed readers a virtual way to attend these events. The Internet and live broadcasting ability of today's technology have made such events even more accessible. Displays of wealth have become tied to the common sense associated with wedding gift giving and materialism. Influenced by the "proper" weddings of the upper class, the form of the wedding in the US transformed from the simple at-home affair in which a bride wore her best dress to a well-planned event requiring the white wedding gown and separate venue for the holding of a postceremony reception.

As the *acta diurna* of modern times, newspaper wedding announcements continue to create an image of bridal loveliness. Today, no matter her social station, the bride becomes a celebrity simply by the public declaration of her wedding. Wedding announcements also serve as a way to examine how women's progress has unfolded in mass media; as news they provide a historical record of wedding practices of private citizens as well as what newspapers have deemed important regarding the reportage of women. What may seem inconsequential actually reflects cultural practices and changes in those practices. Wedding announcements thus serve as a venue to study such changes, and serve as data for examining the practice of a woman's changing her given surname to her husband's as well as assessing feminist attitudes among women (Goldin & Shim, 2004; Hatch & Hatch, 1947; Hoffnung, 2006). The inclusion of a bride's occupation, once a nonissue in this type of news, also became commonplace during the 1970s, when the Second Wave of feminism made its mark on U.S. society. By the early 2000s, same-sex wedding announcements became a regular part of wedding news ("Times Will Begin Reporting," 2002; Venema, 2003).

The range and scope of the bridal media milieu described in Chapter 3 provide a sense of just how much the media industry has been infiltrated, for lack of a better term, by the wedding business and the popularity of weddings as gossip and entertainment. Bridal magazines, web sites, and reality television programs all contribute to the forwarding of a hegemonic version of the wedding. Just as in "real" news on the front page of newspapers and in television broadcasts, these all focus on the bridal appearance. The consumerism associated with weddings, especially as it pertains to the costs required for the creation of (a) the bridal image and (b) a lavish reception, becomes the centerpiece, so to speak, of this media genre. Marriage serves only as an afterthought; these media accounts of "true love" and romance lack any true inspection or introspection regarding the quality and strength of relationships. In this way, the treatment given to weddings—spectacles featuring beautiful brides and beautiful settings—reinforces unrealistic versions of romance so common in Hollywood films and television programs, as described and critiqued by Galician (2004).

Television programs featuring celebrity weddings continue the tradition of published gossip, with emphasis on wedding accessories and costs. Indeed, many of the celebrity couples who have over-the-top weddings, with massive diamond rings, designer gowns, and sumptuous receptions, have become subjects of follow-up programs featuring their breakups. Treatments of weird weddings frame deviations from the white wedding format as tasteless and irresponsible; these and blooper-style programs of weddings gone wrong further trivialize unusual (nontraditional) weddings by making fun of them. By extension, the marriages created by those "different" weddings become trivialized as well, which further underscores the unimportance of the love relationship within both the wedding industry and bridal media in general.

In Chapter 4, I analyzed how the focus on the bridal appearance serves as another of the myriad ways that mass media tell women that their physical appearance is the most important thing about them. The requirement that the feminine woman needs to take great care to make herself look attractive becomes magnified on her wedding day. Indeed, it is the one day in her entire life that really matters—the day she becomes a wife. Reality wedding programs of the late 20th and early 21st centuries, such as TLC's *A Wedding Story* and *Say Yes to the Dress*, FitTV's *Buff Brides*, and WE tv's *Bridezillas*, emphasize the costume required for a woman to be called a bride. They tell us that the wedding dress serves as the ultimate cue of femininity, and without the perfect dress a woman cannot truly be considered nor feel like the perfect bride. Indeed, perfection is not only desired, but also required for a legitimate wedding. This perfection applies to the superficial quality of weddings as portrayed in media; the perfection has to do with the "packaging" of the bride and the packaging of the wedding rather than the essence within (Goldstein-Gidoni, 1997).

When logically connected, the superficiality of weddings infers the superficiality of women: weddings serve as a plaything for women, distracting them from the real world of work, politics, and serious matters—the world of men (Felski, 2000). Thus, when considered as a whole, the sum of these portrayals that show women undergoing the transformation to become perfect brides, all similar in sequence and result, creates a picture of women as interchangeable. I see the repeated footage in these reality programs as a bride factory where the individuality of women becomes negated and replaced with the bridal persona. Even though men, too, may appear similar in their required uniforms of tuxedo and suit, the amount of effort and time invested in their appearance does not even come close to that willingly given by women.

The "penguin suit"—slang for tuxedo—is used as a comical reference that pokes fun at the stereotypical aversion that "real" men have to getting dressed up in formal attire. However, for women, the bridal gown is serious business, both literally and figuratively. While dressing up may be presented as a fun diversion for women, bridal media portray the search for the perfect dress as a stressful, painful test of endurance. Indeed, the pain associated with the attainment of beauty was the focus of FitTV's *Buff Brides*, as the women in that program spent hours exercising in addition to all their other responsibilities, worried over their extra body fat, and denied themselves food, all for the goal of fitting into their dream gown. Men in these reality programs are never seen worrying over their looks; a corresponding program, with a title such as *Buff Grooms*, documenting the angst and stress of grooms trying to lose weight in order to fit into their "dream" wedding tuxedo likely would never exist.[2]

The transformation from mere woman to perfect bride involves work, and lots of it. So does the perfect day. In Chapter 5, I examined how bridal media in the form of reality programs offer a backstage view of the wedding production process that continues to reaffirm the idea that weddings are mostly the woman's responsibility. Until her docile body undergoes the process of becoming beautiful, the bride is allowed a degree of agency. She becomes the director of her own production and in control of her wedding universe. That is, until the obstacles to wedding perfection appear. Bridal media present the wedding as a monumental task, so important that one must devote every extra minute to ensuring its perfection. Indeed, doing wedding work at work becomes normalized in bridal media, and even in other venues, such as entertainment television. For example, during 2006, the NBC prime-time comedy *The Office* depicted women employees doing wedding work at the workplace with no real consequences.[3] The uninterested bride is a rarity in these portrayals. So, too, are brides who appear relaxed and happy. Rather, the stress of creating the perfect wedding and making sure everything is perfect replaces whatever joy and happiness might be associated with marriage to a partner one loves and values.

An extreme form of Boden's (2003) superbride, the bridezilla persona allows women to exert power and ensure their desires are realized. While one could take the view that the bridezilla forwards a positive image of the decisive, independent woman, the manner in which she achieves her goals ultimately reinforces negative stereotypes of the hysterical woman. Add to this the active exclusion of men from wedding planning and the overall impression of the bridezilla shows that she is also a male basher—openly expressing that all grooms (and men in general) know nothing about weddings, and, thus, are useless in this capacity. If one associates feminism with egalitarianism, then the bridezilla certainly does not forward gender equality. The dominion of the bridezilla is the wedding, which serves as a place where women can have their way in a patriarchal world. This gender territoriality tells men to "keep out" and gives the bridezilla a sense of power and control. However, that power ends once the wedding day is over. Thus, even after all the work, time, effort, and emotional investment put into her one special day, her reward *might* be a perfect wedding. Indeed, several bridezillas in the eponymous reality series I studied *still* found fault with their perfect day even after it concluded.

The reality television programs discussed in Chapters 4 and 5 provide some sense of brides' identities in terms of occupation and education, but for the most part this aspect of their lives tends to be ignored. Whether or not the editing process disallows the inclusion of such information, what appears onscreen leaves the critical viewer with more questions than answers regarding who these women really are. Their role as bride naturally takes center stage, but unless their personal data appears in onscreen graphics or in the narrative itself, one gets only a vague idea of their nonbridal identity. Some programs, such as Oxygen's *Real Weddings From The Knot* and FitTV's *Buff Brides*, mention women's job titles. *Real Weddings From The Knot*'s Internet component offered detailed profiles of featured couples. Others, such as TLC's *A Wedding Story* and *Say Yes to the Dress*, generally ignored this information.

The issue of brides' (and grooms') age also seemed irrelevant, except when they were very young, such as in the second season of WE tv's *Bridezillas*. At most, viewers can ascertain demographic information from visual cues, but one gets no real sense of where these women are in their lives in terms of educational attainment, career achievement, or other information that defines them other than female. Even though most may have demanding professional careers that require a high degree of education and skill, the brides in these programs put aside their other roles as they work at getting their weddings organized.

The notion that weddings are women's work becomes more pronounced when one considers the appearance (or disappearance) of grooms in these programs and in bridal magazines. Although not completely absent in programs such as TLC's *A Wedding Story* and Oxygen's *Real Weddings From The Knot*, grooms still generally take only a limited role in wedding planning. Mostly, they assist with any preparations, perhaps accompanying their future wives to appointments to choose floral arrangements or to decide on a wedding cake. They may help make party favors, or take a more active role, especially for more downscale weddings that require a degree of handicraft. In these instances, wherein one sees both brides and grooms engaged in preparatory chores, the wedding work done by such couples appears to anticipate the partnership symbolized by the impending marriage. Among the exceptions to the women-only rule regarding wedding work I found from viewing these various programs over the years, *A Wedding Story*'s episode of Jessica and Michael showed that this hegemonic notion also has it counterhegemonic instances. Michael designed the bridesmaids' dresses for their wedding and footage of him using a sewing machine revealed just how involved he was in the preparation for his and Jessica's big day.

The potential for weddings to become viewed as partnered work exists, as these reality programs demonstrate. The issue is to what degree these programs, and bridal media in general, present such divergent portrayals that eventually may influence or reflect actual values and attitudes regarding an egalitarian assignment of wedding chores. As long as purveyors of current wedding etiquette such as *TheKnot.com* keep telling women that men do not want to participate, or give them advice to avoid involving their male partners altogether, such as in the article "Wedding Planning: How to Plan Your Wedding at Work" (Wood, 2009), then such changes may not occur.

Similarly, as long as women view weddings as *their* purview, their private domain over which they (seemingly) have power and control, then the possibility for feminism—with its goal of egalitarianism—to infiltrate this bastion of gendered work appears limited. The *gestalt* of portrayals, attitudes, perspectives, and values that permeate bridal media in the US at the beginning of the 21st century offers a cultural space where decisive, career-oriented women can indulge in feminine fantasies. White bridal gowns, custom-made wedding cakes, and sophisticated flower arrangements grace the covers of magazines and have become de rigueur for television programs featuring celebrity weddings and those of everyday folks.

This version of the wedding so familiar and so well marketed belies the leaks that challenge commonsense notions regarding gender roles, consumerism, and the assumed heterosexuality of the wedding script. Chapter 6 focused on alternative brides and grooms whose wedding stories departed from that script, and serve as examples of what I see as wedding counterhegemony. Within the reproduction of ideology comes contradictions, and reality TV allows for deviations to the extent that the status quo remains intact. The story of Clementine the reluctant bride from TLC's *A Wedding Story* stands out because she actually questioned the whole wedding process and the need for an elaborate celebration. Comparatively a low-key affair, her wedding day and its supposed necessity challenged her values and self-perception as an educated woman who wanted to elope. Symbolic of the difficulties one faces when challenging the dominant viewpoint, Clementine's angst—which one can view as feminist-based—alas turned out to be a nonissue. Her wedding day unfolded as planned, and her wedding story became just another episode in a series built on ensuring that viewers would see a happy ending. That her open expressions of doubt were included in the narrative, complete with a wedding-day discussion about how she really just wanted an elopement, evidences the openness of hegemony in media depictions of "real life" weddings.

Low-budget weddings among the frothy, white affairs in Oxygen's reality series *Real Weddings From The Knot* offered viewers a glimpse into the do-it-yourself approach. Deviations represented by homemade, down-home weddings showcased alternatives that still followed the white wedding format, enough to both show viewers there are other ways of celebrating and to reaffirm the appeal of the dominant version. To offer more than a smattering of these simpler versions would jeopardize the status quo. After all, bridal media depend on advertising to survive; without a thriving wedding industry, their existence would be threatened.

Same-sex weddings clearly challenge the presumed and "required" heterosexuality of weddings that Ingraham (2008) noted. Some wedding media entities, such as Internet retail sites and *TheKnot.com*, had already targeted same-sex couples by the early 1990s. In the sense that "wedding" referred to a celebration patterned after the so-called traditional wedding that incorporates a marriage ceremony and reception, same-sex weddings in reality uphold the status quo—at least regarding the ritualistic and consumerist aspects embodied in media portrayals. The reality television program *Gay Weddings* essentially treated same-sex unions in the same manner as other video vérité wedding programs. Considering the history of the marriage ceremony and weddings as ritual, the counterhegemonic-yet-hegemonic portrayals offered by *Gay Weddings* support Geller's (2001) observation: "Because it de facto represents a tradition, no wedding, conventional or innovative, occurs autonomously" (p. 259).

However, when compared to other reality wedding shows in existence at the time of *Gay Weddings'* debut, the openness with which the participants talked about the stress and anxiety they encountered while planning their weddings far exceeded that of heterosexual couples in other reality television wedding programs (*Bridezillas* notwithstanding). This opening of the backstage presented a sympathetic portrait of couples who simply wanted the same recognition and public acknowledgement that heterosexual couples enjoy. In this way, these portrayals imply that the couples also endorse the hegemonic form of the wedding and a presumed desire to conform to marriage based on the pair bond.

Reality television treatments of the wedding largely exclude weddings that do not conform to the ideal so often depicted. In that viewers never see elopements or quickie weddings that do not involve thousands of dollars or hundreds of hours of planning, the resulting message to the women who consume bridal media is that in order to display love properly, one must also have a big wedding reflective of that love. Elopements certainly don't require the same level of spending as a "real" wedding, and thus have no place in advertisement-based bridal magazines. Aside from their element of surprise, elopements would not be included in reality television weddings, and it's unlikely that couples who do elope would want to take part in the creation of such shows. Instead, these counterhegemonic (in the sense that eloping couples reject the common sense of weddings) versions are treated by media in the same way as weird weddings: suspect and clearly not holding the same respectability as those patterned after the commonsense version. To ignore these alternatives thus helps to sustain the dominant viewpoint; it is unlikely that elopements will ever overtake the white wedding, given the current bridal media environment.

The Expanding Bridal Media Universe

As noted in Chapter 3, bridal media have a vested interest in making sure only a certain picture is presented to their audience—a picture that supports the retailers who make the existence of such media possible. In this sense, hegemony and political media economy[4]—the interrelationships between media industries and other economic sectors in a capitalist system—become so intertwined that the culture being produced in bridal media has commodified the concept of love (expressed through the wedding)—and the meaning of "woman." Herein lies the obvious connection between cultural hegemony, media, and capitalism: by ensuring the appeal of the white wedding, framed as romantic, feminine, and fantastic, the owners of bridal media companies remain in business. The manufacturers, service providers, and artists who work in the wedding industry need bridal magazines and reality programs to keep showing their customers the must-have products that make a wedding legitimate. These media versions of weddings become especially problematic when idealized, high-priced weddings presented in bridal magazines cannot be realized within a couple's decidedly lower budget.[5]

A scan of the recent reality television landscape shows that big weddings appear more popular than ever. The number of wedding-focused programs continually increases, especially among cable channels that target largely female audiences. Indeed, the seemingly exponential increase in the number of bridal-themed magazines, television programs, and Internet sites makes it difficult to offer a definitive analysis; even as I was writing Chapter 3, "The Bridal Media Milieu," I was gathering new examples of bridal media and found even more bridal programs. Any documentation of bridal media requires constant surveillance, as further fragmentation appears endless, at least for the near future. The following lists and descriptions must be qualified as incomplete, and reflecting only those available media I found among U.S. outlets as of the first decade of the 21st century.

Weddings galore on cable television

In 2011, the WE tv network counted among its lineup several programs with a wedding theme. Offerings on this clearly feminine-themed outlet emphasizing marriage and motherhood include: *Bridezillas* (still going strong with 141 total episodes as of August 2011[6]), *Platinum Weddings* (weddings for which price is no object), *My Fair Wedding With David Tutera* (a wedding makeover show), *Rich Bride Poor Bride* (the perfect wedding on a budget), *Amazing Wedding Cakes* (an entire series just on wedding cakes), and *Wedding Cake Wars* (featuring wedding cake competitions) ("WE tv Shows," 2011). Included among the titles under WE tv's *Wedding Central Presents* umbrella of programs were *Amazing Wedding Gowns; Bling on the Bride; Little People, Big Day; Sin City Weddings;* and *Wedding Planners* (parts 1, 2, 3, and 4) ("Wedding Central Presents: Episodes," 2011). Other titles of WE tv wedding specials included *Wedding Place*, a one-hour program consisting of tips from wedding planners on ensuring the perfect reception, and *Wedding Cake Masters* ("Wedding Central Presents: Episodes," 2011). In 2009, WE tv premiered *Girl Meets Gown*, a reality program set in a Texas bridal salon and based on TLC's *Say Yes to the Dress* ("Girl Meets Gown: See It on WE tv!" 2009).

Any indications of a reversal of the white wedding ideal appear nonexistent, at least on WE tv, a cable channel aimed at women. Indeed, instead of toning down the consumerist aspect of weddings, WE tv has "amped up" the wedding with its numerous offerings, especially *Platinum Weddings*, an entire series featuring extravagance and luxury. *Platinum Weddings* amplifies the importance of creating a fantastic, lavish change in habitus that the wedding as social event provides. It distinguishes the "super" wedding from other, less extravagant but still pricey events while also adding to what Foster (2005) saw as a denial of class and class struggles; the "spectacle of opulence and outra-geous expense" cultivated by wedding media makes budget weddings even more undesirable (p. 74).

Platinum Weddings bills itself as "the ultimate wedding show that captures the drama and decadence of wedding planning on an extraordinary budget!" The program's logo invokes all the familiar clichés associated with the big wed-ding: "The perfect wedding is priceless," reads the banner complete with pic-tures of diamonds on the program's web page ("Platinum Weddings," 2010). Price tags for various wedding elements appear onscreen during the 30-minute episodes; viewers learn about weddings of the very rich and over-the-top receptions that characterize the meaning of "platinum."

These big, white weddings redefine the word *big*. For example, the episode of *Platinum Weddings* featuring the wedding of Shane and Monet, a young couple in their twenties, had a price tag of more than $250,000. Described by Monet's mother as a "fairy-tale wedding, fairy-tale couple, fairy-tale life," their wedding story included a $30,000 diamond wedding ring, a $42,500 reception for 270 guests, a $14,000 custom-made mother-of-the-bride dress encrusted with Swarovski crystals, and not one, but two wedding gowns (totaling $11,900).[7] Synopses of earlier episodes reflect the opulence associ-ated with these truly "platinum" weddings: Kim and Ken's dream wedding included $75,000 worth of orchids; Lauren and Kristopher had a "half-mil-lion dollar" budget that gets "blown out of the water when Daddy's Princess gets every wish she ever desired"; Tanya and Jonathan's wedding cake cost $30,000; and Liane and Danny's wedding story began with a $250,000 engagement ring ("Platinum Weddings: Episodes," 2010).

Wedding Central was a digital cable channel that offered a range of real-ity style programs solely about weddings from 2009 to 2011. Among its offerings were WE tv's *Amazing Wedding Cakes*, *Bridezillas*, and *My Fair Wedding with David Tutera*; some 47 programs were listed on the Wedding Central web site during its short existence ("Wedding Central Shows," 2010). Additional titles in early 2010 included *Bride vs. Bride*, a wedding competi-tion show; *How to Marry a Prince*, a reality program on the demands faced by royal brides; and specials such as *Wedding Gown Secrets Revealed*. The existence of an entire cable network devoted to weddings illustrates the continuation of wedding hegemony and consumerism. In 2011, Wedding Central was dropped by its parent company AMC Networks; it became subsumed as a web page on WE tv's web site (Umstead, 2011).

The range of lifestyle and home improvement cable outlets also draws on weddings as subject matter for reality programming. The Style Network, a fashion and style cable channel, offered several wedding-themed programs in 2010, including the regular series *Whose Wedding Is It Anyway?* The reality program centers mostly on wedding planning and coordination from the wedding planner's point of view. *Whose Wedding Is It Anyway?* has included same-sex commitment ceremonies since its debut on Style in 2003 ("Whose Wedding Is It Anyway? Seasons 1–8 Episode Guide," 2010). In addition to this regular programming, Style has offered several wedding specials, including the 2007 program *My Celebrity Wedding With The Knot*, which re-created the wedding of pop singer Christina Aguilera ("Behind the Scenes," 2009), and the wacky wedding-style, documentary treatments *Weddings From Hell* and *Most Outrageous Weddings*.

Similar to FitTV's *Buff Brides*, the Fine Living Network's reality makeover program *Bulging Brides* uses the motivation of the perfect wedding dress to "whip the bride into shape—and make sure every bulge disappears before she walks down the aisle" ("Bulging Brides," 2010). *Bulging Brides* made a brief run on the WE tv network before moving to Fine Living. In early 2009 it began its second season. In early 2010, the show's web site listed 26 episodes, with titles such as "Big Fat Italian Bride," "Two Sizes Too Big," "Last Minute Squeeze," "Stressed to the Max," and "Bursting at the Seams" ("Bulging Brides Episode Guide," 2010).

TLC, the home of *A Wedding Story*, the progenitor of the reality wedding program, continues to give viewers bridal-themed reality fare. Although *A Wedding Story* has ended its run, weddings serve as a cornerstone content topic, with the returning series *Say Yes to the Dress*, described and analyzed in Chapters 4 and 5. In early 2010 TLC's wedding-themed series included *Masters of Reception*, a program on a family catering business that manages four different facilities that can "do" 10 weddings at a time ("Masters of Reception: About the Show," 2010). The bridal competition program *Four Weddings* premiered in 2009; it centers on four brides who judge each other's weddings on the key elements of "food, dresses, venues, and overall experience" ("Four Weddings: About the Show," 2010). The three other brides attend each wedding in *Four Weddings*, and act as guests, tasting food, assessing reception décor and colors, and then give a score for the four factors. For example, the traditional Indian wedding of one of the brides in the episode " . . . and a Boat to Catch" received an overall experience score of 8 out of 10 by another bride, who deducted points because the Indian food served at the reception was too spicy for her.[8] The brides with the highest ratings win a "fabulous, five-star honeymoon." In addition to these offerings, the "wacky weddings" compilation show *Wild Weddings* continued to enjoy occasional showings on TLC as well, including a mini-marathon of several editions in late 2009.[9]

Reality television treatments of weddings have extended beyond the niche, "boutique" cable channels described here. In 2009, the major cable channel TNT presented an "unscripted" wedding program produced by Mark Burnett, the creator of the CBS network's reality program *Survivor*. Titled *Wedding Day*, the ten-episode run featured "real-life dream weddings with profound backstories" ("Wedding Day: Show Overview," 2010). Episodes began with the story of a couple, nominated by family and friends, who deserved but couldn't afford their special dream wedding. The episode featuring Sara and Bryan, for example, told viewers how Sara had become a single mother at age 23 and never thought she would ever find her "dream husband." Bryan became a widower in 2003 after his wife died of ovarian cancer, leaving him with two small children.[10] Backstories were told by the couple as well as their family members and friends, with their on-air narratives accompanied by melancholy-sounding music.

Invoking the familiar wedding clichés such as "wedding of their dreams," and Sara's trying on of wedding dresses that made her look "like a princess," TNT's *Wedding Day* relied on the "misery show" format of women's television described by Cassidy (2005) in *What Women Watched: Daytime Television in the 1950s*. In a review of *Wedding Day*, television critic Mary McNamara of the *Los Angeles Times* called it "essentially a 'Queen for a Day' battle of pathos, with the couples sending 'audition' tapes to prove that they are worthy enough to receive a bunch of really good free stuff" (McNamara, 2009). McNamara also pointed out that the program's emphasis on the pageantry of the white wedding turned it "into a big satin and sequin raspberry to those who can't legally enter into the state of matrimony and undercuts those who argue that civil unions allow gays and lesbians the same legal rights as marriage." McNamara compared *Wedding Day*'s format to ABC's "failed" wedding-themed version of its Extreme Makeover reality franchise, *Extreme Makeover: Wedding Edition*.[11]

The connection between weddings and one's physical body also continues to inspire new reality competition programs as of this writing. The 2010–2011 series *Bridalplasty* on the E! Entertainment Channel offered plastic surgery and the dream wedding as the prize for its female competitors, as mentioned in Chapter 1. In early 2011, reality wedding game shows took on a slightly more egalitarian tone by including grooms in the CW network's *Shedding for the Wedding*, which featured overweight, engaged couples competing in a weight-loss contest in order to get their "fantasy wedding" ("Shedding for the Wedding—About," 2011).

Wedding news and celebrity gossip

The appeal of weddings and wedding gowns, especially of celebrities, continues unabated as well. On any given day, one can find gossip magazine covers announcing the latest marriages and engagements of pop singers and movie stars among the expected divorces and breakups of same. Weddings appear to become even further removed from any sense of real commitment or relationship quality required for successful couplehood.[12] Celebrity gossip instead continues to focus on the superficial cues that have come to represent romance and love. Despite their accomplishments, female artists in the music and film worlds gain even more status as brides or brides-to-be.

The weddings of film stars don't even have to have occurred yet to receive headline treatments in the popular press. For example, "intimate details" of Hollywood brides-to-be were promised by the headline "My Dream Wedding" for the "exclusive" cover story of the August 10, 2009 issue of the supermarket periodical *In Touch Weekly*. The eight-page spread "Stars Share Their Dream Weddings!" gave readers all the wedding details of upcoming Hollywood weddings, with some based solely on wedding experts' opinions on what those weddings should include rather than any facts about them. Hypotheticals, such as which designer's wedding gown would look best on brides-to-be such as actresses Penelope Cruz and Anne Hathaway, were mixed in among the juicy details on ideal (and real) locales, dresses, cakes, rings, and floral arrangements. Completing the media industry circuit between television, magazines, and the wedding industry, the article cited WE tv wedding planner extraordinaire David Tutera of that cable channel's series *My Fair Wedding With David Tutera*. Tutera summarized the conspicuous consumption appeal of the celebrity wedding: "Celebrities need to out-do all of the lavish parties they are invited to on a regular basis. . . . Most couples will spend what they can to make their wedding perfect—celebrities just have a bigger budget to do just that" (p. 29). The magazine's cover featured actresses Penelope Cruz, Rachel Bilson, and Anne Hathaway in white gowns (one surmises that their photographs were taken during red-carpet events). The pink lettering of the headline and hot pink background on the cover's left hand column of mini-headlines clearly evoked an appeal to the feminine. The juxtaposition of "My Dream Wedding" in supersized font with the mini-headlines of rocky celebrity relationships ("Brad and Angelina—Fight Over Maddox" and "Nick's Date with Jessica Look-Alike") served as a representation of the two major themes of gossip magazines: romance that ends in a wedding or romance that just ends.

More magazines

Clearly, updating the bridal media milieu requires a vigilance that limits a comprehensive description. However, I need to mention just a few more examples of this ever-growing subgenre of mass media aimed primarily at women. An example of the continuing narrowcasting of bridal magazines comes in the form of publications based on ever-more specific geographical locations, which I saw with the 2009 issues of *Southern Weddings, Brides Florida* ("from the publisher of Brides and Modern Bride"), and *Gulf Coast Bride* ("Real Brides, Real Weddings—From Destin, Seaside, 30A, and Panama City Beach, Florida to Orange Beach, Alabama"). All three covers featured brides in white, with only *Gulf Coast Bride* including a cover photo of a rare image of a groom *and* bride on a beach (with the bride dressed in a formal white gown and the groom in a white tuxedo, barefoot). The cover copy on these publications promise readers tips for choosing the "perfect dress," "perfect destination wedding," the "hottest rings, bouquets, fab finds," and finding out all one needs to know about photography and videography.[13]

Among the pages of *Southern Weddings*, I found even more bridal media venues in "A Day in the Life: Top Wedding Bloggers" (2009–2010). In addition to short profiles of four wedding blog authors, the article provided a list of ten Internet wedding sites that offer tips, product descriptions, personal stories of weddings, and additional links to vendors of wedding services and items. These sites not only offer repeated images of party favors, invitations, and dresses, but generally uphold the white wedding ideal. Several also provide even more links to other Internet wedding-product sites and blogs. In short, the Internet is home to an almost infinite number of cyberspaces where one can find not only wedding items, but cultural reinforcement of feminine consumerism and identity. Beyond a focus on the bride, these web sites are useful in that they serve as ideal paths for future research on the interrelationships between capitalism, patriarchy, and the status of feminism within the world of weddings and the worldwide web.

A book such as this, which endeavors to document the amount and types of bridal media one can find easily at retail outlets, supermarkets, and bookstores, would need updating every few years or sooner. In early 2011, as I was making revisions to this manuscript, I visited a major bookseller and picked up even more bridal magazines that I had not seen during my previous years of research for this project. These included *Beverly Clark's 2011 Elite Wedding Collection, Get Married, Uptown Weddings & Travel, Bella Bride*, and *Cosmopolitan Bride* (a British publication). These magazines' cover lines reiterated the themes of perfection and romance promised by material goods and services that the lavish, white wedding requires: "The Luxe List: Your City's Top Florists, Caterers, Jewelers, Designers, and More," "Fabulous Dresses Hot Off the Runway," "Fabulous Engagement Photos," "Hottest Trends in Design, Catering, Cakes and Florals," "Reception Perfection: Dreamy Details and Stunning Real Weddings."[14]

I also found what looks to be a revival of the men's wedding magazine similar in content to *For the Groom*, which I described in Chapter 3. Styled as "the men's guide to happily ever after," the Spring 2011 issue of *Sophisticated Groom*, published by Powell II the People, featured a James Bond-type theme on its cover, with the cover lines "Get Your 007 Physique," "Time to Role Play," and "Honeymoon Royale: Every Story Has a Beginning." *Sophisticated Groom*'s cover stories did not mention party favors, reception menus, cakes, or other related party items. Further illustrating the contrast between wedding planning and emphasis on appearance stressed by bridal magazines and the more serious topics faced by grooms, this narrowcasted publication included articles on making the marriage proposal and ensuring the approval of future parents-in-law (reflected by the "5 Step Guide to Asking P.I.L.'s [parents-in-law] Blessing"). However few, groom-targeted publications such as *Sophisticated Groom* provide yet another way to examine how media communicate hegemonic notions about masculinity versus femininity and how they reproduce the gendered binary that casts masculinity as male and femininity as female to "delimit the terrain of what is considered 'normal' gendered practice," to borrow Vavrus's words (2002, p. 358).

Opening the Door to Resistance and Opposition

This book has focused on nonfictional versions of weddings. I find important that even with the "wacky" weddings and "indiebrides," reality television and accounts of actual weddings of actual, real-life people lack the imagination and progressiveness ironically offered by fictional weddings. For example, as unlikely as it may seem, I found a counter to the big, white weddings frequently featured in Hollywood movies in the 2008 film *Sex and the City: The Movie*, based on the long-running HBO series. In it, main character Carrie Bradshaw (played by Sarah Jessica Parker) finally marries John Preston, her "Mr. Big" (played by Christopher Noth). The series *Sex and the City*, as a woman-centered media phenomenon, has been described as postfeminist, illustrating the "women-can-have-it-all" theme that reflects a world in which feminism as a political and social movement no longer finds relevance: its women are independent, sexually aggressive, mothers and careerists, and proud, conspicuous consumers (McRobbie, 2004). Romance and sex were treated as separate entities by female characters in the series, even though traditional, mythic themes about love abounded and the search for "the one" ended with three of the women getting married. Even the fiercely independent Samantha for a time lived within the confines of a monogamous relationship. Throughout the course of the show, its writers gave viewers both big, traditional weddings (as in the case of Charlotte's two large weddings) and a low-key, intimate ceremony (for lawyer Miranda).

In *Sex and the City: The Movie*, Carrie and John begin planning their wedding, which first starts out as a small affair. Carrie had already purchased an unlabeled, cream-colored vintage suit in hopes of one day marrying John. Its low-key, rather dowdy style failed to impress her friends, but she had her heart set on someday wearing it as her wedding outfit. However, given Carrie's various contacts in the fashion industry and friends in the wedding business, her dream wedding soon becomes an overblown production with an ever-growing guest list set at the New York Public Library.

The very fact that she was about to become a first-time bride at 40 spurred Enid, her still-unmarried editor at *Vogue* (played by Candice Bergen), to feature Carrie in the magazine's annual "age" issue; Carrie would represent 40, and her new status as bride-to-be would serve as the focus of her story. Thus, Carrie's impending marriage garners her even more notoriety than her previous success as a columnist and book author. During the photo shoot for the *Vogue* story, Carrie narrates a list of the designer names of the opulent wedding dresses she models: Vera Wang, Carolina Herrera, Christian LaCroix, Lanvin, Oscar de la Renta, and Vivienne Westwood. The film also includes the familiar image of onlookers becoming emotional when seeing the "perfect" wedding dress on a bride, as in the bridal reality program *Say Yes to the Dress* described previously in Chapter 4. Carrie's cynical friend Samantha (played by Kim Cattrall) attends the photo shoot, and is moved to tears when she sees Carrie's bridal splendor.

As if to add a touch of fairy godmother magic, Carrie receives the lush, voluminous gown she wore in the photo shoot's "grand finale" as a wedding gift from its designer, Vivienne Westwood. The designer gown replaces her dowdy suit as her wedding costume. The treatment Carrie receives as a bride at 40 further evidences the upgrade in status that women achieve when they marry. Carrie's haute couture wedding gown serves as the diametric opposite to the understated, secondhand outfit she had first chosen, her new bridal look and accessories definitely high-fashion and worthy of a cover for *Vogue*. The replacement designer gown symbolizes the desirability and appropriateness of the white wedding gown over her first choice; her modest suit serves as a throwaway symbol for the low-key wedding she had envisioned. Instead, Carrie gets swept up in the hegemonic, big, white wedding, which appears to hold more value and worth than her true desires.

Although the stood-up-at-the-altar plot device that causes Carrie to break up with John might have been nonrealistic (he gets cold feet on the wedding day), the denouement of the film reveals the significance of their marriage over the big, out-of-control wedding that began to overwhelm them. After eventually reconciling, the two finally make their commitment legal at a simple city hall ceremony. Carrie wears her vintage suit after all, and John surprises Carrie by inviting "the girls" and their families to celebrate at a diner-style restaurant; no "fancy, designer reception," but "just food and friends," as Carrie tells the viewer in her voice-over of the scene (King, 2008).

Regardless of any criticism the series or film had garnered concerning the essence of the story lines among the four lead characters, the understated, unglamorous treatment given to Carrie and John's wedding day offers a counterhegemonic version of today's white wedding that truly befitted her individualistic style. Further, it provides an example of the anti-wedding that emphasizes relationships over consumerism, substance over style. In the film version of *Sex and the City*, a program that hinged on designer labels and status symbols, Carrie Bradshaw's simple wedding—and wedding dress—offers an example of a movie bride who found a way to eschew the trappings of the big wedding and make her own rules.[15]

The anti-bride bridal guides and Internet sites described in Chapter 6 may offer cosmetic changes that give the impression of counterhegemonic weddings. However, a truly counterhegemonic wedding would be no wedding—and no marriage in the first place. The web site *Unmarried.org*, which I found through a link on the *FeministWeddings.com* site, serves as the online home for The Alternatives to Marriage Project (AtMP), "a national non-profit organization advocating for equality and fairness for unmarried people, including people who are single, who choose not to marry, cannot marry, or live together before marriage" ("*Unmarried.org*," 2010). Visitors to the site can learn about "ways to be unmarried," including living single, cohabitation, polyamory (nonmonogamous relationships), and being unmarried with children. The "GBLT" page offers a discussion of the pros and cons of same-sex marriage, while the "MarriageFree & Boycott" page explains how The Alternative to Marriage Project supports same-sex marriage to call attention to people's right to choose whether or not to marry; the choice to remain unmarried serves as one way to support gay rights and same-sex marriage ("MarriageFree & Boycott," 2010). Rather than arguing against marriage altogether, even this anti-wedding site has a page on commitment ceremonies, which supports the idea of monogamy without using or advocating weddings as the only way to validate relationships.

The open-access nature of the Internet, which allows for "organic intellectuals" to voice their philosophies, thus provides avenues for some incursion of difference (Gramsci, 1999, p. 131).[16] On one hand, these efforts may serve to reaffirm the "rightness" of the dominant portrayal of weddings forwarded by bridal magazines, television programs, and retail-based Internet web sites. On the other, they illustrate the potential for resistance and change that Gramsci envisioned. Indicative of hegemony's vulnerability to subversive philosophies, examples of resistance to the wedding ideal forwarded in the wider bridal media milieu demonstrate the possibility and reality of communicating critical awareness of one's external environment to others. Gramsci asked if it was better to think critically about one's world or take part in a conception of the world imposed by one's external environment and the social groups to which one automatically belongs. He categorized this type of critical thinking as the step following the "slightest manifestation of intellectual activity" (p. 626).

In terms of feminism, web sites by women for women that explicitly forward feminist ideals—in whatever form—align with Steiner's (1992) definition of "alternative feminist media": media distinguished from mainstream newspapers, magazines, television, and radio that target women for marketing purposes that operate to "express and celebrate viewpoints of specific groups of women" (p. 123). Alternative feminist media are not profit-motivated; instead, they serve women through communities in which "source" and "receiver" are the same. Steiner described these feminist channels as challenging the dominant structure and ideology while also deriving "considerable intellectual and emotional satisfaction from producing and supporting their own women-controlled, women-oriented media" (p. 121).

The potential of alternative feminist media to subvert hegemony, make others critically aware of the meanings and effects of following current wedding practices, and create new worldviews requires further investigation. Such an inquiry would add to the understanding of hegemony theory in this era of Internet accessibility and media in which message producers can directly reach their intended—and even unintended audiences—without the filter of profit-dependent entities. In these alternative versions of bridal media, the reason for the wedding and its fundamental ritualistic foundation is not questioned. Rather, it is the way in which that ritual is reified through artifacts and interaction that the authors of these alternative media question.

The way in which tensions between dominance and resistance are resolved further points to the need to examine the strength of hegemony concerning media's systematic tendency to "reproduce the ideological field of society in such a way as to reproduce, also, its structure of domination" (Hall, 1977, p. 346).[17] The strength of hegemony, as noted by Zompetti (1997), originates in not only acceptance by the subaltern, but in the desire of what that hegemony offers. Just as the hegemonic mindset did not develop overnight, nor through coercive means, neither did common sense-based wedding practices that require a white gown, party, and specialized objects. Similarly, the pushback articulated by the new bridal identities offered in these alternative bridal media—the anti-bride, the offbeat bride, and the indiebride—likely will not reverse the momentum of materialist-oriented bridal media overnight, either.

Economic forces affect the wedding industry just as they do other types of spending related to luxury or leisure; every economic downturn since 1945 resulted in a decline in weddings, according to the 2009 Bloomberg news article "Brides Kiss Dream Weddings Goodbye as Vendors Shut" (Leondis & Hester, 2009). The average cost of the U.S. wedding fell from $28,730 in 2007 to $21,810 in 2008, a 24% drop.[18] Business failures by florists, bridal boutiques, caterers, and venues resulted in some couples scaling back their weddings. Examples of downsizing included the replacement of lavish sit-down dinners with cocktail parties, use of fewer fresh flowers, and cupcakes instead of multitiered wedding cakes. Less lavish weddings were also attributed to the loss of employment by parents, resulting in smaller wedding budgets. Citing the same Bloomberg article, the Yahoo News story "Love in the Time of Recession" reported that 75% of brides surveyed by the national bridal apparel chain David's Bridal had downsized their weddings (Louie-Garcia, 2009).

Aside from the ups and downs of a capitalist economy, changes in actual wedding practices have the potential to become realized when counter-attitudes find a voice. For example, in the *USA Today* article "Wedding Redux," Barker (2007) told readers about issues surrounding the etiquette of second weddings. Barker offered varying opinions on the taste factor of second weddings, especially the question of whether or not they should look like first weddings or reflect a less luxurious air. The author noted that while second weddings today look more and more like first ones, with sit-down dinners and white gowns, there are parents and in-laws who still think second weddings should be "quiet courthouse affairs, the bride dressed in a skirt suit that's probably beige and definitely not white." Reporting that The Knot had seen a "surge of interest" in its "second-wedding section" in recent years, Barker also cited how the editor of *Encore Bride* saw big second weddings as minimizing the significance of marriage. In this sense, negative perceptions of extravagant second weddings may lead to practices that tone down the luxury factor for second (and third) weddings.

The illusory properties of weddings served as the cover topic of a 2009 issue of *Time*. The cover image featured a bride and groom cake topper sinking into a wedding cake with the headline "Unfaithfully Yours" touting an article on the decline of marriage. In that article, "Why Marriage Matters," author Caitlin Flanagan (2009) reiterated how big weddings distract from the seriousness of marriage by emphasizing the celebratory party rather than the relationship. She wrote:

> the middle class has spent the last 2½ decades—during which the divorce culture became a fact of life—turning weddings into overwrought exercises in consumer spending, as if by just plunking down enough cash for the flower girls' dresses and tissue-lined envelopes for the RSVP cards, we can somehow improve our chance of going the distance. (p. 48)

Flanagan has described herself and been criticized as being "anti-feminist" (Frey, 2004). However, I find her observations in "Why Marriage Matters" highly relevant and valid in that any move toward creating greater consciousness and awareness regarding the connection between the wedding and the serious nature of marriage, especially on the part of women, requires this kind of commentary and criticism from the press. Just as Scanlon (1995), in *Inarticulate Longings:* The Ladies' Home Journal, *Gender, and the Promises of Consumer Culture,* saw *The Ladies' Home Journal* as forwarding a covert, consumerist message to women, so, too, do weddings envelope this gender expectation within the packaging of fantasy and loveliness. The absence of any counterhegemonic messages from the journalism arena guarantees the continued, unquestioned acceptance and "inarticulate longings" for wedding pageantry created by seemingly innocuous bridal media.

Full Circle: Why Study Wedding Media?

The pressure to conform, the pressure to consume, and the pressure to ensure a successful bridal appearance results in women spending an inordinate amount of time and energy toward their one special day. This pressure comes from the overwhelmingly similar images of beautifully packaged brides—no matter what their cultural or economic backgrounds—in the bridal media described in this book which promise the elements of "fantasy and performance" embodied in the bridal appearance, as noted by Jellison (2008, p. 216). It also comes from other women, especially mothers. For example, mothers often express their dreams of seeing their daughters in the perfect wedding gown in the TLC reality series *Say Yes to the Dress.* The bridal identity, as discussed in Chapters 4 and 5, becomes paramount in these depictions—often erasing individual brides' self-identity. Furthermore, the label "bride" relegates these high-achieving women to the same role with the same costume and packaging. In a broader sense, we can consider the roles of women depicted in bridal media as representations of gender in "real life."

The other implication for feminism, defined in Chapter 1 as the progress of women toward egalitarianism, in large part relates to women's financial dependence on others for wedding expenses. In the sample of reality television programs I examined, I found several examples that openly mentioned that the wedding couple is footing the bill, or that parents are paying or helping to pay for the entire affair. However, the question of who pays for what remains largely ignored in the bridal media forms I examined; certainly one assumes that the bride herself is not using her own funds to create her special day. While this may appear gauche in terms of proper etiquette and simple manners, it also assumes that women should not or cannot be concerned with money. This kind of vagueness perpetuates traditional gender expectations regarding what the feminine woman cares about—surely someone else is looking after her and her money, just as someone else certainly is taking care of the expenses for her wedding.

Etiquette rules regarding what the bride's family pays for and what the groom's responsibilities are regarding ceremony costs, rings, flowers, rehearsal dinner, and all the other accoutrements associated with weddings have become antiquated in an age when women can and do earn their own money and when couples often cohabit prior to marriage. Indeed, many of the couples in WE tv's *Bridezillas*, TLC's *A Wedding Story*, and Oxygen's *Real Weddings From The Knot* appeared to be living together already, and several had children. In fact, footage of brides and grooms arguing about costs and party particulars was included in several episodes of *Bridezillas*, further enhancing the bridezilla image of the difficult, demanding woman. As a symbol of postfeminism, wherein femininity and feminism no longer represent opposing viewpoints or life choices, the bridezilla offers an image of the modern woman who gets what she wants. In this case, however, what the bridezilla wants also represents her traditional role as wife, and her quest for perfection reifies the ephemeral nature of the wedding day, rather than any "real" change in the world.

Bridal media offer women the chance to be in control, to make decisions, and to have the spotlight focused on them and only them. However, that control is illusory in that rather than being in control, the bride herself is controlled by the bridal rules that dictate how she should look, what she should wear, and what she should be concerned about. Ultimately, her status as bride negates all other roles she plays. The control, in the end, is really over the trivial, the domestic, the superficial. The appeal of the wedding as reflected and forwarded by the images, emotional narratives, and promises of happiness depicted in the bridal media described here has become so strong that challenges to this "common sense" appear nonexistent. Given the pressure of others' desires and expectations—including those of other women—such as in the case of Clementine in an episode of TLC's *A Wedding Story* from more than a decade ago, I wonder if women as a group can reverse what is happening.

Future bridal media researchers also should look at the status of feminism in the Third Wave and the effects of postfeminist thinking in a time when women still need to question the hegemonic practices that reaffirm patriarchy and gendered divisions of labor. Women and men need to ask themselves what they *really* want, and seriously think about the practical considerations of wedding expenditure, not only in terms of the monetary cost, but the time and effort involved as well as the political implications regarding gender and class. We need to educate young women about the foundations of feminism and the still-held-to traditional gender roles that prevent progress toward true and realistic egalitarianism.

Ironically, the same women who have the ability to transform this still-patriarchal society are the ones who still adhere to those practices that distract them, as Bowlby (1996) asserted, "from what would otherwise be their true identities, as humans and/or as women" (p. 381). Naomi Wolf's beauty myth becomes reified and reaffirmed in bridal media; the wonder and fantasy offered by Brideland which she herself could not resist represents a multibillion-dollar roadblock to women's progress toward gender equality.[19] I see the seemingly harmless content of bridal media as undermining the progress of the modern woman—and, as a result, the progress of our society as a whole.

I end here with an observation of the toy section of my local Target department store. Browsing the offerings in the Barbie doll aisle in early 2010, I noticed a new line of Barbies exclusive to Target titled the "i can be…" series. The various identities Barbie holds at the beginning of the 21st century include: pet vet, kid doctor, rock star, ballerina, race car driver, dentist, and, of course, bride. The message "i can be…a bride"—with the lower case "I" opening the slogan to a reading of minimal self worth—on bridal Barbie's packaging upholds a status quo that continues to tell girls that "bride" is a goal, rather than a fleeting identity. Placed within a series of occupations, the "i can be a bride" entry in this series (presumably designed to instill in girls career aspirations) implies that bride is a career like the others. Aside from the marketing advantages of dressing Barbie in a pretty, white dress and creating an aesthetic appeal for young girls, the message that "bride" holds equal status to the other occupations and careers reflects the status given to the role of bride in a wider sense. When considering the wedding-themed milieu of mass media, the persona of bride as a "job" and life goal has become commonplace and commonsensical. In this manner, the hegemonic version of woman/female/girl as potential bride remains firmly in place.

In the same pink-tinged aisle, I found a series of reproductions of vintage Barbie personas from the 1960s called "My Favorite Career." Reissued some 45 years later, the packaging of these reproductions symbolizes the continuing dichotomy between feminism represented in new identities and gender freedom and the femininity of traditional gender roles and expectations. The "My Favorite Career" series features Barbie in three jobs. Although clearly departing from her original identity of "teenage fashion model," the packaging of Barbie's alter egos in the "My Favorite Careers" series says something about the tension between femininity and feminism, at least as portrayed in the early 1960s. Even as Barbie pursued new careers, ones requiring a high level of education that would likely earn Barbie a pretty good salary, she was still very much concerned about clothes and fashion. For example, the reproduction of Barbie as a student teacher from 1965 has a caption on the packaging stating, "I chalk it up to my Ph.D. in fashion." The 1961 registered nurse reproduction Barbie instructs, "Get new shoes and call me in the morning." The reproduction of the 1965 version of astronaut Barbie announces, "Yes, I am a rocket scientist!" This declaration embodies both a confidence and a defensive tone, as if to tell the onlooker not to be so surprised that Barbie— a female—could actually be an astronaut (hence, the exclamation point).

I consider it ironic that even as Barbie expanded her career horizons nearly 50 years ago, her career as bride remains a key element of Mattel's newest Barbie offerings in the 21st century. I look forward to the day when Barbie the feminist—with the caption "Yes, I am a feminist!" (the exclamation point serving as more of an emphasis than a defense)—becomes a bestseller, offering girls an alternative identity to the fairy princesses and bride versions of Barbie that continue to define what it means to be female in American society. Ideology embodied by gendered toys such as bridal Barbie helps to keep in place a cultural hegemony that reaffirms not only traditional ideals of masculinity and femininity, but the very nature of personal relationships that underlie the very need for the wedding industry. Only when the glamour and fantasy of the bridal role become passé in the "real world" will Barbie, too, escape the bride factory.

Notes

1. The escape from "spinsterhood" provided by marriage allows for not only the continuing appeal of weddings, but of other mythic notions regarding being incomplete without a partner. Galician (2004) traced love myths to mythological stories of Cupid's arrow and other ancient tales. Foster (2005) also offered a critique of the wedding industry and the costs associated with the upward mobility promised by lavish weddings.
2. The CW network's 2011 reality "game-show" program *Shedding for the Wedding* did include grooms, but rather than following them, à la FitTV's *Buff Brides*, this competition show offered a free wedding as a prize for couples who lost weight.
3. For example, in *The Office* episode "Conflict Resolution" from Season 2 (original airdate May 4, 2006), Pam became the subject of a complaint over her wedding planning activities during office hours. Ironically, the complaint was made by her future husband, Jim.
4. Political media economy or political economy of the media refers to the study of power relations between media companies and other industries in capitalist societies. This area of study looks at how communication is used to "reinforce, challenge, or influence existing class and social relations," according to McChesney (2000, p. 110).
5. I must note that even as the wedding industry relies on the demand for wedding products advertised in bridal media, not all professionals endorse exorbitant wedding

expenditure. For example, florist Patty Singer-Buckley, co-owner of Fenton Flowers in Fenton, Missouri (a suburb of St. Louis) believes bigger doesn't always mean better. Rather than doing one large, expensive wedding, she prefers doing many smaller ones. Couples with a "$1,000 budget and champagne taste" run into problems when their budget does not match their ideal, she says. Flower arrangements and bouquets presented in bridal magazines may contain flowers out of season, which can cause brides to pay higher prices during out-of-season periods, for lower quality flowers. At the very minimum, Singer-Buckley says every bride should have a bouquet, "even if it's just a clutch of daisies" (personal communication, August 13, 2011).

6. "Bridezillas Episodes on WE" (2011); "Bridezillas on WE: Episodes" (2010).

7. Episode title: "Shane and Monet," recorded January 23, 2010 (original airdate June 17, 2007).

8. Episode title: " . . . and a Boat to Catch," airdate January 31, 2010.

9. For example, several episodes were run during a mini-marathon on December 30, 2009, of which I recorded three.

10. Episode title: "Sara and Bryan," airdate July 5, 2009.

11. Callaway (2005), author of "Nina's Wedding Blog," described *Extreme Makeover: Wedding Edition*, which aired in 2005; its first episode featured a groom who was a four-time cancer survivor.

12. For a summary of various relationship theories and elements of marital satisfaction, see Chapter 3 in Galician's (2004) *Sex, Love, and Romance in Mass Media*.

13. Publication titles, dates, and publishers: *Southern Weddings*, 2009–2011, published by Bliss Event Group; *Brides Florida*, Fall–Winter 2009, published by Condé Nast; *Gulf Coast Bride*, Winter 2009–2010, published by 3G Media, LLC.

14. Publication titles, dates, and publishers in order: "Luxe List" in *Uptown Weddings & Trends* (Spring 2011), published by Uptown Media Group; "Fabulous Dresses" in *Get Married* (Spring 2011), published by Get Married Media, Inc.; "Fabulous Engagement Photos" in *Beverly Clark's 2011 Elite Weddings* (Spring–Summer 2011), published by Beverly Clark Enterprises; "Hottest Trends" in *La Bella Bride* (2011), published by K La Fay publishing; "Reception Perfection" in *Cosmopolitan Bride* (February–March 2011), published by The National Magazine Company/Hearst Communication.

15. A similar rejection of the big, white wedding appeared at the end of the hit Broadway musical and later 2008 Hollywood blockbuster *Mamma Mia*, which used a wedding as the backdrop for its story about independent mother Donna and her soon-to-be wed daughter Sophie. Based on the music of the pop group ABBA, the play/film centers on Sophie's search for her biological father; she invites three men from Donna's past to the wedding to find out which is her real father. The climactic wedding scene, set in a chapel with numerous guests, results in Sophie's last-second decision not to marry her fiancé Sky—even as she and Sky are about to say their vows. Sophie realizes that she is too young to marry; her decision not to go through with the marriage ceremony represents a rejection of marrying early, and, in a sense, the empty symbolism of weddings not based on a solid, mature relationship. The film could have ended here, leaving viewers with the message that white weddings do not ensure happiness nor represent lasting love. Instead, Donna and Sophie's real father take their place and exchange vows, thereby "saving" the wedding and ensuring at least one happy ending.

16. Organic intellectuals originate from the nondominant class; they come from outside the category containing what Gramsci (1999) called "intellectuals" (creators of science, philosophy, and art) and "administrators" (those who simply convey "traditional, accumulated intellectual wealth") (p. 146).

17. Regarding the reproduction of ideology by media, Hall (1977) noted that cultural work cannot be carried through without also the dissemination of contradictions within that ideology.

18. Leondis and Hester (2009) reported the average dropped by 24%. Actual wedding cost average figures are from "Avg. Wedding Cost 1945–2010" (2011).

19. Wolf addressed the created need that tells women they must purchase beauty products and follow beauty practices in *The Beauty Myth* (2002), and explained the allure of the bridal image and fantasy of the wedding in "Brideland" (2003). In a real sense, I have worked to uncover the myth of Brideland here.

8. Conclusion

I BEGAN STUDYING WEDDING MEDIA MORE THAN TEN YEARS AGO, WHEN I noticed some marked differences in the way women and men appeared in the TLC reality television series *A Wedding Story*. While most brides spent their time on their wedding day preparing themselves for the bridal appearance, being made up, having their hair done, and putting on their wedding gowns, more of the bridegrooms engaged in a variety of activities, such as playing sports. The rush and angst that brides appeared to experience on their wedding day stood in stark contrast to the more leisurely way their future husbands appeared to approach this landmark and life-changing event. Thus began my journey exploring bridal media at the turn of the 21st century.

As I have shown throughout this book, the taking on of the responsibilities of wedding planning by women, for the most part, provides a demonstration of power in the sense that the bride controls her wedding day. But this power is fleeting, and overseeing the most intricately detailed, well-orchestrated event of one's lifetime presents the illusion of female control over the ultimate expression of love, romance, and commitment. The wedding industry, which provides livelihoods for those who work in it or depend on its success, relies on "tradition." This tradition upholds commonsense values embodied in the concept of hegemony as it functions in civil society. In that weddings serve as the physical representation of the beginning of marriage, they also incorporate aspects of the state, with state-sanctioned marriage ensuring the smooth functioning of a nation, as explained by Cott (2000). In that marriage symbolizes the application of the law to private life, then marriage equality serves as an indication of a society's treatment of all its participants in terms of its citizens' rights, including the right to have the pair bond recognized as a legal entity. As of this writing, the New York State Senate approved same-sex marriage, the sixth U.S. state to do so in addition to Washington, DC.[1] The desire for equality in legality, however, inherently assumes a certain viewpoint, namely, the desire to formalize the pair bond in the first place. When one examines the issue of gender status within the practice of heterosexual marriage, the assumptions associated with the typical wedding ritual seen in the bridal media discussed in this book open the door to a deeper look at the issue of equality. More to the point, the hegemonic thinking and acritical approach towards weddings and the subsequent marriages they endorse become a means to perpetuate an implicit imbalance of the sexes. The "exchange of women," explained by Rubin (1997) as a means by which men could ensure smooth social interactions, becomes even more apparent when one considers the escorting of brides by their fathers to the bridegroom. Indeed, one often sees the father shaking hands with his soon-to-be son-in-law as he "hands over" his daughter. If one takes Rubin's view, this gesture implies the agreement between men that they are allies, in a sense, and that the daughter/gift is a symbol of goodwill between them and a guarantee of nonaggression. In essence, this exchange translates to "I will not fight you, and as a gift to confirm this, I present you with this female." According to this explanation, then, in societies where men run the show, they make sure that they keep running the show by imposing this gift status upon females. In a sense, by following the "tradition" of being given away by a male to another male, the bride essentially becomes an *object* of exchange. Similarly, I see bridal media as a factory that manufactures a carefully constructed image of women. This process treats them as objects to be transformed from mere females to perfect brides.

Certainly, I am not saying that women are still chattel within patriarchal Western culture. Yes, women control their own lives and make their own decisions, including the decision to marry a mate of their choosing. However, the way in which the bridal media examined here present us with "real" depictions of real weddings continues to reflect archaic notions regarding the assumed duties of human beings based on sex. Modes of power still retain their male-dominant origins—we still get stories from real couples in which the marriage proposal is made by "the man," who is expected to present his woman with an item of jewelry to seal the deal. The economic forces that drive notions such as the perfect diamond engagement ring, which one learns needs to cost the man two months of his salary, and overall perfection regarding wedding dresses, wedding cakes, wedding receptions, and all the supposedly important things needed for the perfect wedding day play on emotional rather than

rational appeals.² The beauty, love, and romance associated with bridal advertising and the false needs they create are aimed at and have become the
purview of women—and, thus, one aspect of everyday life that women are
taught to become and see themselves as the experts.

Rather than controlling the world of business or politics, women's wedding work allows them to think they have domination over at least one aspect
of their existence. If postfeminism embodies the notion that feminism is obsolete, the bridezilla persona offers evidence that women have *achieved* something, namely, that women can have power and wield it in an almost
masculine-like fashion—at least in the world of weddings. However, the
bridezilla persona becomes problematic when viewed through a critical lens.
A woman who knows what she wants and gets it might give the impression
that brides need not be "blushing" and demure, but powerful and strong. It
seems as if the bridezilla is *taking* power and using it to get something very,
very important (her dream wedding). However, I say the demanding, mon-
strous bridezilla is *given* the space to break both the rules of politeness as well
as the stereotype of the accommodating female. She may think she is taking
that space without impunity. Consequences of rudeness and bad behavior in
"normal" social interactions disappear in the world of the bridezilla; in the end,
she does have her wedding, whatever the hitches and problems that threaten
its success. In this manner, the bridezilla is treated like a spoiled child, indulged
by a society (akin to the spoiled child's parents) who lets her treat others—
including other women—horribly because it is easier to let her do so than to
stand in her way. As I pointed out previously in Chapter 5, the framing of the
bridezilla as a foul-mouthed "bitch" does nothing to promote or forward gender equality. Instead, it results in the reaffirmation of the hysterical female
whose all-important goal is to have the wedding of her dreams, the ultimate
feminine achievement that combines her successful escape from spinsterhood
with the presentation of her body in its most visually appealing form possible.
Perfection becomes a desirable burden, and the bridezilla willingly takes on
the quest. At the same time, her control allows for the dismissal of men. In
this sense, we see the realization of the fantasy world of Brideland, where men
become subservient and *women* rule.

What the combination of gender-related messages from wedding-centered
media tells us is this: Give the bride whatever she wants on her wedding day,
no matter the cost in money or time, because it is her one day to be happy and
the deserved center of attention. Give her this one thing, because, in reality,
once the magical day is over, she will go back to her place and will know it.
This is what I see as being the problem with weddings: aside from all the good
feelings we associate with two persons declaring their love for each other in a
public venue, the wedding is a shiny object used to distract women from ques-

tioning WHY the perfect wedding and perfect bridal appearance are so important. More to the point, the quest for the perfect wedding requires time and energy that might be better used by women to empower themselves and attain true gender equality in the world outside Brideland.

I find so important to this inquiry Suzanne Leonard's (2006) keen observations regarding marriage envy as the manifestation of the competiveness among women associated with the life goal of "finding a man." The resulting jealousy felt by still-single women toward their married and soon-to-be-married cohorts is a form of infighting among women as a whole. Finding an appropriate partner with whom to share one's life can be a beneficial, wonderful thing.[3] However, the directive to women that they need a (male) partner in order to fulfill the role of "woman" underlies the negative effects of such a goal, namely, the acceptance of an inappropriate or even abusive partner, as noted by Rich (1980). This, coupled with the love myth that the right mate "completes you," promoted by mass media depictions of romance, socializes women and girls to consider themselves incomplete without a man (Galician, 2004).

The directive to women to avoid spinsterhood at all costs remains alive and well in the 21st century. Add to this the "wedding pageantry" associated with marriage, and the result points to a sustained, continued socialization of women to adhere not only to compulsory heterosexuality, but the notion that the bridal role is essential to their self-identity and well-being (Rich, 1980, p. 645). In short, the consequences of marriage envy lead women to compete with each other rather than with men—further distracting them from "taking care of business" and establishing egalitarianism throughout all facets of human interaction.

The special status given to brides as the stars of their fairy-tale fantasies come true further underscores the difference between women who have succeeded in securing a male mate versus those who cannot or never will. The overarching and never-ending "job" women have of making themselves appealing to men has become in essence a career unto itself as explicated by Wolf (2002) and Kilbourne (2002). While the beauty industry surrounds us with a barrage of messages on how to improve ourselves by buying the correct and corrective products, becoming a bride takes this job to a new level; the manufacturing of the perfect bridal appearance requires the perfect dress *into* which she must conform, both physically and symbolically. Weddings and bridal gown fittings have become a familiar and recognizable scenario in the world of advertising. Indeed, just as I began work on this conclusion, I noticed a television commercial for vegetable juice touted as a low-calorie beverage. It featured a young woman sipping it as she successfully fit into her wedding gown. With a triumphant "Yes!" and raised arms, the bride celebrated her apparent accomplishment of weight loss in the setting of a bridal salon. Not only that, she had lost weight to fit into her wedding gown, inferring that her impetus for losing weight was to look good on her wedding day, rather than a goal in and of itself. The reason for her weight loss in the context of this particular commercial is implied and understood, and any health implications are ignored. A seconds-long message like this might appear innocuous, but it becomes part of the never-ending media barrage aimed at women that tells them over and over again that their bodies are in need of discipline, whether or not it relates to their physical well-being.

"Everybody loves a wedding," the saying goes, and thus to *not* love a wedding calls into question the critical observer's motives. Leonard (2006) pointed out that marriage envy can be used by women against each other to alleviate the threat of criticism leveled against weddings. Research on weddings has become "legitimate," if one considers the scope and range of scholarship published in recent years, but serious *critique* makes the critic suspect. To point out all the things wrong with weddings and the bridal industry opens up oneself to attack: the critic is bitter because she didn't have a wedding, bitter because she has not been or does not want to be a bride, bitter because she is *still* single. In short, she suffers from both marriage envy and wedding envy. Thus, the critic's critics contend, the reason why the critic deconstructs weddings is because she is jealous: she could not partake in the celebration experienced by other, "successful" women who found a husband, therefore she has no recourse but to complain about it. In other words, the reason she does not see a wedding or the bridal role as desirable is because she has failed to get either. The application of Aesop's fable of "sour grapes" used by the critic's critics to explain her "problem" then becomes a way to dismiss such critique and rationalize hegemonic thinking.

Feminism as an investigative tool thus becomes a liability, especially if we see the existence of postfeminism as an accurate description of this moment in history. Inquiring women who question the need for weddings, and even the need for marriage, are told to "get over it" and live and let live. We are seen as attacking love, attacking joy, and attacking a good time; we are bitter killjoys who can't appreciate the celebration and happiness that weddings represent. For men who didn't or don't "get" feminism in the first place, the investigation of weddings becomes another petty "woman thing" to be dismissed as childish and petty.

So, are bridal media feminist or not? I invoke the answer I was taught as a graduate student: It depends. If one looks closely enough, one can certainly find evidence for "anti-feminist" instruction within bridal magazines, reality television, news, and popular films. I see these media as overpromoting ideals of femininity, especially regarding the vital importance placed on women's physical attractiveness. The notion of perfection that permeates the bridal media world amplifies this notion—the perfect dress, the perfect hair, the perfect makeup, the perfect bride. The magic associated with the bridal appearance underscores the importance of the dress, especially, allowing for a bridal mythology that helps us to rationalize the expense, time, and emotional torture of finding it, let alone enduring hours of discomfort while wearing it.

If femininity is used to attract and secure a man, the other overriding lesson these media give women is that accomplishing this goal is both extremely important and unimportant. Let me explain. On one hand, the wedding serves as proof that the woman in question was able to get a husband. On the other, men in Brideland are, ironically, unimportant. I see this in wedding planning programs, such as *Bridezillas*, where women are the ones in charge and making decisions to ensure the realization of the perfect wedding day. I use the term *gender territoriality* to describe the enforcement of the "rules" governing the space for wedding planning, namely, that the wedding is firmly entrenched within the realm of the feminine. The message to men is "keep out," and it further demarcates the responsibilities and work assigned to men and women. The time, labor, and stress involved are taken on willingly by brides—to the point where wedding planning becomes a part-time, or even full-time, job. This job allows women to wield their expertise over their men, who are deemed too dumb and stupid to say anything useful or give a valid opinion concerning what is supposed to be the couple's special day. In sum, even though a "man" has been secured by the woman, in Brideland he is dismissed, unimportant. His dismissal symbolically allows *women* to rule, thereby escaping patriarchy, at least for a little while.

Given these dominant messages, however, I invoke again the usefulness of hegemony theory as a theoretical tool to examine how common sense as forwarded by bridal media becomes disseminated and incorporated into everyday life. Gramsci saw the potential for changing common sense in the sphere of the civil, and I see glimmers of hope for this happening with the alternatives presented by individuals and groups with access to media outlets, such as the Internet. The Alternative to Marriage Project and web sites such as *FeministWedding.com* and *Offbeatbride.com* provide evidence for the existence of counterhegemonic messages. The dilemma faced by "anti-bride" authors and programs such as *Gay Weddings* is that they already are created within the assumed and established paradigm of marriage as a desired and desirable state of couplehood, or, at least, the accepted and "normal" way romantic partners are supposed to signify their partnership. To say one has eschewed tradition by having an untraditional wedding (a female best man, a male maid of honor, the wearing of colors and clothes other than a white dress for women, and even same-sex weddings) is a misnomer because these occur with an acceptance of an approved-of way of being (Geller, 2001). To rethink marriage or reject it altogether certainly would qualify as counterhegemonic. However, given the staying power of marriage and of weddings, I foresee transformation of gender-based inequities as happening from within, as egalitarian ideals are brought in and forwarded by those who do decide to participate.

Acquiescence to marriage does not negate the potential for achieving the goals I see forwarded by feminism. Several examples from the bridal media presented and analyzed in Chapter 5, "Working the Part: Bride as Actor," offer portrayals of brides and grooms contributing equally to the planning of their weddings, most notably in reality television programs that feature couples as they approach their special day. Just as with housework, wedding work certainly can, and should, be shared. On one hand, these portrayals provide evidence that such couples do exist. On the other, they are much too few and far between, if we consider the preponderance of bridal media that continue to show that the work of weddings mainly belongs to women.

What are the implications for the media literate viewer/reader? First, it must be acknowledged that one seeks bridal media—that is, it is produced and marketed to a specific audience: those seeking or wanting information or entertainment about weddings. Thus, these media are preaching to the choir, a self-selected audience for whom criticism of weddings might be avoided or dismissed *a priori*. Given this, it is even more important to look at such media with a critical eye and open mind. The viewing of the "real" weddings I am concerned with here requires the realization on the part of the viewer that they do not represent the universe of weddings of soon-to-be married couples. When considering one's own wedding, one must "know thyself": the media literate consumer needs to ask, "What do I really need?" rather than, "How can I make my wedding look like those I see on TV or in magazines?" Last, one needs to realize the costs associated with weddings, both financial and in terms of time and effort. Popular money expert Suze Orman's question "Can I afford it?" needs to become the guideline for wedding spending, regardless of who does the paying.[4] The costs beyond those related to money or time and labor, however, require a deeper look at one's own conscience, especially regarding family wishes. For this, I am afraid, I have no advice to offer.

The economic dictates of the mass media industry limit the probability that bridal media, as they exist today or in the very near future, will ever devote a larger portion of their space to *marriage* planning than to wedding planning. The frothy, lace-drenched, flower-laden images of weddings that provide a respite from everyday life and change of habitus in which anyone can be a celebrity—at least for one wonderful, perfect day—trump any images of couples engaged in serious discussion about the legal and financial implications of marriage. Bridal media imply that weddings are the denouement of romantic relationships rather than the beginning of a (supposedly) life-long partnership. They tell us that the work of weddings is difficult, yes, but worth it. After all, if one can get through planning a wedding and seeing it executed correctly without major snags, then the rest certainly must be easy.

The work required to sustain a relationship in which compatible partners thrive, and set and achieve individual and shared goals, one that nurtures and expands the crucial elements of intimacy, passion, and commitment—what Sternberg (1998) called "consummate love"—really has nothing to do with a wedding.[5] This aspect of marriage, I believe, is sorely lacking and more important than anything advertised in today's bridal media that sell a superficial sense of happiness based on the accumulation and display of material goods and practices that continue to highlight gender difference. As media consumers, we need to look past the window dressing and packaging of weddings we see in the media and think about what we *really* mean when—or if— we ever decide to say "I do."

Notes

1. The New York State Senate approved the Marriage Equality Act with a vote of 33 to 29 on June 24, 2011 (http://open.nysenate.gov/legislation/bill/A8354–2011).
2. The NBC comedy *The Office* incorporates humorous commentary on issues presented here, as previously mentioned in Chapter 7. In the Season 7 episode "Garage Sale," aired on March 24, 2011, Michael Scott proposed to his girlfriend, Holly Flax, in the office, with the help of his office employees. The ring he bought to present to her shocked his co-workers because of its overly large size. He responded to their surprise at the ring's dimensions by saying it cost two years' salary, which was his misinterpretation of the familiar two-months' salary guideline conveyed by diamond industry advertising.
3. As Glebatis (2007) noted in "'Real' Love Myths and Magnified Media Effects in *The Bachelorette*," desiring a partner with whom to share one's life is not necessarily a bad thing, as long as that partner is the *right* one.
4. During the time of this writing, CNBC's *The Suze Orman Show* featured a segment in which financial advisor Orman considered costs of items viewers want to purchase, using an assets versus liabilities assessment. Based on this, their requests were either approved or denied. Wedding expenses appeared frequently, with items such as wedding gowns and chair rentals for receptions among the items viewers requested in episodes I had seen as a casual viewer.
5. In *Cupid's Arrow*, Sternberg (1998) outlined his Triangular Theory of Love, in which the concept of consummate love incorporates its three essential elements: intimacy (bonded feelings), passion (sexual desire), and decision/commitment.

References

About Oxygen. (2007). Retrieved from http://www.oxygen.com/basics/about.aspx (no longer available).

About Say Yes to the Dress. (2008). Retrieved from http://tlc.discovery.com/tv/say-yes-dress/about.html

About WeddingChannel.com. (2009). Retrieved from http://wedding.weddingchannel.com/about_us/article_1318.asp

About WE tv. (2009). Retrieved from http://www.wetv.com/about-we-tv.html

Acosta, B. (1999, December 28). Veg-all TV. *The Austin Chronicle*. Retrieved from http://www.weeklywire.com/ww/12-28-99/austing_screens_tveye.html (no longer available).

A day in the life: Top wedding bloggers. (2009–2010). *Southern Weddings, 2*, 108–109.

A dress for the ages. (2011, May 16). *People: Special collector's issue*, 88–91.

A fox caught. (1882, February 23). *Los Angeles Times*, p. 0_3.

Against the odds. (2005). *People: I do! The great celebrity weddings*, 100–101.

Alison Geraghty, Andrew Bethke. (2009, April 19). *The New York Times*, p. ST12.

All Access: Episodes. (2009, October 2). Retrieved from http://www.tvguide.com/tvshows/access/episodes/281364

Allen, E. (2003). Culinary exhibition: Victorian wedding cakes and royal spectacle. *Victorian Studies, 45*(3), 457–484.

Alphonse, L. M. (2011, April 29). Royal wedding mysteries, solved. Retrieved from http://news.yahoo.com/s/yblog_royals/20110429/wl_yblog_royals/royal-wedding-mysteries-solved

Alter, E. (2002, August 29). *Gay Weddings* a different reality. *Media Life*. Retrieved from http://209.61.190.23/news2002/aug02/aug26/4_thurs/news5thursday.html (no longer available).

America gets married. (2009, July–August). *Brides*, 270–291.

Amnéus, C. (2010). Wedded perfection: The evolution and aesthetics of the wedding gown in Western culture. In C. Amnéus (Ed.), *Wedded perfection: Two centuries of wedding gowns* (pp. 14–62). Cincinnati, OH: Cincinnati Art Museum.

Anderson, S. H. (1981, July 30). The dress: Silk taffeta with sequins and pearls. *The New York Times*, p. A10.

An elegant wedding. (1882, November 10). *Los Angeles Times*, p. 0_1.

Angelic angling. (1882, May 9). *Los Angeles Times*, p. 0_3.

Apple, R. W., Jr. (1981a, July 29). Charles and Lady Diana wed today: Beacons burn across a joyful Britain. *The New York Times*, p. A1.

Apple, R. W., Jr. (1981b, July 30). Amid splendor, Charles weds Diana. *The New York Times*, p. A1.

Artz, L., & Murphy, B. A. O. (2000). *Cultural hegemony in the United States*. Thousand Oaks, CA: Sage.

Ask Carley. (2009, Fall–2010, Winter). *The Knot*, 18.

Average cost of a wedding increases 23% in 2010 to $24,066. (2011, January 10). Retrieved from http://www.theweddingreport.com

Avg. wedding cost 1945–2010. (2011). Retrieved from http://www.theweddingreport.com/

Bacchilega, C. (1997). *Postmodern fairy tales: Gender and narrative strategies*. Philadelphia, PA: University of Pennsylvania Press.

Baldrige, L. (2000). *Legendary brides: From the most romantic weddings ever, inspired ideas for today's brides*. New York, NY: HarperCollins.

Balz, C. (2006, August 7). Weddings: A veil of sadness. *Newsweek*, 13.

Barker, O. (2007, June 17). Wedding redux: The thrill is gone for resentful guests. *USA Today*. Retrieved from http://www.usatoday.com/life/lifestyle/2007–06–17-second-weddings_N.htm

Barovick, H. (1999, October 18). Labor, love and ratings. *Time*, 103.

Bartky, S. L. (1988). Foucault, femininity, and the modernization of patriarchal power. In I. Diamond & L. Quinby (Eds.), *Feminism and Foucault: Reflections on resistance* (pp. 61–86). Boston, MA: Northeastern University Press.

Bartky, S. L. (1990). *Femininity and domination: Studies in the phenomenology of oppression*. New York, NY: Routledge.

Baumgardner, J., & Richards, A. (2010). *Manifesta: Young women, feminism, and the future* (10th anniversary ed.). New York, NY: Farrar, Straus, & Giroux.

Bechtel, S. (2000). For better or worse. *For the Groom*, 82–85.

Behind the scenes: 'My Celebrity Wedding With The Knot.' (2009, March 6) Retrieved from http://wedding.theknot.com/wedding-themes/choosing-wedding-themes/articles/my-celebrity-weddings-with-the-knot.aspx

Behm-Morawitz, E., & Mastro D. (2008). Mean girls? The influence of gender portrayals in teen movies on emerging adults' gender-based attitudes and beliefs. *Journalism and Mass Communication Quarterly*, 85(1), 131–146.

Belsky, G. (2000). Here and eloping in Las Vegas. *For the Groom*, 86–91.

Berger, J. (1998). Ways of seeing (excerpt). In L. Peach (Ed.), *Women in culture: A*

Women's Studies anthology (pp. 97–104). Malden, MA: Blackwell.

Berlant, L. (2008). *The female complaint: The unfinished business of sentimentality in American culture*. Durham, NC: Duke University Press.

Blitzer, P. (2005, Winter). Get ready to look great. *InStyle Weddings*, 235–240.

Boden, S. (2003). *Consumerism, romance and the wedding experience*. New York, NY: Palgrave Macmillan.

Bordo, S. (1993). *Unbearable weight: Feminism, Western culture, and the body*. Berkeley, CA: University of California Press.

Boswell, J. (1994). *Same-sex unions in premodern Europe*. New York, NY: Villard Books.

Bowlby, R. (1996). Soft sell: Marketing rhetoric in feminist criticism. In V. de Grazia & E. Furlough, *The sex of things: Gender and consumption in historical perspective* (pp. 381–387). Los Angeles, CA: University of California Press.

Brady, L. S. (1997). *Vows: Weddings of the nineties from* The New York Times. New York, NY: William Morrow.

Bravo fact sheet. (n.d.). Retrieved from http://ncta.com/guidebook_pds/Bravo.pdf (no longer available).

Bridezillas: About the brides. (2010). Retrieved from http://www.wetv.com/bridezillas /about-the-brides

Bridezillas: About the brides, Adrianna-Korliss. (2006). Retrieved from http://games. amctv.com/bridezillas2005/about.hmtl (no longer available).

Bridezillas Episodes on WE. (2011, August 19). Retrieved from http://www.tvguide. com/tvshows/bridezillas/episodes/191423

Bridezillas on WE: Episodes. (2010, January 29). Retrieved from http://www.tvguide.com /tvshows/bridezillas/episodes/191423

Bridezillas' wedding details. (2007, August 24). *New York Magazine*. Retrieved from http://nymag.com/metrotv/bridezillas/resources.htm

Brown, J. (1999, August 25). Fairytale weddings get TV treatment. *The Detroit News*. Retrieved from http://detnews.com/1999/entertainment/9908/25/08250087.htm (no longer available).

Brown, M. E. (1989). Soap opera and women's culture: Politics and the popular. In K. Carter & C. Spitzack (Eds.), *Doing research on women's communication: Perspectives on theory and method* (pp. 161–190). Norwood, NJ: Ablex.

Budget etiquette. (2011). Retrieved from http://www.brides.com/wedding-answers-tools/wedding-etiquette/2010/05/budget

Bulging Brides. (2010) Retrieved from http://www.fineliving.com/fine/bulging_brides (no longer available).

Bulging Brides episode guide. (2010) Retrieved from http://204.78.50.142/fine/ episode_archive/0,1663,FINE_32916_983,00.html

Bush wants marriage reserved for heterosexuals. (2003, July 30). Retrieved from http:// www.cnn.com/2003/ALLPOLITICS/07/30/bush.gay.marriage/

Butler, J. (1999). *Gender trouble: Feminism and the subversion of identity*. New York, NY: Routledge.

Butler, J. (2002). Is kinship always already heterosexual? In W. Brown & J. Halley (Eds.), *Left legalism/left critique* (pp. 229–258). Durham, NC: Duke University Press.

Buy, buy love. (2001, Spring). *InStyle Weddings*, 176–183.

Callaway, N. (2005, May 4). Extreme Makeover: Wedding Edition. Retrieved from http://weddings.about.com/b/2005/05/04/extreme-makeover-wedding-edition.htm

Calvert, C. (2000). *Voyeur nation: Media, privacy, and peering in modern culture*. Boulder, CO: Westview Press.

Cambridge Women's Pornography Cooperative. (2009). *Porn for the bride*. San Francisco, CA: Chronicle Books.

Capsuto, S. (2000). *Alternate channels: The uncensored story of gay and lesbian images on radio and television, 1930s to the present*. New York, NY: Ballantine Books.

Carragee, K. M. (1993). A critical evaluation of debates examining the media hegemony thesis. *Western Journal of Communication, 57*(3), 330–348.

Cass, J. (1967, January 15). Lovely brides brighten the midwinter scene. *Chicago Tribune*, p. A5.

Cassidy, M. F. (2005). *What women watched: Daytime television in the 1950s*. Austin, TX: University of Texas Press.

Choney, S. (2011, April 29). Royal wedding breaks Internet records. Retrieved from http://digitallife.today.com/_news/2011/04/29/6556575-royal-wedding-breaks-internet-records

Cochran, S. (2011, April 27). Short history of 'Waity Katie' to Britain's future queen. Retrieved from http://news.yahoo.com/s/ac/20110427/en_ac/8372019_short_history_of_waity_katie_to_britains_future_queen_1/print

Cole, P. M. (1893). New England weddings. *Journal of American Folklore, 6*(21), 103–107.

Condit, C. (1994). Hegemony in a mass-mediated society: Concordance about reproductive technologies. *Critical Studies in Mass Communication, 11*(3), 205–230.

Cook, J. (2003, July 22). Bravo launches two gay-themed shows. *Salt Lake Tribune*. Retrieved from www.sltrib.com/2003/Jul/07222003/tuesday/77539.asp (no longer available).

Coontz, S. (2005). *Marriage, a history: From obedience to intimacy or how love conquered m marriage*. New York, NY: Viking.

Corrado, M. (2002). Teaching wedding rules: How bridal workers negotiate control over their customers. *Journal of Contemporary Ethnography, 31*(1), 33–67.

Cott, N. F. (2000). *Public vows: A history of marriage and the nation*. Cambridge, MA: Harvard University Press.

'Country Wife' gets updated. (1972, May 22). *Chicago Tribune*, p. B12.

Couple updates: *A Wedding Story*. (2009). Retrieved from http://tlc.discovery.com/fan-sites/weddingstory/updates/updates.html

Currie, D. H. (1993). 'Here comes the bride': The making of a 'modern traditional' wedding in Western culture. *Journal of Comparative Family Studies, 24*(3), 403–421.

David, N. (2001, Fall). Renewing your vows. *Bride Again. 3*(3), 22–24.

Davis, A. M. (2006). *Good girls and wicked witches: Women Disney's feature animation*. Eastleigh, UK: John Libbey.

de Certeau, M. (1984). *The practice of everyday life* (S. Rendall, Trans.). Berkeley, CA: University of California Press.

Dees, M., with S. Fiffer. (2001). *A lawyer's journey: The Morris Dees story*. Chicago, IL: American Bar Association.

dellaCava, M. (2006, June 7). Grooms are getting more engaged in wedding planning. *USA Today*, p. 6D.

Directory: Making faces. (2005, Spring). *Bride Allure*, 67–68.

Doane, M. A. (1989). The economy of desire: The commodity form in/of the cinema. *Quarterly Review of Film and Video, 11*(1), 23–33.

Dobscha, S., & Foxman, E. (1998). Women and wedding gowns: Exploring a discount shopping experience. In E. Fischer & D. Wardlow (Eds.), *Proceedings of the Fourth Conference on Gender, Marketing and Consumer Behavior* (pp. 131–141). San Francisco, CA: San Francisco State University.

Donald, J., & Hall, S. (1986). Introduction. In J. Donald & S. Hall (Eds.), *Politics and ideology: A reader* (pp. ix–xii). Philadelphia, PA: Open University Press.

Dougherty, C. (2010, September 29). New vow: I don't take thee. *The Wall Street Journal*. Retrieved from http://online.wsj.com/article/SB10001424052748703882404575519871444705214.html?mod=wsj

Dow, B. (1990). Hegemony, feminist criticism and *The Mary Tyler Moore Show*. *Critical Studies in Media Communication, 7*(3), 261–274.

Dow, B. (1996). *Prime-time feminism: Television, media culture, and the women's movement since 1970*. Philadelphia, PA: University of Pennsylvania Press.

Dow, B. (2001). *Ellen*, television, and the politics of gay and lesbian visibility. *Critical Studies in Media Communication, 18*(2), 123–140.

Dress prediction: Final rumor round-up. (2011, April 26). Retrieved from http://unveiled.blogs.cnn.com/2011/04/26/dress-prediction-final-rumor-round-up/

Dwyer, L. (2009, July–August). Secret to a great marriage. *Brides*, 182.

Edwards, T. (2006). *Cultures of masculinity*. New York, NY: Routledge.

Eight-tiered cake wows guests at wedding reception. (2011, April 29). Retrieved from http://news/yahoo.com/s/afp/20110429/If_afp/britainroyalsmarriagefood (no longer available).

Elias, N. (1978). *The civilizing process: The history of manners* (E. Jephcott, Trans.). New York, NY: Urizen Books.

Elser, D. (2009, August 7). Waity Katie needs to get a life. *The Punch*. Retrieved from http://www.thepunch.com.au/articles/kate-middleton-needs-to-get-a-life

Emanuel, D., & Emanuel, E. (2006). *A dress for Diana*. New York, NY: Collins Design.

Engstrom, E. (2003). Hegemony in reality-based TV programming: The world according to *A Wedding Story*. *Media Report to Women, 31*(1), 10–14.

Engstrom, E. (2006). What women watched: Daytime television in the 1950s. [Review of the book *What women watched: Daytime television in the 1950s*, by M. Cassidy]. *Journal of Broadcasting and Electronic Media, 50*(2), 338–341.

Engstrom, E. (2007). The 'reality' of reality television wedding programs. In M.-L. Galician & D. L. Merskin (Eds.), *Critical thinking about sex, love, and romance in the mass media* (pp. 335–354). Mahwah, NJ: Lawrence Erlbaum.

Engstrom, E. (2008). Unraveling The Knot: Political economy and cultural hegemony in wedding media. *Journal of Communication Inquiry, 32*(1), 60–82.

Ensnared by Cupid. (1892, September 25). *Chicago (Daily) Tribune*, p. 27.

Episode detail: Weddings of a Lifetime. (2009, September 28). Retrieved from http://www.tvguide.com/detail/tv-how.aspx?tvobjectid=205400&more=ucepisodelist&episodeid=888356

Eva Longoria: I'm no bridezilla. (2007, July 12). Retrieved from www.gmanews.tv/story/50667/Eva-Longoria-Im-no-bridezilla

Faludi, S. (1991). *Backlash: The undeclared war against American women.* New York, NY: Crown.

FAQ, FeministWedding.com. (2011). Retrieved from http://www.feministwedding.com/faq.html

Felski, R. (2000). *Doing time: Feminist theory and postmodern culture.* New York, NY: New York University Press.

FeministWedding.com. (2010). Retrieved from http://www.feministwedding.com/index.html

Feuer, J. (1983). The concept of live television: Ontology as ideology. In E. A. Kaplan (Ed.), *Regarding television: Critical approaches—an anthology* (pp. 12–21). Frederick, MD: University Publications of America.

55 million saw wedding. (1981, July 31). *The New York Times,* p. C23.

Filak, V. F. (2002). *Marriage, magazines and makeup tips: A comparative content analysis of* Brides *magazine and* Glamour *magazine.* Paper presented at the meeting of the Association for Education in Journalism and Mass Communication, Miami, FL.

Filene's Basement bridal bargain. (2002, August 16). *News Three at four* [Newscast]. Las Vegas, NV: KVBC-TV.

Fine, J. (2001, October 22). Mag ad pages plummet 9.2%. *Advertising Age,* 20.

Flanagan, C. (2009, July 13). Why marriage matters. *Time,* 45–49.

Ford, C. (1988). *Etiquette: Charlotte Ford's guide to modern manners.* New York, NY: Clarkson Potter.

48 hour wedding. (2002). Retrieved from http://www.pax.tv/specials/48hourwedding/?cmp=IL5113 (no longer available).

Foss, K. A., & Foss, S. K. (1989). Incorporating the feminist perspective in communication scholarship: A research commentary. In K. Carter & C. Spitzack (Eds.), *Doing research on women's communication: Perspectives on theory and method* (pp. 65–91). Norwood, NJ: Ablex.

Foster, G. A. (2005). *Class-passing: Social mobility in film and popular culture.* Carbondale, IL: Southern Illinois University Press.

Four Weddings: About the show. (2010). Retrieved from http://tlc.discovery.com/tv/four-weddings/about.html

Freeman, E. (2002). *The wedding complex: Forms of belonging in modern American culture.* Durham, NC: Duke University Press.

Frey, H. (2004, Winter). Back to the kitchen, circa 1950, with Caitlin Flanagan. *Ms.* Retrieved from http://www.msmagazine.com/winter2004/backtothekitchen.asp

Frisby, C., & Engstrom, E. (2006). Always a bridesmaid, never a bride: Portrayals of women of color in bridal magazines. *Media Report to Women, 34*(4), 10–14.

Frye, N. (2000). *Anatomy of criticism.* Princeton, NJ: Princeton University Press.

Galician, M.-L. (2004). *Sex, love, and romance in the mass media: Analysis and criticism of unrealistic portrayals and their influence.* Mahwah, NJ: Lawrence Erlbaum.

Gamble, S. (Ed.). (2001). *The Routledge companion to feminism and postfeminism.* New York, NY: Routledge.

Garnet. (2004, September 20). Anyone else feel icky about bouquet/garter toss? [Online forum comment]. Retrieved from http://www.indiebride.com/kvetch/index.php?t=msg&goto=182907&S=02f95f0ef3fe2cc9e1cc59b19cec1705#msg_182907

Gay weddings go prime time. (2002, October 3). Retrieved from http://www.thedaily-beast.com/newsweek/2002/10/03/gay-weddings-go-prime-time.html

Geller, J. (2001). *Here comes the bride: Women, weddings, and the marriage mystique.* New York, NY: Four Walls Eight Windows.

Gerin, C., & Rosenbaum, S. (2002). *Anti-bride guide: Tying the knot outside of the box.* San Francisco, CA: Chronicle Books.

Gerin, C., Hughes, K., Hornick, A. G., & Tubkam, I. (2004). Anti-bride wedding planner: Hip tools and tips for getting hitched. San Francisco, CA: Chronicle Books.

Gibbons, S. (2003, June 4). Bridal media promote merchandise, not marriage. *Women's eNews.* Retrieved from http://womensenews.org/article.cfm/dyn/aid/1353/context/archive

Girl Meets Gown: See it on WETtv! (2009). Retrieved from http://www.amspictures.com/page.php?page=%3Ci%3Egirl-meets-gown%3Candi%3E

Gitlin, T. (1987). Television's screens: Hegemony in transition. In D. Lazere (Ed.), *American media and mass culture: Left perspectives* (pp. 240–265). Los Angeles, CA: University of California Press.

Glebatis, L. M. (2007). 'Real' love myths and magnified media effects of *The Bachelorette.* In M.-L. Galician & D. Merskin (Eds.), *Critical thinking about sex, love, and romance in the mass media* (pp. 319–334). Mahwah, NJ: Lawrence Erlbaum.

Goffman, E. (1959). *The presentation of self in everyday life.* New York, NY: Doubleday.

Goldin, C., & Shim, M. (2004). Making a name: Women's surnames at marriage and beyond. *Journal of Economic Perspectives, 18*(2), 143–160.

Goldstein-Gidoni, O. (1997). *Packaged Japaneseness: Weddings, business, and brides.* Honolulu, HI: University of Hawai'i Press.

Gramsci, A. (1999). *Selections from the prison notebooks of Antonio Gramsci* (Q. Hoare & G. N. Smith, Trans. & Eds.). London, UK: Electric Book.

Gramsci, A. (2000). *The Antonio Gramsci reader: Selected writings, 1916–1935* (D. Forgacs, Ed.). New York, NY: New York University Press.

Gross, L. (1989). Out of the mainstream: Sexual minorities and the mass media. In E. Seiter, H. Borchers, G. Kreutzner, & E.-M. Warth (Eds.), *Remote control: Television, audiences, and cultural power* (pp. 130–149). New York, NY: Routledge.

Hall, S. (1977). Culture, the media and the 'ideological effect.' In J. Curran, M. Gurevitch, & J. Woollacott (Eds.), *Mass communication and society* (pp. 315–348). Beverly Hills, CA: Sage.

Hall, S. (1996). What is this 'black' in black popular culture? In D. Morley & K.-H. Chen (Eds.), *Stuart Hall: Critical dialogues in cultural studies* (pp. 468–478). London, UK: Routledge.

Hall, A., & Hebert, L. (2004, August). *The evolution of the makeover from print to television: An analysis of the social construction of the female body image.* Paper presented at the meeting of the Association for Education in Journalism and Mass Communication, Toronto, Canada.

Harrington, C. L. (2003). Homosexuality on *All My Children*: Transforming the daytime landscape. *Journal of Broadcasting and Electronic Media, 47*(2), 216–235.

Hatch, D., & Hatch, M. (1947). Criteria of social status as derived from marriage announcements in the *New York Times. American Sociological Review, 12*(4), 396–403.

Haugland, H. K. (2006). *Grace Kelly: Icon of style to royal bride*. New Haven, CT: Philadelphia Museum of Art/Yale University Press.

Hennessy, R., & Ingraham, C. (Eds.). (1997). *Materialist feminism: A reader in class, difference, and women's lives*. New York, NY: Routledge.

Herr, R. (2005, May). *The dream and the reality of the American wedding: Taste, style, and reality television*. Paper presented at the meeting of the International Communication Association, New York.

Hochschild, A. R., with Machung, A. (1989). *The second shift*. New York, NY: Avon Books.

Hoffnung, M. (2006). What's in a name? Marital name choice revisited. *Sex Roles*, 55(11–12), 817–825.

Hough, J. (2007, March 21). The Knot marries fast growth, obscene margins. *Smart Money*. Retrieved from http://www.smartmoney.com/investing/stocks/the-knot-marries-fast-growth-obscene-margins-20976/

How to submit an announcement. (2009, April 24). *The New York Times*. Retrieved from http://www.nytimes.com/pages/fashion/weddingss/index.html

Howard, V. (2006). *Brides, Inc.: American weddings and the business of tradition*. Philadelphia, PA: University of Pennsylvania Press.

Hutchison, C. (2010, September 20). 'Bridalplasty': Plastic surgery as a TV prize? Retrieved from http://abcnews.go.com/Health/Wellness/bridalplasty-compete-nose-jobs-implants-dream-wedding/story?id=11663378

Inbar, M. (2009, July 15). Runners sprint to wedded bliss live on *Today*. Retrieved from http://today.msnbc.msn.com/id/31922530/ns/today-today-weddings/

Indiebride: Our vow. (2008) Retrieved http://www.indiebride.com/ourvow/index.html

Indiebride: Trousseau. (2008) Retrieved http://www.indiebride.com/trousseau/index.html (no longer available).

Ingraham, C. (1999). *White weddings: Romancing heterosexuality in popular culture*. New York, NY: Routledge.

Ingraham, C. (2008). *White weddings: Romancing heterosexuality in popular culture* (2nd ed.). New York, NY: Routledge.

In social spheres. (1892, January 2). *Los Angeles Times*, p. 5.

Ives, N. (2006, April 4). Conde Nast unites bridal titles online. *Ad Age*. Retrieved from http://adage.com/article/mediaworks/conde-nast-unites-bridal-titles-online/108294/

Jane Crawford officer's bride in New Guinea. (1945, August 30). *Chicago (Daily) Tribune*, p. 19.

Jellison, K. (2008). *It's our day: America's love affair with the white wedding, 1945–2005*. Lawrence, KS: University Press of Kansas.

Jellison, K. (2010). The commercialization of weddings in the twentieth century. In C. Amnéus (Ed.), *Wedded perfection: Two centuries of wedding gowns* (pp. 78–95). Cincinnati, OH: Cincinnati Art Museum.

Jensen, R. (1996). The politics and ethics of lesbian and gay 'wedding' announcements in newspapers. *The Howard Journal of Communications*, 7(1), 13–28.

Johnson, S., & Prijatel, P. (2007). *The magazine from cover to cover* (2nd ed.). New York, NY: Oxford University Press.

Jung, P. B., & Smith, R. (1993). *Heterosexism: An ethical challenge*. Albany, NY: State

University of New York Press.

Kate Middleton: Snapshot. (2011, March 23). Retrieved from http://www.people.com/people/kate_middleton

Kate Walsh's bridezilla moment. (2007, August 29) Retrieved from http://www.theinsider.com/news/332206_Kate_Walsh_s_Bridezilla_Moment (no longer available).

Katherine Dudley Hackstaff married to Lt. Robert Reis. (1945, January 1). *Los Angeles Times*, p. A5.

Katie: My dream wedding! (2006, December 4). *Life & Style Weekly*, pp. 28–33.

Katz, G. (2011, April 18). From Waity Katie to Princess Catherine. Retrieved from http://www.komonews.com/news/entertainment/120065124.html

Kay, R. (2011, April 30). From that kiss to William's smile, Diana and haunting reminders of the last great royal wedding. *Daily Mail*. Retrieved from http://www.dailymail.co.uk/news/article-1382092/Royal-wedding-2011-Haunting-reminders-Princess-Diana.html

Kennedy weddings. (2005) Retrieved from http://www.lifetimetv.com/shows/weddings/kennedy/index.html (no longer available).

Kilbourne, J. (2002). *Killing us softly III: Advertising's image of women* [DVD]. Northampton, MA: Media Education Foundation.

Kim, J. L., Sorsoli C. L., Collins, K., Zylbergold, B. A., Schooler, D., & Tolman, D. L. (2007). From sex to sexuality: Exposing the heterosexual script on primetime network television. *Journal of Sex Research*, *44*(2), 145–157.

King, M. P. (Producer, Director, & Writer). (2008). *Sex and the city: The movie.* [Motion picture]. USA: New Line Cinema.

Kipnis, L. (2006). *The female thing: Dirt, envy, sex, vulnerability.* New York, NY: Pantheon Books.

Krane, V., Choi, P., Baird, S., Aimar, C., & Kauer, K. (2004). Living the paradox: Female athletes negotiate femininity and muscularity. *Sex Roles*, *50*(5–6), 315–329.

Kuczynski, A. (2000, April 11). A little light reading, anyone? When weighty issues are the magazines themselves. *The New York Times*, p. C1.

Landy, M. (1994). *Film, politics, and Gramsci.* Minneapolis, MN: University of Minnesota Press.

Lauraska. (2007, March 29). Am I being too uber-feminist, here? [Online forum post]. Retrieved from http://www.indiebride.com/kvetch/index.php?t=tree&th=26371&S=e840823d316e2f97c9fd5777f7c86253

Lears, T. J. (1985). The concept of cultural hegemony: Problems and possibilities. *American Historical Review*, *90*(3), 567–593.

Leeds-Hurwitz, W. (2002) *Wedding as text: Communicating cultural identities through ritual.* Mahwah, NJ: Lawrence Erlbaum.

Leonard, S. (2006). Marriage envy. *Women's Studies Quarterly*, *34*(3–4) , 43–64.

Leondis, A., & Hester, E. (2009, April 13). Brides kiss dream weddings goodbye as vendors shut. Retrieved from http://www.bloomberg.com/apps/news?pid=newsarchive&sid=aDVUEORQd3Pc

Letter from the editor. (2009, September 25). *Signature Bride.* Retrieved from http://www.signaturebride.net/editor2.html

Levant, R. F., Good, G. E., Cook, S. W., O'Neill, J. M., Smalley, K. B., Owen, K., & Richmond, K. (2006). The normative male alexithymia scale: Measurement of a gender-linked syndrome. *Psychology of Men and Masculinity,* 7(4), 212–224.

Levine, E. (2005). Fractured fairy tales and fragmented markets: Disney's *Weddings of a Lifetime* and the cultural politics of media conglomeration. *Television & New Media,* 6(1), 71–88.

Lewin, E. (1998). *Recognizing ourselves: Ceremonies of lesbian and gay commitment.* New York, NY: Columbia University Press.

Lewis, C. (1997). Hegemony in the ideal: Wedding photography, consumerism, and patriarchy. *Women's Studies in Communication,* 20(2), 167–188.

Lin-Eftekhar, J. (2002, October 8). Indie filmmaker documents real life. *UCLA Today.* Retrieved from http://today.ucla.edu/portal/ut/021008indie_filmmaker.aspx

Lockford, L. (1996). Social drama in the spectacle of femininity: The performance of weight loss in the Weight Watchers program. *Women's Studies in Communication,* 19(3), 291–312.

Louie-Garcia, A. (2009, April 20). Love in the time of recession. Retrieved from http://news.yahoo.com/s/ynews/ynews_bs304

Lowrey, T. M., & Otnes, C. (1994). Construction of a meaningful wedding: Differences in the priorities of brides and grooms. In J. A. Costa (Ed.), *Gender issues and consumer Behavior* (pp. 164–183). Thousand Oaks, CA: Sage.

Lull, J. (2011). Hegemony. In G. Dines & J. M. Humez (Eds.), *Gender, race, and class in media: A critical reader* (3rd ed., pp. 33–36). Thousand Oaks, CA: Sage.

Lyall, S. (2011, April 29). To fanfare, William and Kate Middleton marry [Original title]. *The New York Times.* Retrieved from http://www.nytimes.com/2011/04/30/world/europe/30britain.html?_.r+1&hp

Magazine ad page leaders for January through March 2007 (2007, April 20). Retrieved from http://adage.com/datacenter/datapopup.php?article_id=116018

Maher, J. (2004). What do women watch? Tuning in to the compulsory heterosexuality channel. In S. Murray & L. Ouellette (Eds.), *Reality TV: Remaking television culture* (pp. 197–213). New York, NY: New York University Press.

Mansfield, S. (2002, September 2). The wedding planners. *San Francisco Examiner.* Retrieved from http://www.examiner.com/ex_files/default.jsp?story=X0902TVw (no longer available).

Many are married. (1893, April 23). *Chicago (Daily) Tribune,* p. 26.

Marikar, S. (2011, July 16). Jennifer Lopez minus Marc Anthony: What happened? *ABC News.* Retrieved from http://abcnews.go.com/Entertainment/jennifer-lopez-minus-marc-anthony-happened/story?id=14086706

MarriageFree and boycott. (2010). Retrieved from http://www.unmarried.org/marriagefree.html

Married. (1851, October 29). *The New York Daily Times,* p. 4.

Marx, L. (2009, April 19). Vows: Christina Matthews and Benjamin Macfarland III. *The New York Times,* p. ST11.

Masters of Reception: About the show. (2010). Retrieved from http://tlc.discovery.com/tv/masters-of-reception/about-masters-of-reception.html

Mather, M., & Lavery, D. (2010). In U.S., proportion married at lowest recorded levels. Retrieved from http://www.prb.org/Articles/2010/usmarriagedecline.aspx

May, L. (2011, April 29). Double kiss, Kate's wedding dress capture memorable moments. *Yahoo News.* Retrieved from http://news.yahoo.com/s/ac/20110429/en_ac/

8390047_double_kiss_kates_wedding_dress_capture_memorable_moments

McChesney, R. W. (2000). The political economy of communication and the future of the field. *Media, Culture and Society, 22*(1), 109–116.

McClanahan, A. M. (2007). 'Must marry TV': The role of the heterosexual imaginary in *The Bachelor*. In M.-L. Galician & D. L. Merskin (Eds.), *Critical thinking about sex, love, and romance in the mass media* (303–318). Mahwah, NJ: Lawrence Erlbaum.

McCracken, E. (1993). *Decoding women's magazines: From* Mademoiselle *to* Ms. New York, NY: St. Martin's Press.

McNamara, M. (2009, June 16). 'Wedding Day' on TNT. *Los Angeles Times*. Retrieved from http://articles.latimes.com/2009/jun/16/entertainment/et-weddingday16

McNeil, A. (1991). *Total television: A comprehensive guide to programming from 1948 to the present*. New York, NY: Penguin Books.

McRobbie, A. (2004). Post-feminism and popular culture. *Feminist Media Studies, 4*(3), 255–264.

Mead, R. (2007). *One perfect day: The selling of the American wedding*. New York, NY: Penguin Press.

Melissa Etheridge's ex opens up about split. (2010, May 24). *SFGate*. Retrieved from http://www.sfgate.com/cgi-bin/blogs/dailydish/detail?entry_id=64267

Miss 'Daisy' Vail married. (1892, September 18). *The New York Times*, p. 4.

Miss Noble married to Lt. Sheafe. (1945, January 7). *Los Angeles Times*, p. C6.

Morales, T. (2002, August 20). Beware of the 'Bridezilla syndrome.' Retrieved from http://www.cbsnews.com/stories/2002/08/20/earlyshow/leisure/books/main519238.shtml

Mulvey, L. (1975). Visual pleasure and narrative cinema. *Screen, 16*(3), 6–18.

Mumby, D. (1997). The problem of hegemony: Rereading Gramsci for organizational communication studies. *Western Journal of Communication, 61*(4), 343–375.

Mundy, D. (2008). *Assimilation and/or distinction: Same-sex wedding announcements, symbolic markers of change in a discourse of tradition*. Unpublished manuscript.

Murnen, S. K., & Byrne, D. (1991). Hyperfemininity: Measurement and initial validation of the construct. *Journal of Sex Research, 28*(3), 479–489.

Naremore, J. (1993). *The films of Vincente Minnelli*. New York, NY: Cambridge University Press.

Natharius, D. (2007). Gender equity stereotypes or prescriptions? Subtexts of the stairway scenes in the romantic films of Helen Hunt. In M.-L. Galician & D. L. Merskin (Eds.), *Critical thinking about sex, love, and romance in the mass media* (pp. 177–185). Mahwah, NJ: Lawrence Erlbaum.

National Heart, Lung, and Blood Institute. (2007). *Body mass index table*. Retrieved from http://www.nhlbi.nih.gov/guidelines/obesity/bmi_tbl.htm

Noxon, C. (1999, July 25). Signoff: Till death do us part. *The New York Times*. Retrieved from http://www.nytimes.com/1999/07/25/tv/signoff-till-death-do-us-part.html?scp=1&sq=till+death+do+us+part&st=nyt

O'Connor, A.-M. (2003, Spring). The wedding dress diet. *Fitness Weddings Makeover Special*, 56–60.

Offbeat bride: About. (2003–2010). Retrieved from http://offbeatbride.com/about

Offbeat bride: Advertise on Offbeatbride.com. (2003–2010). Retrieved from http://offbeatbride.com/pr

Offbeat bride: Altar your thinking. (2003–2010). Retrieved from http://offbeatbride.com

Offbeat name-changing kit. (n.d.). Retrieved from http://www.thenamechanger.com/offbeat.php (no longer available).

Offbeat bride: Wedding porn. (2003–2010). Retrieved from http://offbeatbride.com/filed/wedding-porn

Oswald, R. (2000). A member of the wedding? Heterosexism and family ritual. *Journal of Social and Personal Relationships, 17*(3), 349–368.

Otnes, C. C., & Pleck, E. H. (2003). *Cinderella dreams: The allure of the lavish wedding.* Berkeley, CA: University of California Press.

Our world famous bridal event. (2009). Retrieved from http://www.filenesbasement.com/bridal.php

Oxygen proposes to The Knot: 10 more episodes of *Real Weddings From The Knot* [Press release]. (2004, March 1). Retrieved from http://www.theknot.com (no longer available).

Page. E. (1966, June 6). June brings nuptial news from afar. *Chicago Tribune*, p. B5.

Padget, J. (2002, August 29). Pomp and circumstance: *Gay Weddings* on Bravo. *Metro Weekly.* Retrieved from http://www.metroweekly.com/arts_entertainment/tv/?ak=78

Palkovic, H. (2005, Summer). Red hot on the paper trail. *Better Homes and Gardens Weddings*, 90–93.

Parsons, S. (2010, October 20). Wedding or not, it's time Waity Katie grew up . . . *Daily Mail.* Retrieved from http://www.dailymail.co.uk/femail/article-1322042/Wedding-time-Kate-Middleton-grew-.html

Patricia Eleanor Hobart wed to Herbert Banta Jr. (1945, January 10). *Los Angeles Times*, p. A5.

Patterson, L. (2005). Why are all the fat brides smiling? Body image and the American bridal industry. *Feminist Media Studies, 5*(2), 243–246.

Peiss, K. (1996). Making up, making over: Cosmetics, consumer culture, and women's identity. In V. deGrazia with E. Furlough (Eds.), *The sex of things: Gender and consumption in historical perspective* (pp. 311–336). Los Angeles, CA: University of California Press.

Penner, B. (2004). "A vision of love and luxury": The commercialization of nineteenth-century American weddings. *Winterthur Portfolio, 39*(1), 1–20.

Pevzner, H. (2008, June). Bride-to-be confessions. *Fitness*, 116–121.

Piepenburg, E. (2002, September 6–12). Going to the chapel: Cable watchers tune in to gays tying the knot. *Gay City News.* Retrieved from http://204.2.109.187/GCN15/thechapel.html

Piercy, M. (1973). *Small changes.* New York, NY: Ballantine Books.

Pioneer wedding. (1851, October 31). *New York Daily Times*, p. 4.

Platinum Weddings. (2010). Retrieved from   http://www.wetv.com/shows/platinum-weddings/

Platinum Weddings: Episodes. (2010). Retrieved from http://www.wetv.com/platinum-weddings/episodes

Pool, C. (2009, November). Planning points! Real advice from Weddingstar brides. *Weddingstar* (November 2008–November 2009), 190–191.

Porn for women. (n.d.). Retrieved from http://www.wannasnuggle.com/index/

Propp, V. (1968). *Morphology of the folktale* (2nd ed.). Austin, TX: University of Texas Press.

Radway, J. (1984). *Reading the romance: Women, patriarchy, and popular literature.*

Chapel Hill, NC: University of North Carolina Press.

Real wedding award winners. (2009, Fall–2010, Winter). *The Knot*, 68–69.

Real weddings. (2009, Fall–2010, Winter). *The Knot*, 58–67.

Receptions and teas. (1892, November 20). *Chicago (Daily) Tribune*, p. 27.

Resources: FeministWedding.com. (2011). Retrieved from http://www.feministwedding.com/resources.html

Rich, A. (1980). Compulsory heterosexuality and lesbian existence. *Signs: Journal of Women in Culture and Society, 5*(4), 631–660.

Rings & fine jewelry. (2005, Spring–Summer). *The Knot Magazine*, 92.

Robinson, B. K., & Hunter, E. (2008). Is Mom still doing it all? Reexamining depictions of family work in popular advertising. *Journal of Family Issues, 29*(4), 465–486.

Roddy, D. (2000, February 26). Picture this: A TV wedding that lasts. *Pittsburgh Post-Gazette*. Retrieved from http://www.post-gazette.com/columnists/20000226 roddy.asp

Rogers, S. (2003, January 7). Fox to air *Bridezilla* special January 27th at 8 p.m. Retrieved from http://www.realitytvworld.com/news/fox-air-bridezilla-special-january-27th-at-8pm-844.php

Rogers, S. (2003, September 12). NBC's *Race to the Altar* finale to air two-hour finale on September 13. Retrieved from http://www.realitytvworld.com/news/nbc-race-to-the-altar-finale-air-two-hour-finale-on-september-13-1728.php

Rosie O'Donnell: 'Lesbians stay connected after divorce.' (2010, January 26). *SFGate*. Retrieved from http://www.sfgate.com/cgi-bin/blogs/dailydish/detail?entry_id=56059

Rowland still mortified about bridal cover after breakup. (2006, July 11). *SFGate*. Retrieved from http://www.sfgate.com/cgi-bin/blogs/dailydish/detail?blogid=7cat=1343&entry_id=6972

Rubin, G. (1997). The traffic in women: Notes on the 'political economy' of sex. In L. Nicholson (Ed.), *The second wave: A reader in feminist theory* (pp. 27–62). New York, NY: Routledge.

Sacks, R. (2010, November 16). Waity Katie no more: Kate Middleton and Prince William to wed in 2011. *Vanity Fair*. Retrieved from http://www.vanityfair.com/online/daily/2010/11/its-official-prince-william-is-engaged-to-marry-kate-middleton-in-the-coming-year.html

Scanlon, J. (1995). *Inarticulate longings:* The Ladies' Home Journal, *gender, and the promises of consumer culture*. New York, NY: Routledge.

Schley, S. (2006, January 16). Invitation to the wedding business: Oxygen campaign revolves around nuptials. *Broadcasting & Cable*, 43.

Schreier, S. (2002). *Hollywood gets married*. New York, NY: Clarkson Potter.

Seelye, K. Q. (2006, April 3). As magazine readers increasingly turn to the web, so does Condé Nast. *The New York Times*, pp. C1–C2.

Shedding for the Wedding—About. (2011). Retrieved from http://www.cwtv.com/shows/shedding-for-the-wedding/about (no longer available).

Shister, G. (2002, August 30). Gay weddings are reality and reality TV. *Seattle Times*. Retrieved from http://seattletimes.nwsource.com/text/134524859_wgayweddings30.html (no longer available).

Signature Bride—The magazine. (2009, September 25). *Signature Bride*. Retrieved from http://www.signaturebride.net/main.html

Signorielli, N., & Morgan, M. (1996). Cultivation analysis: Research and practice. In D. W. Stacks & M. B. Salwen (Eds.), *An integrated approach to communication theory and research* (pp. 106–121). Mahwah, NJ: Lawrence Erlbaum.

Slaughter, J. (2011). Gramsci's place in women's history. *Journal of Modern Italian Studies, 16*(2), 256–272.

Snedeker, L. (2007, October 25). What's hot in magazines: Bridal titles. *Media Life.* Retrieved from http://www.medialifemagazine.com/artman2/publish/Magazines_22/What_s_hot_in_magazines_Bridal_titles_printer.asp

Sniezek, T. (2005). Is it our day or the bride's day? The division of wedding labor and its meaning for couples. *Qualitative Sociology, 28*(3), 215–234.

Society. (1895, March 31). *Los Angeles Times*, p. 21.

Society topics of the week. (1887, October 23). *The New York Times*, p. 16.

Spaemme, N., & Hamilton, J. (2002). *Bridezilla: True tales from etiquette hell.* Salado, TX: Salad Press.

Stallings, A. M. (2006). *Offbeat bride: Taffeta-free alternatives for independent brides.* Berkeley, CA: Seal Press.

Stanley, A. (2011, April 29). Passion versus pageantry in royal wedding reports. *The New York Times*, p. A6.

Stanley, A. (2002, November 20). TV memo: Forget the sex and violence; Shame is the ratings leader. *The New York Times*, p. A1.

Stars share their dream weddings! (2009, August 10). *InTouch Weekly*, 28–35.

Steiner, L. (1992). The history and structure of women's alternative media. In L. Rakow (Ed.), *Women making meaning: New feminist directions in communication* (pp. 121–143). New York, NY: Routledge.

Stephens, M. (2007). A *history of news* (3rd ed.). New York, NY: Oxford University Press.

Stephens, R. L. (2004). Socially soothing stories? Gender, race and class in TLC's *A Wedding Story* and *A Baby Story*. In S. Holmes & D. Jermyn (Eds.), *Understanding reality television* (pp. 191–210). New York, NY: Routledge.

Sternberg, R. J. (1998). *Cupid's arrow: The course of love through time.* New York, NY: Cambridge University Press.

Stewart, E. (2011, April 29). Kate Middleton's wedding dress revealed! And it's *amazing.* Retrieved from http://www.eonline.com/uberblog/b239184_Kate_Middletons_Wedding-Dress_Revealed_And_Its_Amazing.html

Stoddard, T. (1992). Why gay people should seek the right to marry. In S. Sherman (Ed.), *Lesbian and gay marriage: Private commitments, public ceremonies* (pp. 13–19). Philadelphia, PA: Temple University Press.

Taylor, K. (2000). Money matters. *Mother of the Bride*, 34–39.

The Knot—About us: Company history. (2005). Retrieved from http://www.theknot.com/au_companyhistory.html

The Knot and WeddingChannel.com enter into a definitive merger agreement [Press release]. (2006, June 5). Retrieved from http://wedding.weddingchannel.com/press_release/pr_2006_06_05.asp

The Knot Magazine debuts on newsstands nationwide [Press release]. (2002, September 18). Retrieved from http://www.theknot.com/09.18.02.shtml (no longer available). Accessible from http://www.writenews.com/2002/092702_theknot_magazine.htm

The May Department Stores Company and The Knot announce marketing alliance [Press release]. (2002, February 25). Retrieved from http://www.theknot.com/02.25.02.shtml

The princess wedding diaries. (2011, May 16). *People: Special Collector's Issue*, 111–120.

The social world. (1874, November 15). *Chicago (Daily) Tribune*, p. 5.

The social world. (1874, December 13). *Chicago (Daily) Tribune*, p. 5.

The wedding album. (2005, March–April). *Brides*, 235–255.

The world of society. (1885, October 4). *The New York Times*, p. 14.

30 co-eds trade caps and gowns for bridal veils. (1938, May 9). *Chicago (Daily) Tribune*, p. 3.

Thompson-Swarts. (2002, March 10). *The Topeka Capital-Journal*. Retrieved from http://cjonline.com/stories/031002/wed_thompson.shtml

Times will begin reporting gay couples' ceremonies. (2002, August 18). *The New York Times*, p. 30.

Timmons, B. F. (1939). The cost of weddings. *American Sociological Research*, 4(2), 224–233.

Today: Weddings. (2010) Retrieved from http://today.msnbc.msn.com/id/23713175/ns/today_today_weddings

Traister, R. (2004, June 18). Bridezilla bites back! *Salon*. Retrieved from http://dir.salon.com/story/mwt/feature/2004/06/18/bridezilla/index.html

Trent, B. (2000). Paaaarty! *For the Groom*, 78–91.

Tropiano, S. (2002). *The prime time closet: A history of gays and lesbians on TV*. New York, NY: Applause Theatre and Cinema Books.

20 co-eds to be commencement wedding belles. (1937, May 17). *Chicago (Daily) Tribune*, p. 22.

Umstead, T. (2011, July 8). AMC Networks divorces Wedding Central. *Multichannel News*. Retrieved from http://www.multichannel.com/article/470699-AMC_Networks_Divorces_Wedding_Central.php

Unmarried.org. (2010) Retrieved from http://www.unmarried.org

Ussher, J. M. (1997). *Fantasies of femininity: Reframing the boundaries of sex*. New Brunswick, NJ: Rutgers University Press.

Vavrus, M. D. (2002). Domesticating patriarchy: Hegemonic masculinity and television's 'Mr. Mom.' *Critical Studies in Media Communication*, 19(3), 352–375.

Venema, S. (2003, January 5). Gay wedding announcements a growing trend. *Women's eNews*. Retrieved from http://www.womensenews.org/article.cfm/dyn/aid/1170/context/archive

'Waity Katie' to wed her William. (2010, November 16). *The Sun*. Retrieved from http://www.thesun.co.uk/sol/homepage/news/3230700/Kate-Middleton-finally-gets-her-Prince-William.html

Walker, L. (2000). Feminists in Brideland. *Tulsa Studies in Women's Literature*, 19(2), 219–230.

Warner, M. [Marina]. (1995). *From the beast to the blonde: On fairy tales and their tellers*. New York, NY: Farrar, Straus, & Giroux.

Warner, M. [Michael]. (2002). Beyond gay marriage. In W. Brown & J. Halley (Eds.), *Left legalism/left critique* (pp. 259–289). Durham, NC: Duke University Press.

Wedded in Christmas season. (1925, January 6). *Los Angeles Times*, p. A6.

Wedding at Pasadena. (1883, August 17). *Los Angeles Times*, p. 0_4.

Wedding bells. (1883, June 6). *Los Angeles Times*, p. 0_6.

Wedding Central presents: Episodes on WE. (2011) Retrieved from http://www.tvguide.com/tvshows/wedding-central-presents/episodes/289828

Wedding Central shows. (2010). Retrieved from http://www.weddingcentral.com/shows

WE corporate. (2007). Retrieved from http://www.wetv.info/corporate (no longer available).

WE tv shows. (2011). Retrieved from http://www.wetv.com/shows

Wedding Day: Show overview. (2010). Retrieved from http://www.tv.com/wedding-day/show/75373/summary.html

Wedding Story on TLC. (2009). Retrieved from http://www.tvguide.com/tvshows/wedding-story/episodes/195607

Weddings. (1874, December 11). *Chicago (Daily) Tribune*, p. 5.

Weddings. (1924, April 6). *Chicago (Daily) Tribune*, p. G3.

Weddings. (1933, December 10). *Chicago (Daily) Tribune*, p. G5.

Weddings special. (2005) Retrieved from http://www.lifetimetv.com/shows/weddings/specials/index.html (no longer available).

Weddings of a Lifetime: Celebrity weddings InStyle. (1999). Retrieved from http://www.lifetimetv.com/onair/shows/woal/celeb_couples.html (no longer available).

Weddings of a Lifetime: D'Earcy Paul Davis & Tracy Lynn Hoyte. (1997). Retrieved from http://www.lifetimetv.com/onair/shows/woal/woal_tracy_paul.html (no longer available).

Weddings of a Lifetime on Lifetime. (2009, September 28). *TVGuide*. Retrieved from http://www.tvguide.com/tvshows/weddings-lifetime/205400

Weiss, T. (2000, April 14). Lights, bride, baby: The Learning Channel reaps high daytime ratings with real-life dating, weddings, births. *Hartford Courant*, p. D1.

Werde, B. (2003, July 28). A first at *Bride's* magazine: A report on same-sex unions. *The New York Times*, p. C6.

Whose Wedding Is It Anyway? Seasons 1–8 episode guide. (2010). Retrieved February 5, 2010 from http://www.tv.com/shows/whose-wedding-is-it-anyway/episodes/

Winge, T. M., & Eicher, J. B. (2004). The American groom wore a Celtic kilt: Theme weddings as carnivalesque events. In H. B. Foster & D. C. Johnson (Eds.), *Wedding dress across cultures* (pp. 207–218). New York, NY: Berg.

Wolf, N. (2002). *The beauty myth: How images of beauty are used against women* (Repr.). New York, NY: HarperCollins.

Wolf, N. (2003). Brideland. In A. Kesselman, L. D. McNair, & N. Schniedewind (Eds.), *Women: Images and realities: A multicultural anthology* (3rd ed., pp. 61–62). New York, NY: McGraw-Hill.

Wood, J. T. (2010). *Gendered lives: Communication, gender, and culture* (9th ed.). Belmont, CA: Thomson Wadsworth.

Wood, K. (2009). Wedding planning: How to plan your wedding at work (without getting fired). Retrieved from http://wedding.theknot.com/wedding-planning/wedding-budget/articles/plan-your-wedding-at-work-without-getting-fired.aspx

Zap, C. (2011, April 29). Kate Middleton wedding dress a success. Retrieved from http://news.yahoo.com/s/yblog_royals/20110429/wl_yblog_royals/kate-middleton-wedding-dress-a-success

Zipes, J. (1997). *Happily ever after: Fairy tales, children, and the culture industry.* New York, NY: Routledge.

Zipes, J. (2006). *Why fairy tales stick: The evolution and relevance of a genre.* New York, NY: Routledge.

Zipes, J. (2007). *When dreams came true: Classical fairy tales and their tradition* (2nd ed.). New York, NY: Routledge.

Zompetti, J. P. (1997). Toward a Gramscian critical rhetoric. *Western Journal of Communication, 61*(1), 66–86.

Index

Note: page numbers in *italics* refer to illustrations; those followed by "n" indicate endnotes. Women are generally posted by maiden name.